Endorsements for
A Beginner's Guide to Day Trading Online

"Every new trader should buy A Beginner's Guide to Day Trading Online. *Toni Turner takes a difficult subject—trading in the stock market—and makes it enjoyable and exciting to learn. I found the book to be highly compelling and a real page-turner. Don't start trading without it!"*

— FERNANDO GONZALEZ, co-author with William Rhee of *Strategies for the Online Day Trader; Advanced Trading Techniques for Online Profits*

(Fernando Gonzalez has been a successful trader for more than 12 years and has conducted training seminars for Newport Exchange, Inc., teaching hundreds of traders how to start their own trading careers.)

✦ ✦ ✦

"Toni Turner's information-packed guide leads you through techniques and tactics you'll need to become a winning trader, and does it in an upbeat, easy-to-understand format. Read this book if you want to know how the market works, and how to make it work for you."

— GREG CAPRA, principal of Pristine.com and co-author with Oliver Velez of *Tools and Tactics for the Master Day Trader; Battle-Tested Techniques for Day, Swing, and Position Traders*

(Greg Capra is the Vice-President of Pristine.com, one of the Nation's leading educational companies for active traders.)

a beginner's guide to day trading online

TONI TURNER

Adams Media Corporation
Holbrook, Massachusetts

Published by
Adams Media Corporation
260 Center Street, Holbrook, MA 02343. U.S.A.

ISBN: 1-58062-272-0

Printed in the United States of America.

J I H G F E D C B A

Library of Congress Cataloging-in-Publication Data
Turner, Toni.
A beginner's guide to day trading / Toni Turner.
p. cm.
Includes index.
ISBN 1-58062-272-0
1. Day trading (Securities). 2. Electronic trading of securities. I. Title.
HG4515.95.T87 2000
332.64'2'0285—dc21
99-055631

This book is not designed or intended to provide or replace professional investment advice. Readers should invest with care, including seeking specific professional advice, since investments by nature involve significant risk and can result in financial losses. The past performance of the investments reported in this book does not guarantee or predict future performance.

I dedicate this book to my daughter, Adrienne. Her intelligence, wit, beauty, and sense of inner balance remain a constant source of joy and inspiration to me.

Contents

Foreword

Day trading in the stock market is exploding as a profession, and savvy traders who have acquired the necessary skills are making big profits. The Dow Jones Industrial Average has doubled since 1995. Currently, one billion dollars a day flows into the stock market, creating immense volatility or dramatic price movements. To take advantage of these volatile stock prices, a growing number of investors have shed the "buy and hold" rule of investing in favor of turning their portfolios over quickly or "trading" their stocks.

I first met Toni Turner some years ago when she attended Pristine.com's "Simple Art of Trading" seminar at my offices in White Plains, NY, where each year I teach hundreds of individuals the art of trading the markets for a living. I was immediately impressed by her inquisitiveness, not to mention her eagerness to learn and the speed with which she grasped the sophisticated concepts that took me over ten years to formulate. It only took me several days of teaching to realize that Toni's insatiable thirst for knowledge, coupled with her wonderful sense of humor, made her very special. I knew she was a winner from the start, someone who was going to make it in this demanding and ever-so-challenging business.

Before becoming a professional day trader, Toni had been an award-winning magazine and newspaper journalist who was known for her ability to "take her readers with her." She has a knack for teaching and explaining new concepts to her readers in a way that both instructs and entertains. Now she has combined her writing talents with her trading abilities and the result IS no less than phenomenal.

This book teaches you, the beginning trader, how to day trade in the stock market safely and profitably. Toni not only teaches market fundamentals and basic technical analysis, she delves into the unique psychological characteristics needed to keep your cool and apply what you've learned when you need to make a split-second decision—something the every day trader does every day. She shows you skills and strategies needed to execute successful trades, addresses money-management techniques, and reveals nitty-gritty information about online brokers and electronic trading.

Technical analysis, or the interpretation of price, volume, and sentiment of the financial markets, coupled with the examination of day trading techniques and intricacies, normally boggles most neophyte traders. But Toni's lighthearted, reader-friendly style makes the usual dry discussions of how, when, and why to place a technically-perfect trade easier to understand. She has spiced up the text with metaphors and personal learning experiences I know you will enjoy. She talks to the reader as one friend talks to another, promoting an "If she can do it, I can do it, too," mentality.

I watched her travel the same road as most traders when she began making money one day and suffering losses the next, but she stuck it out. When she rose to the ranks of a consistently winning trader, and decided to combine her writing and trading skills into a book from which others could learn and travel an easier path to profits, everyone at Pristine.com cheered. And so will you.

A Beginner's Guide to Day Trading Online is not, however, a get-rich book. Many books and television commercials tout big profits that can be made in the market. Few tell the truth: most novice traders who jump into the market anticipating big bucks crash and burn, destroying their trading accounts and their self-esteem.

Toni's strategy is to guide you around the "booby traps" and market "landmines," that lie in your wait. She has set out to teach you to protect Your Principal, and to Trade to Trade Well.

I was particularly impressed with her one-page "Center Points," inserted between chapters, designed to maintain serenity and balance in the roller coaster market environment. I'm going to try to put these to work myself, the next time the market decides to roar with anger.

Some of the principles and techniques you find in the following pages you can adapt immediately. Others will take a bit longer to "sink in." My advice to you is to go slowly and cautiously. Don't think about the money you're making or going to make; instead focus on implementing safe and sound trading techniques. If you do that, the money will follow!

Whether you're a brand-new trader who wants to form a firm foundation of knowledge you can build on, or a more experienced one who wants to "brush up" on fundamentals, *A Beginner's Guide to Day Trading Online* will point you on the path to success.

Best wishes and happy trading!
Oliver Velez, President, Pristine.com
Co-author of *Tools & Tactics for the Master Day Trader, Battle-Tested Techniques for Day, Swing, and Position Traders*

Acknowledgments

So many people have come into my life during the shaping of this book at exactly the right time, with exactly the right words and support, that it leads me to believe "synchronicity" and "miracles" are not theories, but rather natural occurrences.

First, to Oliver Velez and Greg Capra of Pristine Capital Management, I give my highest appreciation. I couldn't have written this book without them. Their teachings and philosophies form the basis of my personal trading foundation. Many of the concepts and techniques contained in the following pages reflect what I learned while attending their classes, studying the Pristine Day Trader, and in one-on-one conversations.

Oliver showed endless patience in answering my endless questions. Greg unveiled the antithetical side of every trading situation I brought to him; in doing so, he encouraged me to think independently.

A thousand thanks, to my "mega-agent," Deidre Knight of The Knight Agency. A high-energy combination of literary agent, business agent, publicist, psychologist, friend; the woman is a wonder!

Heaps of gratitude also, go to Anne Weaver, my editor, whose consideration, understanding and support brought this book to its final form.

Thanks to Bruce and Linda Seiden for setting me on the path to trading. More to my writing cohorts, David Kohn, who planted the seed for this book in a conversation over lunch, Pat Laye and Anita Bartholomew, who pushed me to continue writing, and Cec Murphey, whose enthusiasm fueled my own.

Greg Barton, computer wizard, has my gratitude for rescuing me many times from the technology jungle, quickly and efficiently.

To Pamela Hastings, Jacqueline Middleton, and Deanne Miller, my appreciation for strong shoulders when I needed them.

To Jerry and Reina Perrault, my gratitude for all those warm hugs and hot dinners, and to Dennis Perrault, who took me for mind-clearing rides on his Harley.

My thanks also to the many others who were instrumental in creating this book. Blessings to you all!

—Toni Turner

Introduction

Welcome to the wild, wild world of day trading! Hang on tight because if you jump aboard, it will be the most exhilarating, most terrifying ride you'll ever take. The stock market is the mother of all roller coasters, lifting day traders to hair-raising highs, then dropping them to the lowest lows, with no regard for their screams. Adrenaline junkies become addicted to the excitement. More timid beings endure or quit.

Day trading—the not-so-gentle art of buying and selling stocks during a brief time period—is exploding as a profession, and savvy traders are making big bucks. The Dow Jones Industrial Average has doubled since 1995, and currently, a billion dollars a day pours into the U.S. stock market. Stock prices have gone wild and show no signs of abating. The resultant volatility has encouraged a growing number of people to forsake the "buy and hold" rule of investing. Instead, they're turning their portfolios over quickly and "trading" in and out of the market to take advantage of the wide price swings.

In earlier years, the most boisterous stocks might add two, maybe even three points (dollars) a share, per day, to a lucky trader's pocket. Some stocks now rocket five, six, even twenty points in a day! They may double in price, yielding dizzying profits to those who have the intestinal fortitude to white-knuckle the ride. When these stocks fall, they tumble even faster, handing the short seller mega-profits. I know of day traders who regularly take home $15,000 a day.

A major contributor to spiraling trading profits, of course, is the mighty Internet. Never before have so many human beings had so much access to so much information. Facts known only to stockbrokers a few years ago are now at our fingertips. We've discovered that the financial markets are not concocted of dark, esoteric secrets understood only by card-carrying members of the Puckered-Brow-in-a-Suit group. We, too, can grasp the simple fact that if inflation threatens to rear its annoying head, the Federal Reserve Board raises interest rates. That forces corporations to pay more for bank loans, thus affecting their earnings. Result? Bad earnings equal falling stock prices.

Besides news and research, the Internet bubbles with up-to-the-minute stock quotes. Want to know the price of Microsoft? Type nasdaq.com in your URL address space. Zap! The Nasdaq Stock Exchange Web site appears with your quote, and more information than you could digest in a month of birthdays.

Also, discount brokers have popped up like mushrooms. Although full-service brokers charge up to $250 commission per trade, a discounter's commission can be as low as $5. Discount brokers don't offer personal service as full-service brokers do, but most offer research tools and online availability, so you can buy and sell stocks with the click of a mouse!

Finally, highly sophisticated trading software and execution systems give serious traders the ability to shoot their trading orders to "the floor" in seconds.

So…in an ideal stock market, we traders can jump onto the Internet and pull up the charts and news we need on a stock. Quickly, we switch over to our online trading execution system, and click the stock we want to buy, at the perfect entry point, of course. Then we sit back with a cup of coffee and rake in the profits. Right?

Right.

Well…*sometimes.*

I've had that exact scenario happen to me. But not always.

Once, early on in my trading career, you would have found me slumped over my keyboard, crying, "What in the heck am I doing wrong?" I watched my trading account lose money by the bucketloads. And it wasn't money I could afford to lose. I *lived* off that account. I pulled the mortgage payment, the electric bill, my daughter's college tuition, and mounting credit card payments out of it. You've never seen an account balance drop so fast!

One day, I sold all of my stocks (it didn't take long, I'd lost a lot) and spent a couple of weeks wandering around in a "blue funk." When I finally finished feeling sorry for myself, I got mad. Madder than mad. Who did this market think it was, taking all of my money? One word kept nagging me: *knowledge*. I didn't know enough.

Some jobs you can fake with a little moxy and a lot of charm, but you can't fake day trading. You can't wander into this rough-and-tumble arena without knowledge. The market eats ignorant players for breakfast.

I know. I was one of them. I made a zillion mistakes. I suffered losses so grim that my friends and family begged me to quit. But I come from a "long line of stubborn."

I persisted. I read books on technical analysis that I didn't understand. I watched CNBC until my eyes glazed over. Then one day, a friend introduced me to a terrific couple who were *real* day traders. They invited me to their home, showed me their computer setup, and explained how they traded. A new world opened to me. I realized day trading was far more difficult and involved than I had previously thought.

A couple of months later, I flew to New York and took a class on trading techniques and strategies taught by Oliver Velez and Greg Capra, of Pristine.com. After I returned home, I studied like crazy. Six months later, when my nontrading friends asked me how my trading was going, I'd grit my teeth and answer defiantly, "I'm losing less."

They rolled their eyes.

After a while, I broke even. Then came the day, nearly a year after I'd started, when I began to make money—consistently. Not gobs of money, but a decent living.

As success became routine, it occurred to me that I could help others do what I do. I imagined there must be many people who would like to work out of their homes, be their own bosses, set their own schedules, and make a tidy profit each week.

Why, though, should these beginning traders make the same mistakes I did—there's standing-room only in the Dumb Mistakes Trading Room—if I can help them skip some of the nastier, account-breaking rungs on the ladder to mastery?

When I started trading, I wished for a book that spoke to me in honest, clear, and direct terms I could grasp quickly and easily. I wished for a book that would tell me, "when the market's doing *this*, don't trade." Or "when a stock's doing *this*, go for it." When my losses finally turned into consistent wins, I decided to write that book.

In the following pages, I'm going to talk to you as one best friend talks to another. If you decide trading is for you, I'll explain how to do it without losing your shirt or blouse. I'll tell you the absolute, nitty-gritty of what you're wading into *before* you make your first trade, not after. I'll show you how to preserve your principal and make money.

I wish someone had explained these things to me, early on, in a way I could understand. It would have saved me big bucks! So here it is, guys and girlfriends, from me to you.

Good luck!

CHAPTER 1

This Ain't No Dress Rehearsal!

BENEFITS OF DAY TRADING: THE GOOD NEWS

Day trading is a made-to-order profession. By and large, you can work when and where you want to. You can structure your days as you chose, working from your office or home, or even when traveling, when need be.

If you think of it as a small business, the initial investment in equipment—a good computer, fast modem, and software—is relatively inexpensive.

You can live anywhere. If you decide to move to Bangor, Maine, from Yeehaw Junction, Florida, just dismantle your electronic monsters, pack them up, and go. If you long to go skiing for a week and can afford it, take your account "flat" (trader's jargon for taking your account to cash), and go.

As a day trader, you're independent and answer to no one but yourself. Forget reporting to a nasty boss. You can stay in bed when you have the flu. You don't have to wear a tie that chokes you or high heels that dislocate your back. You can trade in a torn T-shirt, wearing your duck slippers.

You'll develop your own style, fast-paced or easy-going. Days when the market is highly volatile, you can, and should, take the day off. Run errands, play with your kids, or go shopping with the money you saved by staying out of the market on a whippy, choppy day.

THE FLIP SIDE: WALL STREET TAKES NO PRISONERS

All of the above is "the good news." Now, let's look at the less-than-charming realities you need to know before you place that first trade.

When I first started trading (that's what *I* called it, anyway!), I crawled into bed one night with a bowl of praline ice cream and *Trading for a Living*.

In the opening pages, author Dr. Alexander Elder says, "Markets operate without normal human helpfulness. Every trader tries to hit others. Every trader gets hit by others. The trading highway is lettered with wrecks. Trading is the most dangerous human endeavor, short of war."[1]

"Humph," I thought. "Dr. Elder certainly has a negative attitude."

A few weeks and one bloodied trading account later, I knew Dr. Elder was right on the money! In the hands of the wrong person, trading can be hazardous to one's wealth.

Here's another reality statement: This business crushes most who enter its doors. Nearly 80 percent of those who try, quit. They lose their trading accounts by ignorance, trading too much, or taking foolish risks. Some can't handle the stress.

You can make boatloads of money day trading. If the rewards are high, however, so are the tradeoffs. The stock market is a ruthless arena. *Newsweek* once called Wall Street "the avenue of avarice." It's inhabited by the sharpest minds in the world, all intent on grabbing your money as fast as possible. It's a greed-against-greed, fear-versus-fear, trader-battling-trader, if-you-die-I-win world. Every day. No mercy. The more you lose, the harder I laugh.

"But buying a stock can be a complacent phone call to my discount broker, or click on my computer screen," you say, puzzled. "I don't see the greed and fear connection."

Take my word for it, please. When I began trading, I didn't see the connection either, but I learned in short order, and the lesson was expensive, very expensive.

The best way to start trading is slo-owly, calmly, armed with knowledge you've *already* accumulated. Watch CNBC every day for several weeks, so you can internalize market rhythms. Soak up the gist of the *if, then* logic. *If* this happens on Wall Street, *then* that usually follows. Stare at market indicators and absorb how they act in relation to one another. Listen to market gurus and note whether they're usually right or wrong. (*USA Today* runs an annual stock-picking contest in which darts thrown at a board of stocks challenge stock picks by top brokers. The darts usually win!)

Place paper trades for a few weeks; I'll explain how in Chapter 3. Keep in mind, though, that while paper trading is good practice, it doesn't accurately portray how real trades play out. Reason? The absence of emotion.

I'm giving you stern warnings because if you listen and heed my advice, it will save you money and headaches. Every warning I give you in the pages that follow comes from a lesson I learned the hard way. If you learn from them, you'll keep your losses small and your gains high.

---

[1] Elder, Dr. Alexander. *Trading for a Living.* (NY: John Wiley & Sons, 1993), p. 26.

I jumped into trading head first, assuming I knew what I was doing. I didn't.

As a successful investor, I imagined trading was the same thing, but at a faster pace. Not true! Comparing trading and investing is like comparing apples with kangaroos. Yes, time frames are different, but mindsets are different, too. So are entry points, exit points, and risk–reward ratios. Traders concern themselves with market and stock trends, whereas investors want stocks that outperform the overall market.

Please go slowly when you enter this profession. A cautious turtle will keep his or her money, then make more. An impetuous hare will end up in the briar patch.

WHAT DOES A DAY TRADER LOOK LIKE?

Traders in the trenches insist we need three things to trade successfully, namely, the "Three B's," or "Bucks, Brains, and Balls." They're right.

First, of course, is "Bucks." Anyone who says you can start trading with $5,000 or less is blowing smoke. Why? Because, at sometime, you are going to lose money. You may make it back, but you will lose it first. Show me a successful trader who says he or she didn't lose money learning how to trade, and I'll show you someone growing a long nose! If losing money stops your heart, trading is not your game.

Next comes "Brains." You must have mental horsepower if you're reading this book.

As for the lower part of the male anatomy, guys already know what I mean. Girlfriends, you might not have them now, but if you stick around long enough, I promise you will grow them! This profession gives you confidence and mental toughness not only when you're trading, but in every area of your life. After all, if you're a day trader, you survive in one of the toughest arenas in the world.

My nontrading friends ask me repeatedly, "How do you *do* that all day? Isn't it *risky*?" You bet. If you don't love jumping blindfolded into the dark unknown, with no guarantee whether you'll land on a pile of feather pillows or into a crater of hot lava, please don't trade!

Successful traders know how to act swiftly. Many times you'll have *one second* to make a decision that may affect your account by thousands of dollars. If your middle name is "Waffle," you'll be happier investing.

The best traders also handle multiple tasks easily. They scan charts, while listening to CNBC, while watching a list of major market indicators and mentally computing their relationship to one another, while keeping an eye on one or more stock positions, while remembering the strategy and stops for each trade, while executing a "scalping play" or two, while....

Women usually pay the most attention to their intuition, but in trading, guys cultivate it also. By intuition, I don't mean they buy a stock because they have a "gut feeling" it's going to fly. That's never a good idea. I mean they use the gut feeling developed by all good traders through experience—the hunch that tells them something in the market is good, or amiss, before the actual event takes place.

The traders holding the fattest wallets can change their minds in a nanosecond. Being right or wrong has nothing to do with it. They know that sticking to a decision they made hours, or even minutes, ago just to insist they're "right" is the worst thing a trader can do.

Emotional discipline is a must. The best traders monitor their emotions constantly. In *Trading for a Living*, Dr. Elder says, "Your feelings have an immediate impact on your account equity. You may have a brilliant trading system, but if you feel frightened, arrogant, or upset, your account is sure to suffer."[2] I've traded while feeling scared, smug, and sad. During those times, I've always lost money.

One emotion I still allow myself, however, is pure, self-congratulation. *After* I close a great trade, I say, "You go, girl!" I punch the air with my fist. I twist my arm over my shoulder and whomp myself on the back or reward myself with a piece of chocolate.

Okay, this is the perfect moment to pause for introspection and a reality check as to whether or not you'd be happy and prosperous as a day trader. Forget your ego. Be completely honest and ask yourself these questions: "Can I chance losing part of my account?" "Do I think fast and stay cool under stress?" "Can I control my emotions?"

TO TRADE OR NOT TO TRADE?

As one of my best friends says about life, "This ain't no dress rehearsal."

Neither is trading. You can't "sort of" ride a roller coaster. Either you're hurtling through space at mach two with your hair on fire or you're standing on the ground below. You can't do both. To hang one foot outside the speeding car is mighty dangerous.

Before you start to trade:

- ✦ Study this book and others on the "Recommended Reading List" located in the back of the book.
- ✦ Explore trading chat rooms on the Internet; analyze what their members say.
- ✦ Consider taking a course in technical analysis and electronic day trading.
- ✦ Attend a "money" show or seminar.
- ✦ Join a local trading group and talk to other traders. You learn from every kind of trader, whether they trade stocks, commodities, or jelly beans.

Happy trading!

---

2 Elder, p. 27.

AUTHOR'S NOTE

Learning to trade successfully was the most vitalizing, yet the most difficult, undertaking of my life.

As with all professions, the good times, when everything fell into place, delivered a sense of self-satisfaction and composure. The not-so-good times, when everything I touched knocked me down, gave way to discouragement and frustration.

To cope with the challenging times, I studied principles gleaned from motivational teachings. I hoped that if I "backed up" from the trading world and observed larger truths of life from a different vantage point, it would empower me to persevere. It did.

Each "Center Point" in this text summarizes various concepts and observations that kept me centered on my goal of becoming an accomplished trader. They also benefited other areas of my life.

I trust you will find these messages to be valuable handrails as you make your way over the stepping stones to success.

✦ ✦ ✦

CENTER POINT

The Power of Commitment

Until one is committed, there is hesitancy, the chance to draw back, always ineffectiveness. Concerning all acts of initiative (and creation), there is one elementary truth, the ignorance of which kills countless ideas and splendid plans: that the moment one definitely commits oneself, then Providence moves, too. All sorts of things occur to help one that would never otherwise have occurred. A whole stream of events issues from the decision, raising in one's favor all manner of unforeseen incidents and meetings and material assistance, which no man could have dreamed would come his way.

—W. H. MURRAY (CLIMBED MT. EVEREST)

When you fully commit to a goal, the focus of positive energy onto a desired result is like programming a missile to "lock on" to a moving target; the missile automatically pursues the target no matter how elusive it becomes. The act of commitment also attracts exciting, new possibilities to your doorstep, leading to dramatic changes in your life.

Perhaps you've noticed that successful people are not always the best or the brightest, the quickest or strongest. Yet they're always the ones who do whatever it takes to succeed.

A goal without a commitment is a nonentity, and usually falls by the wayside from lack of interest by its beholder. Only when we fully commit to a dream are we able to access the highest possibilities of our being.

Commitment requires you to identify a clear and positive goal that's in harmony with natural laws. Next declare your intention to achieve that goal, while maintaining the belief that it's *already a reality* in your life. If your inner commitment to your goal remains strong and unwavering, it will remove obstacles that fall onto your path and deliver you to your objective.

Personal greatness comes from fully engaging and fully participating with the process that generates life by drawing on your inner, transformative resources. When you do that, the universe responds to the endeavors of your soul!

✦ ✦ ✦

CHAPTER 2

Wall Street: A View from the Top of the Skyscraper

THE FIRST TRADERS

The act of trading dates back to Uggh and Oog, the original cave neighbors. One day, Uggh reflected that he, himself, was darn good at hunting animals for meat, while his neighbor, Oog, was a heck of a fisherman. So, Uggh motioned Oog over and grunted his observations to him. The two men agreed to swap meat for fish, and day trading was born.

THE BIRTH OF WALL STREET

Fast-forward a million years or so to a more civilized world. In 1644, the Dutch West India Company, in New Amsterdam (later named New York City), decided too many cows wandered around the island of Manhattan. The company decreed, "Resolved, that a fence shall be made, beginning at the Great Bouewery, and extending to Emanuel's plantation, and all are to repair thither on Monday, 4th April, with tools to build a fence." The resulting barricade was an earthen embankment, studded with uprooted tree trunks, at the southern tip of Manhattan.

A few years later, in 1653, Governor Peter Stuyvesant knew that the British were about to attack and guessed they would arrive by land. He ordered local residents, mostly soldiers and Dutch colonists, to raise the fence and dig a moat the length of it.

But Stuyvesant missed the boat. The British didn't attack by land. They came by sea in 1664, anchored off Coney Island, and captured the settlement without firing a shot. Later, they burned the wall. The street that ran alongside survived, though, and retained its name—Wall Street.

The New York Stock Exchange was born in New York City, when the first Congress met in Federal Hall in 1789 to assume the debts of the new colonies and government. The Congress issued about $80 million in government notes, creating an exciting new market in securities. These securities, along with additional stocks, bonds, orders for commodities, and warehouse receipts, were put up for sale to the public. Traders gathered each day under the sycamore tree at 68–70 Wall Street to buy and sell.

To participate in this market, many investors helped fund American companies by buying shares of ownership. Therefore, they had "equity" and could prove so by the certificates of stock issued by the company in exchange for the equity capital given by the investor. That stock proved the investor's participation, and so secured the debt. That's why shares of stock are alternately called stocks, equities, and securities.

The stock market began trading formally in 1792, and public auctions of securities were halted to regulate business. Two dozen brokers formed a club. They continued to meet under the sycamore tree, or in the Tontine Coffee House at the corner of Water and Wall streets. Fierce competition ran rampant among them. They fought to protect themselves and their commissions, rather than their customers. Gradually, the brokers formed brokerage houses that offered stocks to the public at fair prices.

In 1827, a new Merchants Exchange building, erected at Wall and Hanover streets, housed the New York Stock and Exchange Board. By 1842, the American Stock Exchange opened its doors. Both exchanges enforced strict rules governing the sale of stocks, and Wall Street began its evolution as one of the world's most important financial centers.

WHO ARE WALL STREET'S BIGGEST PARTY ANIMALS? THE BULLS AND THE BEARS

New York City gradually swallowed Manhattan's farmland, but references to animals carried through on Wall Street.

No matter which exchange we participate in, four animals describe the types of traders: bulls and bears, hogs and sheep. An old Street saying goes: "Bulls make money, and bears make money, but hogs get slaughtered."

A bull fights by striking up with his horns. If you're a "bull," you believe the stock market is going to rise in value. You're a buyer.

Bears fight by striking down with their paws. As a "bear," you speculate that stock prices will fall and make your profits from a declining market. Therefore, you're a seller.

Have you already figured out who the "hogs" are? Right on! Hogs bet all of their money on big, risky positions, then get slaughtered when the market turns against them. The market *always* knows when hogs overeat—it skewers greedy gluttons every time.

Instead of relying on their own knowledge and experience, sheep follow tips, gurus, anybody with a tambourine! Sometimes they tie on bullhorns, sometimes they roar like bears. But when the market turns suddenly volatile, the pitifully bleating sheep get shorn in a hurry!

Each day in the market is a giant tug-of-war between the bulls and the bears. As a trader, you'll decide *before* you put on a trade who is in power. In a strong, rising market, bulls rule, profiting from the soaring prices. Unless you're a contrarian (a market participant who takes the opposite side of the current trend—not a good idea for a new trader), you'll strap on your horns and buy. When the market turns weak and prices fall, bears rule, profiting as prices trend lower. In a bear market, you either stand aside or learn the art of selling short.

When your volatility indicators show that the bulls and bears are engaging in a no-win battle, wise traders observe from the sidelines. *Knowing when to trade and when not to trade is the hallmark of a seasoned trader*. Believe it or not, it takes immense discipline to watch the market whirl around you, and not jump in. Forcing trades when market conditions are whippy and unpredictable is labeled "greed." And we know what happens to hogs!

THE LAND OF GREED AND FEAR

Greed and fear rule the financial markets. These two emotions motivate nearly all market players—institutional managers, stockbrokers, investors, traders, the taxi driver that plays "hot tips"—and you.

"Me?" you holler. "Not a chance! I'm a very nice person. Greed and fear will never rule any part of *my* life."

Sure they will. As a brand-new trader, greed and fear will be your constant companions.

Is that something to be ashamed of? Absolutely not. Are you the only trader experiencing these emotions? Nope! There's standing room only in the Land of Greed and Fear. One of our goals in this book is to face these emotions and understand them. That way, you can get them behind you, where they belong.

What do these emotions look like?

Say you buy a stock at the perfect entry point (you'll learn this later), and it rises exactly as you expected. A little voice whispers in your ear, "This baby's gonna fly. Why don't you take all the money in your trading account and buy as many shares as you can? You'll make a killing." Greed.

Or you buy a stock, and it moves up two points. It's your predetermined profit exit, and you think, "This is the sensible place to take profits. But this stock might push higher. I'm staying in." Greed.

Typically, when strong stocks explode in a bull market, greed explodes in direct proportion. But there's a downside. These same stocks fizzle as fast as, and usually faster than, they mushroom. The falling price detonates panic (fear), and everyone runs for the door with less money than they came in with!

Another example: Convinced a particular stock would shoot up at the market's open the following morning, you took a hefty position home the night before (greed). The next morning, though, the market opens way down (fear). Your stock crashes like a boulder off a cliff, as selling runs rampant. Panic twists your heart and your stomach. The blood pounds in your ears as you watch a big portion of your trading account dissolve with the red blinking prices on your monitor.

Gulp. "Is there a way around this?" you ask. "Can I trade without greed and fear?"

Absolutely. If you learn how to control these two destructive emotions by replacing them with positive ones, if you read this book and others, if you study and apply what you learn in a disciplined, cool-headed fashion, then you'll have the edge over 99 percent of all market players.

SUPPLY AND DEMAND, OR HOW MUCH WILL YOU PAY FOR THAT COOKIE?

Think back to your childhood to when you were a little kid. Remember the day you misbehaved, and your mother punished you by forbidding you access to the cookie jar?

For the last couple of days, you hadn't thought about cookies at all, hadn't even asked for one. Now cookies were off-limits, and you could think of nothing else. You stood and stared at the big earthenware jar, picturing the mouth-watering goodies inside. You wished more than anything in the world that you could nibble on the crunchy oatmeal and taste the soft, sweet, morsels of chocolate melting on your tongue. At that moment, you'd give a week's allowance for a cookie.

Why did you ignore the cookies one day, and focus on them the next? Supply and demand. Suddenly, your *supply* was cut off. Human nature dictates that when *supply* gets low, that item becomes intensely desirable, or in high *demand*.

Let's say the following day, your mother decides you've been punished enough and returns your privileges to the cookie jar. You quickly push a chair up to the counter, scramble onto it, and stand on your tiptoes until you reach the jar. You can't wait to taste those cookies. Smacking your lips in anticipation, you lift the lid. One, lonely cookie stares back at you. *Only one?* Well, heck it's better than none.

Suddenly, behind you, you hear the sound of scuffling feet. Your older brother runs into the kitchen. He shoulders you aside, nearly knocking you off the chair, and jams his hand into the cookie jar. "Only one cookie?" he yells. "It's mine." (demand)

"No, it's *mine*," you reply. (demand)

He's taller than you, and he holds the cookie (limited supply) over his head, taunting you. "What will ya' give me for it?"

Your mind races. You've already spent most of your allowance this week, but now you're willing to give up the rest of it for what seems to be the only cookie in the world (demand). "I'll give you fifty cents."

He sneers. "You gotta be kidding. It's worth more than that. Remember, this is the only cookie left, and I have it." He waves the cookie higher over his head. "How much?"

Your mind races to another quarter you'd seen earlier on your dresser. "Okay. Seventy-five cents. That's all I have!"

He agrees, and you run upstairs, promptly returning to exchange money for the cookie.

A minute later, you sit on the back stoop, taking tiny nibbles of the cookie, savoring every crumb of it. Why didn't you pop it in your mouth, chew absent-mindedly, and gulp it down, as you usually did? Because your *supply* was limited, which added value to the cookie.

The next afternoon, a bunch of the neighborhood kids come over. While you and your friends play, your mother dons her apron and starts to bake. Soon, she holds out a platter of freshly baked cookies. You and your friends grab handfuls of cookies and gobble some down, maybe shoving one or two in your pockets for later. After mumbling your thanks, you run outside to play.

Why didn't you savor each bite, as you did the day before? Because now there's an abundance of *supply*. Everyone can have cookies, with plenty left over. The *demand* has lessened.

Supply and demand manipulate human emotions, which turns full circle to manipulate supply and demand. Just as a cookie shortage causes children of all ages to desire them more, the shortage of an attractive stock at a given price causes market players to desire it more. Those who control the stock demand higher prices because buyers agree to pay those prices.

Limited supply equals high demand. How high a price will you pay? That depends on your level of risk and the perceived reward.

Here's a classic case of supply and demand: A desirable stock breaks through its daily high of $49, a good omen for it to rise even higher. You manage to buy a few hundred shares just over the breakout price, at $49 1/4. Within an hour, the price rises a point, to $50. Coincidentally, $50 is yesterday's high, or the highest price it reached during yesterday's trading.

Let's backtrack. Yesterday, when it reached that high of $50, many traders bought it there, thinking it would go higher. Instead, it fell to $45.

As it fell, the traders who bought at $50 and held on, said, "If this stupid stock ever goes back up to fifty, I'm getting rid of it. At least I'll get out even."

Okay, we're back to the present day, and the stock just hit $50, yesterday's high. Blamm! All the traders who are waiting to get out even sell at $50. *Supply!* Lots and lots of *supply!* (big platter of cookies). To make matters worse, traders who bought the stock today—you included—notice the supply, predict a selloff, and offer theirs for sale.

Now, there's too much stock for sale at $50 (supply) and nobody's buying, meaning no demand. To get rid of it, sellers try to make it more attractive by lowering the price. They offer it out at $49 3/4, then $49 5/8 and $49 1/2.

Finally, at $49 1/4, the "selloff" peters out. Supply dwindles (most of the cookies have been eaten). At $49, the stock's price looks attractive once again, and buyers start nibbling. Demand increases, sellers raise their prices, and the process repeats itself.

PRICE: THE BOTTOM LINE

Just as the most important aspect of real estate is "location, location, location," the most important aspect of the stock market is price, price, price. Price is the bottom line, the end result, the last word. All analyses, whether fundamental or technical, all guru proclamations, all market movements, whether ruled by greed or fear or even uncertainty, boil down to a single element: *price*. Simply put, price rules.

For every transaction in the stock market, there has to be a buyer and a seller. You, the buyer, and the person who is the seller agree on a certain value of a given equity at the same time. Equity and money exchange hands. Price represents a shared consensus at the moment of transaction.

Does this agreement on price mean you have the same emotions about that stock? No. Just the opposite. You have opposing feelings! At the moment you buy the stock, you believe it's a bargain. You think it will increase in value so you can sell it at a higher price and pad your pockets from that increase. The trader who sold it to you, however, feels sure that stock will fall and is delighted to dispose of it.

Please keep this in mind whenever you place a trade. *The trader who is buying the stock from you, or selling it to you, feels the exact opposite of how you do about the trade*. The minute you complete the trade, you're both at risk because the next "tick," or price movement in the stock, will prove which of you was right. And only one of you gets to win!

Why do prices up and down? They move because of supply and demand, coupled with our old buddies, greed and fear. When you, the buyer, and the other guy, the seller, disagree about the value of the stock in question, the disagreement causes the stock price to change.

This change, or fluctuation, creates opportunity for you to make money. You assess the risks in the fluctuating prices and act according to your risk tolerance. The trick is to predict price movement accurately enough of the time that your profits are larger than your losses.

THE NEW YORK STOCK EXCHANGE, "THE SUNSHINE MARKET": HOW IT OPERATES

The present-day New York Stock Exchange (NYSE) was established on the principle that customer orders must be handled in a fair and efficient manner, and that the investor's interest comes first. It's called "The Sunshine Market" because all business carried on at the NYSE is open to full public view.

Located at 11 Wall Street, the NYSE (www.nyse.com) lists more than 3,700 stocks. In terms of capitalization, the NYSE is the largest U.S. stock market. You can observe the floor of the NYSE live, every weekday morning when you watch CNBC's *Squawk Box* on television before the market opens.

The stocks traded on the NYSE are referred to as "listed" securities and generally represent companies with large capitalizations and stable earnings. They're the icons of American industry, such as General Electric, AT&T, Johnson & Johnson, and General Motors.

Thirty NYSE equities make up the Dow Jones Industrial Average. "The Dow," as it's often referred to, is the most closely watched market indicator and is generally perceived to mirror the state of the American economy.

The Dow Jones 20 Transportation Average and the Dow Jones 15 Utilities Average serve as colleagues to the Industrial Average. The NYSE Composite Index reflects the price movements of all stocks listed on the New York Stock Exchange.

Most listed securities behave in a more dignified manner than Nasdaq stocks. Their prices usually move up and down at a more reasonable pace than their wilder, more volatile counterparts. That means NYSE stocks are easier for traders to "catch" at the proper entry point, so there's not as much tendency to chase them.

The NYSE operates on a specialist central auction system. Different "posts," each representing a different stock, pepper the floor of the Exchange. At each post, a specialist (think "auctioneer") conducts a two-way auction between buyers and sellers and provides a market for that stock. Only one specialist represents each stock; for example, GE has only one specialist. Specialists, however, can represent more than one stock.

WHERE YOU COME IN

Say you want to buy 100 shares of Lucent Technology (LU) "at market," meaning at the current posted price. Basically, your order can be filled one of three ways.

1. You call your broker, or you place the order through your broker on the Internet. Your broker sends your order to the floor of the NYSE. A floor-broker representing your broker walks (running is against the rules) to the post where LU is traded and asks the LU specialist for a market. The specialist announces the "size" of the market, meaning the number of shares of LU offered for sale at the best price, and the number wanted to buy, and that best price. Your order is filled, and your broker confirms the price to you.
2. Again, you give your broker the order by phone or Internet, and he or she enters it onto a SuperDOT (designated order turnaround) machine, a computerized system that shoots your order to the specialist, who fills it and sends it back to the clerk. The clerk informs your broker of the "fill" (the precise number of shares and price your order was filled at), and your broker informs you.
3. You execute your order yourself, on a level II order entry software system (detailed in the next chapter) with a SuperDOT button incorporated into it. This zaps the order from you to the specialist, and you usually receive the fill information in less than a minute.

When we say the specialist announces the "market" in Lucent, an example would be 104 x 104 1/8, size 5,000 x 10,000. The "x" translates into "by."

In this case, it means there is a buyer, or buyers, waiting to buy a total of 5,000 shares of Lucent, and willing to pay $104 per share. And there is a seller, or sellers, offering a total of 10,000 shares, at $104.13 per share.

The specialist's responsibility is to keep a fair and orderly market in his or her stock by consolidating all incoming buy and sell orders, both verbal and SuperDOT, in an equitable manner. The specialist may match my order to buy 500 shares of Lucent at $104 with your order to sell 500 shares of Lucent at the same price. This pairing of orders takes place about 75 percent of the time, and the specialist receives a small fee from the participating broker. Specialists usually fill orders in seconds, but according to exchange rules, they are allowed two minutes.

When you place a limit order, in this case meaning you want to buy a stock at a certain price below the current offer, the specialist records your order in his or her electronic "book" and fills it as soon as a matching order to sell at that price appears.

If the stock becomes illiquid, meaning there is a lack of volume (volume = shares exchanging hands between buyers and sellers), specialists must fill any orders presented to them by the customers from their own accounts. Specialists are required to provide liquidity in the stock they represent, much as a retail store manager continually restocks shelves with merchandise.

Consequently, specialists sometimes have to trade the stock themselves, buying it as it falls, and selling (shorting) it as it rises to cushion sharp price variations. Specialists risk their capital to bridge temporary gaps in public supply and demand, which reduces volatility and stabilizes prices.

Remember when we first talked about Lucent's price of $104 x $104 1/8? The difference between those two prices is 1/8th of a point, or .125 cents, or "an eighth." That eighth of a point is referred to as "the spread."

The spread is the monetary difference—on the NYSE, usually 1/16 to 1/8 of a point—between the posted buy price and sell price. A savvy specialist will "make" that spread and usually better: He or she buys LU at $104 from sellers, and sells it at $104.13 (or above) to buyers, earning 1/8, or nearly .13 cents per share. Multiply thirteen cents by hundreds of thousands of stock shares per day, and you know why, in your next life, you want to come back as a specialist!

THE NASDAQ–AMEX, "THE MARKET OF MARKETS"

Until recently, the Nasdaq Stock Market and the American Stock Exchange were two separate markets. On October 30, 1998, the two joined forces under one corporate umbrella to create the Nasdaq–Amex Market Group.

Since the two markets operate independently of one another, and since differences still exist between the two of them, we will refer to them separately.

THE NASDAQ STOCK MARKET: HOW IT OPERATES

The Nasdaq Stock Market (www.nasdaq.com) opened in February 1971. Currently, it lists nearly 5,400 companies and trades more shares per day than any other major U.S. market.

Formerly, NASDAQ designated an acronym that stood for the "National Association of Securities Dealers Automated Quotron." Now, the word *Nasdaq* stands on its own.

The NASD, or National Association of Securities Dealers, operates this computer-based stock exchange, and all transactions take place electronically. You won't see "the floor of the Nasdaq" on any television program because there is none. The Nasdaq operates from a gigantic computer housed in Trumbull, Connecticut.

This market lists all types of equities, from small-cap (small capitalization) companies to large-cap giants, representing every conceivable business enterprise.

Many times, when announcers and journalists refer to the Nasdaq, they describe it as "tech-heavy" because technology stocks take up a large share of the Nasdaq pie. When there's a "tech-wreck," technology stocks crash. Since these stocks tend to move in tandem, when a tech-wreck occurs, it usually pulls the entire Nasdaq market down with it.

You're familiar with many of the Nasdaq leaders, such as Intel, Microsoft, Cisco Systems, and Amazon.com. The Nasdaq 100 Index lists one hundred of the top representative stocks in the market, whereas the Nasdaq's National Market System Composite is an index comprising all issues traded on that exchange. Both the Nasdaq 100 and Composite are important indicators that traders watch throughout the day.

Active Nasdaq stocks are the day trader's playground. Trading many of these issues makes a roller coaster ride feel like a quiet walk in the park. The more attention a Nasdaq stock receives, the more volatile it can be, skyrocketing up 10–20 points or more in an hour or two, then falling even faster, taking a boatload of screaming traders with it!

Since I am adamant about keeping one's trading account on the plus side, I suggest new traders buy and sell the kinder, gentler NYSE stocks when they begin. There's less chance of losing one's shirt or blouse.

The Nasdaq's version of specialists are called market makers. With no central marketplace, they use computers and telephones to execute orders for their firm's customers, trade their firm's account, and maintain liquidity in the stock, which is their responsibility.

Unlike listed stocks where a single specialist orchestrates all the trades, Nasdaq stocks allow many market makers to participate at any given time.

A NYSE stock has one "ruler" (specialist) who matches all the orders and controls the price and order flow. Although registered market makers have a responsibility to keep their stocks orderly and liquid, Nasdaq stocks are governed more like a democracy, sort of "by the people, for the people."

When you call your broker or go online and ask for a quote for Dell (DELL), for instance, your answer might be 43 1/4 x 43 5/16. That means 43 1/4 is the "inside bid," or highest price you can demand if you want to sell Dell as a market order. Forty-three and five-sixteenths is the "inside offer," or "ask." ("Offer" and "ask" are interchangeable terms.) It represents the lowest price you can buy Dell if you want to buy at the market price. When you get a quote from any exchange, whether verbal or written, the bid is always announced first, the offer second.

Although the inside bid and offer are the prices given to you on request, if you saw the big picture—as you do if you're trading on a NASDAQ level II system which displays market participants for a selected stock—you'd see that active Nasdaq stocks boast a long line of market makers waiting at the bid, and another waiting at the offer, or ask, showing different prices. Many of these market makers represent brokers such as Goldman Sachs (GSCO), Merrill Lynch (MLCO), Morgan Stanley (MSCO), and Piper Jaffray (PIPR). Independent market makers also jump in and out of the lines.

The other primary market makers are the ECNs (electronic communications networks). They might be described as co-operatives for individual traders like you and me. Some ECNs you see most frequently are Island (ISLD), Instinet (INCA), and Terra Nova Trading (TNTO).

No one person, be it market maker or day trader, knows everything that's going on with a particular stock at a given moment. Though a NYSE specialist knows of every buyer and seller who comes in and out of his or her stock, no one player in a Nasdaq stock knows everybody else's business.

That's why actively traded Nasdaq stocks resemble high-stakes poker games, as the players attempt to shield their cards (orders) and true intentions from the others. Winning means outwitting your opponents by any means possible!

For instance, say you're the 800-pound gorilla broker known as Goldman Sachs. One of your institutional customers, a huge mutual fund, places an order with you to buy 500,000 shares of Microsoft (MSFT). You sure as heck aren't going to alert the other market makers that you have a juicy order by posting a single buy order for 500,000 shares. If you did, everyone would raise their prices (remember supply and demand?). Instead, you slip in and out of the market, buying up smaller lots of MSFT as quietly as you can. That way you can keep your client happy by getting a good price, and when MSFT rises, as it will from all the shares you absorbed, you can sell off some from your own account and pocket a tidy profit!

Like skilled specialists, savvy market makers rake in huge sums of money for themselves each year.

WHERE YOU, THE TRADER, COME IN

Basically, you, as the trader, can buy and sell Nasdaq stocks two ways.

1. If you place an order with your broker, either by phone or Internet, to buy 100 shares of Amazon.com (AMZN) at the market, the broker sends your order to a market maker, who fills the order and informs your broker. Your broker then tells you.
2. If you're trading with a sophisticated order entry system, you bring up AMZN on your level II screen, and click on the "buy" button. Instead of

waiting for the confirmation to return to you as you do above, either you see the order filled instantly or you see it jump into line as an ECN order, along with the market makers.

If you trade with a level II system, lots of strategies exist on how to "play market maker." You're going to learn them later in this book.

THE AMERICAN STOCK EXCHANGE, OR AMEX

The American Stock Exchange, or Amex (www.amex.com), is the third most active market in the United States, after the NYSE and Nasdaq. The exchange was founded in 1842, in New York City, and it still resides there. Most stocks traded on it are those of small and midsized companies.

The Amex trades similarly to the NYSE, with specialists maintaining orderly markets through the auction system. Amex stocks are also referred to as "listed" securities and, like NYSE stocks, can be recognized by their three-letter symbols.

Although highly respected companies, the majority of these stocks usually trade with less volatility and liquidity than the NYSE or Nasdaq. For a quick look at how the Amex is doing as a whole, check the Amex Composite Index, which includes all common stocks listed on the Amex.

THE RINGMASTER, CNBC

The CNBC (www.cnbc.com) television network covers the world's markets and keeps us informed on a minute-by-minute basis of important events pertaining to global finances. CNN also reports business news, Bloomberg provides excellent television and radio coverage, and you'll want to read the various financial papers. Still, when the market is open, virtually every trading room across America tunes in CNBC.

As important as it is to stay informed on financial news, take care how you apply the news to your trades. News can work for you or against you. Let's say that it's midmorning on a bullish day, and your positions are edging up nicely. Suddenly, Alan Greenspan appears on CNBC, and tells the world that U.S. stocks are overpriced and have displayed "irrational exuberance." A statement like that from someone as powerful as our Federal Reserve Chairman nearly always sends everyone running for the doors.

If you started taking profits at the same time Mr. Greenspan came to the end of the sentence, you did the right thing.

Far more often, you'll hear CNBC interviewing financial gurus. So-called experts, including mutual fund managers, prominent technical advisors, CEOs of companies, and authors of how-to financial books—once in a while they flavor the soup with a market astrologer—forecast their opinions about the markets' future or a particular stock's future.

Wanna see a stock move fast? Watch what happens to the price of Simple Software the moment Marvin Mutual Fund Manager swears it's going to be the next Microsoft. It rockets straight up, point after point. Finally, it quivers for a second, then—look out below! Observe it out of curiosity. Enjoy watching it as amusing entertainment. But no stock chasing, please. When stocks run on news, wise traders keep their mitts off the keyboard and telephone. Why?

First of all, word leaks out early in the morning on which stocks the experts will tout, so the stock may have already absorbed a lot of buying and is ready to pull back.

Second, if a stock split is announced on CNBC—news that many times drives stock prices skyward—it was broadcasted over the professional Bloomberg news system earlier in the day. Institutional and trading offices across the country become aware of the news long before CNBC announces it to you.

Third, those who already own a touted stock use the run-up to take unexpected profits.

For these reasons, be assured if a stock runs on news, it's usually the amateur traders who give it a quick upwards throttle. The market makers sit in the corners, drooling, waiting for these traders to run the stock up, so they, the market makers, can short it and drive it back down. Neophyte traders end up buying at the highest price of the day, then watch it fall in horror, with no buyers to sell it back to. Don't let that be you!

In conclusion, a wise trader uses news as he or she uses an indicator, as a temperature gauge for the markets. A wise trader leaves impulse buying to those with disposable trading accounts.

Okay, guys and girlfriends, this is an interactive book. So, it's your turn! From now on, at the end of each chapter, you will find a quiz. Please don't skip it. Completing the answers by writing them down will make you a better trader, faster.

QUIZ

1. True or false? When volatility indicators show the bulls and bears are fighting a volatile battle, and neither is winning, wise traders stand aside.
2. What two emotions rule the financial markets?
3. Which two fundamental principles dictate stock prices? Give a brief explanation.
4. True or false? Since price equals a shared consensus of the value of a stock, the buyer and seller also share the same opinion of the future worth of the stock.
5. On what kind of system does the New York Stock Exchange operate?
6. True or false? NYSE specialists have only one responsibility—to pair orders between buyers and sellers.
7. Define the term *spread*.
8. Overall, which industry dominates the Nasdaq?
9. True or false? Unlike NYSE stocks, which have one specialist per stock, active Nasdaq stocks have many market makers fielding orders at one time.
10. True or false? The safest strategy for making big bucks is to wait for a CNBC expert to tout a stock, then buy it fast.

ANSWERS

1. True. Successful, seasoned traders recognize whippy, trendless, market patterns and refrain from trading.
2. Greed and fear.
3. Supply and demand. Limited supply of a desirable stock causes high demand. Oversupply of a stock at prices perceived to be inflated causes low demand.
4. False. The buyer and seller have opposite opinions of the future worth of the stock. The buyers assumes it will rise in value; the seller assumes it will decrease.
5. The NYSE operates on a specialist central auction system.
6. False. Specialists not only pair, or match, orders, they also act as the customer's agent by recording and matching limit orders; they provide liquidity by filling orders from their own accounts when necessary; and they keep a fair and orderly market in their stock(s).
7. The spread is the monetary difference between a stock's posted bid and offer price.
8. Technology.
9. True.
10. Very, very false!

✦ ✦ ✦

CENTER POINT

Empower Your Personal Beliefs

Your potential is unlimited. Aspire to a high place. Believe in your abilities, in your tastes, in your own judgment. Imagine and perceive that which you wish to be. Back your image with enthusiasm and courage. Feel the reality of your "new" self; live in the expectancy of greater things and your subconscious will actualize them.

—BRIAN ADAMS

Our personal beliefs form the texture of our lives. When nourished with energy and action, our self-beliefs act as powerful forces for achieving our goals and dreams. They access resources deep within us and direct these resources to support and achieve desired outcomes.

Those who go about their day-to-day lives without positive belief systems about themselves resemble airplanes with no flight crews and no autopilots. They flounder about, with no goals or destinations and so end up with life's "leftovers."

Those who believe they are drawn to magnificent possibilities, and feel confident in their abilities to handle the challenges along the way, find their paths consistently strewn with new opportunities.

When you establish a belief about yourself, the process is an internal one; each belief, consciously or unconsciously, begins with a choice. After that choice is made, be it positive or negative, it filters communications with the world outside you and colors your perceptions with certain attitudes. The more ingrained those beliefs become, the more difficult they are to change.

Beliefs are the most powerful force in the world. On a global scale, diverse belief systems cause cultures to draw boundaries, ideologies to clash, and wars to be fought.

On a personal level, what we believe to be true about ourselves appears in our lives *as* our lives.

What do you believe about yourself? Do you see yourself as a strong and capable person who will succeed in attaining the vision you hold for yourself? Or do you see yourself as ineffective and overwhelmed with limiting circumstances? Either way, you'll be right! Either way, your beliefs will dictate the circumstances in your life—your reality.

If we want to succeed and achieve our highest potential, we must replace any negative beliefs we hold about ourselves with positive ones, much as an electrician rewires circuits in a faulty electrical system. Once attained, that foundation of powerful beliefs will speed us on our path to success and fulfillment!

✦ ✦ ✦

CHAPTER 3

Day Trading Is Your Business: Let's Set It up That Way

Day trading is a business, just like any other, and in this chapter we'll talk about setting it up quickly and efficiently.

First, we'll identify your trading objectives. Are you a part-time trader or a full-time trading jock? Next, we'll talk about the nature of the money you plan to trade with, and make sure it's in your best interests to use it. You'll decide on your weapon, be it an Internet broker or a Nasdaq level II software system. We'll streamline a custom brokerage account, define slippage, commissions, and margin. You'll make sure your environment, whether in your home or community trading room, is "trading-friendly."

Finally, we'll look at the pros and cons of paper trading.

YOUR DAY TRADING STASH: A REALITY CHECK

By now, you've probably allocated a sum of money you intend to use for your trading account. Let's talk about the nature of that money, and take a hard, but necessary, look at reality.

The cardinal trading rule of all time is that you *never trade with "scared money."* That means you never, *ever,* trade with money that, if lost, will diminish your lifestyle or that of your family. Why? When you trade with scared money, fear colors your decision-making abilities. You'll make the worst possible trading choices and lose the money—fast. Trust me. I've done it!

That leads us to the second cardinal rule, which is a variation on the preceding theme: *Trade only with money you can afford to lose.*

It's unfortunate, but true. Novice traders lose money. I know many traders who've lost their entire trading account, and worse—houses, furniture, cars, you name it—when they started. Please don't add your name to that casualty list! If you can't afford to lose the money you've buttonholed for trading, don't touch it. Postpone your trading career until you've pocketed a separate, expendable, stake.

Once you've targeted the money for your account, figure it's going to take from six months to a year before you consistently take money out of the market.

WHAT TYPE OF TRADER ARE YOU: PART-TIME OR FULL-TIME JOCK?

Before you start trading, you need to establish your goals. How much time to you plan to devote to this profession? Do you intend to be a part-time trader or full-time trading jock or jockess?

Most traders glue their backsides to their chair from market's open until it closes, taking advantage of every profit nuance offered during market hours. Others work at alternative jobs and trade two or three days a week. I know a few hot-shot traders who trade two hours a day, during the market's most volatile periods, from the open at 9:30 a.m. (Eastern Standard Time) to 10:30, and then again from 3:00 to 4:00 p.m., when the market closes. As with any business, though, the most prosperous traders are those who spend the most time there.

Now that you've defined the time you wish to devote to trading, let's take a closer look at your objectives:

- ✦ Do you plan to place five or fewer trades during the day?
- ✦ Are you content to be a "swing" trader or short-term investor, meaning you're happy to hold a position for two days to two weeks or longer?
- ✦ Do you intend to study trading as much as possible in your spare time, but have no intention of giving up every waking minute to it?

If these objectives describe your plans, you're probably a part-time trader, and an online account with a discount broker should be sufficient for your needs. You'll probably choose to establish an office in your home or other office area, where you can set up a computer and plug in a television.

The following defines the serious trading jock or jockess:

- ✦ Do you plan to trade every day the market's open and place more than five trades a day?
- ✦ Is your goal to execute trades precisely, often splitting or playing the spread (we'll learn how later) as much as possible?
- ✦ Do you want to make fast profits, maybe jumping in and out of a stock within minutes?
- ✦ Are you dedicated to studying technical analysis and charts until your eyes cross?
- ✦ Is your objective to eventually trade for a living?

If these objectives describe your trading goals, you'll need to consider an order entry system with either an Internet, cable modem, or dedicated phone line. You can work out of your home, or trade in one of the trading centers opening all over the United States. To locate a trading center in your community, check the financial section of your local newspaper.

TRADING ONLINE WITH AN INTERNET BROKER: WHICH ONE IS RIGHT FOR YOU?

Trading on the Internet with an online broker has revolutionized the stock market.

In the "old" days, you drove downtown and entered a stately looking office building. Soon, a dignified stockbroker wearing a dark suit and a condescending manner ushered you into a mahogany-paneled office and opened an account for you. When that broker bought or sold stock, the commission cost you upwards of $100 per trade. Of course, the broker researched the stock, and if you made a nice profit, it covered the commission.

How things have changed! Nowadays, online brokerage houses offer an array of inexpensive services and eagerly await your business. You'll probably never see their office or personally meet their staff. Instead, you choose a brokerage house and request an application form through the mail.

After the account is opened, *you're* in control of your money. You have definite goals and your own trading style. You can research your targeted stocks online, then buy or sell with the click of a mouse. Of course, you can also place your order by telephone. But once you get used to trading via the Internet, placing orders on telephone will seem slow and cumbersome!

If you're going to rely solely on an Internet broker, you'll want to find one that offers:

- A Web site that is accessible and easy to navigate, with graphics that snap on the screen rapidly. Also, you want a site that doesn't slow to a crawl when you move from screen to screen.
- A well-organized trading screen with safety catches built in to guard against data entry errors.
- Access to real-time quotes—for traders, they're a *must*. Real-time quotes mean stock prices are current when displayed. Some companies give "delayed" quotes, which are 15–20 minutes old.
- A quick confirmation system, current portfolio updates, and account balances.
- Alternative ways of reaching them. What happens when the market plunges 300 points, as it did on August 4, 1998? Were orders accepted and filled, or did their system jam? If the site went down, could the broker be reached by phone?

- Low margin rates; you'll be surprised at how they differ.
- A reasonable minimum dollar amount to open an account—if any.
- Buy or sell stops, even on Nasdaq stocks. All will set stops on NYSE stocks, some will on Nasdaq issues as a customer service. Ask if the buy and sell stops are "day" orders or can be "good-till-canceled" (GTC). GTC sell stops are particularly useful if you want to keep a core holding in your account while you go on vacation. (If the designated price hits your sell stop, it triggers a market order, and the position is automatically sold.)

When it comes to brokers, I believe in word of mouth. Ask other traders which Internet brokers are reliable and efficient, then call the most highly recommended ones and ask them to mail you information. Take your time and do as much research as possible. If you sign up with the wrong house, it can make your trading life miserable!

Here is a selection of popular online brokers:

Ameritrade	www.ameritrade.com	1-800-454-9272
Brown & Co.	www.brownco.com	1-800-822-2021
DLJdirect	www.DLJdirect.com	1-877-355-5557
Datek	www.datek.com	1-888-463-2835
E*Trade	www.etrade.com	1-800-387-2331
Muriel Siebert	www.msiebert.com	1-800-872-0444
National Discount Brokers	www.ndb.com	1-800-888-3999
Quick & Reilly	www.quickwaynet.com	1-800-837-7220
Schwab	www.schwab.com	1-800-435-4000
Suretrade	www.suretrade.com	1-800-394-1452
Waterhouse	www.waterhouse.com	1-800-934-4448

Some new traders start with an Internet broker, later adding or substituting the sophisticated order entry system that we'll talk about next.

ADVANTAGES OF USING A LEVEL II ADVANCED ORDER ENTRY SYSTEM

A major reason day trading has exploded as a profession is the rapid advancement of technology made available to the public. Now you can look inside the market and see the same financial information that used to be privy only to stockbrokers. Customizable charts, ticker tapes, up-to-the-minute news, and real-time price quotes are as close as your computer. So is the data that shows not only inside bids and offers, but all the tiers below those prices. You can watch all the market makers on a Nasdaq issue—meaning who wants to buy and sell, and how much.

If you plan to be a serious trader and play with the pros, you need access to all this information, plus an order entry system that gives you split-second access to the markets.

When it comes to placing orders, speed is *the* essential weapon in your arsenal. Speed gives you the edge over other market players who want your money. The speed with which you and your equipment act not only levels the playing field, it can tip it in your favor. Jump in before everyone else does. Hop out with a fistful of bucks before the rest of crowd realizes you were there!

For optimum trading speed and accuracy, your orders need direct routing to the exchanges. Serious traders don't have time to call a broker or wait for their Internet broker to fill an order. They click on a "buy" or "sell" button on their system's order entry screen. In a split-second, they see their order displayed or filled. These order entry systems that incorporate Nasdaq Level II quote systems are known as level II.

Currently, three basic quote systems define the trading scene: level I, level II, and level III. A level I quote is what you see when you ask for a quote from an Internet broker, or the inside bid and offer. Level III quote screens are used strictly by professional market makers and allow them to change the price of buy and sell orders.

Day traders use the level II quote system. A level II quote is actually a moving screen, constantly being updated. It shows the various prices and lot sizes at which a stock is bid and offered, and the regional exchanges (NYSE) or market makers (Nasdaq) involved. Most traders add a "time and sales" screen to their level II. Time and sales displays the actual "prints," meaning the trades that are taking place and the time they were executed. We'll talk in detail later about how to use this screen. Figure 3-1 shows a sample level II screen of the Nasdaq stock, Dell Computers (DELL), with a time and sales added.

Order entry systems using level II screens are currently available to traders. Since technology will have advanced or changed these systems by the time you read this, and because new systems will have appeared on the market, I've given only brief descriptions.

The Executioner is offered by Terra Nova Trading, www.executioner.com. Features include level II quotes and order entry system, real-time charts, customized ticker tapes, access to the NYSE and Nasdaq-Amex, and an educational support system.

All-Tech Investments offers Attain, http://www.attain.com, which features level II quotes, real-time charts, and customized ticker tapes. Access to Nasdaq only.

DELL COMPUTER CORP <32T,0969,YTPT,36005655>

DELL	42 1/16	↑ +1 1/2	2300	t	10:20
Bid ↑	42	Ask	42 1/16	Vol	6523400
# Bid	17	# Ask	1	Spread	1/16
High	42 1/8	Low	40 1/16	Close	40 9/16

Name	Bid	Size	#Best
SNDV	42	10	1
MSCO	42	10	12
USCT	42	2	3
DBKS	42	10	1
REDI	42	12	19
WARR	42	7	10
HMQT	42	9	4
SLKC	42	10	35
GSCO	42	10	9
SBSH	42	10	13
DKNY	42	1	37
BTRD	42	10	44
INCA	42	103	50
MWSE	42	3	4
MASH	42	1	11
PRUS	42	1	10
ISLD	42	50	90
JPMS	41 15/16	1	13
MLCO	41 15/16	10	5
WETH	41 15/16	50	0
RAJA	41 15/16	30	4
MADF	41 15/16	4	2
RSSF	41 15/16	10	11

Name	Ask	Size	#Best
USCT	42 1/16	5	6
PIPR	42 1/8	1	1
SWCO	42 1/8	10	0
NEED	42 1/8	1	1
DEAN	42 1/8	9	0
DLJP	42 1/8	10	1
NFSC	42 1/8	25	15
REDI	42 1/8	10	17
COST	42 1/8	10	16
PERT	42 1/8	4	8
MADF	42 1/8	17	15
ARCA	42 1/8	15	16
DKNY	42 1/8	1	13
BTRD	42 1/8	1	10
INCA	42 1/8	31	54
MWSE	42 1/8	13	9
RSSF	42 1/8	10	0
MASH	42 1/8	1	31
ISLD	42 1/8	40	107
SLKC	42 3/16	10	10
NITE	42 3/16	5	31
LEGG	42 1/4	1	0
AANA	42 1/4	1	0

Price	Size
42 1/16	1000
42 1/16	1000
42 1/16	2600
42 1/16	900
42	1000
42 1/16	500
42 1/16	100
42 1/16	100
42 1/16	1000
42	100
42	4000
42 1/16	5000
42	100
42 1/16	5000
42	1500
42 1/16	300
42 1/32	500
42 1/32	200
42 1/32	500
42 1/16	500
42 1/16	700
42 1/16	300
42 1/16	500
42	300
42 1/16	600
42 1/16	2000
42 1/16	400
42	400
42	200
42	300
42 1/16	500
42	1500
42 1/16	100
42 1/16	2300

Figure 3-1

This is a level II screen of the Nasdaq stock, Dell (DELL). The top portion shows current bid and ask prices, the current day's high and low prices, price change, and volume. Below that, the market maker Soundview (SNDV) is on the inside bid at 42. U.S. Trading Corp. (USCT) is on the offer at 42 1/16. The time and sales screen on the right shows actual trades, lot sizes, and the time they took place. (The time isn't showing on this screen, but every time it advances a minute, it appears on the screen.)

Chart Courtesy of *The Executioner*©

Pacific Day Trading offers software at www.day-trade.com, and offers level II quotes, charts, and ticker tapes. Access to NYSE and Nasdaq.

There are others, and more are coming onto the market. Check out as many as you can. Ask the company for information, then most important, talk to other traders to find out which systems they use, and how well they work.

Here are some things to consider and ask when checking out a level II system.

1. Make sure the system gives you access to all the exchanges, SuperDOT for the New York and American Exchanges. You'll also need SOES (Small Order Entry System), Island, and other access to other ECNs (electronic communications networks) for the Nasdaq.

2. How fast does the system execute trades? Remember, speed is one of your primary weapons and saves you money, especially when you need to beat a hasty exit! Don't worry about paying a little extra for faster executions. You'll come out ahead in the long run.
3. Are the keystrokes trader-friendly? Easy to use? You shouldn't have to type out the order. A click of the mouse or keystroke should do it. Are the "buy" and "sell" boxes easy to differentiate between? Learning how to trade on an electronic system can produce enough ulcers, without the system itself adding to the confusion. Like me when I was a new trader, you may sell when you meant to buy, and vice-versa!
4. Is the system reliable? How often does it go down, cutting off your access to the market? This is important because the trading god has a nasty sense of humor: At the exact moment your account is maxed out with volatile Internet stocks, a sadistic analyst will downgrade the entire Internet industry. Then, as Internet stocks crash and burn, your system will go down! So, grill the system's customer's representative: How many customers use the system? How accessible are they by phone if a problem arises? (Remember, they fib!) The best vote of reliability will come from talking to other traders who know about, or use, the system.
5. Is everything on one page? Shifting back and forth between pages to see your account positions and orders pending and executed, as well as level II screens and charts, will drive you bonkers. The fewer pages, the better.
6. How's the portfolio tracking? You should be able to see your current positions, trades completed, and real-time profit and loss statistics at all times. You'll also want your interest list in front of you, meaning the list of stocks you're watching, their current price, and change on the day.
7. Does the system offer an S&P futures feed? *Very important*. Please make sure the system you use gives you access to a real-time quote and chart of the S&P 500 futures. If you have to pay extra, do it. We'll discuss it later, but for now, know that it's the indicator used by every market pro, every minute of every trading day. Don't trade without it!
8. Does the system provide real-time charts? Personally, I could not trade without charts. Charts are pictures (a zillion words!) that show at a glance how a stock is performing. When I'm not watching minute-by-minute charts of the stocks I'm in, I'm skipping through others, searching for the next money-making opportunity. Chart packages differ; some are high, and some are low quality. You don't want bar charts; they don't give you enough info. You want candlestick charts and indicators, such as Bollinger bands, moving averages, MACD,

Commodity Channel Index, volume, and more. I'll explain these indicators later. For now, just inquire about the system's charting capabilities.

9. How does the charge work—by the number of shares or by trade? Are there different charges depending on whether it's a listed or Nasdaq stock? Some firms charge more or less depending on which market maker or ECN fills the trade. Some add on charges for DOT trades. Get a comprehensive list of *every* charge they can levy.
10. Is there a monthly charge for the system? Do you have to make a minimum number of trades per month? Do the number of trades you make affect the monthly charge?
11. How's their bookkeeping? Does it make extra work for you? Example: You place an order to buy 500 shares of AOL on the order entry system. It's filled in three separate orders consisting of 300 shares, then 100 shares, and then 100 shares. You should pay only one commission. Still, some systems automatically charge for each fill, then *you* have to ask for a refund on the other two commissions. Pain in the patootie.
12. Does the system use the Internet or a dedicated telephone line? There's the good news/bad news element to both. Internet servers go down with regularity. Cable modems that access the Internet may be faster and more reliable, but they cut off occasionally. Dedicated phone lines are the most reliable, but can cost a fortune if you're on long distance all day.
13. What are the margin rates? Do you receive interest on cash balances? Make sure their margin rates are competitive, and that they pay you interest on credit balances.
14. Do they require a minimum opening balance?
15. Does the system offer alarms? If so, you can set them to sound off when specified stocks hit a certain price.
16. Does the system offer news? What's the extra charge?
17. How secure is their system? In other words, who, besides you, has access to your account? Are there enough safeguards—codes, passwords, and so on to assure no hacker will break into your account?

I encourage you to research at least three systems before you chose one. Ask each company to send you information, then note how fast each responds. Their attitude right out of the gate will tell you something! Call them on the phone. How fast do they answer? Do they answer at all, or does a canned voice ask you to leave a message?

Are their customer representatives friendly and knowledgeable? Ask a technical question: "If a position is held overnight, and then sold the next day, is my account credited with the full amount at the moment of sale?" Some systems credit your account with only 25 percent of the proceeds from the overnight hold on the day you sell it.

Next, drive a few miles if you have to, but find a trading center or office that has a system comparable to the one you're considering, and check it out. Ask the traders who use it how it behaves. Listen to their gripes and praise.

The day trading business is so new most of the technology is still in the trial-and-error stage. Some of it is cutting-edge, but I've experienced times when that edge is as dull as a cardboard nail file! Only traders who have been-there, done-that, got-the-T-shirt, will tell you the unvarnished truth. And the truth is important when it's your money on the line!

SHOULD YOU OPEN TWO TRADING ACCOUNTS?

I have always maintained two trading accounts: one for day trades, one for swing/intermediate-term trades.

I keep the first account strictly for day trading. It is part of my level II order entry system, and I trade actively on it. The commissions are higher with this system than with my online broker, but since it executes rapidly and with precision, and since I "play market maker" with it, that makes up for the higher rate. I close out positions before the market closes each day, rarely holding a position overnight.

I maintain a second, intermediate-term account with an online broker for three reasons. First, my online broker allows me to place sell stops on all of my positions, even Nasdaq issues. This way, I can take a day off without worrying, knowing that if the stock falls, it will be sold if it hits my stop.

My second reason: *margin calls happen!* You can hold a position overnight that opens way down the next morning, causing a margin call. And during market hours, we traders move so fast, and calculate numbers so quickly in our heads, we've been known to make mistakes and slip over margin limits. Some brokers automatically cut you off if you try to overshop. Some don't.

Either way, you're phone will ring the day after the slipup, and an ominous voice will announce, "You have Regulation T margin call. Failure to send us the entire amount of money within three days will cause us to deactivate your account." *Gulp*.

I don't know about you, but I don't keep a zillion dollars in cash under my pillow, or even in my checking account. So I go to my other trading account and pull out the funds to pay the margin call. You can switch the money back in a few days if you want to after the call is satisfied.

The third reason I keep two accounts: *technology glitches happen*. And, wow, can they be costly. There you are, frantically trying to get out of a position that's

Hot Tip

If you use the Internet to trade on, make sure you have a backup Internet server. Even cable modems, though fast and efficient, are known to fail in bad weather. If your hookup is a cable modem, please maintain an alternative telephone line as well, with an alternative ISDN. If your hookup is a standard phone line, maintain an alternative server. The $20 or so extra cost per month equals peanuts if you compare it to losing a point or more in a 500-share position because your server went down!

going against you, and—whap—your screen freezes. A server goes down. After shouting "oh, golly, darn," you switch to your other account (assuming it's got a different connection) and if the situation's drastic enough, hedge your account that crashed. Also, the automatic sell-stops you have on open orders in that second account will provide a safety net for them.

The bonus reason for trading two accounts: When I started trading, I lost money with many of my day trades. Yet, my longer, intermediate-term holds made money. At the end of a brutal trading day, I'd turn my weary eyes to my intermediate-term account, and notice that GE, or AT&T, had made money. Those gains bolstered my flagging self-esteem, as well as offset the losses of my day trading account.

The important thing to remember when maintaining two accounts is to keep a separate mindset, or discipline, with each. Don't use your day trading account for long-term holds. Don't use your intermediate-term account for day trades. If either account crosses the line into the other, the value of trading two accounts is lost, and you'll have chaos on your hands.

Also, if you decide to go with dual accounts, consider going with a "plain vanilla" Internet broker who gives good fills on your orders, but charges low commissions. Remember, the higher commissions you pay, the more bells and whistles you have access to. Your level II account should provide you with all the research you need. Plus there are a truckload of sites on the Internet that offer free stock news and research. Check out the list of financial information sites in Chapter 14.

SLIPPAGE AND COMMISSIONS: HOW THEY AFFECT YOUR WALLET

Slippage takes place when your order is filled at a different price than the one displayed when you placed the order. Market makers, particularly, use it to pad their pockets when unsuspecting traders and investors issue market orders to buy or sell stocks.

Say you go to the Web site of your Internet broker and bring up the price for Igloo Ice Cream. The offered price is $29 1/2. So you place a market order to buy 500 shares of Igloo at the market (current asking price). When your order is confirmed, you find you bought 500 shares of Igloo at $29 5/8! What happened?

That's 1/8th of a point higher than you intended to buy it. On 500 shares, that equals $62.50.

Slippage hurts even more when you're selling at a loss. Say you buy 800 shares of Wacky Widgets at $50. Suddenly, the trade turns sour and starts to plummet, hitting $48 1/2, your "sell stop," or the predetermined price you exit the position at if the trade goes sour. You see the stock's selling off so fast, you panic and put in an order to sell at market. When your confirmation comes through, the actual price your order was filled at was $47 7/8. That's 3/8 of a point lower than when you placed your order, or $300. Add that to your loss of $1,200, and you're chewing on a $1,500 loss—before commissions!

I've watched stocks trade quietly at the same price for minutes, even an hour at a time. Keeping an eye on my level II screen, I've decided to sell a position I'm holding, and for fun, put it in at market. Click. The order is sent. And somebody saw it coming! I watch the price drop 1/8th of a point, and my confirmation appears. You guessed it. The market maker "dropped the bid," or lowered the price he or she had been advertising on my screen for the past hour! A quick profit, at my expense!

Remember when I told you in Chapter 1 that the stock market is sometimes a vicious arena? A dog-eat-dog world? This represents one example, and it happens all the time.

How do you cure the slippage malady? By placing limit orders, where you specify the exact price you're willing to pay for, or sell, the stock. I'll go into detail about limit orders later. Just remember that slippage will gobble chunks out of your profits if you're not careful.

Commissions also gobble up profits. They're a necessary business expense since, by law, your trades have to go through a registered broker. Still, neophyte traders typically overtrade, meaning they trade much more than they should, or need to, then wonder why commissions swallowed their profits.

It's extremely common for an active trader (20–30 trades per day), and more especially momentum traders (100 or more trades a day), to be "up on the day," and end up with a loss after commissions.

Say you're trading 500-share lots of Terrific Truck Lines. You're in and out of the stock all day, trying to buy the pullbacks and sell the rallies. (I don't suggest this for new traders, but your broker will urge you to—guess why?) Anyway, you trade your brains out, and at the market's close, you tally your profits and losses and see you made $600 on the day. Hey, this trading thing isn't so hard after all!

You puff out your chest and brag to your friends. Then you glance down at your trade sheet. Oops, you forgot to subtract the commissions. Let's see, you made 30 trades total, or 15 round trips. There's a $25 commission each way, or

$50 per round trip. Hmm, 30 trades multiplied by $25 each equals $750. Profits are $600. Subtract commissions, $750. *Gulp*. You lost $150 dollars!

When you come out of shock-mode, you can do a little more math. Excepting holidays, there are about 20 trading days in a month. Let's get conservative and say you average 10 trades, or 5 round trips per day at $25 per trade. In commissions, that equals $250 per day. Times 20 days a month, that comes to $5,000 per month! Huh? Really? Mercy!

Wanna keep going? You probably don't, but we're going to, anyway. There are about 250 trading days in the year. Multiply that out, and—please sit down before you read this—you're paying $62,500 in commissions per year!

Stops your heart, doesn't it? I know it does mine.

It also gives you a clue as to why trading centers are springing up like mushrooms! Ninety percent of the time, the broker makes much more money than the traders in the room, even after expenses.

What's the cure for paying hefty dollars in commissions every day, month, and year? There isn't one, really, except for a few common sense ideas I'll throw out now.

- I mentioned earlier in the chapter that you might consider maintaining two trading accounts. If you do, pay up for speed and accuracy on your level II account, but open your Internet account with a plain vanilla broker who charges minimum commissions. As of this writing, $5 commissions are being advertised. Every little bit helps.
- Don't overtrade. This is one of the biggest mistakes new traders make. Instead of letting the market "come to them," they buy anything that moves. They trade during lunch (bad odds), and when the market is going against them. Spastic trigger finger. Big losses. Add commissions to those losses. Ouch!
- Keep a realistic attitude. Remember, when you open a trade, you are starting out at a loss (commission) that you have to earn back before you can even begin to make a profit. Unlike you, your broker gets paid whether you win or lose. If you're trading on margin and holding a losing position, the knife plunges deeper: You're paying a commission on borrowed money that's shrinking in value, *and* paying interest on the commission.

I hope this dose of slippage and commissions reality sobers you enough so you don't overtrade, or chase stocks, or have unrealistic expectations of profits when you begin to trade. Please be a wise and cautious trader. Then you'll beat the system and make money despite the odds.

TRADING ON MARGIN: HOW TO DO IT AND STILL SLEEP AT NIGHT

Margin is a loan given to you by your stockbroker. Just like any bank, your broker charges interest on it. When you open your trading account, you'll want to designate it as a margin account, usually called a "50 percent margin account." The margin, or loan amount (no interest is charged until you actually use the money) matches your deposit amount. If you open your trading account with $50,000, your broker will give you access to another $50,000. Suddenly, you have $100,000 to trade with. Hey, let's go shopping!

Hold it right there. One of the riskiest things you can do as a new trader is max out your entire trading account, margin and all. Please understand that when a stock you are holding on margin tanks, you lose *twice* as much money as you would if you were playing with just your own cash.

As a safety measure, when you first begin trading, forget you have a margin account and use only your original equity to trade with. Keep a portion of your account in cash at all times, and keep any overnight holds to the bare-bones minimum. Sound boring? Don't worry, no matter how cautiously you trade, the market will provide plenty of entertainment and excitement along the way!

WHERE WILL YOU TRADE: YOUR HOME OR A TRADING CENTER?

The terrific thing about day trading is that you can do it from almost anywhere. Still, no matter what environment you trade from, be it home office, alternate office (some professional types are "closet day traders;" they sneak into their offices between patients or clients and trade away), or trading center, certain criteria apply.

To trade properly, you need to be able to maintain a positive mindset, concentrate, and be able to execute trades in a disciplined manner.

We'll start with the home office. Some of the following is obvious, some you may not have thought of:

- ✦ If possible, make sure your office has a window, or natural light. It's psychologically positive and easier on your eyes to have natural light streaming in the windows.
- ✦ Your computer should be up to date, with the fastest modem available.
- ✦ If you trade with a level II system, consider using a second monitor. That way you can watch twice as many charts, market maker screens, and ticker tapes. Windows 98 allows for multiple monitors on one computer.
- ✦ Don't forget your backup Internet server. The extra cost per month is a drop in the ocean compared to the losses you might incur when the system goes down.

- Install a television and leave it permanently tuned to CNBC.
- Learn how to ignore phone calls. You can't discuss the Mets, or give opinions on the newest nail polish, and trade well at the same time. I've lost hundreds of dollars by politely talking to friends while trying to trade. Explain to everyone who's likely to call that you can't chat during market hours. Then let the machine or voice-mail service answer the phone.
- Make sure your office is quiet. Kids running around, a noisy dog, or well-meaning spouse running the vacuum all interrupt concentration.
- Keep your desk cleared, except for your trading log. When your largest holding looks unhappy, it's a real tooth-grinder to push papers around searching for a trading log with the sell stop written on it. Mess causes stress!
- Don't leave volatile positions open and wander out to the mailbox, or wash your car. I once lost $500 in Intel because I visited the ladies' room!

If you trade from an alternative office where you work at another job, it's already set up by now. Please provide yourself with the peace and privacy to make clear-headed decisions.

Several considerations come into play if you open your account and plan to trade in a day trading center or office.

- Are the surroundings clean, efficient, and positive? I once walked into a grim and gray, windowless trading center. It housed the unhappiest-looking traders I've ever encountered! No one looked up, no one spoke. Now I know that's common when the market's volatile and concentration levels are strained. Yet, after the closing bell rang, these traders' expressions didn't change. Eventually, the manager approached me and we talked, but I kept one eye on the traders. They left without saying a word to each other. Conclusion? Virtually everyone there was losing money.
- Beware of centers that offer you four-to-one margin, or more. When they try to pooh-pooh your concerns, close your ears. If you trade there, they usually expect you to make *hundreds* of trades a day. With the commissions they make, they don't care if you crash and burn. There's another fool waiting in line to take your seat.
- Beware of centers that goad you into momentum trading—trading actively for tiny profits of a "teeny" (a sixteenth of a point), or an eighth—especially before you are ready. Momentum trading is not for beginners, and most lose everything. (People who argue this point are usually on the receiving end of commissions!)

- Ask how many traders in the room are truly making money on a consistent basis. Is there proof?
- Will the center train you how to use the system before you place your first trade, or do they expect you to already know the basics? Trading on an unfamiliar system can cost you, big time. Don't do it.
- Ask (the traders if you can) how often the system goes down. *This is very important.* If the system does fail, is there a backup? If the computer assigned to you acts cranky, is a technical assistant available? How fast does the assistant show up?
- How long of a drive is it from your house to the trading room? Do traffic tie-ups consistently make you late for the market's opening bell? Are you stressed out before you arrive at the trading room?
- Try to find a trading center that offers trading courses, not just on their equipment, but on trading techniques as well.
- Ask the other traders if they are happy trading there.

PAPER TRADING: SHOULD YOU DO IT?

Some trading teachers advocate beginners trade on paper—trade without putting real money on the line—for weeks or months prior to placing the first real trade. Others think it's a waste of time.

I believe paper trading can be a valuable tool, as long as you focus as though the money aspect is real. It aids in teaching internal rhythms of the market, and you can become familiar with the personalities of different stocks and indexes.

You may "make" a lot of money when you paper trade and mistakenly think real trading is just as easy. One component is missing from paper trading: emotion. Heck, real trading is just like paper trading—only with a loaded gun pointed at your head!

QUIZ

1. Name the two rules that define the money with which you open your trading account.
2. Describe the three levels of quote systems currently at use for trading.
3. Give three advantages to opening two trading accounts.
4. Define slippage.
5. Name three ways to avoid overpaying on commissions.
6. Give one safety measure to avoid margin calls.
7. Is paper trading a good use of time?

ANSWERS

1. Never trade with "scared money." Trade only with money you can afford to lose.
2. Level I is a stock's real-time inside bid and offer displayed upon demand. Level II is the moving screen showing all the bids and offers, and can be used to initiate orders by traders. Level III is used exclusively by market makers, allowing them to refresh their orders and alter their prices.
3. Three advantages of splitting your money between two accounts, one day trading, one swing trades/intermediate-term: (1) In case of a margin call, funds to cover it can be accessed from the alternative account. (2) In case of a technical failure, you can hedge one account with the other. (3) The intermediate-term account may contain core holdings that bolster and hedge any losses in the day trading account.
4. Slippage takes place when your order is filled at a different price than the one displayed when you placed your market order.
5. To avoid giving back all of your profits in commissions: (1) Open two accounts, and keep your swing/intermediate-term account with a good online broker who charges minimal commissions. (2) Don't overtrade. (3) Remember, you have to earn the commission back before you begin to make a profit.
6. One way to avoid getting a margin call is to refrain from taking home overnight positions.
7. Paper trading can teach the novice trader different stock personalities and relationships between indicators, and help the trader to internalize market rhythms.

✦ ✦ ✦

CENTER POINT

Your Vision: Life's Invitation to Greatness

What would you do if you knew you could not fail?

—DR. ROBERT SCHULLER

Deep within you lives your vision—it's you in the form of your purest potential, your real self. Your true vision is your core being telling you who you really are. It defines your personal greatness.

To see your vision and mold it into a recognizable thought form, you must sweep aside old, limited beliefs of who you *thought* you were, and see your *true* self—the self who is made from innate wisdom, power, and intelligence. That self can reach for your highest potential and establish a life built on clear purpose.

Once your vision is clear to you, you may not know how to accomplish it. Few of us do! But just as a seed planted in warm earth and sunlight knows exactly how to grow into a plant, your vision has within it the cosmic wisdom to bring itself into fruition.

In order for your vision to germinate, you need only listen to your inner guidance. Act upon what it tells you. Take one step, then the next. Just as attention from sunlight and rain nourishes the seed into a strong, healthy plant, the more energy you shower onto your vision, the more it will grow. You'll be guided automatically to the right people, places, and situations to move you ahead on your journey.

The vision growing within you is the unlimited you, the powerful you, the wise you. It's the you who knows perfect harmony, the you who knows you deserve to live your highest possibility, your fondest dream.

Your vision is the truth of your being. Hold your vision in front of you like a lamp, and let its light show you the way to attainment.

Your vision is life's invitation to greatness. Do you accept the invitation?

✦ ✦ ✦

CHAPTER 4

The Winning Market Mentality That Leads to Profits

Experts say good sex is 10 percent in your body and 90 percent in your head.

Believe it or not, good trading evolves from the same ratios—about 10 percent methodology, and 90 percent mental discipline. You can study charts and indicators until your eyes cross, but unless you develop a specific mindset that guides your trades, you'll be walking a tightrope without a safety net!

To start with, let's establish two, etched-in-stone commandments to live by the rest of your trading life.

- The First Commandment: Protect your principal
- The Second Commandment: Trade to trade well (not to make money)

Do they sound too simple to be true? Trust me, they're not! They're much easier promised than accomplished, but they can be mastered. Virtually everything you learn in this book points back to these two commandments. If you keep them uppermost in your mind, and implement them into every trade, you'll travel the road to riches!

THE FIRST COMMANDMENT: PROTECT YOUR PRINCIPAL

Successful professionals in occupations the world over use tools to accomplish their goals. Whether intangible, such as knowledge and discipline, or tangible, such as stethoscopes, violins, or race cars, these tools are cared for.

Dr. C. Everett Koop doesn't drag his stethoscope on the floor behind him as he makes hospital rounds, Stradivarius didn't toss his violin out in the rain, and Michael Andretti doesn't push his racing car into the path of an oncoming train.

As a successful trader, your tools consist of market knowledge, mental and emotional discipline, and *your trading account.* Protect the money in your trading account at all times. Don't abuse it, treat it carelessly, or allow others to take it from you. This money is your most cherished tool, and you must guard it with your life!

"Yeah, yeah, I already know all that stuff," you reply. "You're oversimplifying. You're going overboard with your explanation."

Am I really? Surely we've both watched television programs that tell the unhappy stories of new day traders who have lost *all their money, and worse.* I bet we've both heard the same statistics—between 80 and 90 percent of all traders crash and burn! As you read this, traders somewhere in the world are "chasing" a stock, ignoring their stops, holding losers, overtrading, taking home dangerous or oversized positions, and buying against a downtrend. Translation? They are treating their precious tool—their trading capital—recklessly.

I work with new traders every day who swear they protect their principal and in the next breath, abuse it by jumping into a careless trade. They get caught up in the thrill of the moment, the excitement of a running stock, the euphoria of buying when everyone else does. Hey, I've been there, too. Took pictures, bought the T-shirt, and lost money!

Even if you avoid all unnecessary risks, a percentage of your trades will lose money. Don't add to these by careless trades, or you'll wake up one morning with assets that total pocket change.

True trading professionals, who rake in profits of five, six, even seven figures a year, protect their accounts like a mother tiger protecting her cub. They trade cautiously. They look at occasional good-trades-gone-sour as routine business expense. And they don't compound them with losses due to carelessness.

Jimmy Rogers, one of the shrewdest investors of our time, frequent guest on CNBC, and now retired and teaching at Columbia University Graduate School of Business, says in Jack D. Schwager's *Market Wizards,* "One of the best rules anybody can learn…is to do nothing, absolutely nothing, unless there is something to do. I just wait until there is money lying in the corner, and all I have to do is go over there and pick it up."[1]

Rogers, like other financial giants, amassed a fortune by protecting his principal. He knows specific signposts that point to a high probability of success and has the mental and emotional control to wait until they appear. You will, too.

---

1 Schwager, Jack C. *Market Wizards.* (NY: Harper Business, 1993), p. 286.

Let's talk about positive, mental devices you can use to protect your principal.

- During the trading day, repeat to yourself over and over, "At all times, I protect my principal." Say it out loud. Don't just murmur it, shout it with enthusiasm! Sound crazy? Try it. It works.
- Before you click on the "buy" button, ask yourself:

1. Why am I entering this trade? Does my trade coincide with the present market trend? Do primary market indicators support my decision?
2. Is my entry point technically perfect?
3. Do I have a rational, thought-out game plan? Where's my sell/cover stop if my trade goes sour? Where's my proper exit point if it performs well?
4. What time of day is it? (Certain time slots during the trading day almost guarantee a trade's failure or success. You'll learn these times in Chapter 5.)

With practice, you'll soon be able to answer the above questions in five seconds or less. If your answers are quick, concise, and positive, then the trade should be as close to a "sure thing" as possible. If you fumble or overjustify one of the answers, reconsider placing the trade at all.

Please take a personal oath right now to protect your principal. Paste the commandment on your monitor. Tape another copy on your bathroom mirror and refrigerator door. Write it on the back of your hand—whatever it takes to etch these words onto your brain and every fiber of your being. Treat your trading account as any professional treats his or her tools, with concern and respect. Protect it at all times, and don't expose it to carelessness or neglect. If you care for it properly, it will care for you—and multiply at the same time!

THE SECOND COMMANDMENT: TRADE TO TRADE WELL, NOT TO MAKE MONEY

It appears to contradict reality, but it doesn't. Traders who routinely rake in big bucks don't mentally count the dollars while they're trading. They don't think, *Wow, I'm up two points in AOL. Let's see, a thousand shares, times two dollars a share, equals two thousand dollars.*

Nothing blows your concentration and clouds your judgment more than keeping a mental calculator running in your head, tallying up the actual dollars you've made and lost each minute.

While we're at it, let's take this a step further. Please don't get up in the morning and announce to your partner/spouse/kids/dog that today, you "have to make a thousand bucks trading." Trust me, you're setting yourself up for failure. I've done it. Other traders have done it. Guaranteed losing mentality.

In fact, stating a set goal in dollars you must bring home every day, or any day, especially if you're a beginner, assures it probably won't happen. The need to make a certain amount of money colors your perceptions of the markets. It pressures you to enter trades that are bad bets because you promised yourself—or worse, someone else—that you would bring home trading "bacon."

Besides, the day you make that promise usually falls on the rockiest market you've witnessed in weeks. Indicators warn you'd be best on the sidelines. But your pledge echoes in your mind, so you force trades. Odds are, you lose money. Now you're embarrassed and annoyed with yourself. That punishes your self-esteem, which automatically leads to more losses.

The cure for this malady: From now on, *your goal is not to make money!*

Your goal is to *trade to trade well.* As of this minute, banish money from your mind. As we say in New York, "Forgettaboudit!" Think of stock prices as numbers and fractions, not dollar amounts.

Good trading is an art form. Throwing a flawless, 30-yard pass to a moving receiver, performing open-heart surgery, and landing a fighter on an aircraft carrier at sea, all require "touch," skill, and sheer determination. So does executing the perfect trade. Money represents the by-product of the art of good trading, and you'll have plenty of time to count it at the end of the day.

Funny thing about trading to trade well: The profits add up a zillion times faster than they do when making money's the primary goal. Why? Traders who trade to trade well cut their losses and let their winners run. They cherish and protect their principal. They leave unnecessary risks to others. They recognize whippy, choppy market conditions and stand aside, content to keep their money safe. They control their emotions. They make no promises to anyone, including themselves, about take-home money.

Traders who trade well "let the market come to them." They insist on entering the trade at the perfect entry point and exiting at the perfect exit point. If those points don't arrive, or are faulty, they automatically discard the trade. Should you point to money left on the table, they shrug and say, "So what?" They know another opportunity is just around the corner.

Traders who trade to trade well don't trade because they're addicted to the thrill, or to get back at someone, or because they're bored. They don't trade when they are exhausted, sick, or hungover. They are calm and confident, but cautious. They keep their list of trading guidelines beside them at all times, and always trade within those guidelines.

To sum it up, traders who trade to trade well are perfectionists about their craft. And wealthy. Make this your goal, too.

WHY THE STOCK MARKET IS ALWAYS RIGHT

If you've chatted with experienced traders, you've heard, "The stock market is always right." A shortened, Zen-like version sounds even more accurate: "The stock market *is*."

A macrocosm of collective energy, the stock market expands and contracts, rises and falls with global news, company earnings, government reports, wars, weather, and more. Traders, investors, gurus, and analysts, all come, participate, and go—and still the self-contained market continues.

Television commentators and journalists judge that the market "overreacted" to bad earnings, or it "underreacted" to a war. Does this ball of energy care what judgment we pass on it? Nope. Just like an 800-pound gorilla, it does what it wants to, when it wants to.

Industries within the market inflate and deflate in value, depending on economic fundamentals or the fickle herd-mentality of market participants. Internet stocks are "in." Retail stocks are "out." Oil stocks are "overvalued." Gold stocks are "undervalued."

Think the price of Microsoft is out of line? Too bad. Like it or leave it. Were you sure that small-cap stock you bought would double by now—and instead it fell by half? "Not fair," you mutter. The market doesn't know or care about "fair."

What you think, expect, want, or believe should happen, carries no weight with the stock market, or any particular stock. If you, the trader, show up and find opportunities in the market, you're welcome to them. If you let money slip through your fingers—the market swallows it, then yawns. It shrugs off excuses, complaints, even thank-yous.

As Mark Douglas says in *The Disciplined Trader*, "The point here is that right and wrong as you may traditionally think of them don't exist in the market environment."[2]

Just as the market is always right, so are stock prices. If I decide to buy, and you agree to sell shares of stock at a specific price—our reasons can be biased, insane, bizarre, and crazy. They can be fear- and greed-ridden, or based on the full moon. Doesn't matter. That's the price, and it's "right" at this moment.

You may contend that you, as a trader, can influence price movement by fancy level II strategies you'll learn in later chapters, or by buying or selling big volume. Sure you can, for a tick or two, but unless you're a major market nabob, you can't change price for any length of time. Soon new forces take over, and with or without you, the price moves depending on the collective mindset of the players involved.

---

2 Douglas, Mark. *The Disciplined Trader.* (NJ: New York Institute of Finance, 1990), p. 36.

How do you survive and prosper in such an environment? By looking at the market as a field of opportunities based on price fluctuations. You assess the opportunities, and then decide whether or not the reward is worth risking your capital.

Think of the stock market as a fruit stand. You visit the stand and look over the various displays. If the fruits are ripe and juicy, you buy and enjoy. If they're rotten and overpriced, you shrug and leave with your money still in your pocket.

Please keep in mind the two phrases, "the market is always right," and "the price is always right." They cultivate an attitude that's extremely important to successful trading. The more you trade, the more you'll agree with me.

THE TRADER'S MOST FORMIDABLE FOE

Another favorite saying in this business: Trading is war. It's absolutely true!

To emerge victorious, you need to identify your enemies quickly, and go into battle with a tough, winning mindset. My goal is to help you achieve that lofty status of a trader who survives and prospers.

With that in mind, let's drag your most formidable foe into the daylight and get a good look at it. By now, you may have guessed its name: *emotion.*

As a trader, you can memorize every nuance of technical analysis, equip yourself with the fanciest computer ever built, install the fastest, high-tech level II system available, and still lose gobs of money. How? By allowing the most lethal enemy of all to wield your trades—*emotion.*

Learning to control your emotions while trading may prove to be the highest hurdle, the tallest challenge you'll face.

In the *Disciplined Trader*, Mark Douglas says, "When asked for their secrets of success, [winning traders] categorically state that they didn't achieve any measure of consistency in accumulating wealth from trading until they learned self-discipline, emotional control, and the ability to change their minds to flow with the markets."[3]

I can say, without hesitation, that the first day I traded with composure as my only emotion was the day I became a winning trader. Period.

Before that, I read charts with the best of them. I deciphered intermarket relations, indicators, and oscillators in a nanosecond. I traded on a high-tech, level II system and made split-second decisions. And I lost money. Lots of money.

"You're kidding," you reply. "Were you dumb, or something?" No, not dumb—just human.

Every day, into every trade, I let greed, fear, the need to be right, anxiety over losses, self-deprecating talk, and a host of other negative emotions accompany me.

---

3 Douglas, p. 4.

The day I started trading from my head—and not my heart—I started making money consistently, trade after winning trade.

At the time, I marveled at the feeling. I didn't plan it to happen although I'd wished for it long enough! How did it feel? As though an internal shift had taken place. How long did it take to come about from the time I first started trading? A year. Why so long? Because to hone myself into a cool, calculating machine, I had to override the core of my being—my humanness, my emotions.

If you took Psychology 101 in college, you may remember the basic premise: A thought plus a feeling, equals an action. That's how we humans operate. Try eliminating one of those components and notice how uncomfortable we get.

First, imagine a thought plus a feeling, minus the action—especially if the action relates to pleasure. Thought: *I've had a long day at work, and a beer would taste good before dinner.* Automatically, you imagine a frosty mug filled with the golden elixir, a foamy top. Feelings: pleasure. Your mouth anticipates the taste of cool, refreshing, robust liquid. Gratification flows through you at the feeling of relaxation that always follows and a reward for a long day. Action: Yes, you'll have a beer. You reach into the refrigerator—but there's no beer. Rats. Now your feelings of expected pleasure turn to irritation. Thought, plus a feeling, minus the desired action.

That's how we humans are built. We think of something, qualify it with feelings, and carry through with action (or inaction). *I'm out of beer* (thought), disappointment (feeling), so you go (or decide not to go) to the store (action).

Thought and feeling also precede automatic actions though they may be lightning-quick, such as sitting down, stepping on the brakes, or kissing a loved one.

You can't eliminate thoughts from the equation; every feeling or action begins with a thought. Feelings were originally installed in humans to tell us whether those thoughts, acted upon, would produce pleasure or danger. So to a greater or lesser degree, feelings control our actions. To control those feelings demands superhuman dedication and resolve.

We humans are built to seek pleasure, and the feelings associated with day trading represent the most incredibly thrilling, exciting, breathless, heart-pounding, "I'm gonna be rich," "I was right on the money about this stock," ego-building sensations you'll ever experience! When you make a big score, it's like winning the lottery! Not only did you make big bucks fast, you get to brag about it to your friends. You're *the man*! Or you're *the woman*!

It may go something like this. Thought: *Hey, look at that action in Dell. It must be a good buy.* Next, depending on the situation, emotions surge through you:

- *Thrills:* Whoa! Look at Dell scream! Everybody in the world is buying Dell right now. They must know something I don't! I better grab some while I can! *Point. Click.*
- *Excitement:* I knew it...Dell's going to the moon and I'm gonna go with it! I'll have to carry my profits home in a moving van! *Point. Click.*
- *Breathless/heart-pounding:* Wait for me, little red Porsche! I'm coming to drive you out of the showroom! Dell's gonna make me big bucks. *Point. Click.* Go, Dell, *Go! Yesss!!!!!!!!*

Unfortunately, this doesn't portray the feelings of most winning traders I know. They do, unfortunately, portray the feelings of the traders who don't make the cut. I remember those feelings well. Lots of losses ago.

Please don't misunderstand me. After I complete a good trade, satisfaction washes over me that I *traded well*, and I give myself a pat on the back. At the end of the day, I feel elated that I came to the market, took winnings from it, and escaped with my principal intact.

The next morning, though, the emotional slate is wiped clean. New day, new market, new set of circumstances.

For professional traders, the scene with Dell goes more like this. Thought: *According to my trading plan, this is the precise entry point to buy Dell.* Quick assessment of market conditions. *Okay, all other systems are "go."* Feeling: calm, confident, and composed. Action: *Point. Click.*

To become a winning trader, then, you must leave thrills and excitement to others, and execute your trades in a calm, controlled manner. You'll experience plenty of excitement after the market closes—when you count your money!

In the following paragraphs, we discuss other emotions you'll enjoy leaving behind.

Confusion runs rampant among new traders. And no wonder!

It's like learning how to snow ski. You feel cold and clumsy. The workings of your equipment remain a mystery to you. You're supposed to coordinate brain and body enough to perform an intricate series of movements while falling mach 2 down a treacherous, icy slope. As if that weren't enough, you're scared spitless. Great, just great.

When you're first learning to trade, the market moves in mysterious ways. You're not yet experienced enough to read signposts that hint at what may happen next. You're trading on a computer (I hope), be it Internet broker or level II system (which is more complicated), and you don't understand what to click on next. Stocks shoot up and collapse for no apparent reasons, and you feel ten steps behind everyone else. You've been told that "the best in the business" lurk in every trade, waiting to grab your money from you. You hate to admit it, but you're scared. Great, just great.

When I first started trading, my hands shook so badly and I got so confused, sometimes I'd buy when I meant to sell, and vice-versa. Soon after I sent a tangled trade into cyber-ether, my online broker would call: "Miss Turner, you bought 300 shares of Igloo Ice Cream. Then you sold 600 shares. Did you really mean to do that?"

Wince. "Um, no. I meant to *sell* 300. Did I sell it twice? Sorry."

Or "Miss Turner, you just put in a buy order for 1,000 shares of Terrific Truck Lines. That puts you, let's see, $20,000 over margin. Did you really mean to do that?"

Gulp. "A thousand shares? *Twenty-thousand over margin?* Rats. I meant to buy a *hundred* shares. I punched an extra zero by mistake. *Wince* Sorry."

Fortunately, experience will diminish much of your confusion, but catastrophes can occur before experience calms you down. To save time and money, take steps early on to avoid unnecessary confusion.

Best Cures for Confusion

1. When you start trading, buy small lots, say, 100 to 300 shares per trade. That way, if the stock tanks, and you accidentally buy more—instead of selling what you have (laugh if you want, but it happens)—you won't swallow as big of a loss.
2. Complete one trade before you enter another. Keeping up with one stock in a fast-moving market is job enough. If you feel like you're missing out on other opportunities, rest assured that more will come along. And you'll still have money to trade with!
3. Paper trade until you feel comfortable placing real trades.
4. Thoroughly learn any new system, especially a new level II system, *before* you attempt your first trade on it. If a trainer isn't sitting beside you when you begin to trade, make sure the system has a trial feature that lets you push buttons and get used to the procedure before you use actual money.
5. Learn one trading strategy at a time. *Then stick to that strategy*, and that one only, one trade at a time. Sound boring? Does making money sound boring?
6. Until you're an experienced trader, don't mix trading time frames, such as putting on a day trade, and while it's still open, diving into a scalp. Maintaining different time frames is too confusing when things get crazy, and too risky.

The need to be right about a stock's future direction plagues every new trader I've ever met. It's a major cause of fat losses. Why?

You'll find "the need to be right" on the flip side of our old nemesis, fear. Insisting that you're right equals the fear of being wrong. Humans in general, and Americans in particular, grow up learning it's important to always be "right." Mistakes, and those who make them, we label stupid and weak. We poke fun at people who are "never right about anything."

Successful people are "right." Those who fail are "wrong." Naturally, we all want to be "right."

The trouble is, "right" can be an illusion. We make choices and act on them. One choice produces one result, another choice a different result.

The need to be right in trading causes enormous losses. For example: Tom Trader buys 500 shares of Terrific Truck Lines at $52, the proper entry point. The stock promptly falls to $50 7/8, hitting his protective sell-stop. Instead of selling without hesitation, Tom grits his teeth. "I'm not selling at a loss. Terrific Truck Lines is a good company, and just announced fantastic earnings. This will end up being a great trade. I know I'm right."

Terrific Truck Lines continues to fall, sinking toward $45, then $40, and Tom Trader holds. Now if he sells, the loss will seriously dent his trading account, as well as his ego. He's no longer a trader. He's an "investor," as traders joke when they knowingly hold onto a losing position. When people ask why he's still holding, his jaw juts out. "It's a good company. It'll come back."

Maybe it will. Maybe it won't, at least for a long time. Meanwhile, the loss is very real (paper losses are real losses), and even if Terrific Truck Lines struggles back to $52, it may take weeks or even months. During that time, Tom could have used that money to make profitable trades. The need to be right cost him, big time.

Cure for the Need to Be Right

1. Practice shrugging and saying "I don't know." Simple yes, funny maybe, but also very powerful. This attitude saves you mega-bucks by alleviating the "need to be right" syndrome. Listen to Jimmy Rogers on CNBC. When an interviewer quizzes him about what will happen next in the financial markets, the wealthy Rogers usually grins and shrugs. Then he answers, "I have no idea."
2. One of the biggest favors you can do for yourself in this profession: When you enter a trade, *don't get attached to the outcome.* Banish expectations of which way the stock will go, or any illusions you have of "fair." That way, you won't have to be right.

3. Plan your trade and trade your plan. We'll talk about how to do this later, but for now, please understand that planning your trades with exact entry points, exit points, and protective stops is one of the most efficient ways to cure "the need to be right." Following your plan assures you limit your risk, keeps your losses small, and your profits big.
4. Stop beating yourself up for making "dumb mistakes." Berating yourself cripples your trading career by paralyzing you when the next good opportunity steps in your path. It will also damage your self-esteem and delay the arrival of that calm, confident attitude you're striving for. You make choices, not mistakes. Different choices produce different outcomes. Each outcome is a learning experience. Study the thinking behind each trade, your choice, and the result. Learn from every outcome, both winning and losing.

Greed motivates new traders and even many experienced traders. Remember the saying we mentioned in Chapter 2? "Bulls make money, bears make money, and pigs get slaughtered." Since I discussed this powerful emotion earlier in the book, the following explanation will be brief.

Don't ask me how, but the market "sees" when greed motivates your trading. If I didn't know better, I'd swear an invisible scorekeeper stands over us with a tally sheet, waiting to punish greedy traders. Don't believe me? Listen to traders talk about the time they "bet the ranch," convinced a stock was going to double. That was usually the last thing they remember before the stock crumbled.

Greed also comes into play when you "chase" a stock, or pay too high a price for it. When you chase a stock, odds are good you'll buy at the top of the move—and sell at the bottom!

Cure for Greed

1. As a new trader, you've already decided to limit your risk by trading small lot sizes. Don't compromise. This alone will temper any notions that "more is better."
2. When you see a stock screaming straight up on your quote screen and you're filled with the urge to join in on the fun—sit on your hands. Go get a cold soda. Play with the dog. Leave the room if you have to, but *don't touch that mouse*! If you insist on staying to watch, notice how fast the stock drops when the buyers leave and the sellers rush in. Falls fast, doesn't it? Ouch. Better them, than you.

For traders, *fear* is the Goliath of emotions. Fear, which ranges from mild anxiety to gut-wrenching terror, causes more havoc in the trader's life than any other entity.

Fact: Fear is nothing trying to be something.

As a child, do you remember the still, dark nights you believed a monster lurked under your bed? Recall the feelings? Your heart pounded, you mouth went dry, and your hands sweated. You curled into a quivering ball and waited for the monster to come and get you!

Of course, no monster lurked under your bed. The sensations of fear were real, but you grew to realize that monsters didn't exist, and your feelings were self-induced.

For a neophyte trader fear takes on many faces, from mild to severe. *Dismay*—you enter a trade properly, then watch the S&P futures dive. Will your stock follow? *Alarm* and *frustration*—your Internet server goes down; you have open positions. *Fright*—your stock is falling a point every five seconds, and you can't sell it to anyone! *Outright panic*—you held a stock overnight, and this morning it opens down thirteen points (yes, it happens).

Fear of losing money can cause you to exit good trades too early, and stay in bad ones too long. Fear of losing may also urge you to ignore information that's telling you what the *real* situation is, not how you want it to be!

Cure for Fear

1. How do you conquer fear? You don't. You displace it.

Just as a rock displaces water in a bucket, you displace fear with a positive foundation of knowledge, experience, and self-trust. Each of these feeds into the next, creating a symbiotic relationship.

Start by displacing fear with knowledge. Most new traders gain a little knowledge, then stop studying. Yet they continue to trade, repeating the same mistakes over and over, until they blow away their trading accounts.

I remember one new trader who took a three-day course, then dove headfirst into the market, buying thousands of shares of anything that moved. When I warned him he didn't have enough trading knowledge to manage so many hefty positions, he replied smugly, "I know enough. I don't think there's a lot more to learn." He went on to crash and burn, losing a great deal of money by anyone's standards.

I promise you this—if you study the art of trading until the sun turns purple, you still won't know everything! Read every trading book you can get your hands on, whether you agree with the system or not. Study chart patterns until you topple out of your chair. Keep a trading journal; record lessons your trades teach you each day. When a CNBC announcer or journalist explains a financial concept that's new to you, write that in your journal, also. Make it a goal to learn at least one new trading gem each day.

Next, you'll displace fear with experience. Experience constantly reinforced with fresh knowledge crafts a powerful trading weapon. Experience teaches you how to internalize market movements and stock movements. It guides you to the trading style that best suits your temperament. Experience helps you identify techniques that work for you, and those that don't. You discover how you, and other traders, react to certain situations, and the best ways to either profit or escape.

As your knowledge and experience expand, they will present you with a priceless gift: self-trust. When you finally evolve to the point that self-trust guides all of your trades, fear will disappear. *Then* you will know you've arrived. You will trade with that calm, controlled attitude I mentioned earlier. The market cannot harm you unless you return to your old ways. Self-trust will permeate you with a new sense of inner assurance, and you'll sense that now you're a "real" trader.

WHY FAITH AND HOPE SHOULD BE LEFT IN A BASKET BY THE DOOR

We were taught as children to embody "faith" and "hope." Those two attributes add to all parts of your life—except trading. Before you enter your trading environment each morning, please leave faith and hope in a basket by the door!

Faith: "I know I should get out of my trade, but I'm going to hold it until the market goes back up. The market has an upside bias, doesn't it? By tomorrow everything will be fine."

Hope: (in form of prayer to the trading god!) "Please, *please* stop this stock from falling. *Please* get me out of this trade before I lose every buck I have. I promise to never, *ever*, ignore my rules again!"

If you find yourself muttering those famous words, "It'll come back," or whispering "*Please* go up" to your stock, you're trading on faith and hope. This means you're not controlling your trade. Instead, your trade's controlling you!

Best Cure for Faith and Hope

1. If you feel a bout of faith or hope coming on, identify it, then quickly reevaluate your trade and take necessary actions.
2. If faith and hope encouraged you to hold onto a losing position, bite the bullet and get out of the trade immediately. The first loss is always the smallest.
3. Remember, faith and hope lose you money. They are emotions you can't afford to have!

WHY "THE DEVIL" MADE YOU LOSE ALL THAT MONEY!

As a new trader, you're about to meet every personality trait you own, up close and personal. Some traits will aid your quest for success; others will need to be reined in. It's best to identify all of your characteristics that will affect your trading, early on. The more you know about yourself, the more it will benefit your trading career.

When you make a questionable move during the trading day, ask, "Why did I do that? Which one of my personality traits caused *that* to happen?"

Was the answer, "I was impulsive"? Do you feel and act first, then think last? That can get you into trouble. Replace impulsive urges with thoroughly planned trades. Refrain from trading on whippy or choppy market days.

Was the answer, "I was optimistic"? Did you hope (oops!) for the best? Optimism is a cousin of faith and hope. Rose-colored glasses distort market reality.

Was the answer, "I was stubborn"? Stubbornness is a cohort of "the need to be right" and will cost you a fortune in losses. Replace it with a "could-be-right, could-be-wrong…whatever," attitude. This frees you up to make winning decisions.

Was the answer, "I wasn't concentrating"? A scattered mind leads to losses. Replace it with razor-sharp concentration. Practice makes profits.

Was the answer, "I was impatient"? New traders are famous for their impatience. Impatience adds to stress. Whenever possible, temper impatience by striving to stay unattached to the outcome of your trades.

CELEBRATE YOUR POSITIVE TRADING CHARACTERISTICS

Do you embody perfectionism? Fantastic! It drives people around you bonkers, but it sure enhances your trading.

Are you methodical, imperturbable, and nonjudgmental? Great. Stay that way!

Another trader-friendly emotion goes by two names. Guys have "gut feelings." Women have "intuition." Properly developed, that instinct becomes a superb tool.

Let's make sure we're talking about the same thing. Trading on a gut feeling that's merely a whim usually gets you into trouble. Trading on a gut feeling that's honed by knowledge and experience can save you money and fatten your wallet.

Even though I'm a female, I absolutely trade from my gut—solar plexus, if you prefer. It's a reliable source for me, and I depend on it. Say all market indicators scream "go," but for reasons I can't see in front of me, my insides tighten, insisting something's amiss. Nine times out of ten, the market will reverse or make an unexpected turn. I've learned to trust my gut feelings. After a while, you will also.

REALITY CHECK: WHAT COLOR IS THE STOCK MARKET?

One of the most challenging mindsets in trading is the ability to look at the market, or a stock, and see what *is*. We all have different perceptions of the same object, and our perceptions are colored by our previous experiences with that object.

Maybe you look at the market as a place of positive possibilities. The trader sitting next to you views it as a terrifying realm of lost money. Guess what? You're both right! The market will be to you whatever you conceive it to be.

How do you perceive the market? Is it an arena of opportunity? Or the opposite? Take a few minutes to reflect. It's important to do this because the perception you carry to the market determines the outcome of your trading career. That's an absolute. Count on it.

DON'T PUSH THE RIVER: SWIM WITH IT AND THE MONEY WILL FLOW TO YOU!

Americans are taught to be proactive rather than reactive, and we constantly think of ways to alter our relationships and environments. If you're dissatisfied with the color of your living room, you paint it. If you disagree with your partner, you take action to change things for the better. If your children misbehave, you ask them to redirect their actions.

The stock market flows like a river. You cannot push it in the other direction. You cannot paint it a different color. You cannot disagree with it, or demand it behave differently. *You can only control yourself and your reaction to it!*

Once you have that concept firmly in place, your goal is to come to the market each day, as professionals do, and regard it with positive objectivity. How does that feel? Like this:

- You observe and interact with the market as it truly *is*, not as you wish it were.
- You feel calm, your self-trust is fully intact, and you feel no pressure to do anything except follow your plan.
- Feelings of fear, rejection, and having made mistakes are nonexistent.
- You focus intently, yet with a certain feeling of detachment.
- When the market gives you a signal to act according to your plan, you execute the trade quickly and calmly.

RESPONSIBILITY AND RESPECT: HOW THEY PLAY LEADING ROLES IN YOUR SUCCESS

As a professional trader, you take full *responsibility* for every action you take during the trading day. Blame is not part of your trading life; it's too destructive. You blame no one, not even yourself, for trades gone bad and lost money.

You do, however, assume responsibility. The market did not "take" money from you, or "give" money to you. You made choices, and you live with the results of those choices.

If you follow a "hot tip" from a taxi driver and get creamed, don't blame the taxi driver. Learn from it. If a trading teacher convinces you to sell a stock, and the next day it doubles, don't rant and rave. You pushed the button.

Professional traders think for themselves. Sure, they may ask for input, but they apply their own criteria to each and every trade they place.

The world's wealthiest traders *respect* themselves and their abilities. Your success as a trader will reflect your own self-worthiness. In the *Disciplined Trader*, Mark Douglas says, "Taking responsibility is a function of self-acceptance."[4] He goes on to say that the more negatively you think of yourself, the less responsibility you take. The higher your self-esteem, the more positive your thoughts, and the more insight you gain from your experiences.

Along with respecting yourself, to be successful, you must respect money. Not just the money in your trading account, but money in general.

Think for a minute…how do you treat your money? Do you pay your bills on time? Do you repay personal debts quickly? Do you spend thoughtfully?

In *The 9 Steps to Financial Freedom*, Suze Orman asks you to take out your wallet. How are your bills organized? Are they all stuffed together in disarray? Do you have to unravel them to see what they are? Keeping your bills in order serves as "a constant reminder" of the respect that both you, and your money, deserve.

As Orman says, "It's very subtle, but the way we treat ourselves and our money touches every aspect of our lives."[5]

---

4 Douglas, p. 55.

5 Orman, Suze. *The Nine Steps to Financial Freedom.* (NY: Crown Publishers, 1997), p. 120.

QUIZ

1 Name the two trading commandments. Give a brief description of each.
2 True or false? The stock market fluctuates according to exact, economic criteria.
3 As a trader, what represents your most formidable foe? Why?
4 Fill in the blanks. A thought, plus a ___________, equals an __________.
5 True or false? You need the component of excitement to make successful, profitable trades.
6 State one cure for greed.
7 Name three important fundamentals that, when achieved, displace fear.
8 Which two "R" words play leading roles in your success?

ANSWERS

1. Protect your principal. As a trader's most important tool, the trading account must be protected at all times and cared for as the valuable asset it is.

   Trade to trade well. The trader's goal is to trade well, not to make money. Good trading is an art form; money is a reward for well-executed trades.
2. False. The stock market fluctuates according to the collective players' opinions as to value at any given moment. That's why the "market is always right."
3. Emotion represents a trader's most formidable foe. Negative emotions, such as greed and fear, color perceptions of reality and motivate traders to make losing decisions.
4. feeling, action.
5. False. Excitement, as much fun as it is in everyday life, can be lethal when it guides trading habits.
6. Trade small lot sizes, from 1 to 300 shares per trade.
7. Knowledge, experience, and self-trust.
8. Responsibility and respect play leading roles in your success.

✦ ✦ ✦

CENTER POINT
Extend Your Reach

The only way to discover the limits of the possible is to go beyond them, to the impossible.

—ARTHUR C. CLARKE

When we realign our personal beliefs to support our vision and hold that vision high in front of us to light our path, life will call on us to grow. To grasp the good, we have to extend our reach.

When we first imagine our highest reality and own the dreams that have hidden in our heart, there's a sense of excitement—it feels like the perfect fit, right and good. Yet we soon realize that to arrive where we want to go, to do this thing we're called on to do, we'll have to change. We have to go places we've never been before, do things we've never done before, interact with people who are strangers to us. In short, we have to move out of our comfort zone.

With that realization of change, internal chatter that's held us prisoner inside our comfort zone suddenly speaks out, loud and clear. It tells us we "don't deserve" that dream, that our dream might be good enough for someone else—but certainly not for us.

If we listen to the doubt instead of the dream, we'll return to that illusion of safety within our comfort zone. Our vision will remain beyond our grasp.

Instead, let's step over our self-doubt and ask, "What must we do to have this? How must we grow and change to be large enough to contain this glorious possibility?"

Affirm your willingness to extend your reach and expand your comfort zone. Then you will become a vehicle for your magnificent idea, and you will travel the road to realization.

✦ ✦ ✦

CHAPTER 5

Trading Fundamentals You'll Build On

Early in my trading career, I attended a weekend course in commodities trading. The instructor, a well-known veteran in the trading community, would say, "The CRB (commodities) Index and Treasury bond yield always run in tandem." Then he'd grin and add, "Except when they don't."

Or "The CRB Futures and Spot (cash) Index always trend in the same direction." Sly smile. "Unless they don't." Or "The price of gold rises during a bear market in stocks. Except when it doesn't."

This man drove me bonkers. No matter what financial market he discussed, or which chart pattern he described, he'd start by saying, "This always happens," then hedge with, "except when it doesn't." I wanted to smack him.

Now that I'm thousands of trades wiser, I ask you to etch the following on your mind for all of your trading days. If you forget, the market will remind you in a hurry. *Nothing "always happens" in the stock market. The only absolute in the market or stock behavior is constant change.* The wealthiest traders know this. And it's true now, more than ever, as global communities affect each other's financial markets on a twenty-four-hour basis.

THE MARKET HAS NO PRICE OR TIME LIMITS

Do the Dow Jones stocks, or the Nasdaq 100, or the S&P 500 have limits as to how high they can soar? Or how low they can drop before they reach zero?

In Jack D. Schwager's *Market Wizards*, CNBC's Jimmy Rogers, says, "The market is going to go higher than I think it can and lower than I think it will."[1]

Besides having no defined limit on price, the financial markets have no time boundaries. Every minute of the day, as markets open and close around the globe,

---

[1] Schwager, Jack D. *Market Wizards.* (NY: Harper Business, 1993), p. 294.

someone, somewhere is trading in financial markets, be it stocks, bonds, currencies, or commodities.

Here in the United States, bond futures trade all night. Traders on Instinet buy and sell Nasdaq stocks around the clock. Many financial gurus insist that in the not-too-distant future, our stock market will stay open twenty-four-hours a day.

Even if U.S. market hours remain as they are, stocks that close at one price Thursday don't necessarily open at the identical price Friday morning.

First, specialists and market makers adjust the price of their stocks each morning according to the orders waiting to be filled.

Second, human opinion changes constantly. Say on Friday just before the market's close, you sold the position you were holding in Halliburton (HAL). The oil service stock had waffled for days, and you wanted to free up the cash. Over the weekend, however, talk of war in Saudi Arabia simmered and gathered steam.

Now it's Monday morning, and the United States readies attack planes to hit this oil-rich nation. Fears of oil shortages mushroom, and by the time the market opens, HAL is rocketing.

In little more than forty-eight hours, fueled by world events, the prevailing opinion of stocks like HAL reversed from apathy to enthusiasm. Emotions and opinions change the value of a stock.

Now, do you have a clearer idea of what I mean by the statement, "The market has no time and price limits"?

FUNDAMENTAL VS. TECHNICAL ANALYSIS

Two basic sectors of reasoning constitute the way investors and traders go about choosing stocks: fundamental analysis and technical analysis. Those who strictly adhere to one method usually sneer at the other, much like the Republicans and the Democrats.

Fundamental analysts enjoy telling anyone who will listen that they've never met a rich technician. Technical analysts laugh at the fundamentalists' insistence that P/E ratios really do matter in a stock's ability to gain value. Of course, just like the Republicans and Democrats, both points of view have their good points.

In very broad terms, investors, both private and institutional, use fundamental analysis as their basis for stock purchases. Short-term traders use technical analysis. Since the risk–reward ratio between investing and trading is very different, and of course, the time horizon for long term versus short term is so diverse, it makes sense that two different methods are employed. By the way, that's also the reason why many people who invest successfully imagine they can jump easily from investing to day trading—then find themselves swimming in troubled waters. Investing and trading are two different animals!

Fundamental analysis relies on economic supply–demand information in the overall picture, and a company's financial health in the smaller picture. It includes such statistics as a stock's annual growth rate, five-year, one-year, and quarterly earnings records, P/E (price-to-earnings) ratios. (P/E ratios are calculated by dividing the stock's price by its earnings-per-share figure.)

Those who rely on fundamentals are more interested in a stock's performance year to year than they are in market behavior. They don't give a rat's patootie that the Dow Jones plunges one day and soars the next. They are satisfied with steady, conservative growth, and their goal is the end result—that their investments eventually provide for their children's college fund, retirement nest egg, or a condo in Florida. That's why, when the market falls hard, or even soars skyward, and CNBC interviews Joe Public for comments, Joe invariably says, "I don't care how the market acts today. I'm in it for the long haul."

Besides long-term investors, many commodities brokers and traders—especially those who trade agricultural futures, including corn, sugar, and pork bellies—rely on fundamentals such as the weather and global shortages. An event as predictable as the arrival of winter can dictate the balance of supply and demand—and so ultimately, the price. Example: winter = cold weather = more natural gas usage = higher demand. Result? Energy and energy services prices rise in autumn months.

One reason stock traders don't delve into fundamental analysis is that though it provides highly valuable information, the research consumes too much time. Most of us don't have an hour or an afternoon to spend researching a single company's new product potential, along with earnings as compared to past earnings.

One fundamental concept statistic, however, that I *do* use whenever possible is a proprietary ranking shown in *Investor's Business Daily*. It's called the EPS, or earnings-per-share ranking. (Earnings per share are calculated by dividing a company's total after-tax profits by the company's number of common shares outstanding.) The EPS rank, published daily in *Investor's Business Daily* combines a stock's percent earnings increase during the past two quarters with the past five-year average percent earnings and compares that figure to every other stock IBD covers. An EPS rank of 95 means that a company's current and five-year historical earnings have outperformed 95 percent of all other companies. Great fundamentals in a nutshell!

When I target stocks to trade, especially for longer-term holds of days to a week or more, I first choose industries that are in an uptrend, then narrow it down to a few of the most promising stocks in that industry by using daily charts. From the best of those, I glance at their current EPS rankings, and usually buy the final choice if the ranking is 90 or better. If the market gets a case of the hiccups, as long as the stock doesn't hit my sell stop, I relax knowing my stock has a good fundamental as well as technical outlook.

Technical analysis is the alternate method of researching stock. It is the study of the study of time and price, and sentiment. The tool used most often by technical analysts is a chart. Charts show a stock's price history, and with practice, we can see everything we need to know about a particular equity in a matter of seconds.

The prices on charts don't get there by themselves! Remember our discussion on supply and demand, and price? Price patterns on charts appear due to the collective mindset of the stock's participants. Patterns repeat themselves because those buyers and sellers operate from memory. They may have never seen a stock chart in their lives, but even Ivan Investor remembers that when he bought Simple Software, it was $50 a share. It fell right after he bought it. When it finally climbed back to $50 a share three months later, Ivan, along with many other investors, sold it to get even and avoid another possible loss. Those actions form chart patterns.

Figure 5-1 shows how you can recognize excited buying mania, uncertainty, panic, and selling frenzies in charts. When up or down energy dissipates, the stock may meander in the same price range for a while because the numbers of buyers and sellers even each other out and neither emotion rules.

Besides time and price, charts can show different indicators and oscillators (overbought/oversold indicators); every trader has his or her favorites. (We'll talk more about these later.) Volume spikes on charts tell how many shares have been traded on a particular day, week, or month. Moving averages indicate a stock's strength by averaging closing prices. Don't worry, indicators sound confusing as heck, but by the end of this book you'll be interpreting them with ease.

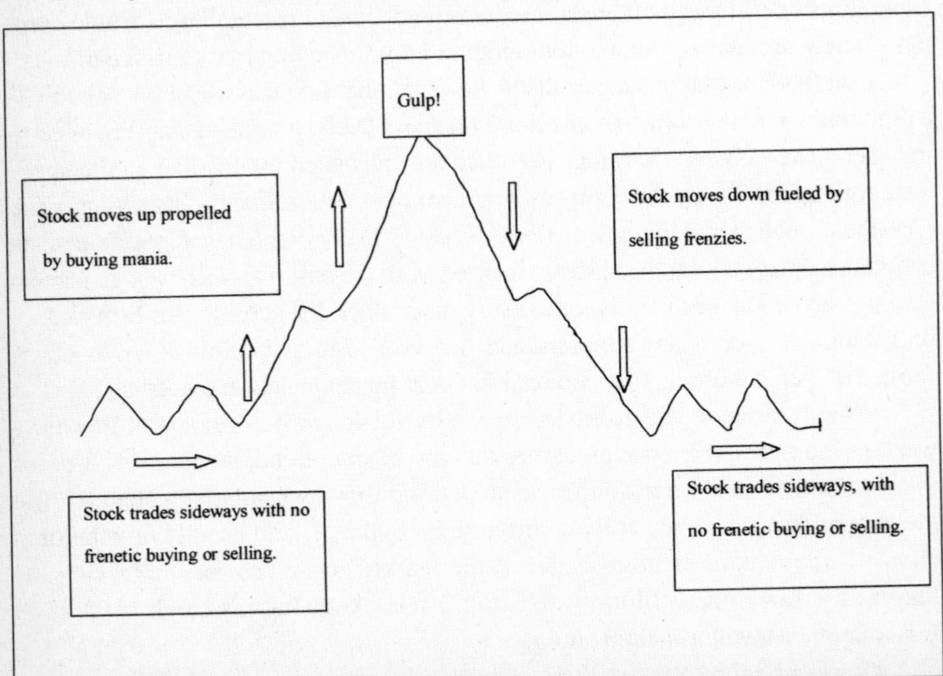

Figure 5-1

Traders also depend on technical analysis to retrieve up-to-the-second information about equities and market indicators. Unlike investors, who may ignore daily market gyrations, most traders pay close attention to major market indices, including the Standard & Poor's (S&P) 500 Index, Dow Jones Industrials, Nasdaq Composite, and more. Charting these indices and other indicators gives insight into which direction the market may move next.

DIFFERENT TRADING TIME FRAMES: WHAT THEY MEAN TO YOU

Traders enter and exit positions within the parameters of four basic time frames. Each time frame has its own expected risk–reward ratios.

1. Short-term investment or intermediate-term trade—stock may be held from one to two weeks, or longer.
2. Swing trade—stock will be held for two to five days.
3. Day trade—stock will be bought and sold (or the reverse) the same day.
4. Scalping play—stock may be bought and sold (or the reverse) within seconds or minutes.

Most traders engage in the last three trades—swing trades, day trades, and scalping plays. I added the first, the intermediate-term trade, for a reason.

In Chapter 3, we talked about maintaining two trading accounts, one for day trading and scalps, the other for swing/intermediate-term trades. In the second account, you may mimic what many seasoned traders do, which is to have a core holding or two that you hold for one week or longer. Just as shopping malls have "anchor" stores—large, well-known department stores that ensure the mall's success—so you may decide to have an anchor stock or two in your account that you hold for a nice, profitable ride.

This *does not* mean you hold onto Igloo Ice Cream because you bought as a swing trade and ignored your sell stop. Then, after it fell like a rock, you were too embarrassed to sell it at a big loss, so you designated it as a "core holding," or "investment."

It *does* mean that you find a stock, preferably a NYSE stock of high fundamental quality such as General Electric (GE) or AT&T (T), or even S&P Depository Receipts (SPY). (Because of their acronym SPDR, these receipts are known as "spiders." Spiders mirror the S&P 500 and trade just like a stock on the Amex, under the symbol SPY.) You buy the core holding at a good entry point and hold until its current uptrend is broken.

Swing trades are positions that you intend to hold for two to five days. In a perfect world (read: bull market!), a nice, easygoing stock may rise from three to five days, then pull back, or rest. In order to catch most of the rise, you enter the stock using the criteria you'll soon learn, hold it overnight for a few days, and sell it just before it reaches its next point of resistance.

Many traders refuse to hold positions overnight. Their reasons are certainly valid. Still, I've made a great deal of money spotting brawny stocks that close on their "high" and then "gap open" (it opens at a higher price than it closed at the preceding day) the next morning, literally making me big bucks overnight.

The downside: You may hold a stock that opens lower because an analyst chooses that morning to downgrade it, or because the market itself opens lower. Holding stocks overnight is risky, but can be profitable. Dealer's choice.

The most common trade executed is a day trade, where we enter the position in the morning, and exit before the market closes the same day.

Scalping plays are performed with lightning speed, and the scalper enters it with the intention of making 1/4 to 1/2 a point. Scalpers buy or short (sell) a stock with the intention of completing the trade within seconds to minutes. Some scalpers make hundreds, even thousands of trades a day. I don't recommend this style for new traders. I prefer to pepper my day trades with scalps when I see an opportunity. Again, dealer's choice.

This is a good time to reflect on your personal risk tolerance. Some people thrive on stress, some buckle under it. All traders endure a certain amount of stress, but you can choose the potency of your poison depending on the time frames you trade in!

Patient plodders enjoy intermediate-term holds and swing trades. Adrenaline addicts prefer day trades and scalping plays.

Experienced traders with guts of steel and superhuman powers of concentration make the best scalpers. They watch a host of indicators out of one eye, and the stock's chart and level II screen out of the other. If the stock so much as breathes funny, they're out.

If you're in a scalping play, you cannot get up to use the bathroom, get a cup of coffee or a sandwich. You cannot talk on the phone or to someone standing behind you. So, if you're a social animal, have to eat the minute you get hungry, or aren't blessed with the bladder of a camel, consider leaving scalping to hardier souls.

As a novice trader, it's best to postpone scalping plays until you learn how to properly execute swing and day trades. Otherwise, instead of being the scalper, you could end up getting scalped!

TRADING WITH THE CLOCK FOR PROFITS

Now that I've hammered home the point that the market is unlimited, unstructured, and timeless, I'm actually going to tell you that key time periods during the trading day do show up with a degree of regularity. "Degree" is the operative word, here. Market reversals and shifts according to the clock fall under the "This always happens, except when it doesn't" premise.

9:30 a.m. EST—market opens
9:50–10:10—first reversal period
10:25—slightly milder reversal
11:20—beginning of lunchtime moody blues
1:30 p.m.—lunchtime moody blues begin to cheer and clear—some stocks start to edge up
2:30—stocks break out (or down) in a more definitive manner
3:00—Treasury bonds stop trading; market breathes a sigh of relief, possible reversal
3:30—mild reversal possible
4:00 p.m. EST— market closes

These times are not exact. Rather think of them as time zones, or areas.

If the market opens in a bullish mode and the indices trend up, by 9:50, they begin to retrace, or pull back. Why? Because when stocks opened up with strong buying, specialists and market makers were forced to take the other side of the longs and sell short. They have no intention of riding losing positions forever. So they start "dropping the bid" (lowering the price at which they'll buy the stock for), about twenty minutes or so after the market opens so they can cover their shorts at a profit.

If the market opens down, or in a bearish mode, when traders sell, specialists and market makers have to buy. Around 9:50 or so, many stocks that have been trending start to turn upwards. You guessed it—specialists and market makers are selling at a profit.

At about 10:10, give or take a few minutes, strong stocks that have pulled back slightly on a bullish day will again turn up. Bearish stocks on a negative day resume their growling.

Greg Capra at Pristine.com drew my attention to the next reversal that begins at 10:25. Here, strong stocks that didn't pull back around the 9:50–10:10 reversal period start topping out. This is an important time to be aware of. If you buy a stock before 10 a.m., and it soars through that first reversal period, don't assume it's clear sailing for the rest of the morning. Chances are the stock will top out around 10:25, and then pull back, or "come in" (retrace price movement back toward opening price or last support area) before it begins its next move.

The lunchtime "moody blues" amble in about 11:20. On an extremely bullish day, the lunchtime blues may hold off till closer to noon. At that time, institutional managers and the majority of players leave their desks for lunch; stock and overall market movement quiets down. Stocks tend to fall off, or slide down slightly or even steeply, depending on their morning's activity and strength. On a bearish day, I've found weaker stocks fall hard at lunchtime.

Experienced traders avoid entering positions at lunchtime. Stock movement, if any, can be whippy and erratic. The majority of breakouts fail. I've known many a trader, myself included, who's made nice profits in the morning and given it all back at lunch. This happens nine times out of ten.

Moral of the story: Go out for lunch. Get out of your office. Take a walk and eat a light, healthy meal. This will clear your head, soothe your eyes, and prepare your body for a productive afternoon.

A few stocks start to perk up around 1:30. Still, if you stay away until 2:30, you probably won't miss that much. (I'm assuming you didn't leave a bunch of volatile stocks in your account during lunch—bad idea.)

By 2:30 on a bullish day, stocks awaken from their lunchtime lethargy and decide where they'll go for the duration of market hours. Later, I'm going to show you some chart patterns that form at lunch and that can give tidy profits for the afternoon.

Treasury bonds stop trading at 3:00 p.m. Bond prices affect the stock market, so when they cease trading, the market breathes a sigh of relief as though it's shooed a cranky child outside to play.

Again, Greg Capra drew my attention to the 3:30 reversal, which may follow through to the market's close.

The way to tell when the reversals are initiating is to watch leading indicators that we'll talk about soon, such as the S&P futures, the TICK, and the TRIN. These indicators act as direction guides, and most stocks follow their lead.

INTRODUCTION TO CHARTING TECHNIQUES

Basically, traders use three types of charts: line charts, bar charts, and candlestick charts. They each tell the same story with a different spin.

Line Charts

Line charts are drawn from the closing prices each day, and so form a line across the chart.

Line charts can be helpful tools to see the big picture, particularly when you use them to overlay on top of each other. For instance, some analysts overlay a line chart of the Transportation Index on top of the S&P futures to note when they move in tandem or when they diverge. The Advance-Decline Line, which we talk about in Chapter 13 is generally shown as a line chart.

For our purposes as traders, bar charts, and more especially candlestick charts, offer more information, faster.

Bar Charts

Bar charts are used by many traders. On a daily chart (see Figure 5-2), the vertical bar shows the price range the stock has traded in during that day.

Highest price of day
Closing price
Opening price
Lowest price of day

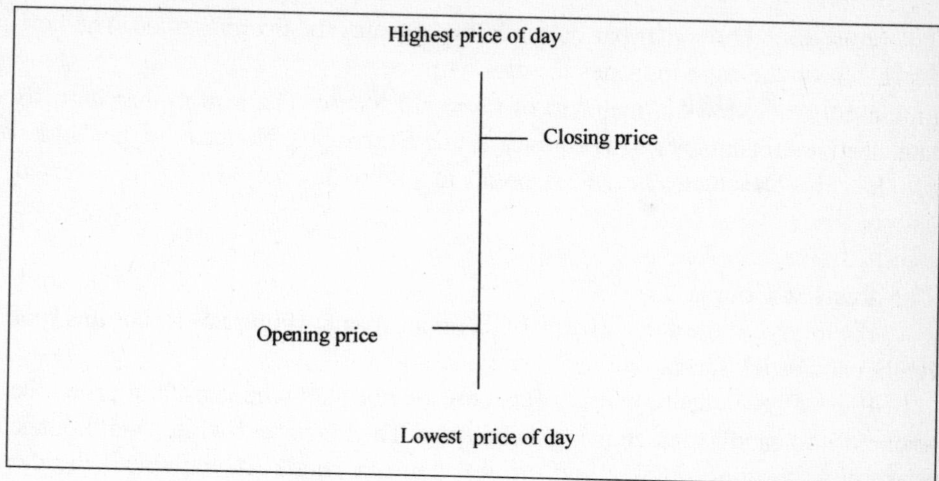

Figure 5-2

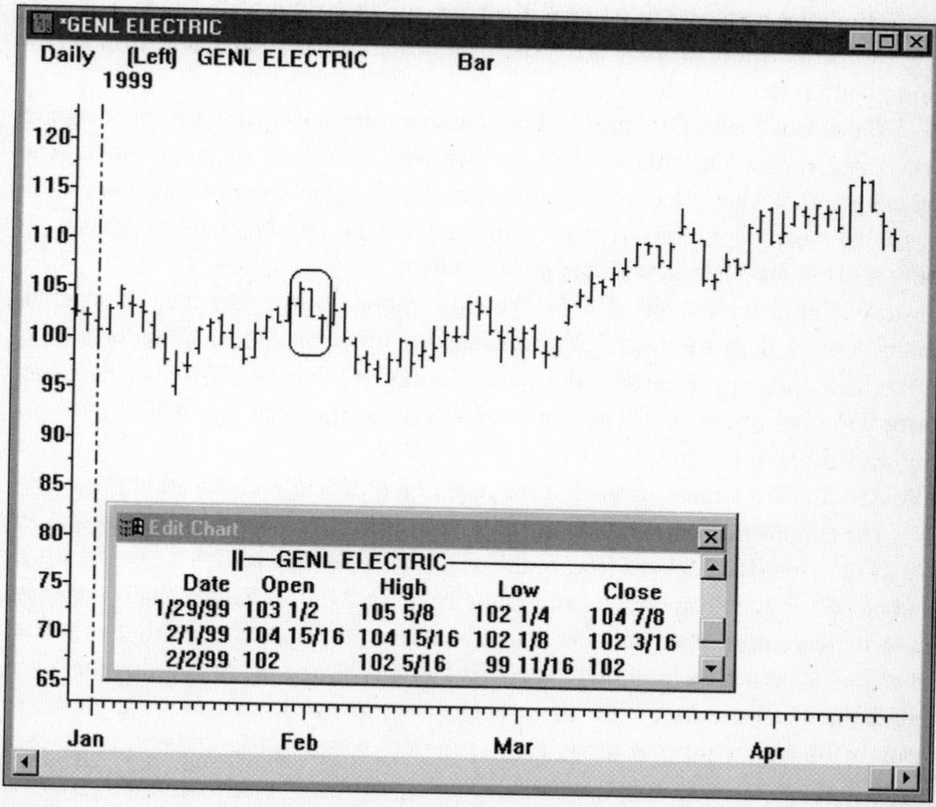

*GENL ELECTRIC
Daily (Left) GENL ELECTRIC Bar
1999
120
115
110
105
100
95
90
85
80
75
70
65
Edit Chart
GENL ELECTRIC
Date Open High Low Close
1/29/99 103 1/2 105 5/8 102 1/4 104 7/8
2/1/99 104 15/16 104 15/16 102 1/8 102 3/16
2/2/99 102 102 5/16 99 11/16 102
Jan
Feb
Mar
Apr

Figure 5-3

Chart Courtesy of *The Executioner*©

The protruding, horizontal bar on the left designates the opening price. The horizontal bar on the right indicates the closing price.

Figure 5-3 shows a line chart of General Electric. The oval in the chart isolates the bars for January 31, February 1, and February 2. Notice how this "bluest of blue chips" fluctuates nearly six points in a three-day period.

Candlestick Charts

Figure 5-4 is the same chart of GE in bar format (Figure 5-3), but this time it's in candlestick format.

Bless a seventeenth-century Japanese rice broker, whose trading principles evolved into candlestick charting techniques. The black-and-white "real bodies" make chart reading quicker and clearer than bar charts. If you spend the day staring at charts, as do most technical analysts, you'll realize how much easier candlestick charts are on your eyes. Candlesticks also interpret stock movement in more detail and give more signals about possible future movement, offering an extra dimension to your analysis. Candlestick charts save you from going blind and broke.

First, let's look at the basics. Like bars, candlesticks use bar forms to designate price range. Then they fatten the bar with a vertical rectangle to indicate opening and closing price comparisons. The Japanese believe opening and closing prices are very important. At those times, traders and investors are most likely to buy or sell their position with the most emotion.

A clear or white body denotes the closing price was higher than the opening price. A black body means the closing price was lower than the opening price. Say, Igloo Ice Cream opened at $17, the low of the day. It closed at $25, which happened to be the high of the day. The candlestick representing that day would look like Figure 5-5(a).

If Igloo Ice Cream opened at the day's high of $25 and closed at the low of $17, the candlestick would look like Figure 5-5(b).

Let's modify it: Igloo's low for the day is $17, the high is $25; it opened at $19 and closed at $23. The body is still white because it closed higher than it opened, but now you can see two *shadows* that indicate the price range, as in Figures 5-6(a). The shadow above the real body is called the *upper shadow*; the shadow below is called the *lower shadow*. If the stock opens at its low and stays above it, the white body will have no lower shadow. That's referred to as a *shaven bottom*. If it closes at the high, and has no upper shadow, it's referred to as a *shaven head*.

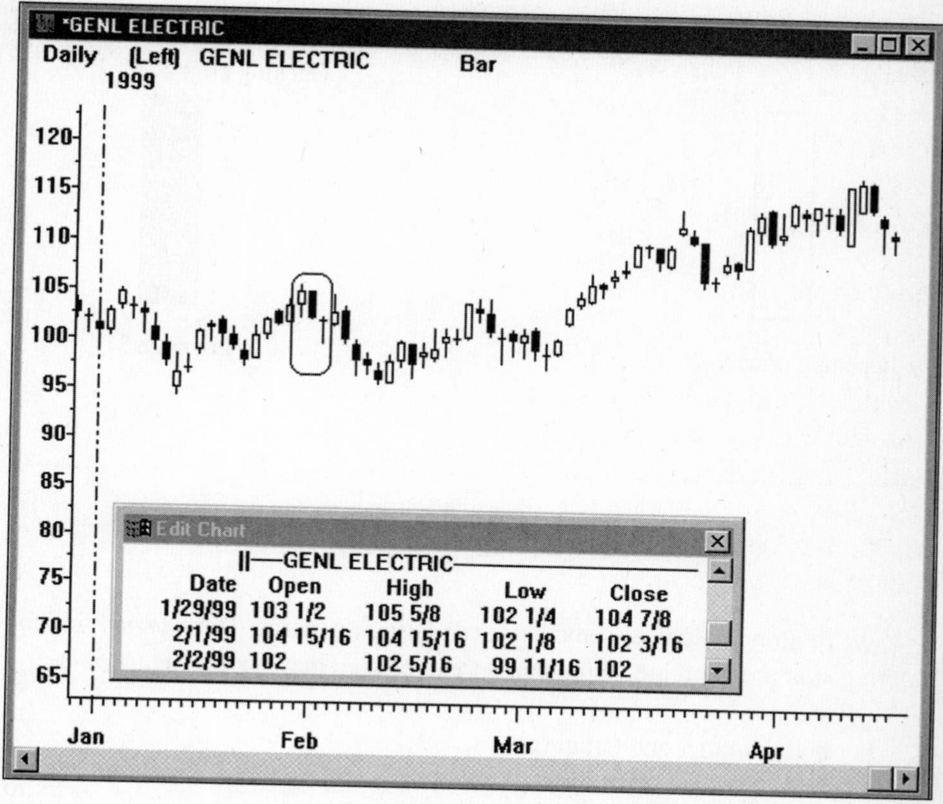

Figure 5-4

Candlestick Chart

Chart Courtesy of *The Executioner*©

If Igloo's price range remains, but it opens at $23 and closes at $19, again, the body is dark, as in Figure 5-6(b).

If Igloo's price range remains the same, but it opens and closes at the same price, for instance $23, the real body is reduced to a line, as in Figure 5-6(c). This candlestick is called a *dogi.*

Candlestick patterns are a valuable tool to traders because, interpreted properly, they forecast reversals, or changes in a trend from mild to moderate.

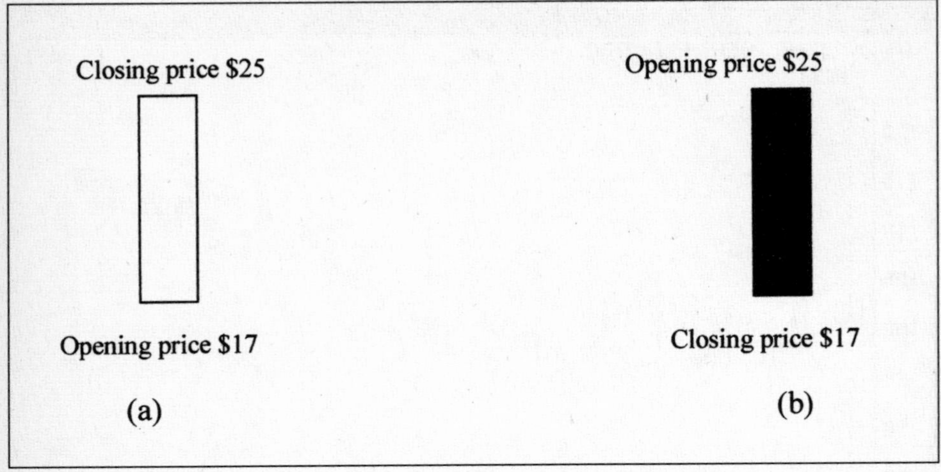

Figure 5-5

We're going to look at some basic candlestick patterns. The *hammer* and the *hanging man* are good indicators that a trend change may occur (Figure 5-7).

For both hammer and hanging man:

- The real bodies are at the top of the day's trading range, the lower shadow should be twice the height of the real body, and it should have a shaven head.

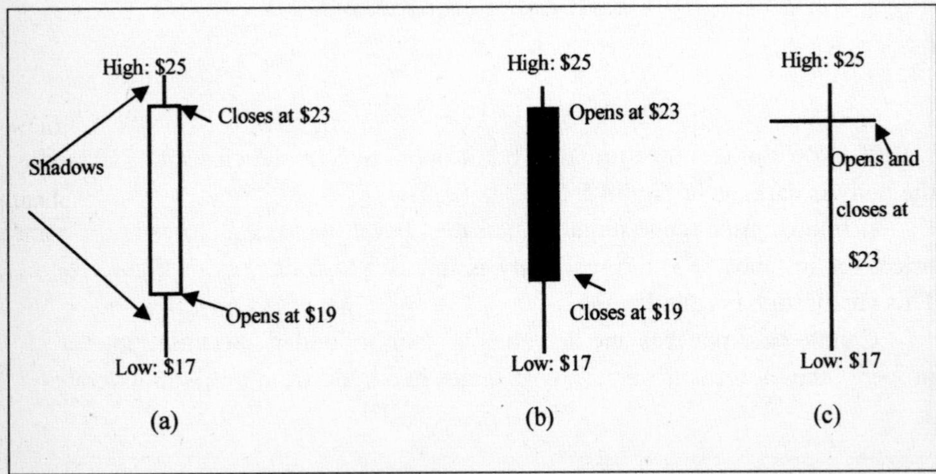

Figure 5-6

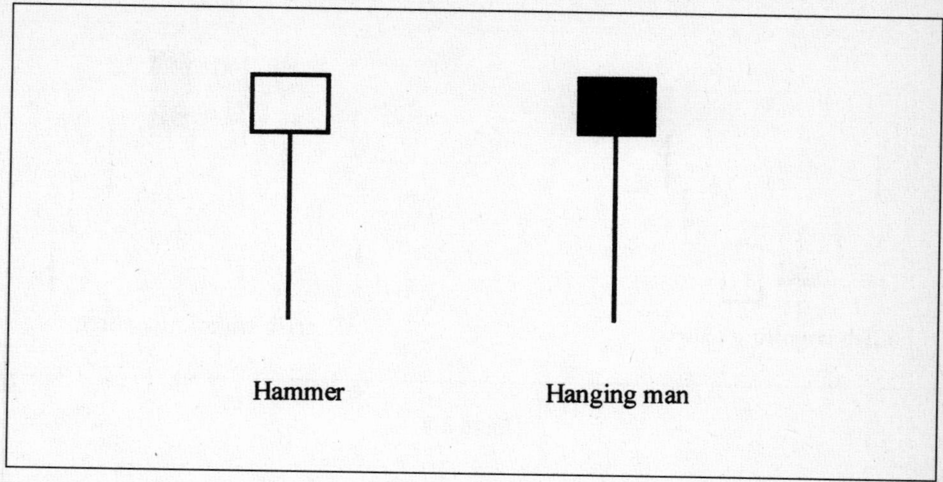

Figure 5-7

- A "hanging man" appears at the top of an uptrend. A "hammer" appears at the bottom of a downtrend.
- Their appearance during a downtrend or uptrend signals the prior move may be broken.

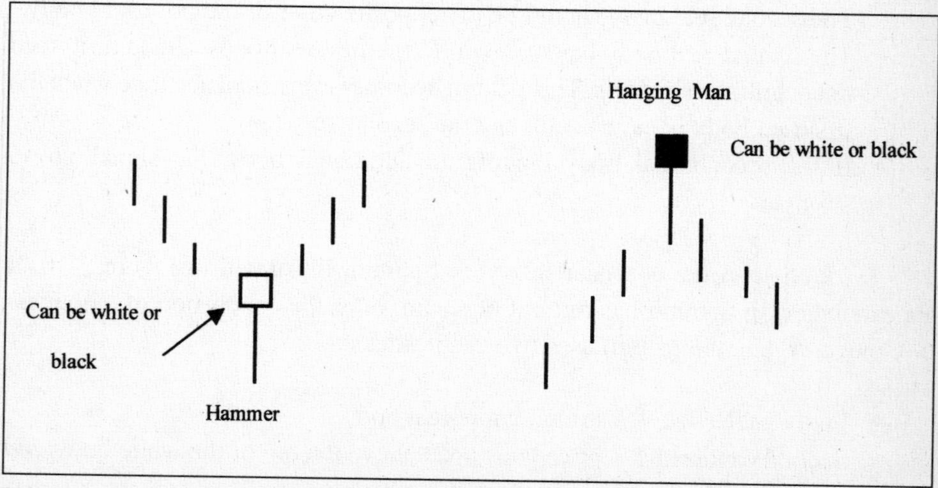

Figure 5-8

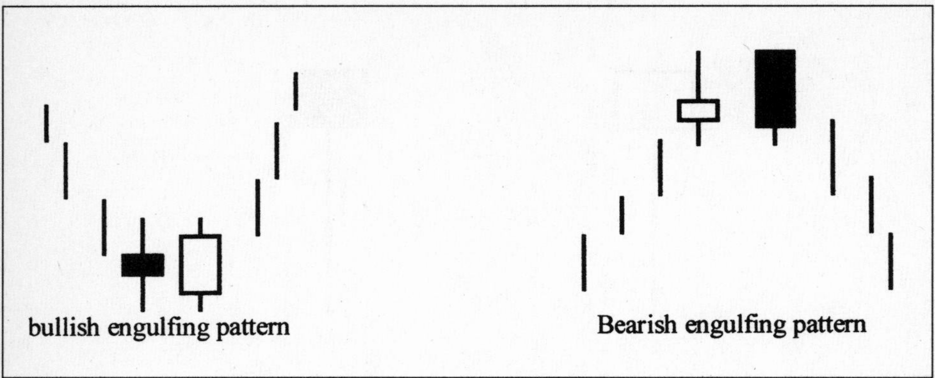

Figure 5-9

As you can see in Figure 5-8, either real body can be white or black, but it is slightly more bullish if the hammer is white and slightly more bearish if the hanging man is black.

Engulfing patterns use two candlesticks to prophesy a major trend reversal. Figure 5-9 shows how a bullish engulfing pattern reverses a downtrend, and a bearish engulfing pattern reverses an uptrend. In *Japanese Candlestick Charting Techniques*, Steve Nison says, "The bearish engulfing pattern can be viewed as a total solar eclipse blocking out the entire sun."[2] So, it covers the entire white body.

- The stock has to be in a definite uptrend or downtrend, even if short term.
- The second real body should be the opposite color of the prior real body.
- The second real body has to "engulf" the first real body although it need not engulf the shadows. This pattern becomes even more accurate when the first real body is quite small, and the second very long.
- If the second real body engulfs an additional body, the signal grows stronger.

Dark cloud cover is a bearish reversal pattern illustrated in Figure 5-10. It appears when an uptrend has run out of steam, or at the conclusion of a congestion move. Again, the pattern uses two candlesticks.

- First candlestick is a strong, white real body.
- Second candlestick's price gaps open above the top of the white body *and* its shadow, if any.

---

2 Nison, Steve. *Japanese Candlestick Charting Techniques.* (NY: New York Institute of Finance, 1991), p. 44.

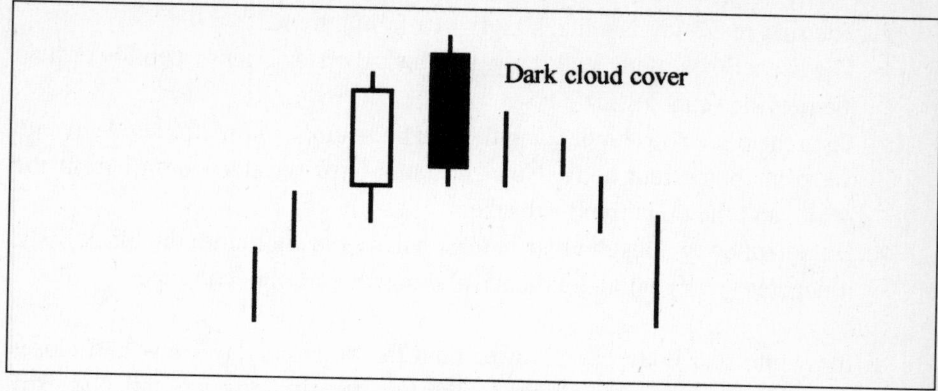

Figure 5-10

- By the end of the move, though, the second body closes well into the white body and near its own low. The more the second, black body moves into the lower part of the first, white body, the higher probability that the bears are taking control and the uptrend is broken.
- If a long, white real body closes above the highs of either the dark cloud cover or the bearish engulfing pattern, it suggests the start of another rally.

The reverse of the dark cloud cover is the *bullish piercing pattern* shown in Figure 5-11. This pattern forecasts the reversal of a downtrend.

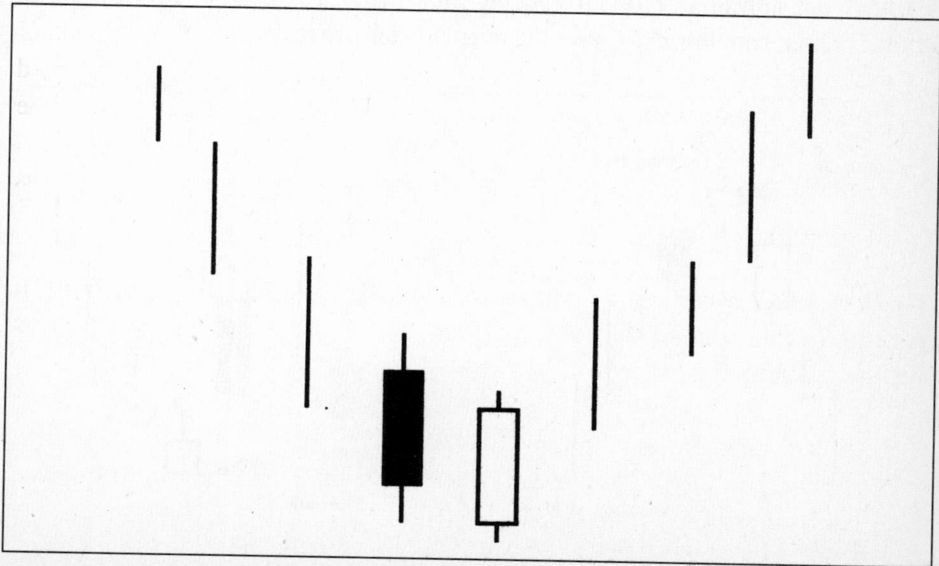

Figure 5-11

- The first real body is a black body in a falling trend.
- The second is a white real body, in which the stock gaps open lower than the previous candlestick's low.
- Then the price rises higher, and the real body closes *more than midway* into the prior black real body. Now the bulls have wrested control from the bears, and the downtrend is broken.
- If the real body doesn't close at least halfway or more into the black body, it negates the signal and indicates the downtrend may continue.

If the white real body opens lower than the previous day's low and closes higher than the previous day's high, in Western terminology we call it a "key reversal day."

"Stars" also warn of reversals. Basic star patterns include the *evening star*, the *morning star* depicted in 5-12, and the *dogi evening* and *dogi morning stars* illustrated in Figure 5-13.

- In each case, the star itself can appear as black or white.
- Technically, the star must gap away from the preceding candlestick, meaning the star's real body must not overlap the previous real body.
- The star's real body is small, indicating that a stock that's had a strong surge up or down is now slowing, and the bulls and bears are deadlocked in battle.

The evening star, Venus, signals the arrival of darkness. In candlestick charting, the appearance of an *evening star* denotes a bearish reversal in an uptrend. Three candlesticks create the evening star pattern:

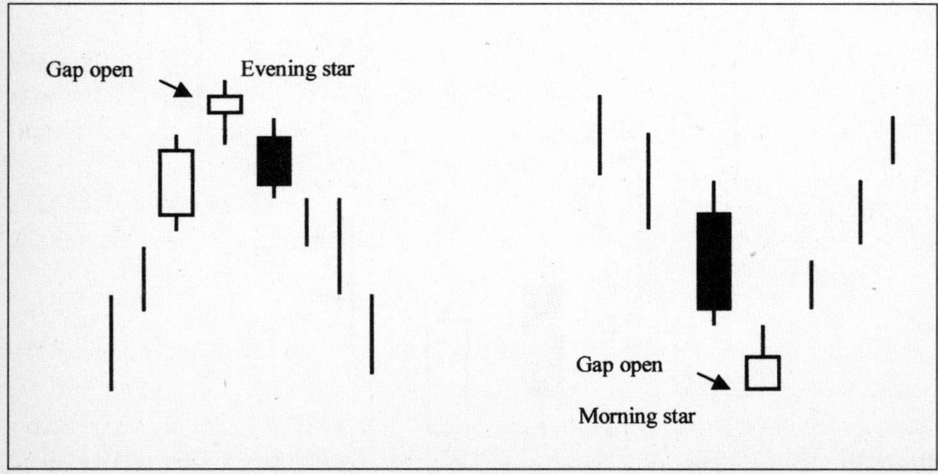

Figure 5-12

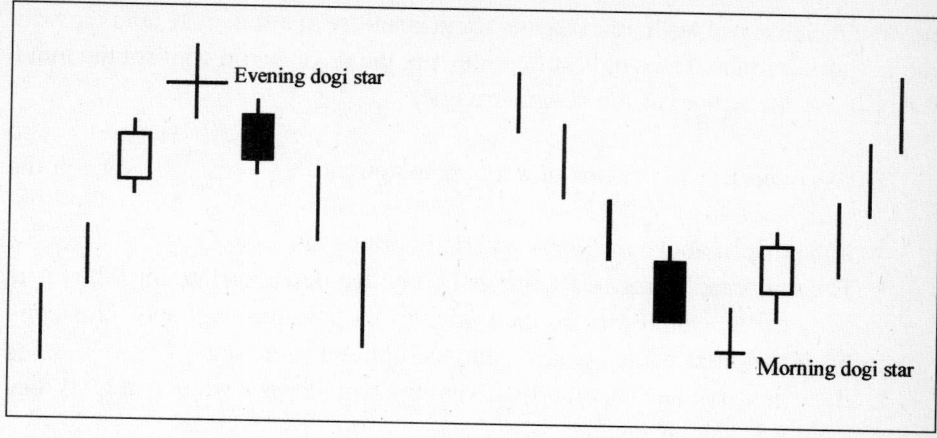

Figure 5-13

- The first two are composed of a long, white real body, followed by a star with a small body, which can be white or black. The star suggests the top of the uptrend.
- The third candlestick is a black real body that drops low into the range of the first, white candlestick. Now the bears are in control, and the uptrend is broken.

The *morning star* derives its name from Mercury, the morning star that appears just before the sun rises. It foretells a bullish reversal in a downtrend. The pattern is the opposite of the evening star and shows three candlesticks in a complete pattern.

- The first two are composed of one, long black body, followed by a star with a small body, which can be white or black. The star gaps open lower that the previous real body's close, then the price rises. This move indicates buying pressure has begun.
- The third star is a white real body that moves into the price range of the first, black real body. Now the bulls have taken control, and the downtrend is broken.

Dogis are created when a candlestick opens and closes at, or very near, the same price; only a lateral line forms the real body. As you can see in Figure 5-13, dogis resemble crosses. *Dogi stars* are dogis that gap open either above or below the previous real body in an uptrend or downtrend. They represent powerful reversal indicators and should be respected when they appear in a strong trend move. It means, once again, that the bulls and bears are at a stalemate, and the next move is up for grabs. The candlestick following the dogi should confirm the trend reversal, and the winner of the power struggle.

An *evening dogi star* warns of a top in an uptrend.

- It gaps open above the white real body prior to it.
- The next candlestick is a black real body that descends into the white real body of the candlestick formed prior to the evening dogi star. This confirms the bears gained control, and the uptrend is broken.
- If the next candlestick after the Evening Dogi Star is a white real body, the Dogi warning is negated.

A *morning dogi star* indicates a possible bottom in a downtrend.

- It gaps open below the black real body prior to it.
- The next white real body opens higher, and the price rises into the area of the black body prior to the morning dogi star. Now the bulls are definitely in control, and the downtrend is broken.
- If the next candlestick after a morning dogi star is a black real body, the dogi downtrend reversal is negated.

On my charts, I have configured the white real bodies to appear green, and the black real bodies to appear in red. This coincides with most level II software systems inclination to show upticks in green and downticks in red, and reinforces a stock's trend at a glance.

There are several good candlestick charting pattern books on the market, and I strongly suggest you read at least one of them. Both of Steve Nison's books are comprehensive and easy to understand: *Japanese Candlestick Charting Techniques* (NY: New York Institute of Finance, 1991), and *Beyond Candlesticks: More Japanese Charting Techniques Revealed* (NY: John Wiley & Sons, 1994).

The charts shown in Figure 5-14 and 5-15 are examples of some of patterns described in this chapter. Please study them so you can learn to spot them quickly. Combined with other technical indicators, they can confirm a pending trend reversal, which is extremely valuable trading information.

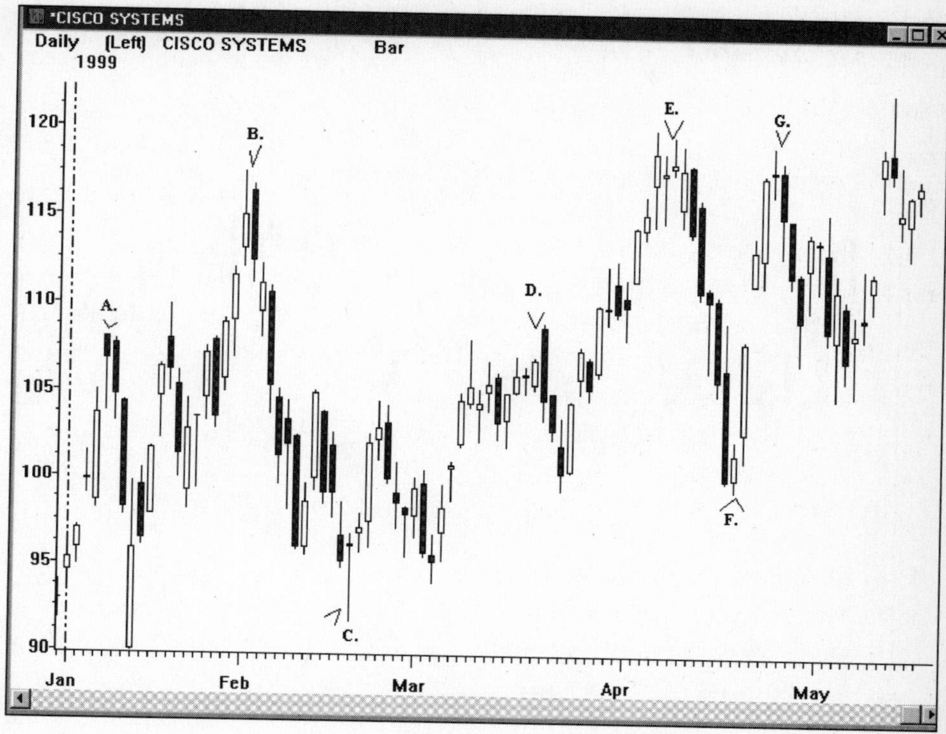

Figure 5-14

A. This Hammer, with a lower shadow twice the length of the real body, foretold the reversal of the prior uptrend.

B. This Bearish Engulfing pattern reliably signaled the end of the previous uptrend.

C. While this doesn't qualify as a Morning Dogi Star because it didn't gap open away from the previous candlestick, it is still a Dogi. When you see a Dogi after a strong up or down move, watch the next candlestick for a confirmation that the present trend is reversed, or at least interrupted.

D. This Bearish Engulfing pattern accurately forecasted a three-day down move.

E. These two narrow white bodies indicate that for two days in a row, Cisco's price opened and closed in a narrow range. After a strong uptrend, narrow-range days signify bulls and bears are undecided. A reversal followed.

F. After a five-day down trend, this Bullish Piercing pattern held near previous support. The next white long body confirmed the pattern.

G. This Dogi Evening Star properly gapped open above the previous candlestick in an uptrend. A reversal followed.

Chart Courtesy of *The Executioner*©

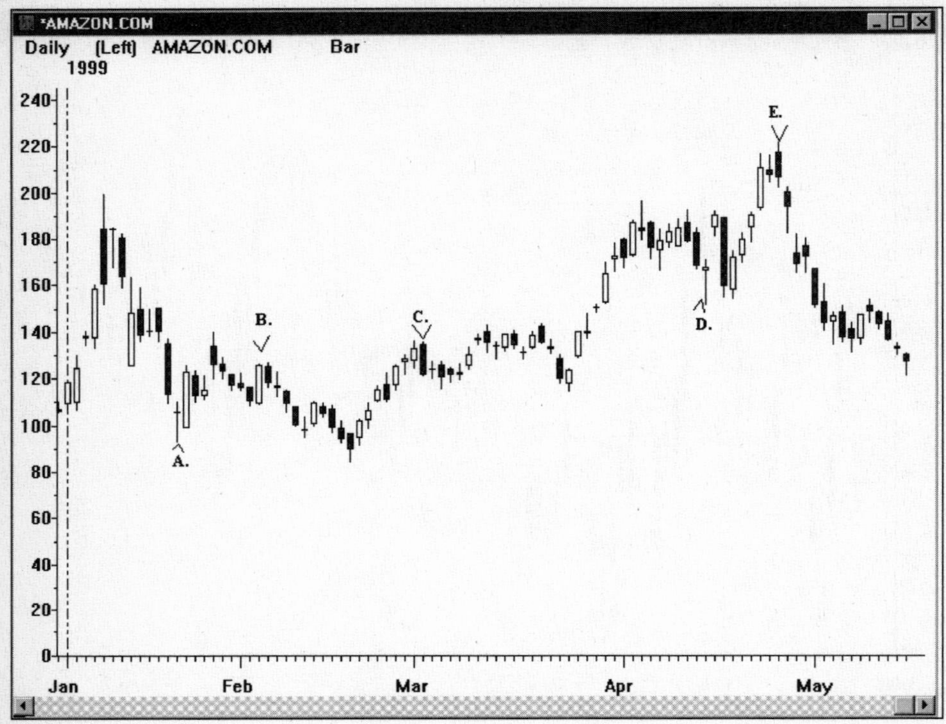

Figure 5-15

A. This Dogi indicates the current downtrend may end. The next long, white real body confirms the reversal.

B. The Dark Cloud here did not close as deeply into the previous white body, but the effect was the same.

C. See how the Bearish Engulfing pattern forecasted a pullback in the prior uptrend.

D. Note how this Hammer, with the small, white real body, which is bullish, foretold a temporary reversal in the prior two-day pullback.

E. Even though the previous candlestick doesn't have a white real body, it is a narrow range candlestick indicating a possible change. The Dark Cloud cover definitely portends an end to the uptrend, and AMZN tumbles obediently.

Chart Courtesy of *The Executioner*©

QUIZ

1. "The only absolute in the market or stock behavior is ________ ________."
2. Give a brief explanation of fundamental analysis. Who uses it most?
3. Give a brief explanation of technical analysis. Who uses it most?
4. Name four trading time frames and their time spans.
5. True or false? During market hours, lunchtime is the best time to trade stocks.
6. Describe the candlestick pattern known as a bullish engulfing pattern.
7. What designates a dogi?
8. What makes a dogi a star dogi?
9. True or false? Dogi stars are highly potent indicators of an impending trend reversal.

ANSWERS

1. constant change.
2. As pertains to the financial markets, fundamental analysis is the study of supply and demand, as well as statistics such as a company's growth rate, quarterly earnings, and P/E ratios. It is used primarily by long-term investors.
3. Technical analysis is the study of time, price, and sentiment as relates to the financial markets. It is used primarily by traders.
4. Intermediate-term trade: one to two weeks or longer; swing trade: two to five days; day trade: position opened and closed during the same day; scalp: trade duration is seconds to minutes.
5. False. Lunchtime (11:30 a.m. to 1:30 p.m.) is the worst time of the day to trade. Stocks either don't move at all or become highly unpredictable.
6. The current stock pattern is a definite downtrend. The first real body is black. The next, white real body opens lower and closes higher than the black one, thus "engulfing" it. Now the downtrend will probably reverse and the stock may break out.
7. A dogi is formed when a stock opens and closes at the same price.
8. A dogi becomes a star dogi when it gaps open above the prior candlestick's real body in an uptrend, or gaps open below the prior candlestick's real body in a downtrend.
9. True. Star dogis are potent trend reversal indicators.

✦ ✦ ✦

CENTER POINT

The Miracle of Giving

He who loves others is constantly loved by them. He who respects others is constantly respected by them.

—MENCIUS (4TH–3RD CENTURY, B.C.)

Would you like to be on the receiving end of prosperity and abundance for the rest of your life? You can be if you expand your experience of giving!

Our world operates through the universal law of cause and effect. Nothing stands still. Life moves continually as energy flows through us and circulates to the rest of the world, then returns to us once more. Your relationships with your spouse, boss, children, and friends constantly revolve in a circle of giving and receiving.

Your career, your health, your spiritual community, your family, and yes, even your bank account, require an energy flow of give and take. If you stop giving to one area of your life, be it knowledge and enthusiasm, food and rest, quest for inner harmony, love and nurturing, or financial support, that part of your life suffers—it returns little to you. Why? You've blocked the energy flow, the circulation. And like a stream, energy must keep circulating to stay alive and vital. Otherwise, it grows stagnant.

Giving and receiving forms a circle, and circles have no end. For each area of our lives to thrive and grow, we need to give freely and receive with gratitude.

Begin the process of circulation by giving what you most want to receive. Would you like more abundance in the form of money? Give what you can, with kind intentions, and no thought for its return. Would you welcome more attention and appreciation? Give honest compliments, do someone an unexpected favor. Give of your time, your caring.

In *The Seven Spiritual Laws of Success,* Deepak Chopra says, "Make a decision to give wherever you go, to whomever you see. As long as you're giving, you will be receiving. The more you give, the more confidence you will gain in the miraculous effects of this law."[3]

Remember, whatever you send out will return to you. So, give for the sake of giving, and your life will overflow with abundance and prosperity.

✦ ✦ ✦

---

[3] Chopra, Dr. Deepak. *The Seven Spiritual Laws of Success.* (CA: Amber-Allen Publishing, 1993), p. 33.

CHAPTER 6

Technical Analysis 101: The Trend Is Your Friend

As we begin our study of charts, you'll notice that stock prices can move only in one of three directions: up, down, and sideways. "Sideways" means the prices changes very little, and so move between an upper and lower price area in what we call a "trading range."

The up, down, or sideways price movements are the only directions prices can take. This is always true. *No other movements are possible.* The only direction remaining is backward, and stock prices cannot move backward because time moves forward. Right? Right!

Note that I said *always* true. This is one of the rare times you'll see "always" appear in connection with the financial markets because, as I stated in Chapter 5, there are precious few times that always applies.

The up, down, and sideways price movements take place whether we're speaking of a macrocosm of months to a year in a stock's life, or a microcosm of seconds to minutes.

Just as each crystal of sand represents a single unit that connects with other units to form an entire beach, each minute, hour, and day of a stock's price movement connects with the next, forming an overall cycle that repeats itself through time.

STOCK CYCLES: HOW THEY HELP YOU PLAN YOUR TRADES

Our world is made up of cycles. Planets orbit our sun on a precise course. On Earth, cycles occur in every nuance of nature. The four seasons follow each other predictably. Tides ebb and flow, birds migrate. As part of this system, we humans tend to think in cycles, or patterns, whether as a collective mindset or as individuals. In short, we expect predictability, and we're comfortable with it.

Our tendency toward cycles reflects in the financial markets. Because the markets and their internal components—whether commodities, options, industry indexes, or individual stocks—are fueled by human expectations, it follows that recognizable cycles emerge.

As traders, we attempt to recognize those cycles and use them to our advantage. Look at a dozen stock charts in a row. See the cycle? A series of peaks and troughs, resembling a mountain range, stretches across the time line of a chart like the Rocky Mountains stretch along our western states (Figure 6-1).

Formations on charts are analogous to mountain ranges. When you stand at a distance, you see only the outline of the major peaks and valleys against the sky. Move in closer, and you notice smaller hills and dales form that mountain. Start hiking up the mountain, and you encounter rock formations and gullies at each rise. From the big picture to the small picture, the cycles evolve, one into the next.

An extended stock cycle may take years to complete. Within that cycle, smaller cycles take place in months, weeks, and days. Within a single trading day, miniature cycles evolve. These cycles, no matter the time frame, can form predictable patterns. Why are they predictable? Because people's emotions are predictable!

Some traders do not use charts to trade. To me, that's inconceivable. Trading without charts is like getting into my car and backing onto the street blindfolded. Trading is hard enough. Attempting to do it without charts accelerates risk immeasurably. Why chance it? High risk = lost money. No thanks!

When the stock is in a valley, or trough, we say it is "basing," or "bottoming." You could say the stock is resting here.

This basing area in a stock's cycle is one of those times brokers call their clients and tell them to buy.

"Remember that high flyer, Igloo Ice Cream? It used to be forty bucks a share, but it's melted down to twenty." The broker chuckles, then his tone turns serious. "We oughtta' pick up some for your account today. It's a heck of a bargain."

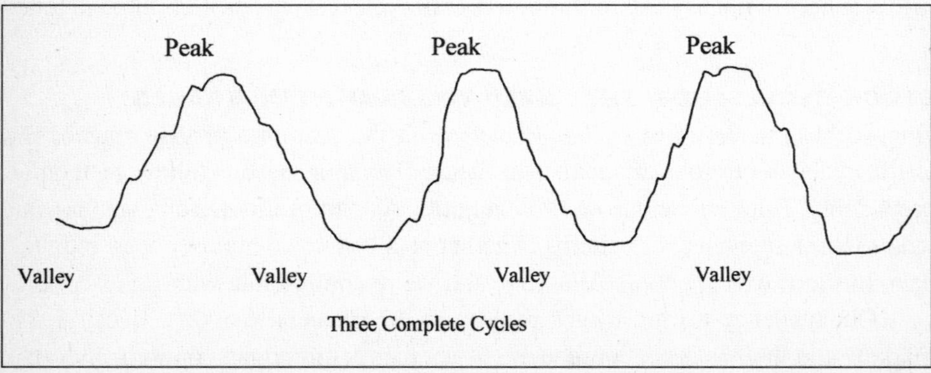

Figure 6-1
Three complete cycles

Maybe. Maybe not. Trouble is, if Igloo has fallen that far, and institutional money managers and investors are ignoring it, it may take weeks or months to rise again. In the meantime, that same capital could have bought a stock catapulting in an uptrend and making money—fast.

When a stock breaks up and out of the valley, then climbs higher and maintains a steady course upward, we call it an uptrend. As a trader, the *uptrend* is the most prevalent pattern you'll search for as you look for stocks to buy. For bulls, this is when the most profits are made. A "breakout" designates the exact point where the stock rises over the valley and leaves the foothills behind to mount a steady course upward.

To remain in an uptrend, a stock must make a series of higher highs and higher lows.

Remember, as we discussed before, stocks move according to supply, demand, and the mindsets of the market players involved. If buyers believe the stock's value will increase and pay higher prices as the sellers elevate the price, the stock moves up. The more volume (volume = number of shares traded) that comes in at this time, the more powerful the move.

Greed and, finally, euphoria (when buyers convince themselves "this baby can rise forever") propel uptrends. At higher highs during uptrends, and particularly as the move nears the top, we call the stock "overbought."

Hot Tip

When you're considering a stock for a swing, day, or scalping trade, develop the winning habit of checking out the stock's daily chart, spanning a few months to a year. This gives you a picture of the stock's true personality and shows how it behaves relative to the overall market.

The nature of cycles, though, dictates that *nothing* goes up forever! When an uptrend starts gasping for breath because buyers close their wallets, the sellers step in. Many of these sellers are previous buyers from the stock's upward move who take profits. Others are short sellers, or bears, who bet the stock is ready to retrace or pullback; they want to profit from the drop. During the pullback, volume typically decreases, indicating a momentary loss in the stock's popularity. Now, buyers wait in the wings for the perfect time to step back in.

As long as the retracement or pullback does not drop lower than the previous low in the trend, the stock technically remains in an uptrend. If, however, the previous low price on the trend is penetrated and broken decisively, technically speaking, the uptrend is over.

When the uptrend concludes, buyers and sellers even out, and the cycle arcs into a sideways pattern. Traders call this movement "rolling over."

The stock may now move sideways for a period of time. Anytime a stock moves sideways, it makes one of three basic patterns. Each tells a different story.

If a stock "trades in a range," it fluctuates between higher and lower price areas in a somewhat predictable, horizontal channel. When it dips to the bottom of the range, or channel, buyers step in and support the price from slipping into a downtrend. When it reaches the top of the range, sellers step in, and the price drifts down again. Sellers who short at the top of the range cover their shorts (buy the stock back) when it nears the bottom of the range, knowing buyers will surely step in and push it back up.

Although most traders hot-foot it to stocks rocketing in uptrends to capture dramatic buying opportunities, or to downtrends to grab shorting opportunities, please consider playing stocks trading in a range. You can make nice chunks of change buying the dips and selling the rallies.

The second pattern—or lack of it—we call "congestion."

Say you have a cold, and your head feels miserable and congested. You can't breathe worth a darn because your nose is all stuffed up. Stocks trading in a congestion pattern feel the same way! No uptrend or downtrend emerges (stock can't breathe) because buyers and sellers won't make up their minds which way this stock should go. Daily price ranges fluctuate from wide to narrow as the stock flounders unpredictably. Tactic: Stay away! You don't kiss your friends who have colds, and you don't trade stocks that trade in congestion patterns, unless you want your trading account to get sick.

The third sideways pattern we label "consolidation." Learn to spot the pattern easily. Whether it appears on daily charts or intraday charts, it will become one of your best friends.

A consolidating stock is doing just that. It marches sideways across a chart in a compact, linear fashion. The price range for each candlestick is short, tight, and orderly. To you, as a trader, it means buyers and sellers are in an even heat, and pressure is building within the compressed price range. When it blows, the stock will move up or down in a fast, furious manner. That volatility makes big profits for traders!

When a stock tires of trading sideways, buyers jump ship. Short sellers attack like hungry sharks, and the stock tumbles into a downtrend.

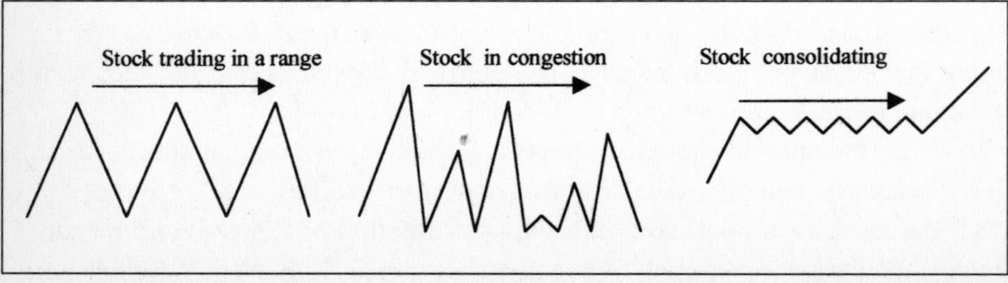

Figure 6-2

A stock in a downtrend makes lower highs and lower lows.

Stocks slide into downtrends on lack of interest alone (low volume). But if volume picks up as the stock falls, that stock has ugly problems. High volume on a falling stock means fear just escalated to panic. Everybody's dumping and heading for the door!

Whether the downtrend is orderly or panic-driven (long, black candlesticks), bears control the helm, and we say the stock is "headed south." If you're like most traders and investors, you look elsewhere for greener pastures. Only grumbling, long-term investors and happy short sellers hang around a stock in a downtrend. For the "shorts," the lower the unhappy stock tumbles, the richer they get. During the downtrend, and particularly near the bottom, we call the stock "oversold."

Nothing goes down *ad infinitum.* Well, almost nothing. I know of a handful of stocks that dropped to almost $0, but they gave early warning signs, and as a savvy trader, I'm sure you wouldn't have been within shouting distance of them.

If a stock represents a decent company that's fallen from grace because of poor, but fixable, fundamentals, or because it's a laggard in its industry group, it usually drops to the levels of its previous valley. There, we hope, sellers have mercy and buyers start nibbling again. It bases, or bottoms, then trades sideways until it gathers enough momentum to begin another uptrend. Then the cycle repeats itself.

Please understand, with the volatility so prevalent in today's market, high-flying stocks can go from an uptrend to a downtrend in a matter of minutes, nearly wiping out any sideways move! Likewise, they can move from a nasty downtrend to an exuberant uptrend quicker than you can say "ticker tape." It's still important, though, to understand the complete cycle so you can identify general pattern and trend changes as you study charts.

Point to remember: On charts, each candlestick represents the indicated time frame. When you look at a weekly chart, each candlestick represents one trading week. On daily charts, each candlestick represents one trading day. Intraday charts are the same: On five-minute charts, each candlestick represents five minutes; on thirty-minute charts, each candlestick represents thirty minutes; on one-hour charts, each candlestick represents sixty minutes; and so forth.

Figures 6-3 through 6-10 show examples of stock cycles. They also show stocks trading in uptrends, downtrends, and the three basic sideways patterns.

Hot Tip

When a stock is getting ready to break out, the farther away the last resistance, the more likely the breakout will succeed. The closer the resistance, the more trouble a breakout will have gaining strength. Why? Because the supply is fresher. Resistance (supply—disgruntled investors or traders who held the stock when it fell) that's a few days or a week old slows a stock down more than resistance that is months away.

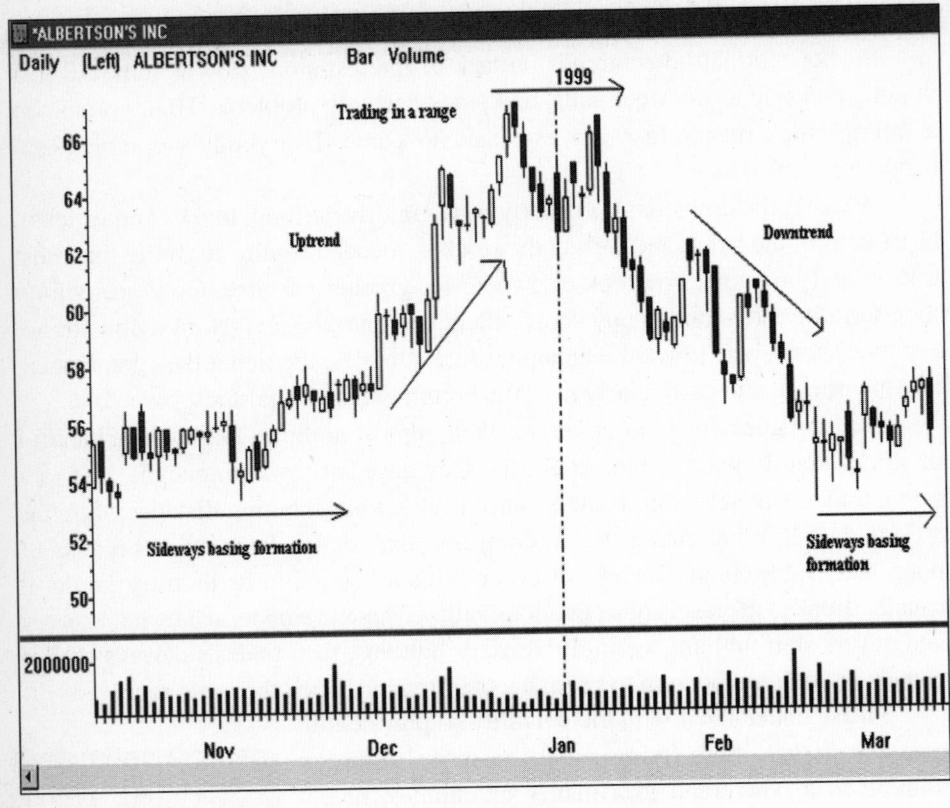

Figure 6-3

Stocks move in cycles. Although variations take place, the theme stays the same: 1. A trough, or valley, where the stock bases. 2. The uptrend. 3. A topping formation, where the stock moves in a sideways pattern, and trades in a range. This can last from minutes to months. 4. The downtrend. After the downtrend completes its move, the stock begins another basing formation and the cycle repeats itself.

Chart Courtesy of *The Executioner*©

SUPPORT AND RESISTANCE: WHAT THEY ARE, HOW TO RECOGNIZE THEM

Support and resistance are perhaps the most widely used of all trading concepts. As a trader, it's important you understand these concepts thoroughly. Every time you look at a chart, be it a one-minute or daily chart, a chart of the S&P futures, or the Nasdaq Composite, the first two questions that should pop into your mind are *Where is support? Where is resistance?*

Support and resistance form an integral part of supply and demand. As you know, stock prices don't rise and fall of their own volition, or at the whimsy of an erratic computer or capricious trading god. Market players virtually draw price movements on charts as they buy and sell. Furthermore, these market players,

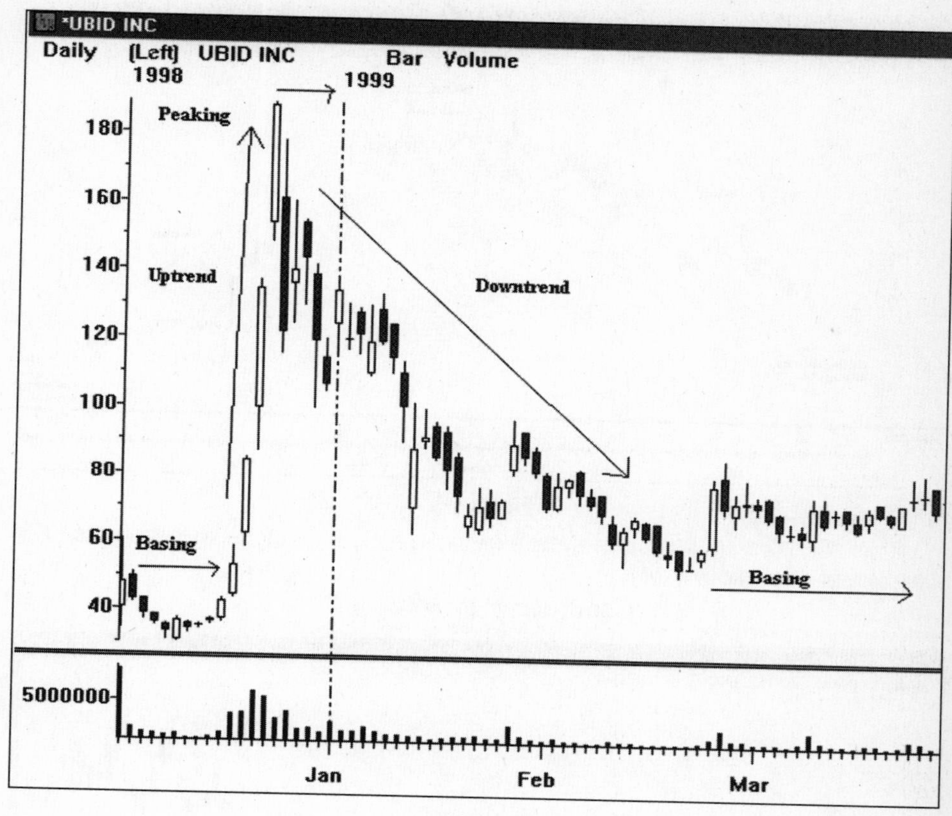

Figure 6-4

Even though some stocks trade in wild, roller-coaster patterns, you can still recognize the basic cycle paradigm. Here, UBID, an Internet stock completes a cyclical move: base, uptrend, brief and volatile peak, downtrend, then back to basing formation.

Chart Courtesy of *The Executioner*©

yourself included, have memories. Human memory, coupled with emotion and fundamental factors create support and resistance.

The stock in Figure 6-11 forms peaks and valleys as it trades in a range between $50 and $60. The pivot points created by price reversal form support and resistance.

Note the word *zone*. Support and resistance are *zones*, or *areas*, not exact prices. Imagine you're standing on a tennis court, next to the net. Lean on the net and feel it stretch. Prices that form support zones or areas are like the net on a tennis court; they stretch a little, both ways.

Another way to think of support and resistance: You are standing in a room on the first floor of a two-story building, holding a large ball. The ball represents

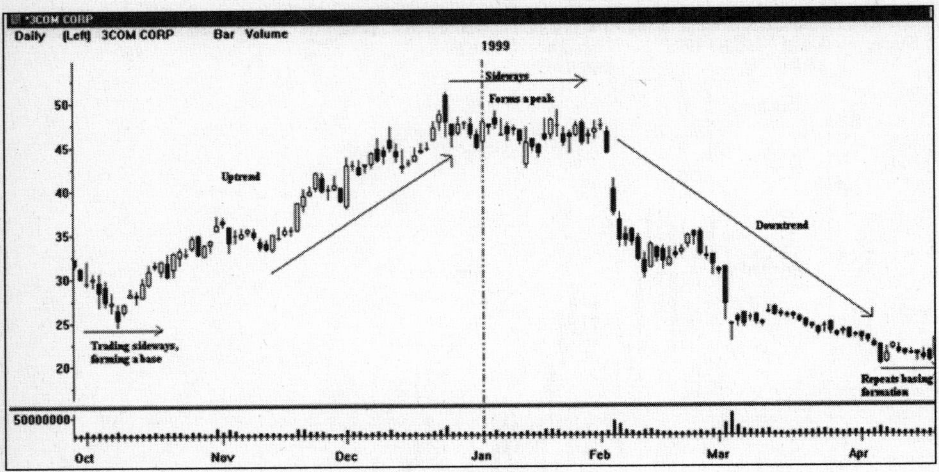

Figure 6-5

Although 3Com Corp., (COMS) can be a volatile day trading stock, as you can see on this daily chart, it has completed a fairly orderly cycle.

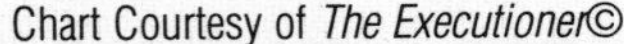

Chart Courtesy of *The Executioner©*

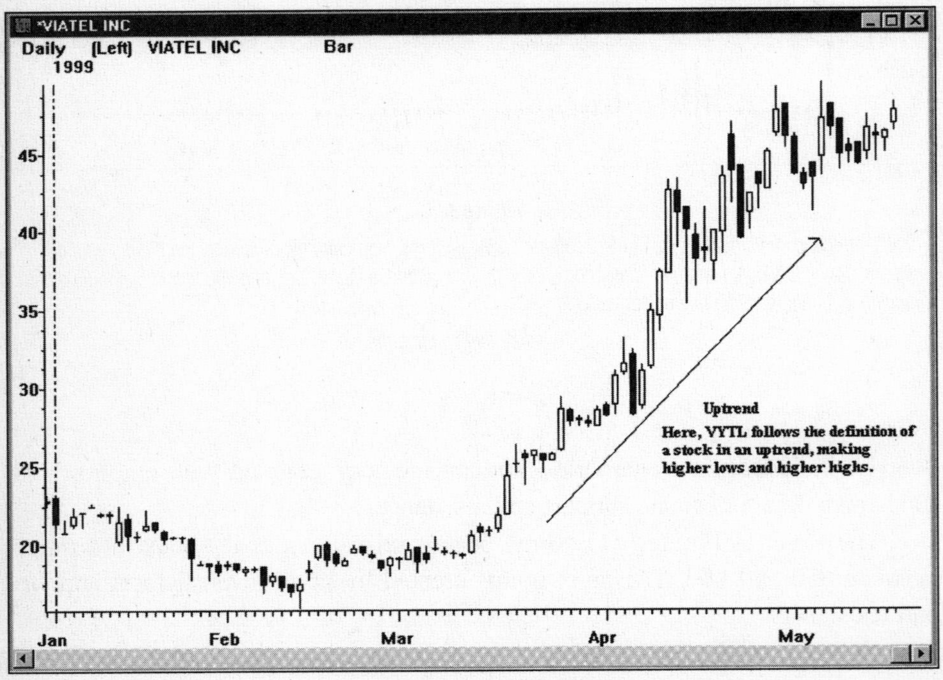

Figure 6-6

In this daily chart of Viatel, Inc., (VYTL), notice what a strong uptrend this stock is in. Practice looking at charts and locating stocks in healthy uptrends. During this uptrend, this stock nearly doubled in price. This presents a good argument for including core stocks as intermediate term holds in your second trading account.

Chart Courtesy of *The Executioner©*

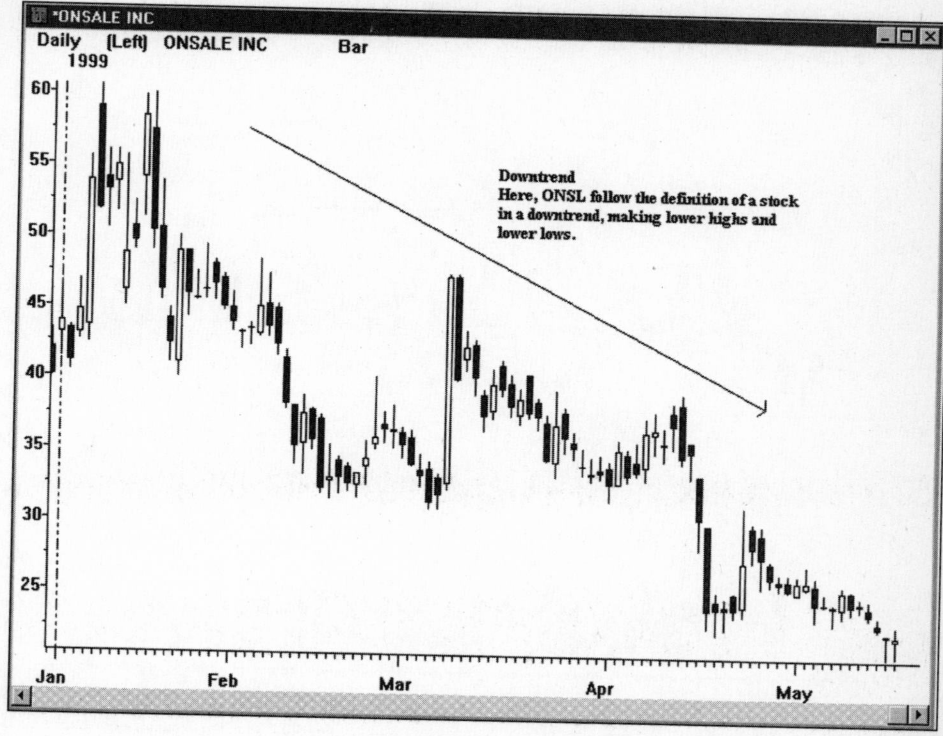

Figure 6-7

Onsale, Inc., an Internet stock, peaks just under 60 in the first week of January. By the middle of May, the stock has sunk to 22. Don't let false breakouts, like the one on March 8, fool you. On that day, the stock rose to a high of 47 1/2. Still, it didn't break the previous high of 48 3/8 on February 4, so the stock continued its downtrend.

Chart Courtesy of *The Executioner*©

"price." You toss the ball up, and it hits the ceiling—resistance. Then it falls, lands, and bounces up from the floor—support. -See Figure 6-12

After the ball bounces from the floor to the ceiling a few times, you catch it and throw it up with all of your strength. It soars upward and flies through a hole in the ceiling, into the story above you. It continues to soar, then gradually loses velocity. When it falls, it lands on the floor above you and bounces up from that. The floor where it lands is the new support for the ball.

Notice how once the ball soars through the ceiling and finally falls, the ceiling becomes a new floor. Former price highs, formed by previous pivot points at $60, are now support. When, or if, the stock moves through the second-story ceiling at $70, $70 (give or take a point or two) becomes the new floor, or support.

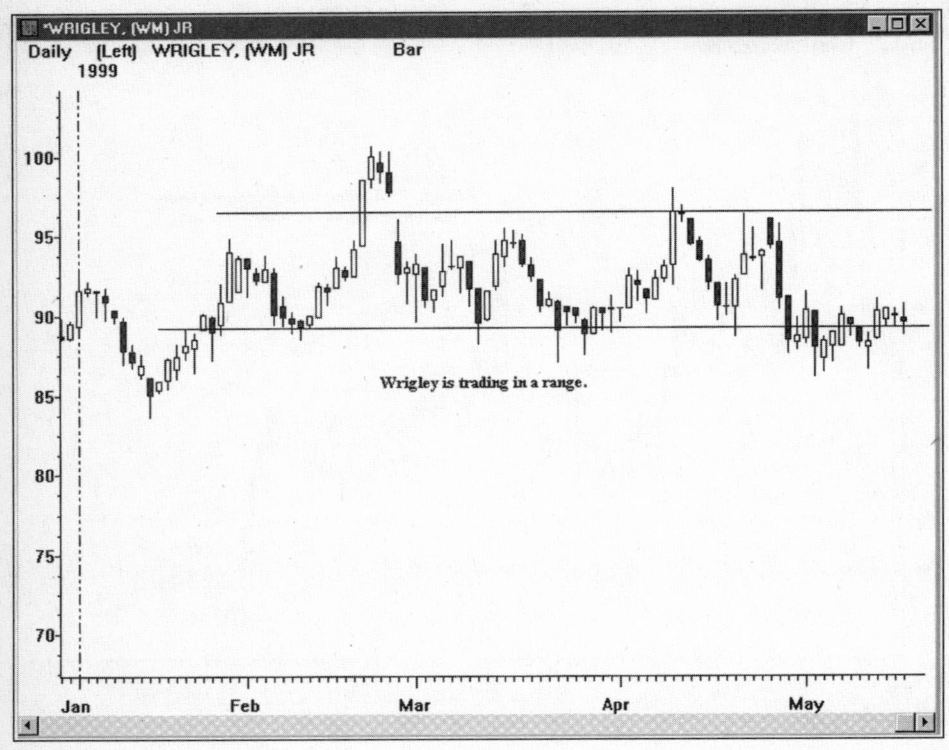

Figure 6-8

On this daily chart of Wrigley (WWY), you can see the stock is trading in a sideways pattern, or trading in a range. For a swing trade, you would buy the dips and sell the rallies, taking chunks of change between 88 3/4 and 95. It's nice to know when you plan your trade that WWY is a listed stock, and rather orderly in its movements.

Chart Courtesy of *The Executioner*©

Imagine the movement reversed as in Figure 6-13. The ball bounces from the first floor to the ceiling a few times. Then you catch it and throw it down, through a hole in the floor. It falls into the basement. When it lands on the basement floor, it bounces. It rises back up toward the floor where you're standing, but it's too weak to propel itself any farther than the basement ceiling, or resistance.

Figure 6-14 exhibits how, when a stock breaks below a major support area to sink even lower, it's usually in deep trouble. If it tests the support area only a couple of times during a short period of time and then violates it, that in itself is a negative signal. But if it bounces off the support many times during a long time period, and finally falls through it, that's an ultra negative signal, and the stock's probably in for a deep decline. *The more times it tests its support area, and the longer the time span it tests it, the more negative the signal if it does fall.* (Think of a perpetual law-breaker. The first few times he's caught for his crimes, he's fined and put on probation. But if he continues to break the law, eventually he's sent to prison!)

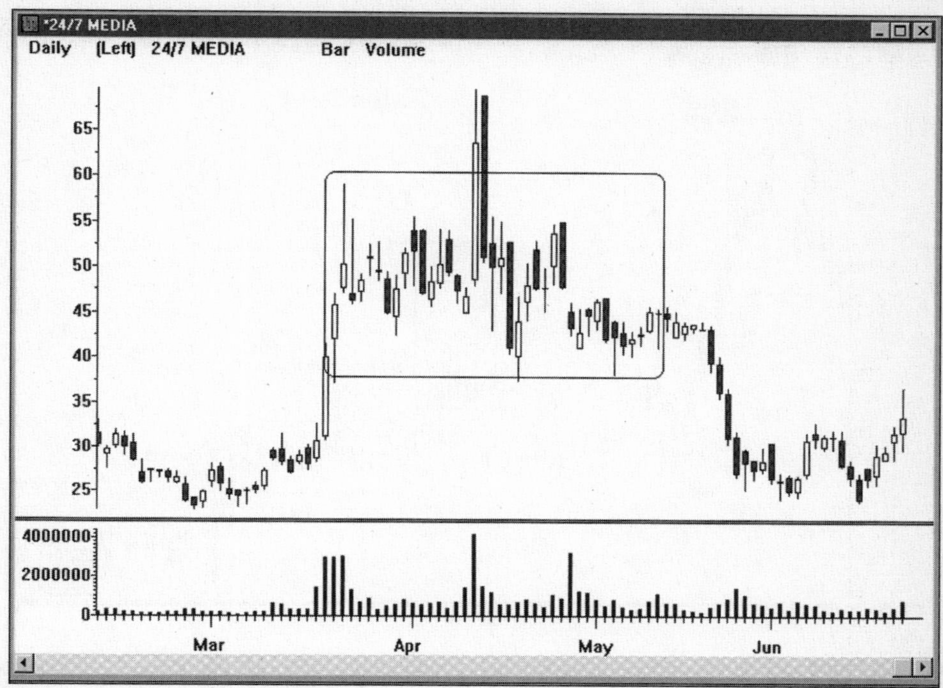

Figure 6-9

In this daily chart of 24/7 (TFSM), the candlesticks within the oval form a congestion pattern. As you can see, no discernible pattern emerged during this sideways movement, and traders, especially those contemplating longer-term trades, should stay away!

Chart Courtesy of *The Executioner*©

If the stock does fall into a deep decline, or downtrend, it will test previous support areas as it falls and will form new ones.

Resistance is the mirror image of support. Resistance is also called "supply," and in trading rooms, the terms are used interchangeably. You already know why. It's the price where a stock's been before, then reversed. It's where all the previous buyers said, "If this #@$*^% stock ever crawls back up to what I paid for it, I'm selling!" Supply = resistance = lower prices.

So, resistance is the "ceiling zone," where a stock feeling its oats will likely get slapped down, at least temporarily. Yet a strong stock will keep bouncing up to that ceiling zone until it gathers enough velocity (buyers) to accelerate through it.

The more times a stock tests resistance, and the more extended time period it does so, the more bullish it is when it breaks through it.

Of course, as the stock advances, it forms more resistance along the way, either succumbing to previous resistance areas or creating fresh resistance by

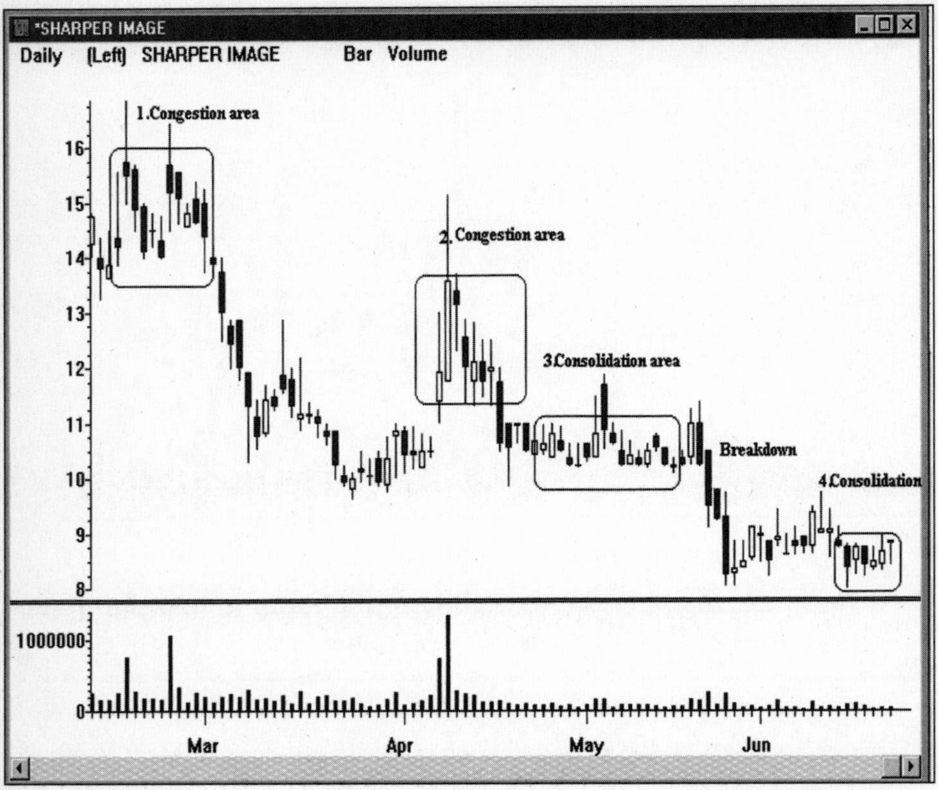

Figure 6-10

Chart Courtesy of *The Executioner©*

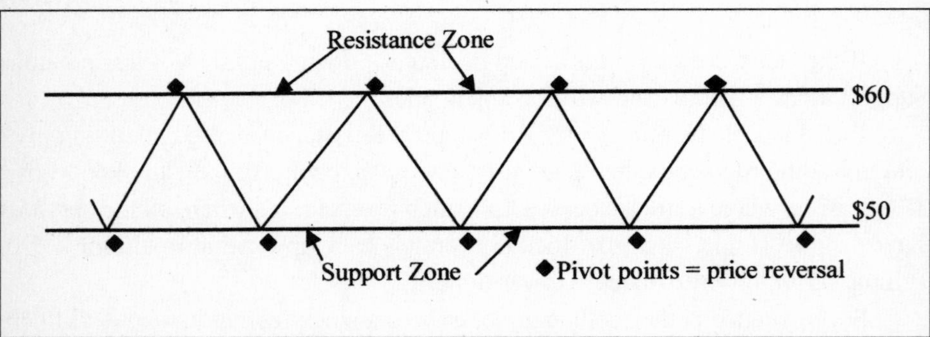

Figure 6-11

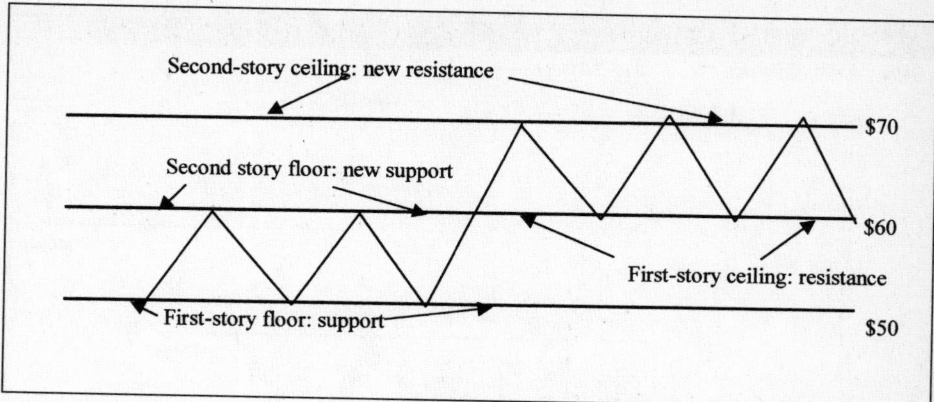

Figure 6-12

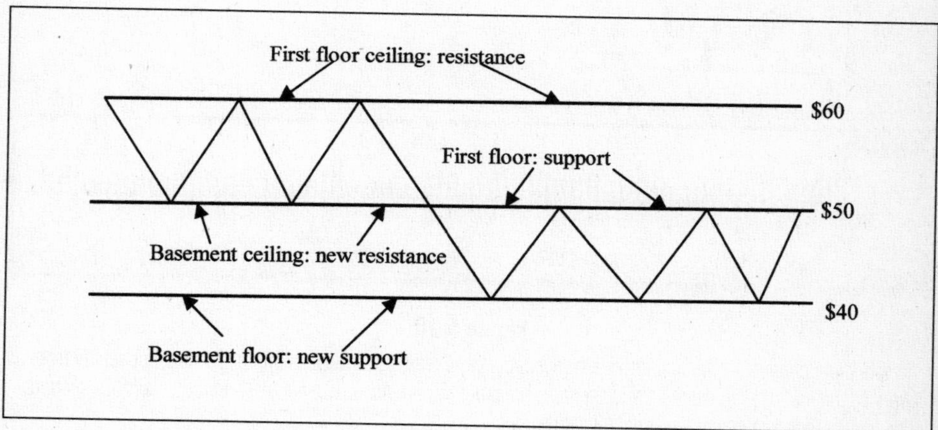

Figure 6-13

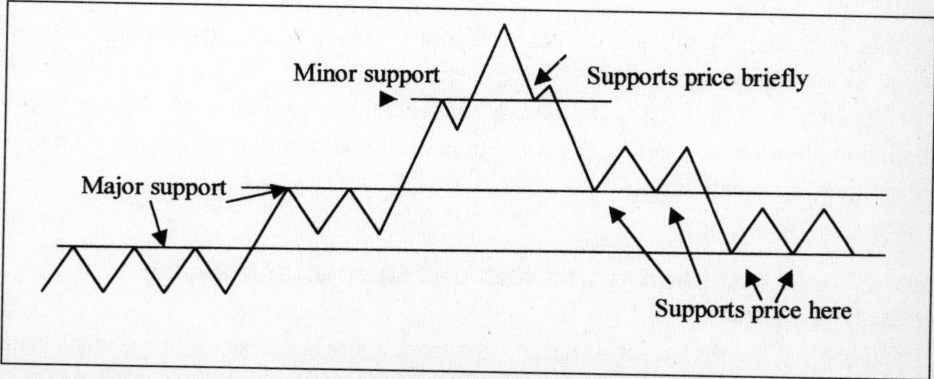

Figure 6-14

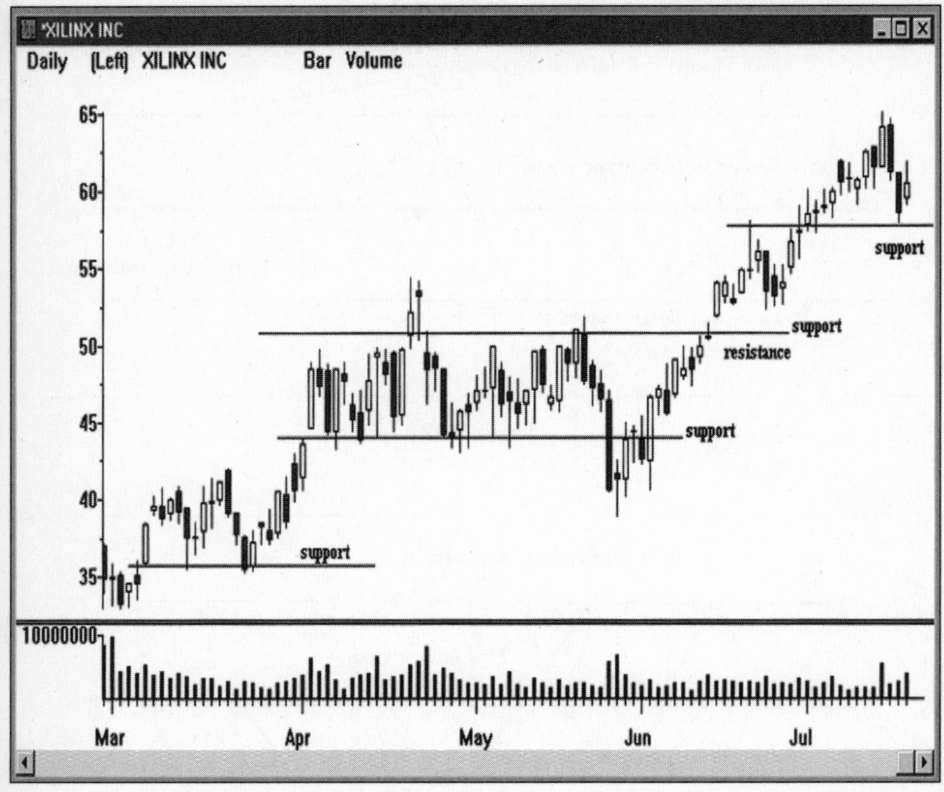

Figure 6-15

In this daily chart of Xillinx Inc., notice how support and resistance play an important role, especially from April to the end of May. Also, look at the false breakout in mid-April. The hammer on the breakout's second day gave a good clue that the breakout would fail.

Chart Courtesy of *The Executioner*©

pulling back due to overall market conditions, news, or the reason that *always* wins: more sellers than buyers!

Figures 6-15 through 6-18 indicate support and resistance levels. Please study them and other charts from your own source until you recognize support and resistance areas automatically.

MONEY-MAKING BREAKOUTS AND BREAKDOWNS: HOW TO IDENTIFY THEM

When a stock breaks out, it turns upward from a sideways move or pullback and rockets through resistance to a new high. It's the same move shown in Figure 6-4 when the ball shoots through the hole in the ceiling. You'll find that *breakouts*

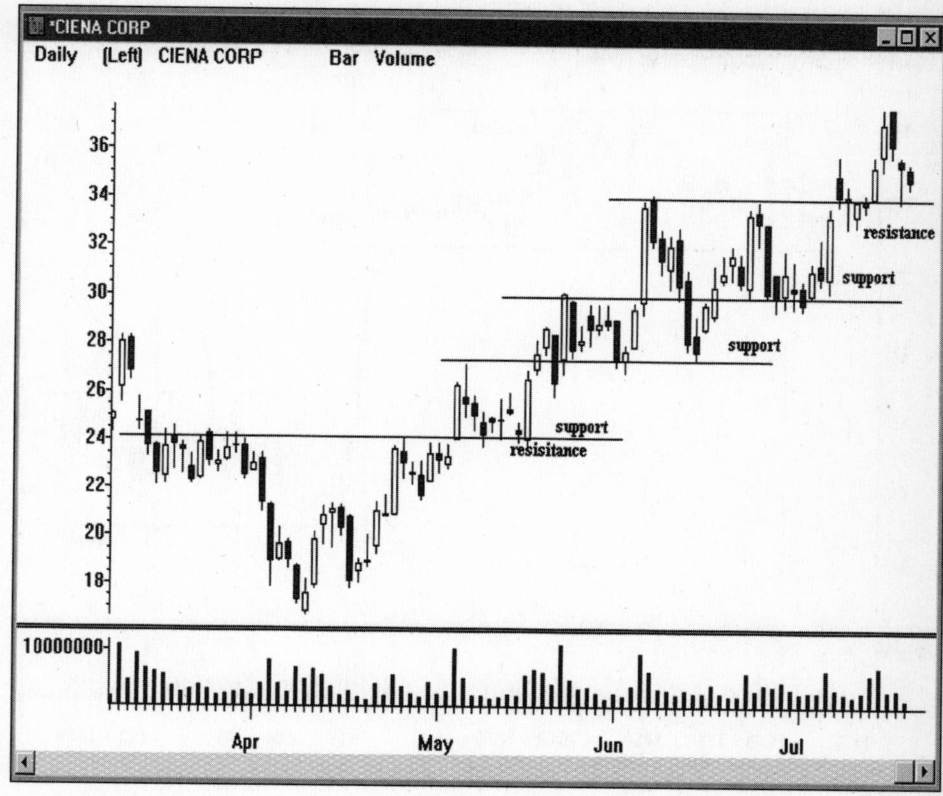

Figure 6-16

In this daily chart of Ciena Corp. (CIEN), even though the uptrend is not the most orderly, definite support and resistance areas are established.

Chart Courtesy of *The Executioner*©

create excellent buying opportunities for all trading time frames, from scalp to intermediate-term hold.

Breakout Steps:

1 The leading breakout: the moment the stock moves above key resistance (when the ball shoots through the hole in the first-story ceiling). If the resistance is at $60, you buy the moment the stock *trades*—not when it's shown at the offer, but *when an actual trade takes place*—at $60 1/16 or $60 1/8. The first price increment *above* resistance is the breakout point. The best leading breakouts are propelled by strong volume.

2 The pullback: As profit-taking sets in, the stock hits resistance (second-story ceiling) and reverses, pulling back toward the breakout price. When the selling recedes and buyers jump back in, the price pivots

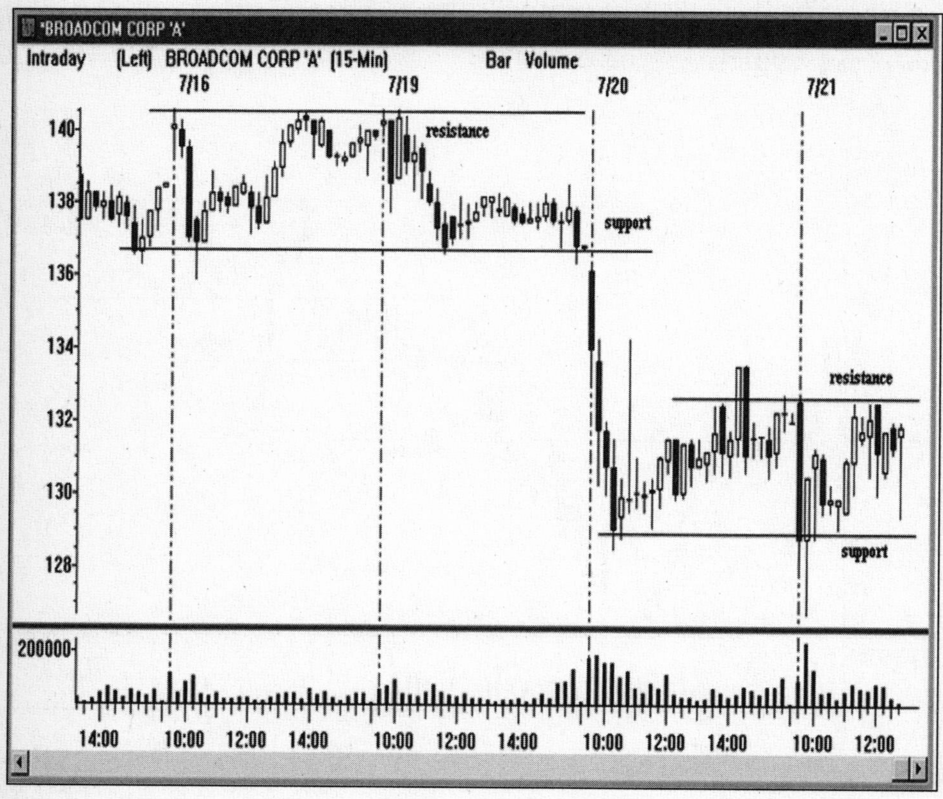

Figure 6-17

On this fifteen-minute chart of Broadcom Corp. (BRCM), notice the strong support that formed in the 137 area for three days in a row. When the stock gapped down at the open on 7/20, it broke support and fell nearly seven points.

Chart Courtesy of *The Executioner*©

(reverses) and heads north (up) again. The moment the price recovers from the pullback and moves up again, it initiates the second entry, or buying point. This is the safest place to buy because the leading breakout established the stock as a muscle stock!

3 The secondary breakout: Now the stock shoots up again, past its former pivot point (second-story ceiling). It accelerates through a hole in the second-story ceiling and flies into the third story. For scalpers and day traders, this point may be too late to buy. For a swing or intermediate-term trade, though, buying here, at the moment it trades *above* resistance, is acceptable.

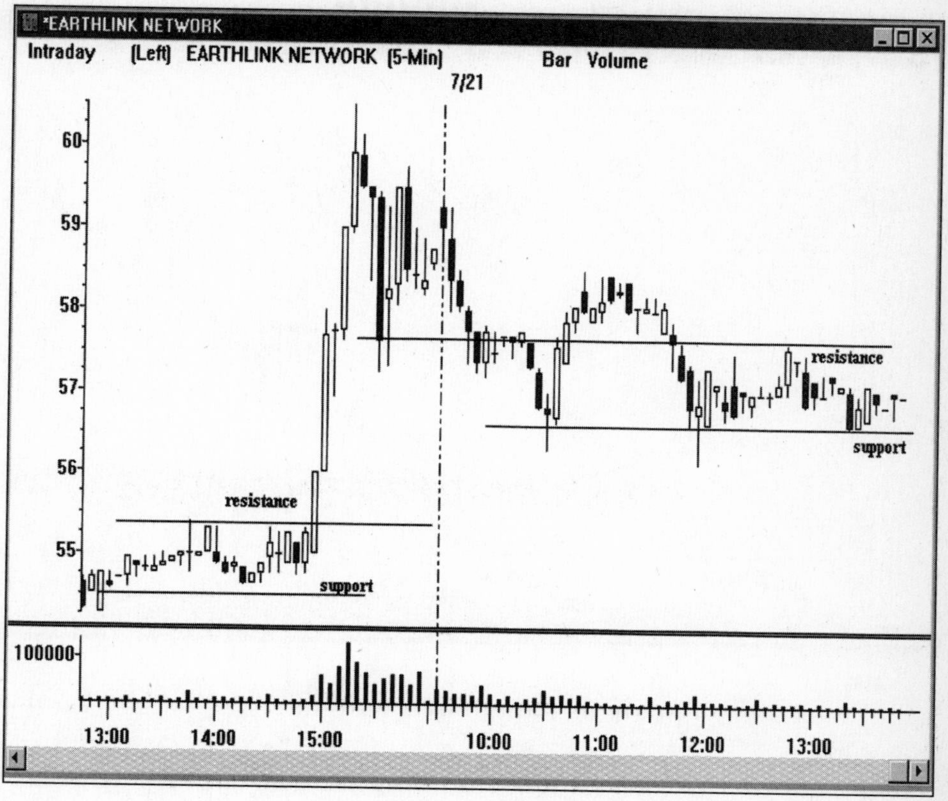

Figure 6-18

In this five-minute chart of Earthlink Network (ELNK), notice how it broke out of its congestion pattern on 7/20, at 55 1/2 and rose in twenty minutes to over 60. On 7/21, a break below 56 5/8 would surely turn into a severe breakdown. The next support would be at the 55 1/2 area.

Chart Courtesy of *The Executioner*©

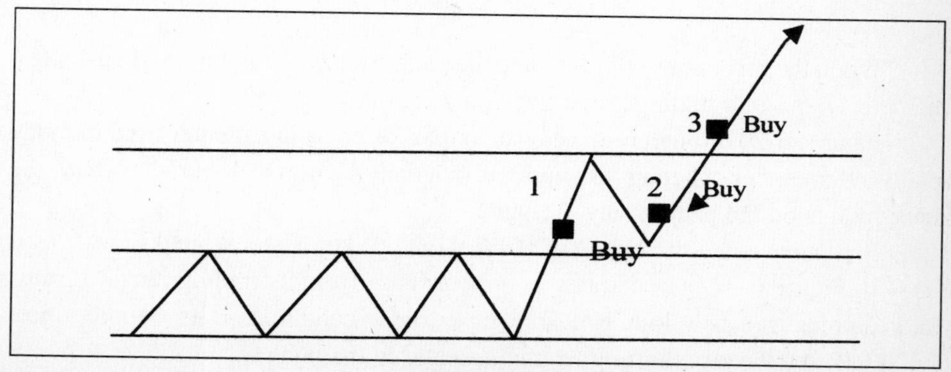

Figure 6-19

Three steps in a breakout

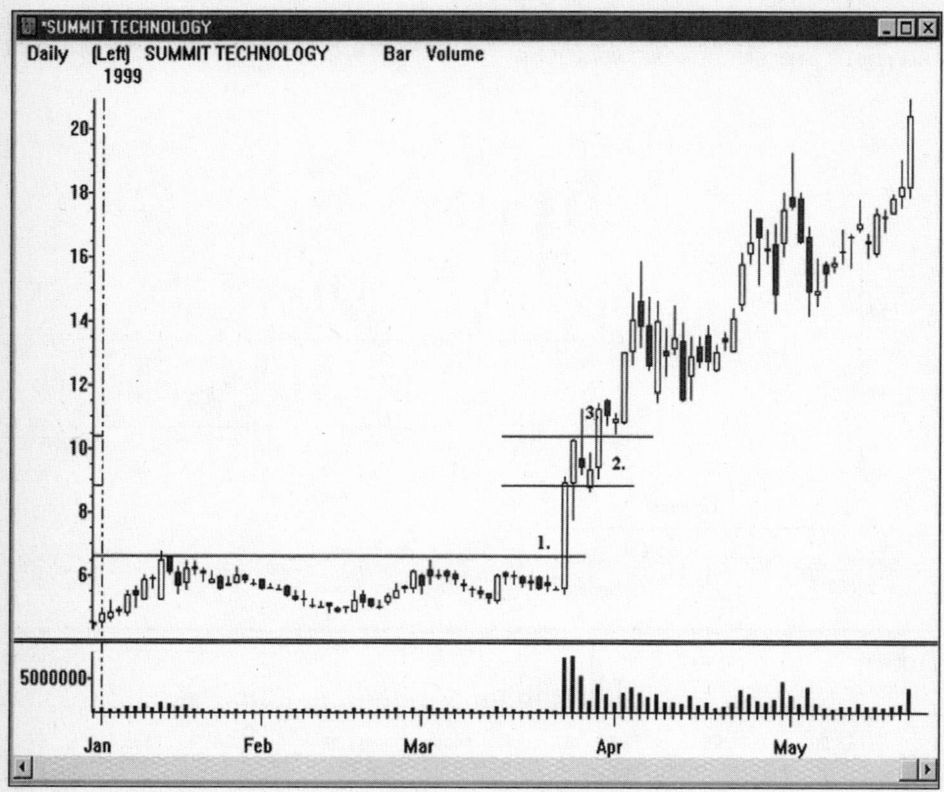

Figure 6-20

1. On this daily chart of Summit Technology (BEAM), you can see that after basing for months, the stock broke out on Mar. 24, rising over previous resistance of 6 5/8. Notice the high volume. Your entry was when it traded over 6 5/8, or 6 3/4. 2. The pullback reversed on Mar. 29, and made a high of 9 7/8. The safest buy point was on Mar. 30, when the stock broke above the Mar. 29 high, or 10. 3. The secondary breakout.

Chart Courtesy of *The Executioner*©

When the breakout steps complete the pattern shown in Figure 6-19, the stock has moved out of a trading range and into an uptrend.

Figures 6-20 through 6-23 show examples of breakouts on daily and intraday charts. Remember, whether you apply it to a daily chart, or an intraday chart, the entry points on the pattern stay the same.

Breakdowns are the opposite of breakouts. When a stock breaks down as it does in Figure 6-24, it penetrates its support base from its trading range or rally, and tumbles to a new low. Breakdowns create excellent shorting opportunities; we'll talk about exact shorting techniques later in the book.

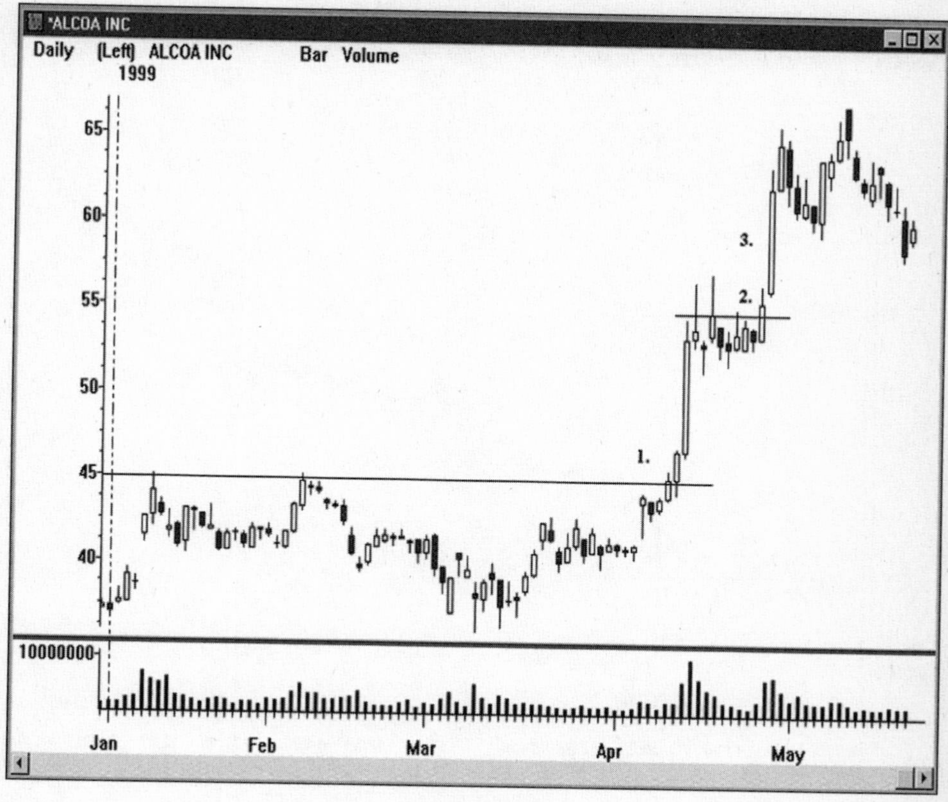

Figure 6-21

1. On this daily chart of Alcoa, Inc. (AA), the stock broke over resistance on strong volume on April 13, at 45. 2. The pullback was slight, then it moved sideways in a consolidation pattern. See how the volume decreased during this time—a good signal. On April 27, AA broke above the closing prices of previous consolidation days. Intermediate-term traders could add to their position here. 3. On April 28, AA continued the breakout, rising nearly eight points on the day. This is a good place to take profits!

Chart Courtesy of *The Executioner*©

Breakdown Steps

1. The breakdown: the moment the stock moves below key resistance (when the ball drops through the hole in the floor). If the resistance is at $60, you sell short the stock when it trades below $60.
2. The stock will decline to its next support area, then bounce, or rally. This rally is the same as a pullback in a breakout, only in the opposite direction. Soon the bears regain control, the bulls surrender, and the stock resumes its downward fall. This is the safest point to short a falling stock.
3. When the price drops below the last support, or pivot point (basement floor), it may be too late to enter for a day trade, but swing traders can

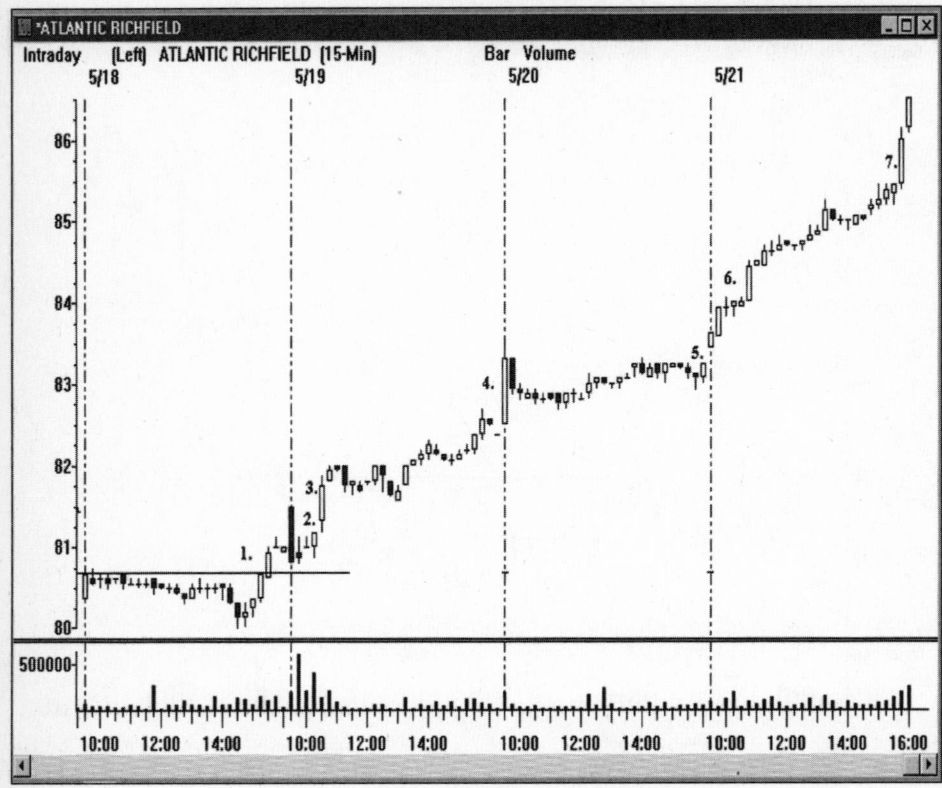

Figure 6-22

On this fifteen-minute chart of Atlantic Richfield (ARC), on May 18, it broke over resistance at 80 11/16. So, buy point was 80 3/4 or 80 13/16. On May 19, it gapped open to 81 1/2, then dropped to 80 13/16, and held there, consolidating. Check out the strong volume. If the oil index was strong, this would be a good entry point for a day trade, or to add to yesterday's position. ARC breaks out again at 10:30. Notice how it continues to rise for the remainder of this day, and the next two, in a gentle, orderly stair-step pattern. Traders could have added to their position at each breakout, and those who bought at 80 3/4 would have gained more than six points in four days. Not bad.

Chart Courtesy of *The Executioner*©

still short here. (I do not recommend new traders enter scalping plays in which they short the stock. You'll understand why later in the book.)

Figures 6-25 through 6-28 show breakdowns on daily and intraday charts. Despite differences in the time frame, the pattern is always the same.

A stock corrects in one of two ways: (1) by moving sideways, or consolidating, or (2) by pulling back. In the case of a downtrend, we call the pullback a "rebound."

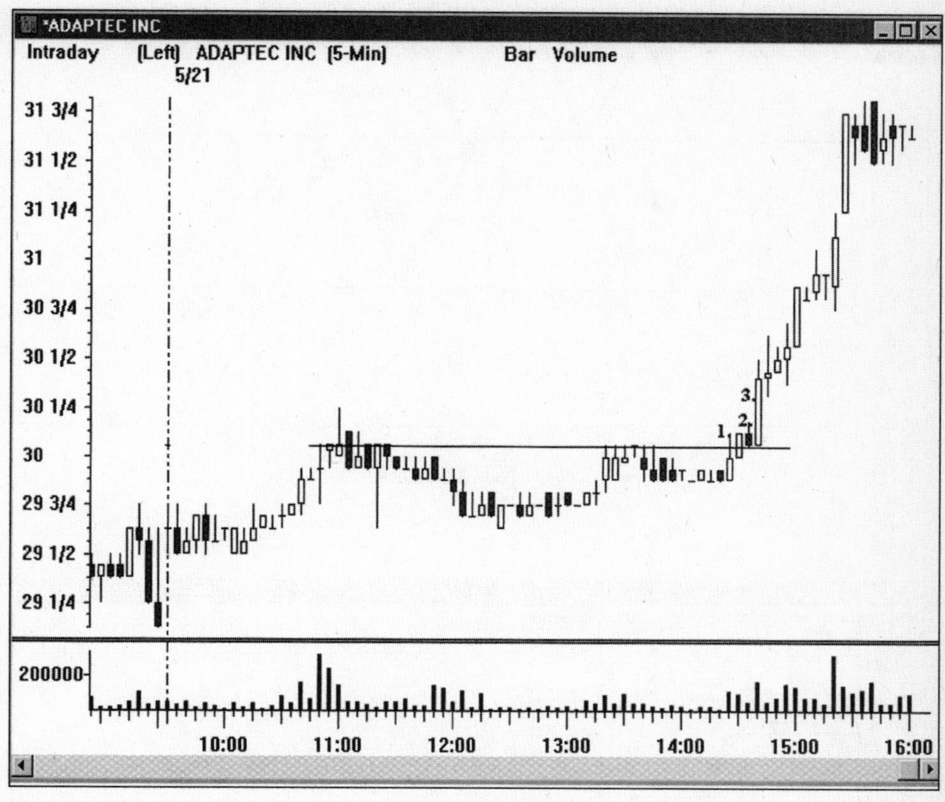

Figure 6-23

1. On this five-minute chart of Adaptec Inc. (ADPT), you can see how it broke over resistance of 30 1/16 at 2:25. (Many breakouts take place about 2:30 on a positive afternoon.) Notice the sudden increase in volume. Traders bought here at 30 1/8 or 30 1/4. 2. ADPT pulled back briefly at 2:35. At 2:40, it passed the high of the previous candlestick. This is a good place to add to your position, or enter if you have not yet done so. 3. The stock never looked back until it topped out at 31 3/4. Day traders exit at 3:35, after a 1 1/2 point ride. Not bad for an hour's work!

Chart Courtesy of *The Executioner*©

Pullbacks occur in an uptrend or downtrend when the stock takes a breather from soaring upward, or trending down.

Review Figure 6-6, and notice how VYTL moved sideways after its first and second breakouts, then retraced during its next two pullbacks. Some traders say that if a stock corrects sideways—as opposed to falling back toward the breakout point—it's stronger and odds are the move up will be powerful! Others say it doesn't matter. Just be aware that when the price moves sideways, the buyers are supporting it by holding—not selling—which in itself is a positive signal.

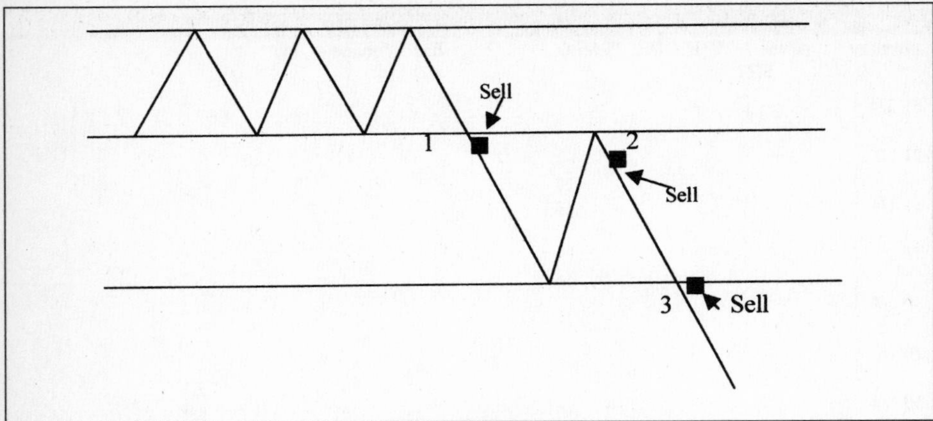

Figure 6-24

Three steps in a breakdown

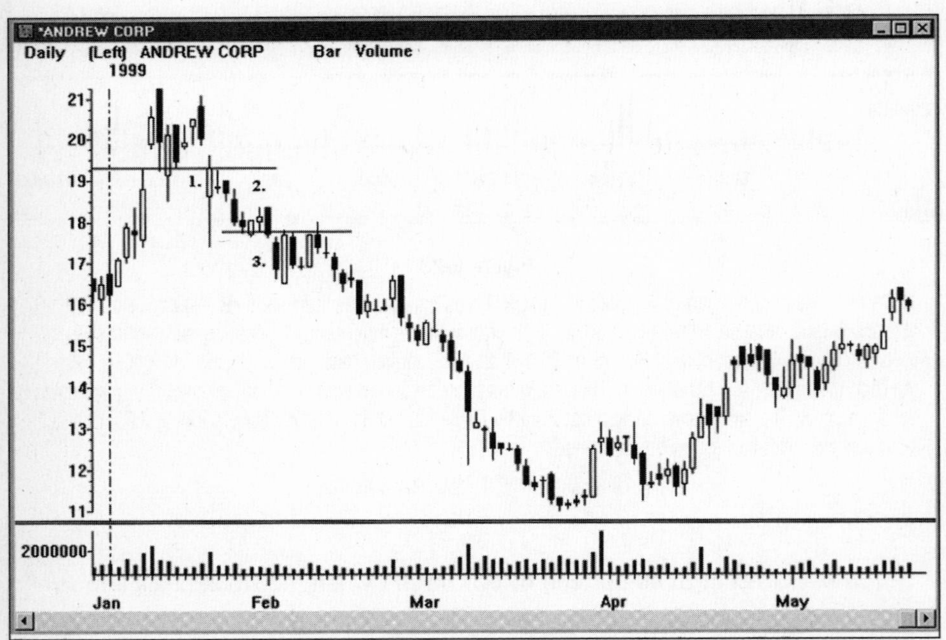

Figure 6-25

1. On this daily chart of the Andrew Corp. (ANDW), see how it gapped down on Jan. 21, down 1 3/8 points from the close of Jan. 20. 2. ANDW had two positive days on Jan. 28 and 29, where it tried to rally a little. 3. On Feb. 2, it gapped down 3/16 of a point, and although it had strong days here and there, it continued to make lower lows through most of March.

Chart Courtesy of *The Executioner*©

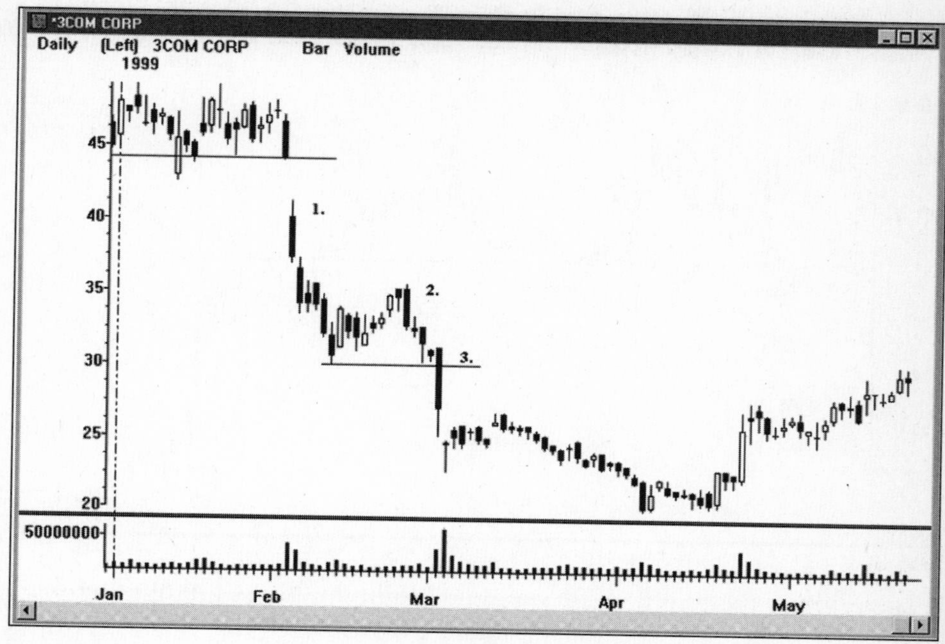

Figure 6-26

1. Poor 3 Com (COMS). On Feb. 3, it gapped down four points from the prior day's close! Notice the high volume—lots of sellers. 2. After a nasty tumble, it tried to rally toward the end of February, but didn't make much headway. 3. On March 2, it fell through support at 30 3/8, and fell to 27.

Chart Courtesy of *The Executioner*©

Either way, if the stock pulls back without falling through support at the breakout point, then turns back up, this is an excellent time to add to your position.

If, however, when the stock pulls back it drops below support, all bets are off. This signals you to exit—fast.

> **Hot Tip**
>
> Things that go straight up come straight down! That includes stocks. If you hang on to a stock that zooms toward the moon for more than two days, the return trip straight down—with no buyers in sight—will make a much more exciting trip than you had planned!

HOW TO DRAW TRENDLINES, OR WHERE TO CONNECT THE DOTS

It's important to get into the habit of automatically establishing trendlines. You can draw them mentally by eyeing the chart, or physically, by drawing the line with your computer.

Officially, you can draw a trendline on a chart by connecting two lows or two highs, using the same technique we use to identify support and resistance on

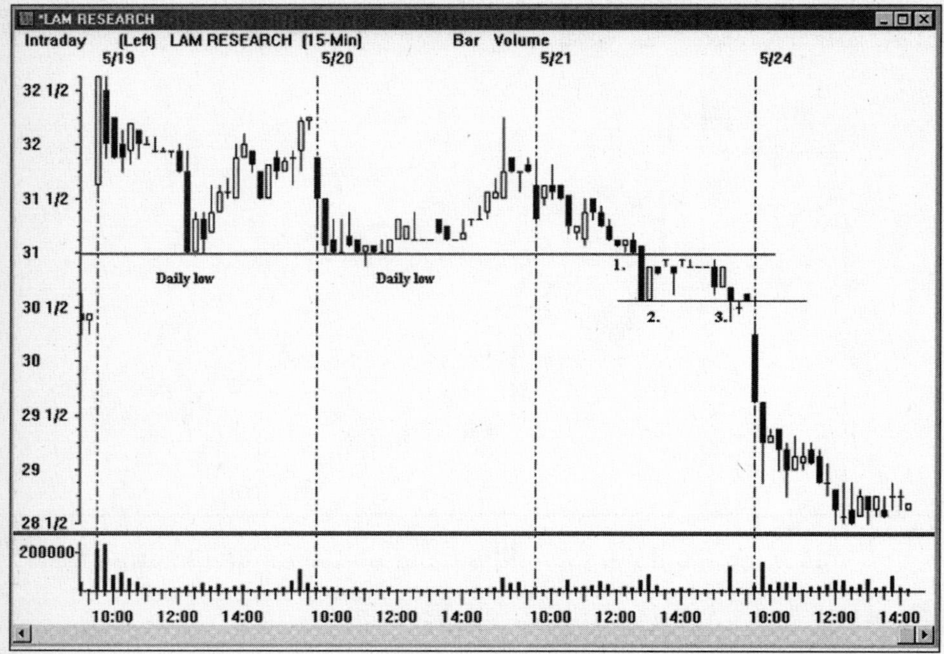

Figure 6-27

1. On this fifteen-minute chart of Lam Research (LRCX), you can see that on May 21, at about 12:45, it penetrated support established by the lows of the previous two days. Traders could have shorted here. 2. It rallied slightly, and consolidated in a sideways move until 3:15. 3. At 3:30, it fell again, making a secondary low. Those who wanted to hold as an overnight short could have sold short here. It closed near the low of the day, and gapped down the following Monday morning. Traders would have covered the short soon after the open Monday for a nice profit.

Chart Courtesy of *The Executioner*©

sideways moves. We're going to be more explicit, though, with our uptrends and downtrends, so they are even more exact.

Properly drawn trendlines make handy indicators with a number of uses. You could call them uptrend or downtrend support lines. They demonstrate where a stock's current trend is expected to go if it continues, and give you a boundary if the trend breaks. Trendlines make excellent, if somewhat tight, sell-stop points.

To draw a trendline for an uptrend, find the lowest low near the bottom of the trend. Next, look for the major low prior to the highest high. Connect the dots (Figure 6-29).

If the price bounces off your advancing trendline three times or more, regard the trendline as highly significant. When, or if, the price penetrates the advancing trendline and breaks below it, that's obviously negative.

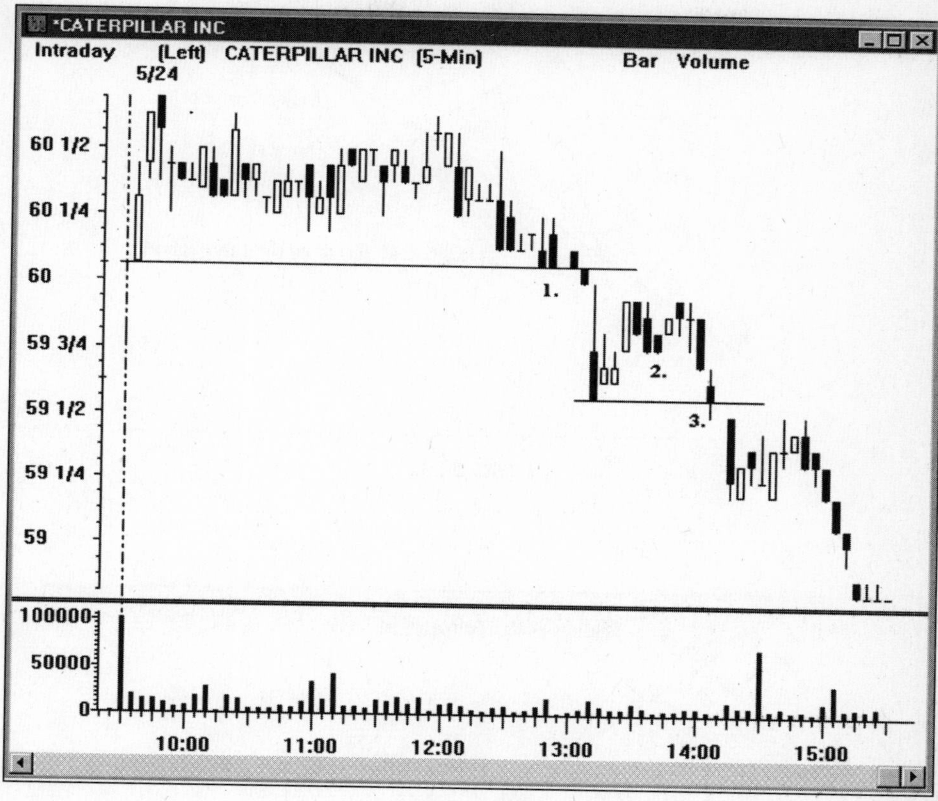

Figure 6-28

1. This five-minute chart of Caterpillar, Inc. (CAT), shows how it broke below the day's low, 60 1/6, at 1:05 p.m. Short sellers could have sold CAT here, about 59 7/8. 2. CAT tried to rebound until 1:55, when a dogi appeared. Dogis warn a change in direction may occur. In this case, the bears took control, and CAT started dropping again. 3. At 2:05, CAT made a secondary breakdown. Short sellers could have added to their position here, and by the close, covered the position for a total of nearly two points.

Chart Courtesy of *The Executioner*©

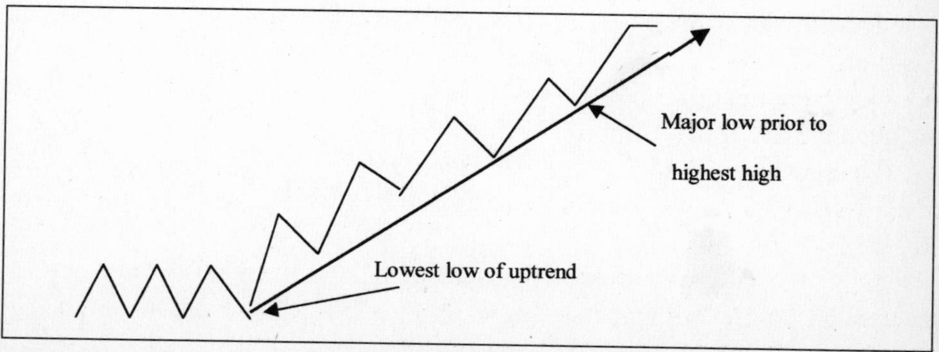

Figure 6-29
Trendline

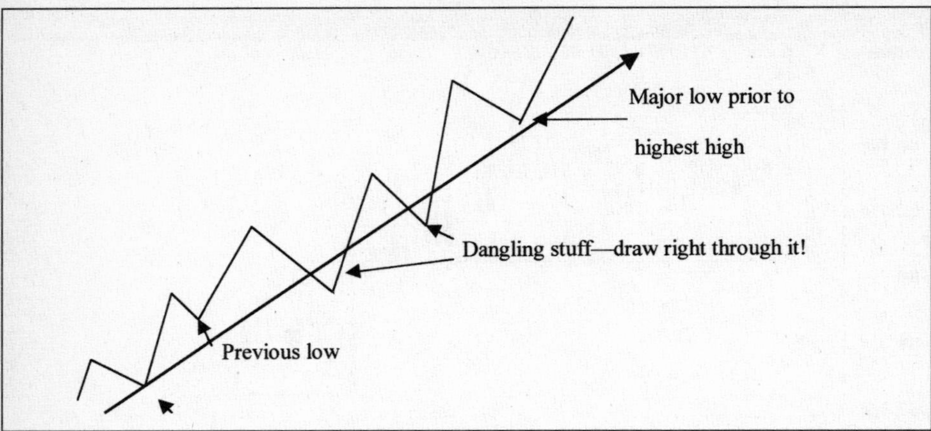

Figure 6-29

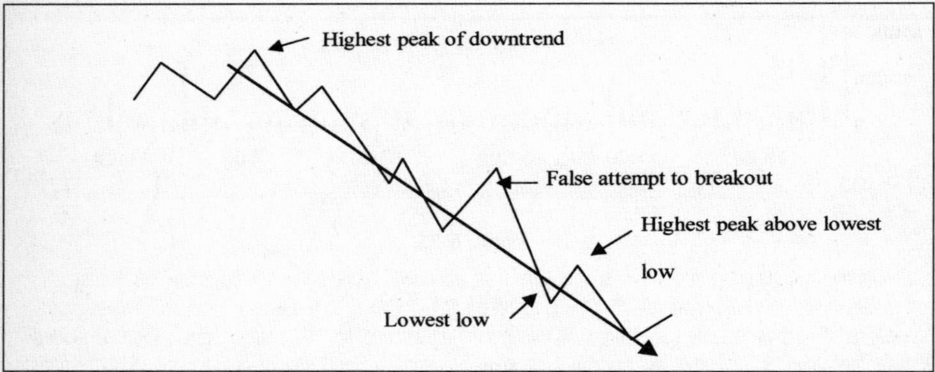

Figure 6-30

Figure 6-32 exhibits how uptrends rise, then roll over and break into downtrends in typical stock cycles. Naturally, the cycle repeats itself.

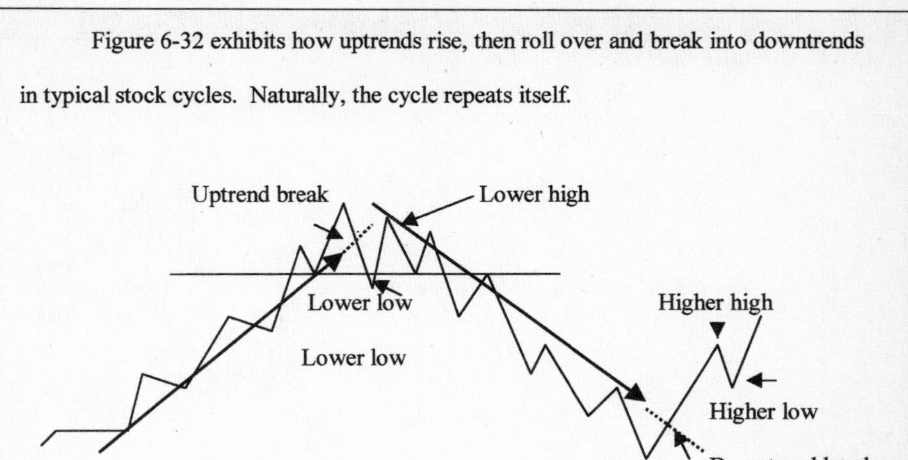

Figure 6-32

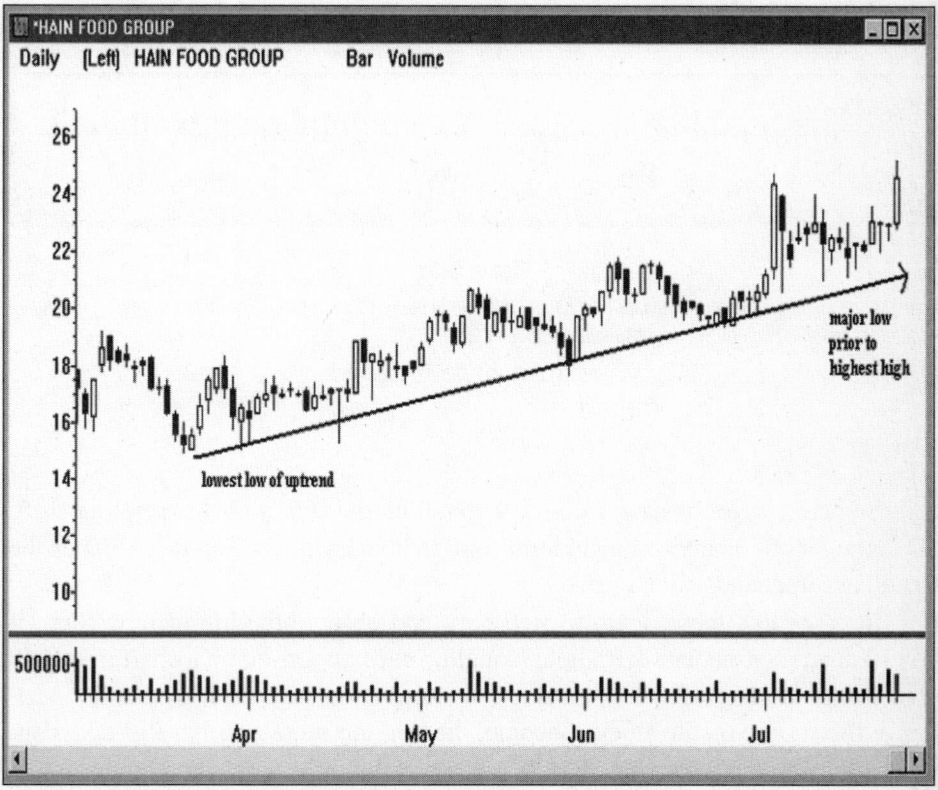

*HAIN FOOD GROUP
Daily (Left) HAIN FOOD GROUP Bar Volume
lowest low of uptrend
major low prior to highest high
Apr May Jun Jul

Figure 6-33

This daily chart of Hain Food Group (HAIN) clearly shows the stock in an uptrend. Draw the trendline from the lowest low of the uptrend to the major low prior to the highest high.

Chart Courtesy of *The Executioner*©

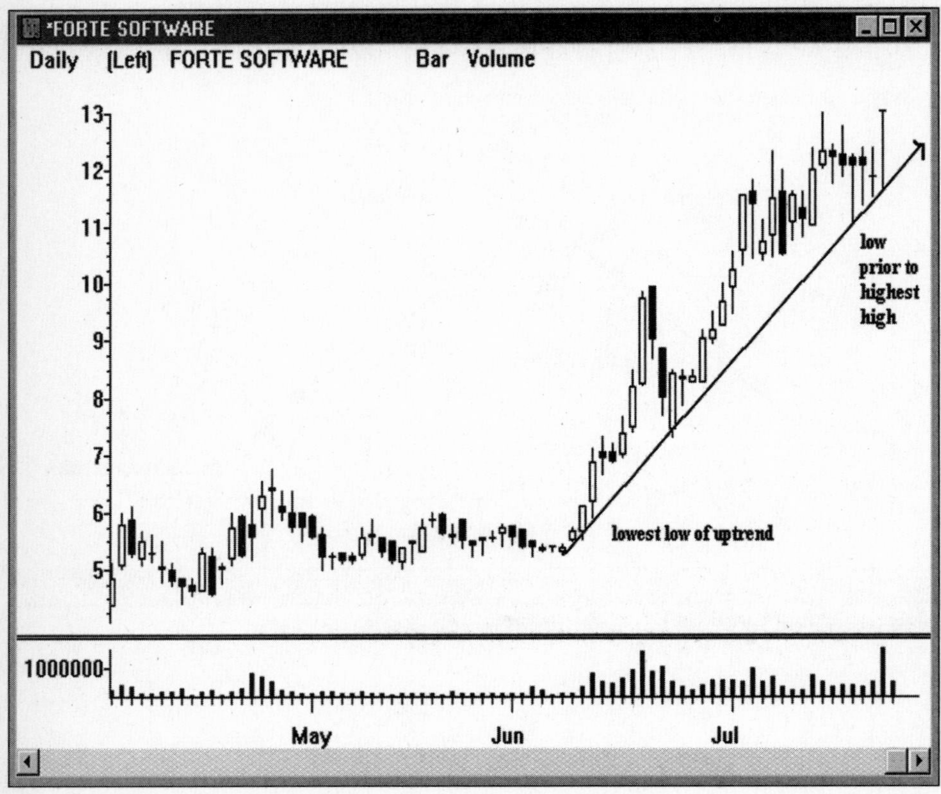

Figure 6-34

On this daily chart of Forte Software (FRTE), the uptrend is obvious. It's a perfect breakout scenario, and an alert trader who bought the initial breakout did very well!

Chart Courtesy of *The Executioner*©

Sometimes you'll have to draw a trendline through a bit of dangling stuff. "Dangling stuff" is my technical term for a temporary price drop that violates the trendline for a candlestick or two.

In cases like these, learn to step back and observe the big picture. Sure, if you're in an intermediate-term hold, dangling stuff appearing on a chart may grab your attention although your sell stop may not be violated. (If it is, exit the position.) The more volatile stocks become, though, the more you have to take dangling stuff into consideration. And, of course, if the little dangle accelerates into a major dangle, that's an alarm to obey!

Note that even though the dangling stuff prices defied the trendline, *both times the lows were still higher than the previous lows*. That's the criterion to

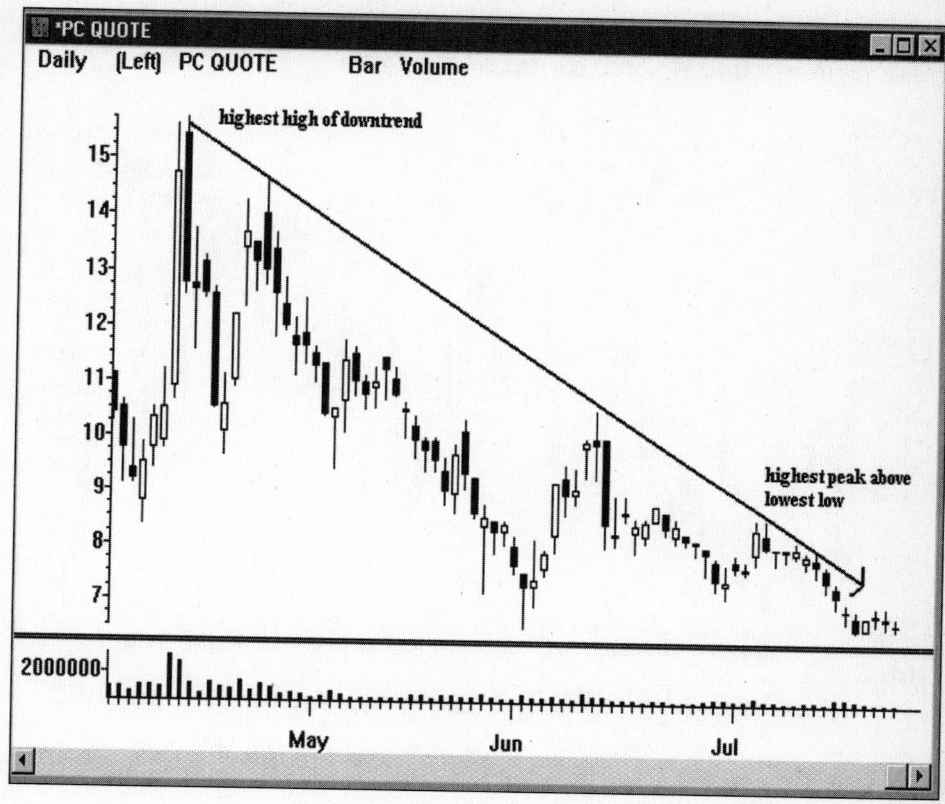

Figure 6-35

On this daily chart of P.C. Quote (PQT), the downtrend starts in mid-April 1999, and doesn't slow until the end of July. PQT tries to reverse in the second week of June, but cannot break through resistance established in mid-May, and so resumes the downtrend.

Chart Courtesy of *The Executioner*©

remember. Since the definition of an uptrend is a stock making higher highs and higher lows, a trendline like the one in Figure 6-30 is not officially broken until a *previous low* is surpassed. When that happens, the trend is at an end!

While you're looking at trends, remember, an uptrend is an uptrend, whatever time frame you're trading in. Are you looking through binoculars at a weekly chart, or a microscope on a one-minute chart? It doesn't matter. An uptrend has the same definition.

For a valid uptrend, the candlesticks must advance with higher highs and higher lows. Three or more touches to the trendline make the line more important. If the stock breaks its uptrend line and that's where you've placed your stop—sell and beat a hasty retreat.

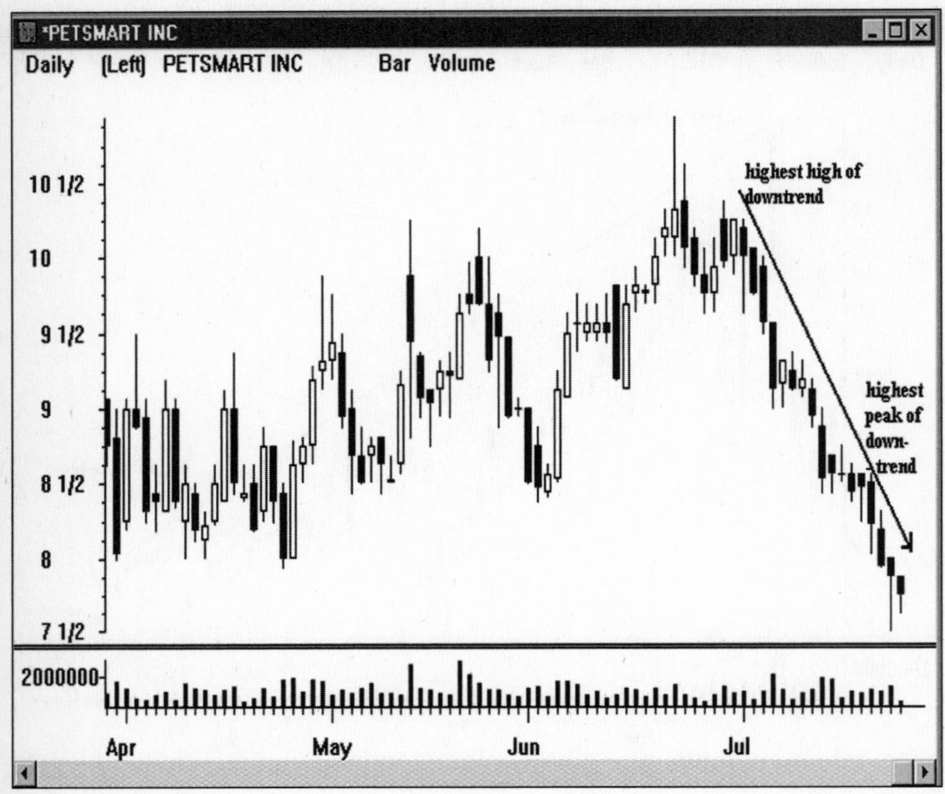

Figure 6-36

Poor Petsmart (PETM)! On this daily chart, we see how it fought valiantly through a congestion period in April 1999, then struggled through a dicey uptrend until mid-May. It fell back to support the first part of June and struggled up again until the last part of the month. The first of July, PETM's party was over for a while. It fell through support into a steep downtrend, showing only two positive days. Short sellers did well with this stock.

Chart Courtesy of *The Executioner*©

For intermediate-term trades and some swing trades, the best-behaving stocks trend up at about a 45-degree angle on a daily chart. Those that trend up steeper than 45 degrees are okay for some swing trades, day trades, and scalps. The sleepyheads that trend up somewhere between horizontal and below 40 degrees don't appeal to most traders because low volatility makes trading Dullsville.

To draw a trendline in a downtrend, find the highest peak, or pivot point above the lowest low. Next, locate the highest peak at the top of the trend. Connect the dots (Figure 6-31).

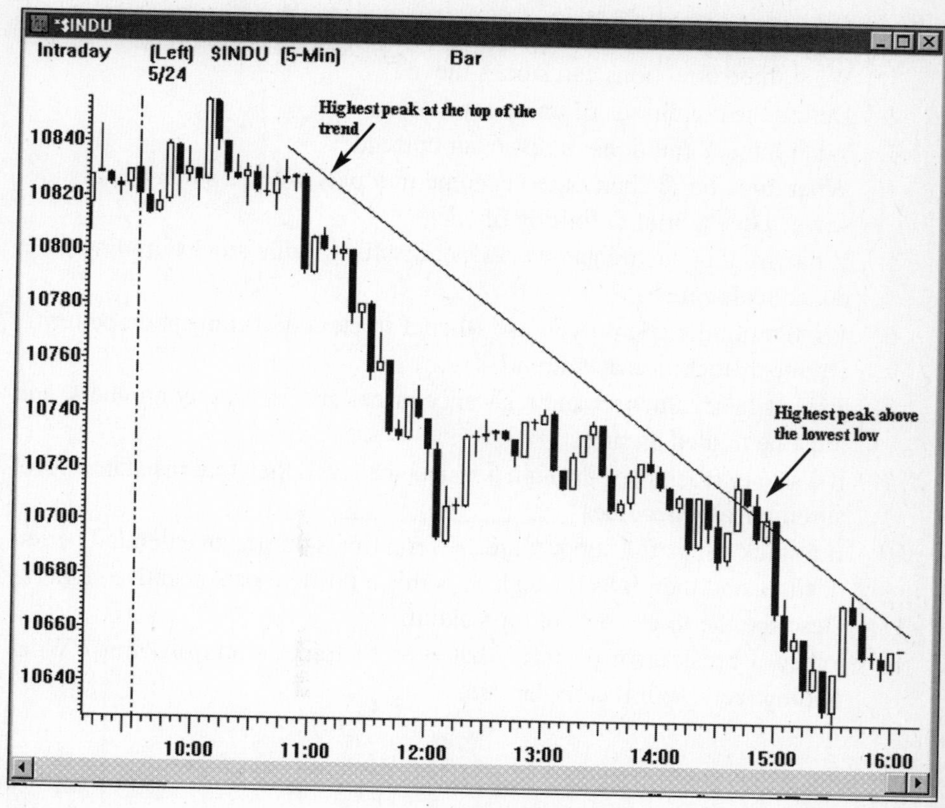

Figure 6-37

On this five-minute chart of the Dow Jones Industrial Average, you can't miss the downtrend on the day.
Chart Courtesy of *The Executioner*©

Notice that when the stock tried to break above the trendline, but couldn't sustain it, that false breakout high was still lower than the previous high. Since the definition of a downtrend is a stock making lower highs and lower lows, a trendline like the one in Figure 6-32 is not officially broken until a *previous high* is surpassed. When that does happen, all short sellers should jump out of the pool!

Figures 6-33 through 6-37 show a selection of the previously illustrated stocks in uptrends and downtrends, with the trendlines properly drawn. After you study these, go to your own chart source. Flip through them and identify stocks in uptrends and downtrends. Identify stocks trading in a range, as well as in congestion and consolidation patterns. Locate stocks breaking up, and breaking down. Where will you draw support and resistance lines? Up or down trendlines?

Analyze charts until the preceding concepts are firmly etched in your brain—or you start to snore—whichever comes first!

QUIZ

1. What three directions can stocks move?
2. Define the conditions of an uptrend.
3. What human emotions motivate an uptrend?
4. What three basic chart patterns come into play when a stock trades sideways? Give a brief definition of each.
5. What trading technique works successfully with stocks trading in a dependable range?
6. What trading tactic do you use when a stock is in a congestion pattern?
7. Define a stock in a downtrend.
8. True or false? Support and resistance prices are firm, exact numbers, and must be treated as such.
9. If a strong stock rises through a resistance level, then that resistance level automatically becomes _______________.
10. If a stock rises off a support area several times during an extended period of time, and then falls through it, is this a positive or a negative signal?
11. Describe the three steps of a breakout.
12. When a breakdown occurs, what type of trader starts drooling? What trading tactic will that trader use?

ANSWERS

1. Up, down, and sideways.
2. A stock in an uptrend makes higher highs and higher lows.
3. The human emotions that motivate an uptrend are greed and, as it reaches the final phases, euphoria.
4. Three basic sideways patterns are trading in a range, congestion, and consolidation. Trading in a range means the stock trades in a fairly predictable pattern, rising and falling between upper and lower, horizontal channel lines. Congestion means no definable trend emerges and traders should stay away. Consolidation means the stock trades in a tight, orderly range and is getting ready to initiate a strong move either up or down.
5. Stocks trading in a dependable range are prime candidates for the trading tactic known as buying the dips and selling the rallies.
6. The trading tactic for stocks in a congestion pattern is to stay away!
7. A stock in a downtrend makes lower highs and lower lows.
8. False. Support and resistance prices denote *areas* or *zones* that must be allowed to stretch a point or two.
9. support.
10. Negative. The more times a stock bounces off support, and the more extended the time period, the more negative the signal when or if it falls below that support.
11. (1) The leading breakout when the stock pushes up through a previous resistance area. Strong volume makes this move more powerful. This is the most profitable time to buy. (2) The pullback; sellers come in to take profits. Soon, though, the bulls take over again, and the stock resumes its upward climb. This is the safest time to buy. (3) The next breakout occurs when the stock makes a new high after the pullback.
12. Traders who drool over breakdowns are bears who can't wait to sell the stock short.

✦ ✦ ✦

CENTER POINT

Coincidence or Synchronicity?

The basics of belief in synchronicity are that every single life has a purpose and a deeper meaning than we are generally aware of. Behind all form is an intelligence that is exquisitely perfect, and that works in synchronized fashion. Everything happens for a purpose, and the puzzle pieces of life fit together perfectly. When you trust and know these thoughts, you will daily recognize evidence for your belief in synchronicity.[1]

—WAYNE DYER[1]

How many times have you lifted the telephone receiver and suddenly known who was on the other end of the line before you said, "Hello"? Or how many times have you thought of someone you've not seen in a while, only to have that person appear in your life the same day?

At a deeper level, have you ever looked back in your life and realized that at the moment you struggled most in a difficult situation—the right person or occurrence appeared out of nowhere to help you over the rough spots? Or have you endured a tough situation that ultimately led to new and surprising opportunities?

Some of us call incidents like these coincidence. Maybe they were. I believe they occurred through synchronicity.

Carl Jung first described synchronicity as "the simultaneous occurrence of two meaningfully but not causally connected events."

The Earth orbits perfectly around the sun; it does not fly off on a path of its own to destruction. Gravity holds each of us on the planet equally, not in spotty chaos. When left alone, nature operates in exquisite synergy, totally synchronized.

If our environment is so perfectly arranged, is it possible our lives are also? Is it possible that each of our lives has an innate purpose? And that each life is orchestrated by an intelligence that works through perfect synchronization to bring about our unfoldment according to a grander plan?

To understand the phenomenon of synchronicity, most of us have to suspend some of our old beliefs that life is random and chaotic. The next step is to become aware of the synchronous events that take place in our lives, and identify them as a wondrous component of our existence.

✦ ✦ ✦

1 1. Dyer, Dr. Wayne. *You'll See It When You Believe It.* (NY: Avon Books, 1989), p. 185.

CHAPTER 7

Choose a Stock to Trade

HOW TO STAY ON THE RIGHT SIDE OF YOUR STOCK

One day, a bit earlier in my trading career, the market was in dire shape. To capitalize on this, I found a weak stock sliding into a breakdown. Then I sold it short at the perfect entry point. Sitting back, I watched with satisfaction as the market continued its free-fall, dragging the stock with it.

Suddenly, with no explanation, my stock suddenly made a U-turn. It reversed, shot straight up, passed key resistance, screamed through the day's high and started for the stars. In shock, I covered the position.

I was in the Pristine Trading Institute, so I jumped up and ran over to Greg Capra. Greg is one of the finest market technicians in the business.

I tapped him on the shoulder. "I just shorted the ugliest stock in town. It fell like a sack of rocks. Then, for no reason, it recovered. Now it's making new highs. Could you please look at it and tell me what happened?"

As other traders crowded behind me, also waiting for the answer, Greg brought up the stock chart on one of five computer screens he stares at all day. He studied the chart, and we all waited expectantly. Surely he'd give us an explanation of intricate technical rhetoric, laced with indicators and oscillators, that would explain this stock's bizarre behavior.

Finally, Greg looked up at me, his brown eyes twinkling behind his glasses. "More buyers than sellers."

"Huh?" Traders standing behind me echoed my keen reply.

"That's it," he said, turning back to his monitors. "More buyers than sellers."

Oh.

Lesson: Keep it simple.

Hot Tip

You're scanning daily charts. Suddenly, you notice one of your favorite stocks. It's in a basing period, but just grew a volume spike so tall, you nearly trip over it! More mysterious, the high volume day didn't rise much at all. You check news sources to justify the volume, but no announcements have been made. Translation: "big volume/little price rise/no news" days may mean institutions are quietly accumulating, rumors leaked of pending news, or insiders (the company's corporate officers) are buying. Whatever the reason, watch it closely and be prepared to enter quickly if it meets the breakout criteria. These stocks tend to sky-rocket—fast!

With all the computerized information we have at our fingertips, it's easy to get caught up in the "paralysis of analysis." If you apply too many concepts to a stock or market index, you can analyze yourself into a corner.

In this chapter and those that follow, you'll learn different indicators, oscillators, and concepts you'll apply to your trades. As you begin to trade, choose two or three—at the most— that work for you, and leave the others to experiment with at a later time.

In other words, keep it simple. If you get confused and find yourself tangled in a maze of information, stop. Back up and look at the big picture. What are the bare essentials? Are there more buyers than sellers? *The stock will go up*. Are there more sellers than buyers? *The stock will go down.* Ninety percent of the time, one of those answers is all you'll need!

VOLUME: A SIMPLE INDICATOR THAT SAYS A LOT

As you've seen in previous charts, volume is displayed in bar form at the bottom of charts. The bars show the number of shares traded for each corresponding candlestick above it.

In Chapter 2's section about Nasdaq market makers and their responsibilities, we painted a scene of broker Goldman Sachs receiving an order from one of its institutional clients to purchase a large block of stock. We stressed that Goldman would slip in and out of the market, buying up small blocks of the stock, careful not to alert the other market players so they would raise their prices. Goldman may hide his true intentions momentarily, but he cannot hide the large order from the volume bar!

Also, in the last chapter, we stressed that high volume powers breakouts and breakdowns. When you notice increased volume on a chart, the higher the bar spikes, the more emotion you're looking at. If it accompanies a strong breakout above key resistance, greedy buyers are grabbing as much as they can. If increased volume coincides with a breakdown below support, then greedy short sellers are having a field day, and unhappy "longs" are dumping and heading for the door (fear)!

A stock experiencing a robust uptrend shows increased volume on positive days, and lower volume on pullback days. Apply this to the time frame you're trading in—if you're trading from an intraday chart, naturally you apply increased volume to the clear, breakout candlestick(s) and lower volume to those black ones indicating a pullback.

As detailed in Figure 7-1, when you see a breakout on high volume, please make sure *the volume takes place on the breakout day*. High volume *after* the breakout, especially on the pullback days, means the stock is selling off as rapidly as it was accumulated on the breakout day.

This action typically takes place with a quiet stock inflated by a single electric news item. Traders buy fast, run it up, then snatch profits and run! Those asleep at the wheel, who thought they had a sweet swing or intermediate-term trade go slack-jawed when the "pullback" slides downhill and drops below the original breakout point.

Also, beware of light volume breakouts . Odds are, they will fail. Why? Light volume on a breakout means no one really cares which direction the stock takes. If no one gives a rat's patootie, even though it breaks to the upside over resistance, the stock still hasn't made up its mind. It might move either way! If you

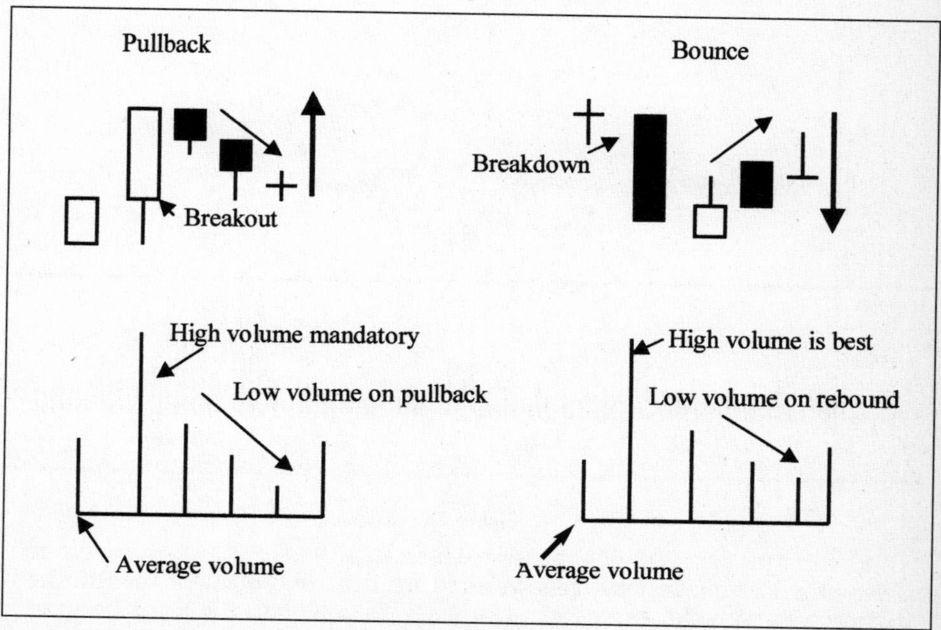

Figure 7-1

Ideal volume setups on breakouts and breakdowns

accidentally jump into a breakout with low or average volume on the breakout candlestick, immediately take a quick profit and look for greener pastures.

For breakdowns, reverse the preceding guidelines. *Volume should be on the breakdown day* (or long, black candlestick), and negative down days, hereafter.

Attention: A stock can fall abruptly without heavy volume and continue into a downtrend, although strong volume accompanies the ugliest breakdowns. Strong volume = strong emotions. That means if a stock falls on strong volume, negative feelings drive it downward. Average to decreased volume on a breakdown might translate into apathy or negative market conditions.

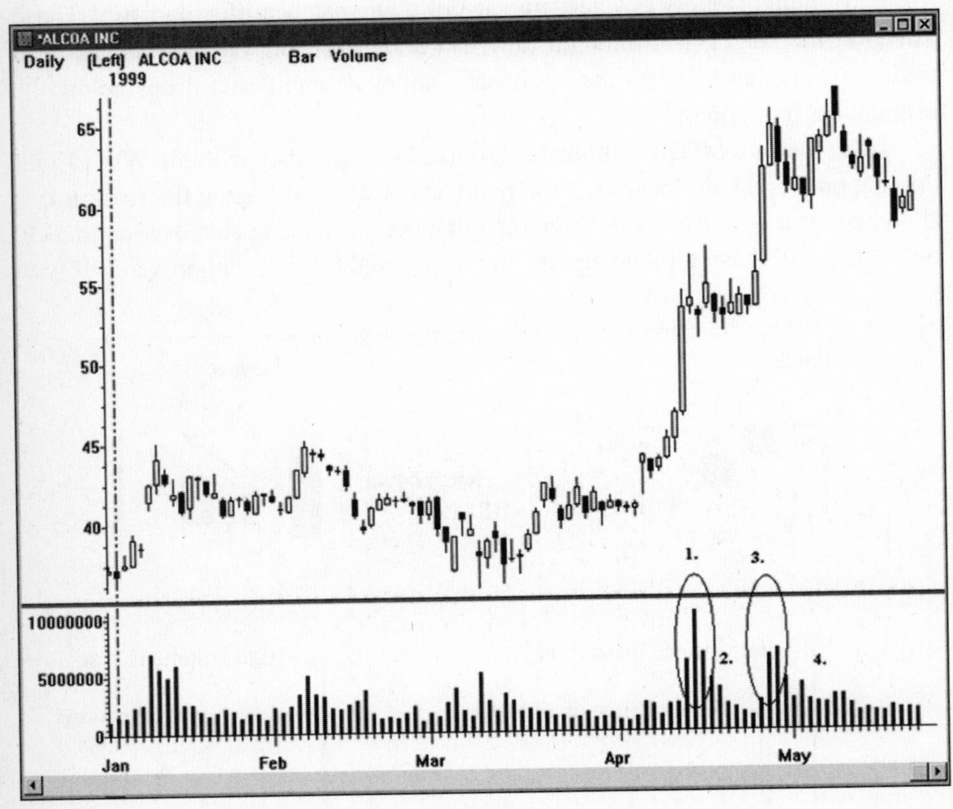

Figure 7-2

1. We looked at this chart in Chapter 6, as an example of a breakout. Notice the big volume spikes on the breakout days. These spikes on breakout days tell you the bulls are buying AA big-time! 2. Now the volume decreases as the stock pulls back and consolidates. This is also bullish. Remember, high volume on the pullback is bearish. 3. When AA starts into its secondary breakout, the bulls come in again, and bring all of their buddies to buy more AA. This repeated, high volume tells you this breakout will also power up nicely. 4. The volume decreases as the breakout, which ran up almost twenty points, slows down, and tops out on lesser-volume. Time to take profits!

Chart Courtesy of *The Executioner*©

Just as pullbacks follow breakouts, rebounds follow breakdowns. When the price rallies after a breakdown, it bounces on decreased volume. Translation: Nobody wants to buy an obvious loser!

A sudden volume increase at the tip of an extended uptrend or downtrend usually means a change lies immediately ahead. When you spot this and you're in a trade, take some, or all, of your profits. If the trend gathers more steam and continues, you can reenter. Otherwise, you have the satisfaction of knowing you took profits at exactly the right place!

Figures 7-2 through 7-6 display breakouts and breakdowns along with their volume signals. Note how the pattern remains the same whether you're looking

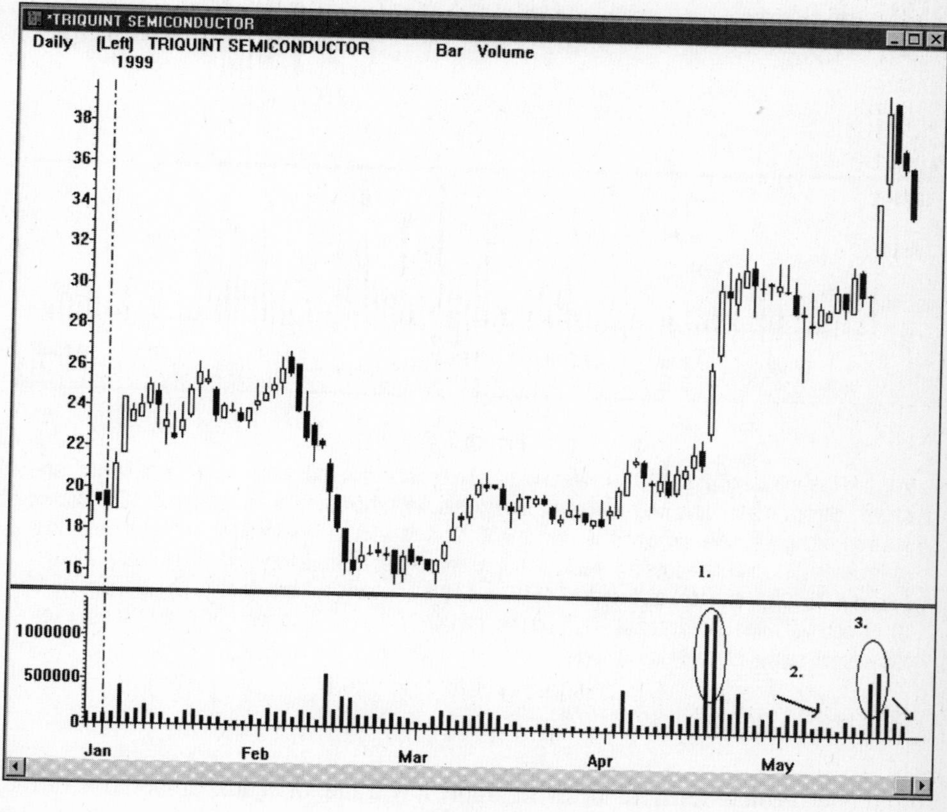

Figure 7-3

1. On this daily chart of Triquint Semiconductor (TQNT), notice the huge rise in volume on the breakout days, April 20 and 21. That tells you this breakout will be a strong one. 2. Decreased volume on the consolidation and pullback is a bullish sign. It means the stock is quietly gathering steam for the next run-up. 3. Volume rises again for the secondary breakout on May 18 and 19. The gap up on the 20th says it's time to take profits. As you can see, volume dropped dramatically for the next three days, and so did the stock!

Chart Courtesy of *The Executioner*©

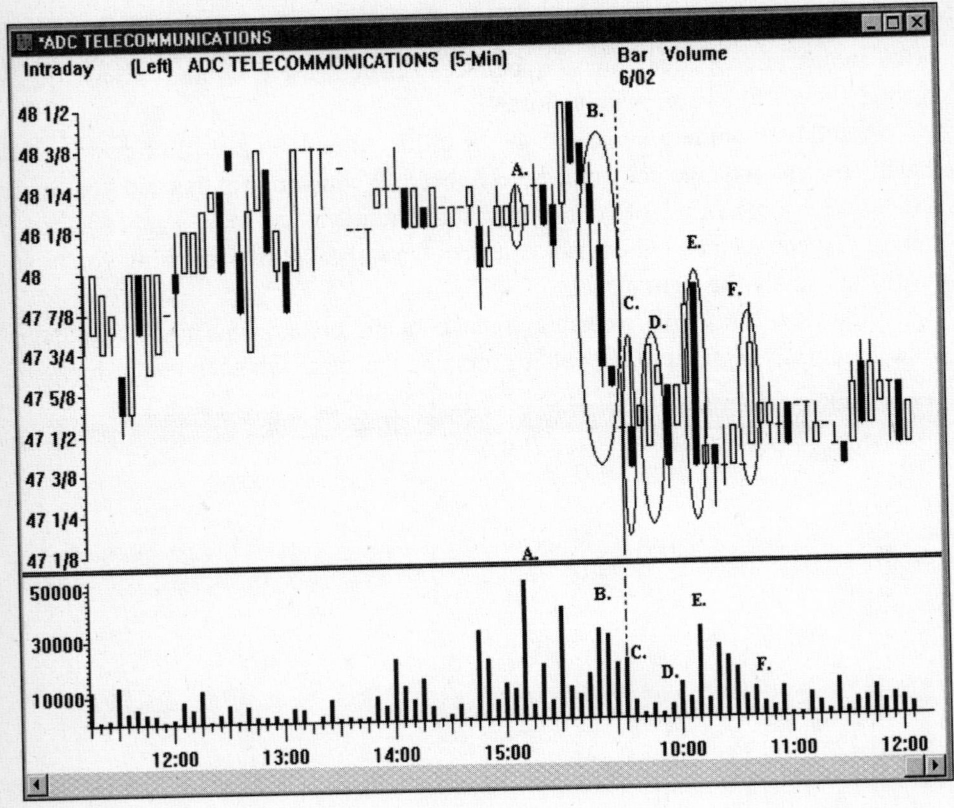

Figure 7-4

A. In this five-minute chart of ADCT,. note the volume spike under this dogi, which went nowhere! This happens on choppy market days when stocks are moving sideways. No cause for excitement. B. ADCT moves down on strong volume at close of day—negative. C. Open is weak, on weak volume—a negative. D. Two white candlesticks indicate possible breakout, but volume is weak. This tells you it will probably fail. And it does! E. At 10:10, the stock falls from 47 15/16 to 47 3/8 on strong volume. Another negative sign. F. At 10:40, optimists who get excited at ADCT's move from 47 7/16 to 47 7/8 should note that the rise is on low volume, so will probably fail. It does.

Chart Courtesy of *The Executioner*©

for an intermediate-term trade, swing trade, day trade, or scalp. In fact, one of the hottest signals a scalper can see is screaming volume on a five-minute candlestick!

Okay, we've talked about volume in breakouts and breakdowns, and it all looks simple on charts we can Monday-morning quarterback, but how do you spot them when the breakouts or breakdowns are about to happen, instead of already over?

For intermediate-term and swing trades on the long side, monitor daily charts from a selection of high-quality stocks that represent industry leaders, and that are basing (moving sideways at the bottom of a cycle), along with their industry. Note the average volume and watch to see if it begins to build, or suddenly spikes.

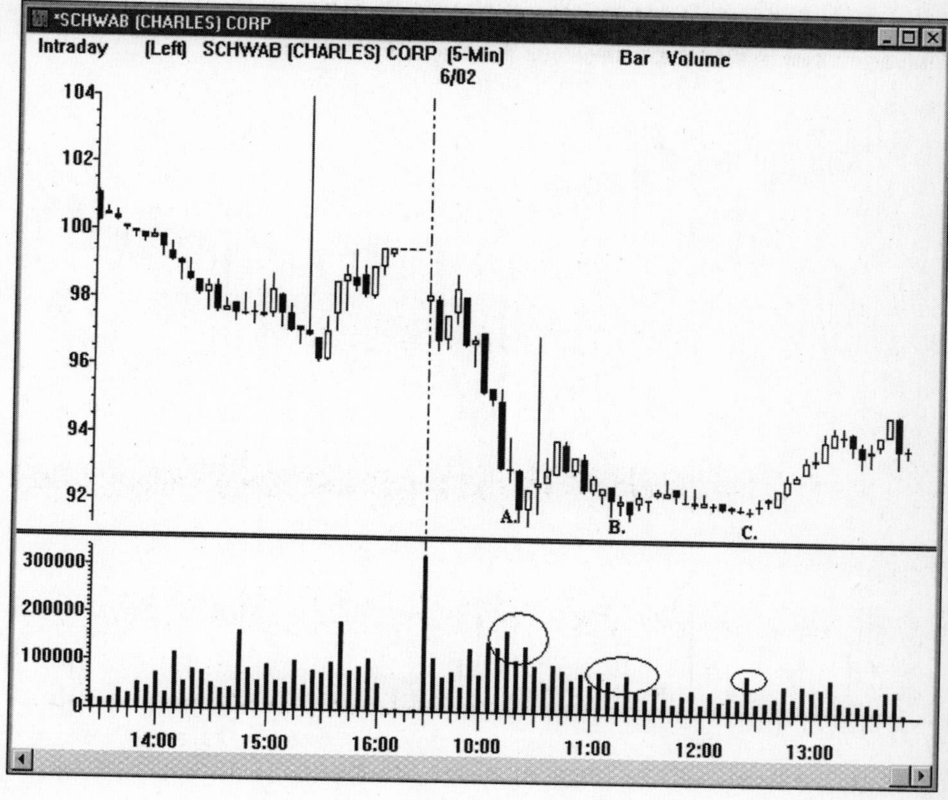

Figure 7-5

A, B, and C. Remember the volume concept that says increased volume after a strong move up or down suggests change? Each of the three times SCH hit a low on the day, the volume increased. Day traders and scalpers who had level II systems on this day would see increased buying each time the low was touched. This tells you buyers are waiting to prop the stock up. This was a negative day in the market, but buyers held SCH at support, and finally drove it higher.

Chart Courtesy of *The Executioner*©

For added information on when industry leaders may start to rise, monitor charts of the industry index it correlates to. Many charting systems will let you chart the oil index (XOI), the banking index (BKX), the gold index (XAU), the Morgan-Stanley High Tech Index (MSH), the S&P 100 (OEX), and more. Also, pay attention to CNBC announcers when they make statements like, "the oil index is finally waking up," or "analysts finally upgrade the downtrodden disk drive makers."

For breakdowns, look for a stock that has concluded a strong uptrend and has rolled over. It should be moving sideways across the top of a cycle, either trading in a range or in a congestion pattern (not in consolidation—that's a positive!). If strong volume appears for several days, and the stock continues to move sideways,

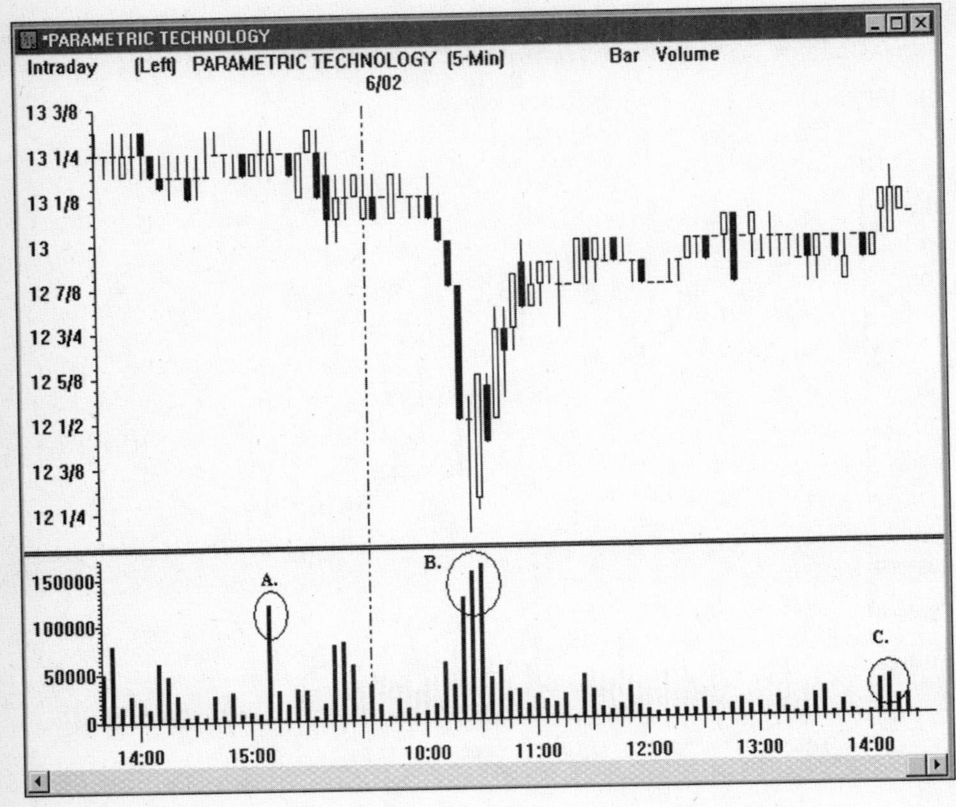

Figure 7-6

A. At 3:10 on 6/01, PMTC showed a volume spike. Again, sometimes when stocks are moving sideways on choppy days in the market, these spikes appear with no price follow-through. B. Another example of strong volume at the end of a downtrend. Note how the dogi ends the move down, then a bullish piercing pattern, both bullish signs. C. At 2:10, increased volume (in this case, it happened with the help of the S&P futures) pushed PMTC over resistance at 13.

Chart Courtesy of *The Executioner*©

it may mean distribution (selling) is taking place and a breakdown is imminent. (In Chapter 11, we'll discuss other criteria you will use to consider shorting a stock.)

With day trades and scalps, volume signals tell the same stories, but at a much faster pace. When the market opens in the morning, you have a list of stocks at your elbow, or typed into your level II interest list, that you'll play if they move as you expect them to.

Here, volume signals are straightforward. If you're trading from a three-minute or five-minute chart, volume either spikes on the breakout candlestick or it doesn't. If it does, good. If it doesn't, forget it.

My rule is this: If I see a possible breakout pattern forming, I get all ready for it—order entry screen up, and finger on the mouse button, ready to pounce. But during the seconds the breakout takes place, if volume doesn't spike, all bets are off. Why? It's probably a false breakout.

A false breakout, one that breaks over resistance for a few seconds or minutes, then comes back in (pulls back to its breakout price), usually comes in fast, with few buyers to take up the supply. False breakouts mean lost money. Even if you break even on the trade, you're still out the commission.

Keep it simple rule: Average volume or less on breakout, no trade. Period.

To short intraday breakdowns, you don't *have* to have strong volume although it confirms your decision. You can short successfully just after the stock falls through resistance and profit from a gradual meltdown to the next support level. Chapter 11 outlines exact shorting techniques.

I never trade stocks that average fewer than 100,000 shares per day of volume. They're okay to hold for investments, but not satisfactory for trading. First of all, a low-volume stock—we call it "thinly traded"—doesn't move very much.

Second, the more active a stock (the more shares per day it trades), the safer you are. Why? Because when the sky falls in an actively traded stock, some fool will likely buy your shares from you.

In a thinly traded stock, when times get rough, you can't always find that fool to dump your shares on. Especially if you're in a hurry! The market makers on a low-volume, crashing Nasdaq stock just turn their backs. When you scream "Aaack! Take it at the market—*anything* to get me out!" they snicker and pay you a rock-bottom price. NYSE specialists don't turn their backs, but you'll still have to sell at market to get out. Actually, I prefer stocks that trade volume of more than 300,000 shares daily, but 100,000 is my rock-bottom number.

VOLUME GUIDELINES

- Strong volume on breakouts or breakdowns means the price will continue in the current direction. Volume = emotion, and it propels price moves.
- Weak volume on breakouts indicates possible breakout failure.
- Strong volume at the end of a trend may stall or reverse the trend.
- High volume on a dogi, evening star, or morning star, where the price stays in a compact range, usually denotes a trend reversal.
- Stocks that trade volume of fewer than 100,000 shares a day make dangerous short-term plays.

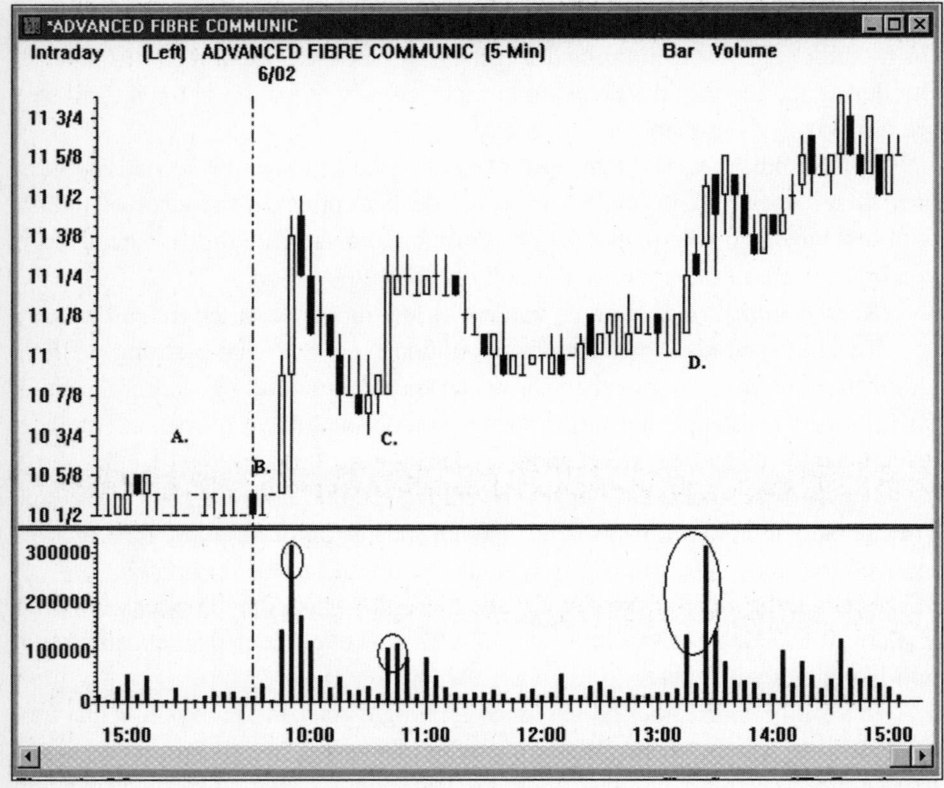

Figure 7-7

A. On this five-minute chart of Advanced Fibre Communications (AFCI), you can see that the stock consolidated into the close, near its high, on 6/01. This makes a good setup for the next day. B. At 9:45 on 6/02, AFCI broke out on strong volume—a perfect buy for a day trade. In the following ten minutes, it ran from 10 9/16 to 11 7/16. C. At 10:40, strong volume at the end of a downtrend forecasts another upmove. The second positive candlestick is a perfect buy point. AFCI moves in the next few minutes from 10 13/16 to 11 5/16, a nice day trade or scalping profit. D. Volume gives another buy signal at 1:15, and confirms it at 1:25, as AFCI soars again.

Chart Courtesy of *The Executioner*©

In Figures 7-7 through 7-11, both daily and intraday, note how the volume tells you when to enter a stock. When you get a practiced eye at spotting volume opportunities, go to your own charting source and scan for instances of high volume, which if acted upon, would have reaped rewards.

MOVING AVERAGES: WHAT THEY ARE, HOW TO USE THEM

Moving averages rank next to volume for being easy to read and dependable as heck. On a daily stock chart, a twenty-day moving average represents the closing

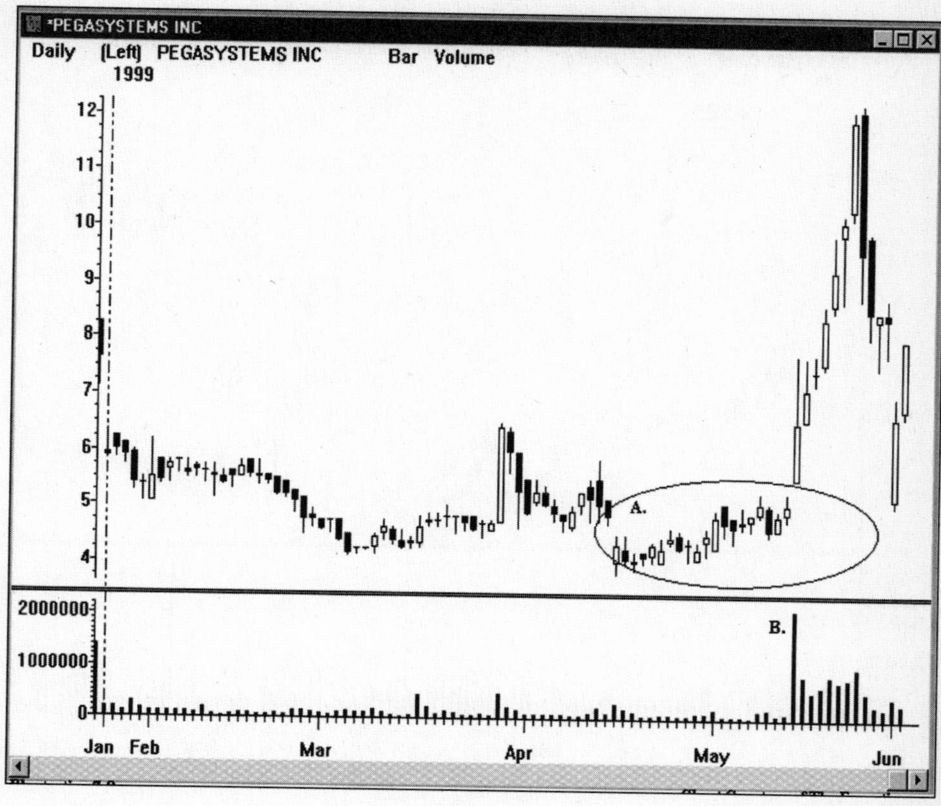

Figures 7-8

A. Note the "island reversal" on this daily chart of Pegasystems, Inc. (PEGA). This happens when a stock trades in a pattern isolated by gaps at both ends. In this case, the first gap is an exhaustion gap; the second, a breakaway gap. When a stock experiences an island reversal, the next move foretells which way the stock will probably trend next. B. On 5/14, PEGA volume traded 104,600 shares. On 5/14, the stock gapped open nearly 1/2 point, and volume soared to 2,106,400! On 5/15, volume decreased by a little over half, yet remained strong enough to carry the stock upward. The seven-day run tops out at 12 1/8, more than a 100 percent run.

Chart Courtesy of *The Executioner*©

price each day for the last twenty trading days, divided by twenty. When you apply this moving average to a chart, it comes out as a line, similar to a trendline. Which makes sense, because it is a trendline!

Major moving, averages used by most traders are 10, 20, 50, 100, and 200 period.

Period = the time frame you're looking at. If you're looking at a 50-period moving average (MA) on a weekly chart, it's averaged from the last 50 Friday closing prices. On an hourly chart, a 50 MA averages the fifty closing prices of the last 50 hourly candlesticks. On a five-minute chart, a 50 MA forms the last fifty closing prices of each five-minute candlestick, averaged, and so forth.

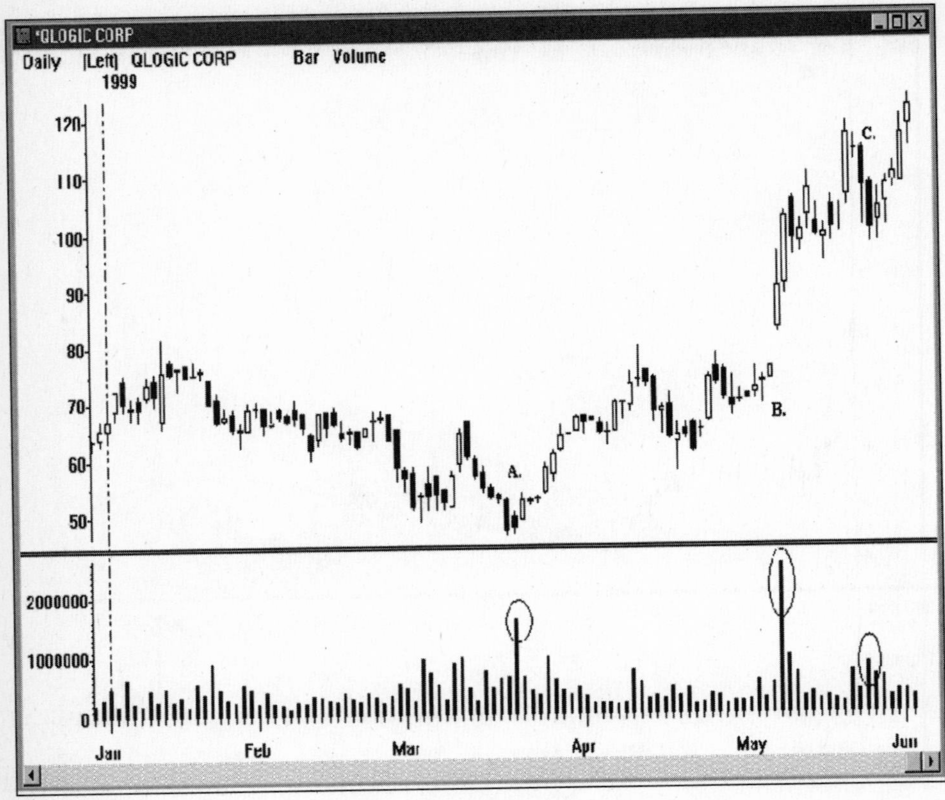

Figure 7-9

A. On this daily chart of QLogic Corp. (QLGC), you see strong volume at the end of a downtrend, which signals a possible reversal. B. On 5/6, QLGC traded 525,900 shares and closed at 77 3/16. On 5/7, it opened at 82 3/4, gapping up and breaking resistance on extremely strong volume. (In this case, you would buy over the first thirty-minute high, a strategy detailed later.) The volume traded on 5/7: 2,537,100. C. On 5/24, high volume at the end of a protracted move down signals a reversal.

Chart Courtesy of *The Executioner*©

As you will see, a 10-period moving average, known in trading jargon as a "10 MA," hugs the prices on the chart much more than the 20 MA, and certainly more than the 50 or 200 MA.

Every trader uses his or her favorite moving averages, and you can use different ones on different time frames.

- Generally, intermediate-term and swing traders use 20-, 50-, 100-, and 200-period moving averages on daily charts.
- Day traders use the 10-, 20-, and 200-period MAs on intraday charts. My favorites: the 20 MA and 200 MA on hourly, fifteen-minute, five-minute charts; and the 10 MA and 20 MA on one-minute charts.

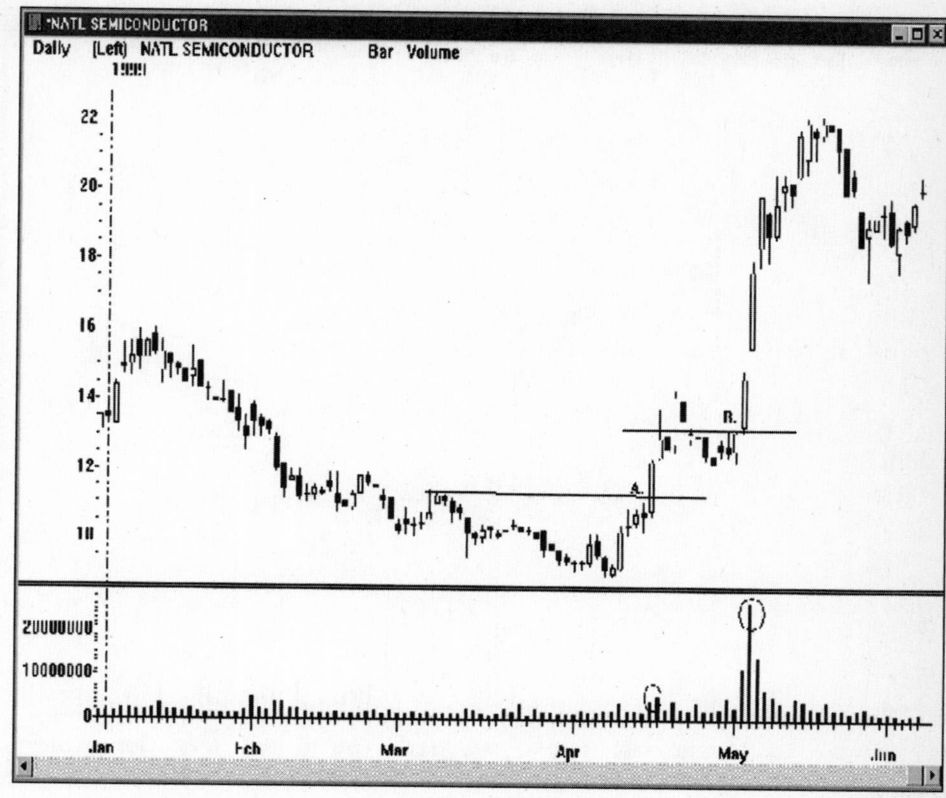

Figure 7-10

A. On this daily chart of National Semiconductor (NSM), strong volume gives clear buy signals. On 4/15, NSM closed at 10 3/8. On 4/16, NSM broke out on high volume, opening at 10 3/4 and closing at 12 1/4. B. On 5/3, NSM closed on increased volume 2,522,700 shares at 13 1/8. On 5/4, it opened at 13 1/4 and on that day traded a whopping 11,129,500 shares. For those who held on until 5/6, it closed at 19 7/8.

Chart Courtesy of *The Executioner*©

If you have level II software and real-time charts, you should be able to specify as many MAs as you want to overlay on your charts. Don't overdo, though. Remember to keep it simple. Three MAs on one chart are enough at any given time. More than three resembles a wad of tangled spaghetti!

When I get confused, I delete them all except for the 20 MA. I find it one of the best storytellers.

Moving averages are the "multiuse" indicator. They're sort of like ketchup—you can put them on everything. Like volume, their message "tells it like it is." If the stock behaves properly depending on where the MAs appear on the chart, enter the play. If it doesn't...don't!

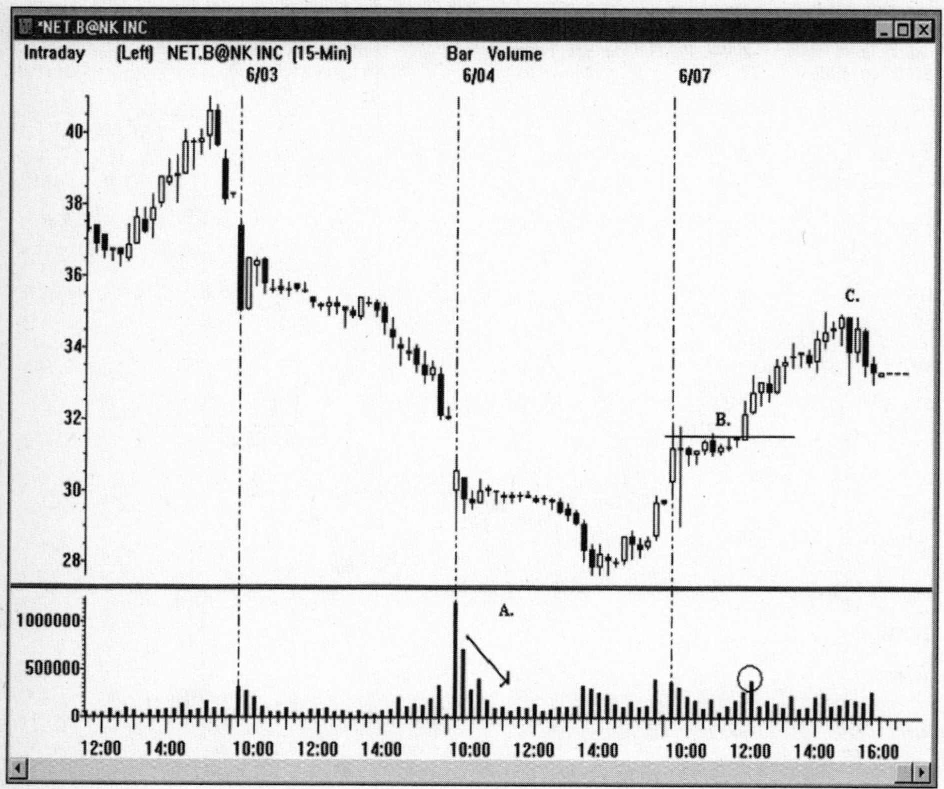

Figure 7-11

A. On this fifteen-minute chart of NetB@ank, Inc. (NTBK), you can see how on 6/04 it opened on high volume, then the volume immediately fizzled. The stock weakened and finally dropped. Finally, around 1:30, the volume picked up a bit, and the stock managed to climb into the close. B. On 6/07, at 11:45, NTBK broke above resistance at 31 1/2, on high volume—a buy signal. It continued the intraday uptrend until 2:45, and topped out at 34 15/16. C. This reversal bar would have stopped us out with a nice profit.

Chart Courtesy of *The Executioner©*

One school of market players claims stock prices make random movements, with no set pattern. To them I say, give me a daily stock chart with 20- and 50-day MAs applied to it, and I'll bet you my mouse pad I can show you a stock with a memory! It's positively uncanny how stocks bounce off these support and resistance lines.

Of course, most of that action takes place because traders agree that moving averages form valid support and resistance boundaries.

For example, say a stock broke out and is climbing nicely in a healthy uptrend. It's above its 20 MA on a daily chart, and whenever it pulls back, it bounces off it like a ball. Experienced traders will buy anticipatory lots when a stock edges down to its 20 MA, anticipating the bounce. (Of course, if the stock falls through the 20 MA, they high-tail it out of their position.) I don't recommend this strategy for new traders; it's safest to wait until the stock actually bounces before buying.

Intermediate-term and swing traders should buy stocks trading above their rising 20 MAs on a daily chart, and certainly above the rising 50 MA.

Never buy a stock that's fallen below its 200 MA on a daily chart, or trading just under it. A stock that's fallen through its 200 MA has a ba-aad case of the uglies! The 200 MA is an extremely powerful indicator. On a daily chart, especially, it weighs a stock down, like a bully repeatedly dunking a struggling swimmer. Odds are, the stock will flounder before it overcomes that 200-pound bully!

You want to play stocks on the long side that ride right on top of a moving average. For instance, if you see a stock on a daily chart in an uptrend, and it's bouncing off its *rising* 20 MA or 50 MA in orderly waves, you can plan your entry point for the minute it bounces. If, however, the stock is flying high above the MA, especially the 20 MA, we say the stock is "overextended," "toppy," or "frothy." Chances are it's ready to pull back to the prevailing MA soon. Wait for the pull-back and a confirming bounce before you enter.

Short sellers should trade stocks trending below its *declining* 20 MA, and better yet, below its declining 50 MA, or even declining 100 MA.

On intraday charts, day traders find success buying stocks that bounce off their rising 200 MA on a fifteen-minute chart. I like the 20 MA on a five-minute chart, and the 10 MA on the one-minute chart as support areas. Short sellers jump in when stocks fall below support areas and under declining moving averages.

Sometimes, when you're day trading and scalping (buying), you'll see the 200 MA above your stock's price, maybe the 100 MA below that, then the 20 and 10. In other words, the moving averages are layered from the slowest to the fastest. This is common in negative markets. It's also a warning to keep your money in your wallet!

Say the market just opened down, and the bears are in control. You're day trading and looking at a five-minute chart of your favorite stock, Simple Software (SS). On the daily chart, it looks ripe for a breakout. But on your intraday chart, it's fallen below the opening price.

Even though the market is down, you believe a reversal to the upside will take place during the 9:50 reversal period. You're watching a five-minute chart of SS bottoming on the day. At the current price of $21 1/8, it's sitting on the 10 MA, which is just starting to turn up. That's positive.

On the downside, the 200 MA, which always slopes more gradually than the others, is declining 3/8 of a point *above* SS's current price, at 21 1/2 (see Figure 7-12). Even if the stock rises on a market bounce, when it reaches the declining

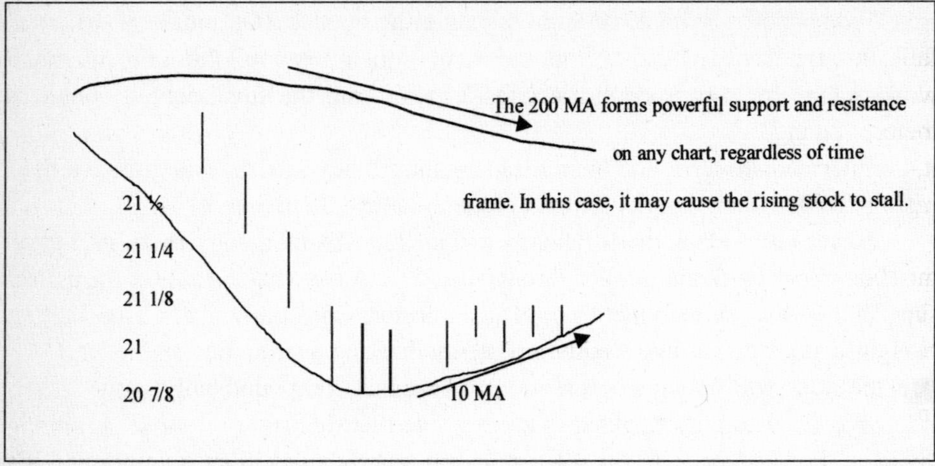

Figure 7-12

200 MA, it may hit its head and fall back down. In a situation like this, you quickly assess the risk–reward odds. Is it worth it? Think: *If I enter this play, am I protecting my principal?* If the answer is *no*, then you know to wait for a better opportunity.

It's always safest to enter a long position, regardless of the time frame you're trading in, when the moving averages support the stock in the most positive order, as shown in Figure 7-13. You won't have all these averages on one chart at once, but if you did, the ideal stacking order is the 10 above the 20, the 20 above the 50, the 50 above the 100, and the 200 way below all of them! Reverse that order for shorting.

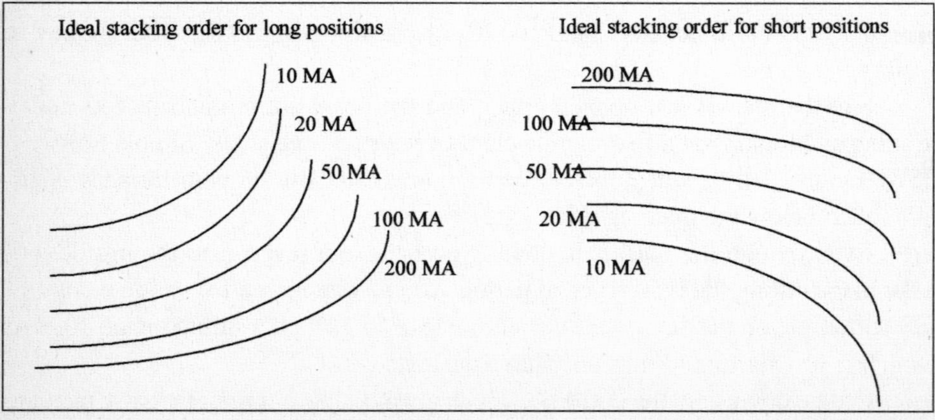

Figure 7-13
Moving Averages

Now that you're an expert on moving averages, the next bit of information falls into the "this is always true, except when it isn't" category. Moving averages work best with a trending stock, that is, a stock moving in an uptrend or downtrend. When a stock is moving sideways, if the MA moves in a horizontal line with it, the MA becomes ineffectual as a storyteller. *When the MA moves laterally, disregard it.* You'll have to depend on other indicators.

Figures 7-14 through 7-16 show the relationships between stocks and their moving averages. Study them and note how trending stocks use the averages for support and resistance.

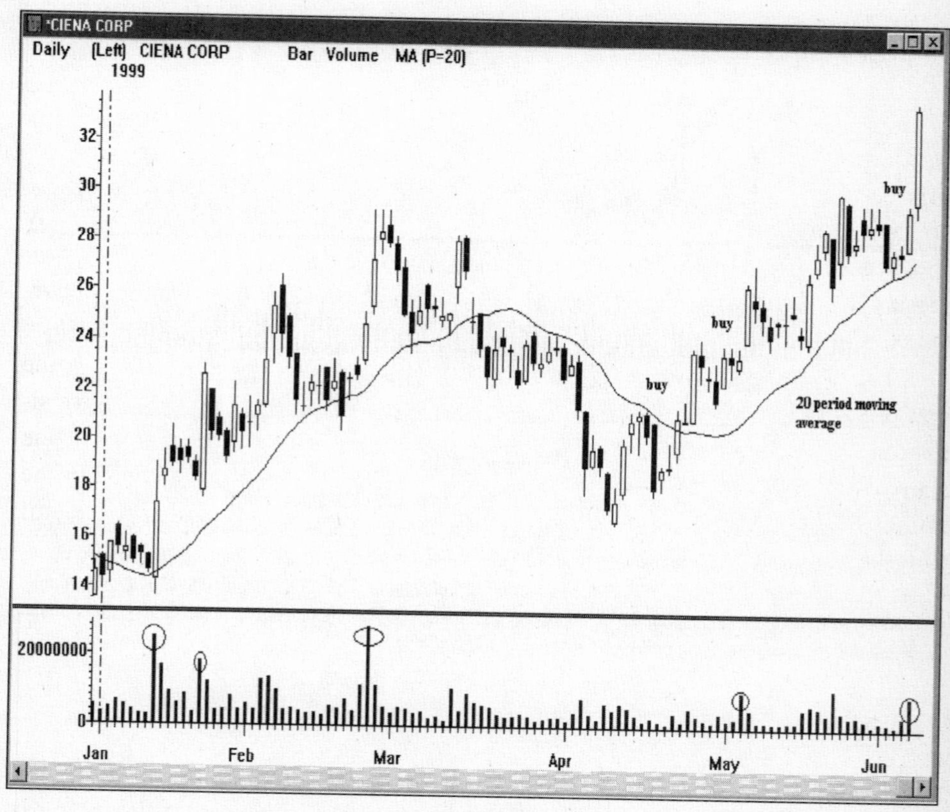

Figure 7-14

On this daily chart of the Ciena Corp. (CIEN), notice how the 20 period moving average acts as support when CIEN climbs in an uptrend, and resistance when it falls in a downtrend.

Also, notice how the volume gave a buy signal at every buy point. Those spikes are hard to miss!

Chart Courtesy of *The Executioner*©

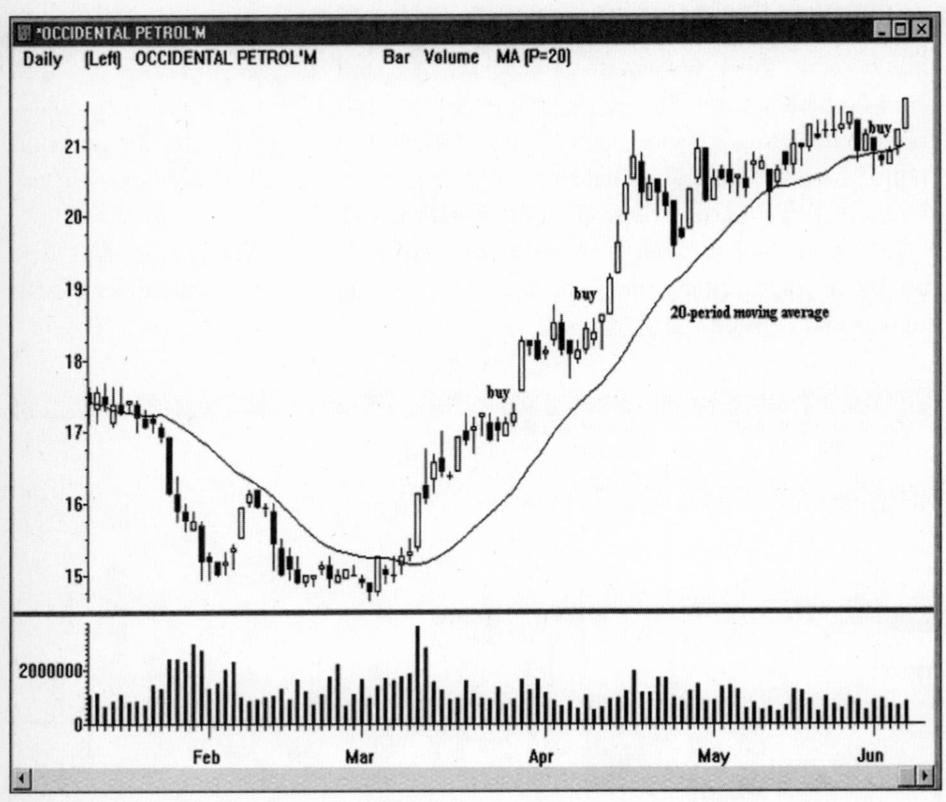

Figure 7-15

On this daily chart of Occidental Petroleum (OXY), notice how this stock obeys its 20-period moving average. Once again, the 20 MA acts as resistance when OXY is in a downtrend, and support when it rises in a sturdy uptrend. Some stocks ride their 20 MA, and some seem to "prefer" their 50-period MA. Both are powerful moving averages. When a stock in an uptrend pulls back or consolidates into its prevailing moving average, then breaks out on high volume, that's a buy signal. Remember, stocks trading under their 200 MAs are very weak, and definitely *not* buying opportunities.

Chart Courtesy of *The Executioner*©

THE FINAL TOUCH: THE COMMODITY CHANNEL INDEX

The Commodity Channel Index (CCI) is a popular oscillator. Oscillators verify whether a stock is overbought or oversold. The CCI works as well with stocks as it does its namesake, commodities. It's easy to interpret and is available on most charting software.

The CCI tells its story best on daily and weekly charts. I position it at the bottom of my charts and use it for confirming setups for swing trades and intermediate-term trades. You can also carry this information into your day trades, meaning you know that on a certain day, the stock is overbought or oversold.

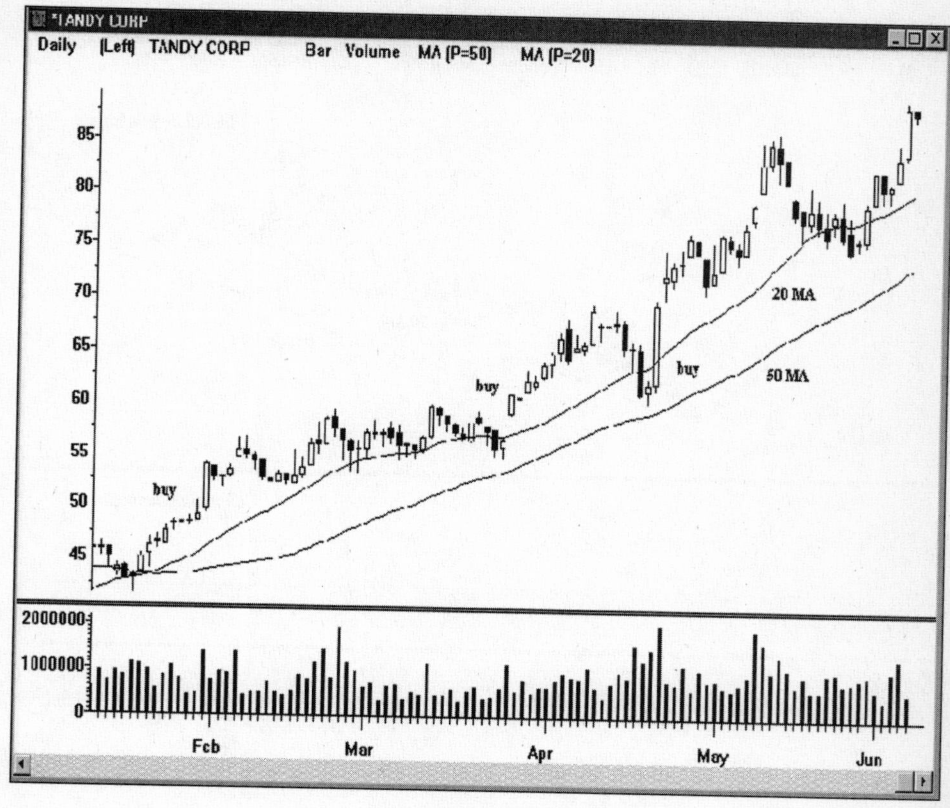

Figure 7-16

It doesn't get any better than this! In this daily chart of Tandy Corp. (TAN), the stock marches up its 20-period moving average in a dependable uptrend. It never penetrates its 50 MA, which many institutional managers watch. Pullbacks to MA support plus volume spikes give TAN several reliable buypoints. By the way, this chart is a nearly perfect example of how you want your moving averages to look, rising with the higher numbers layered under the lower numbers.

Chart Courtesy of *The Executioner*©

As you'll see in charts 7-17 through 7-19, the CCI is, in effect, a line chart. It acts as a gauge, measuring a stock's current price in comparison to its statistical mean. If that explanation intimidates you, don't worry about it. Just learning how to read it is enough, and you're going to do that in the next couple of seconds!

The CCI oscillates (fluctuates) between ± 100. On some charts, it reads ± 200. Readings above +100 (or +200) suggest the stock is overbought. *This is a sell signal.* If it dips below –100 (or –200), then the stock is oversold. *This is a buy signal.* Easy, huh?

When you enter a trade, it helps to know whether the stock is overbought or oversold. As you can guess, an "overbought" stock means values are extremely

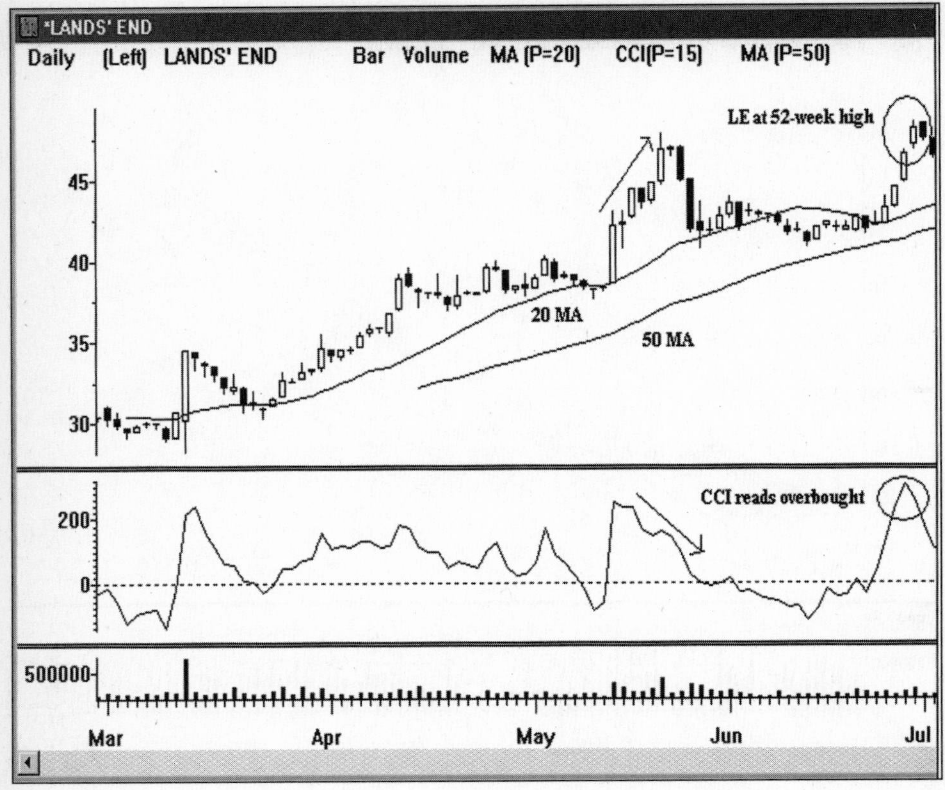

Figure 17

On this daily chart of Land's End (LE), you can see how the CCI acts as a leading indicator. Notice the divergence between the CCI in mid-May, shown by the arrows LE continued to rise, while the CCI fell. That tells you the stock will probably fall soon—and it did! Of course, it's obvious that LE overbought at the end of June and was due for a correction.

Chart Courtesy of *The Executioner*©

high compared to average prices. Much more buying than selling has taken place. "Oversold" means the stock is trading at low values from its statistical mean prices. More shares have been sold than bought.

On a daily chart, if the Commodity Channel Index tells you the stock you're thinking of buying is overbought, chances are it will pull back. If, however, the CCI indicates the stock is oversold—that's the perfect icing for a breakout play. It gives you one more odd that the stock will move up—and as traders, we're grateful for all the odds we can get!

If you really want to get fancy, here's the CCI's second, or alternative use. When you see a divergence between the CCI and the stock's current price (the

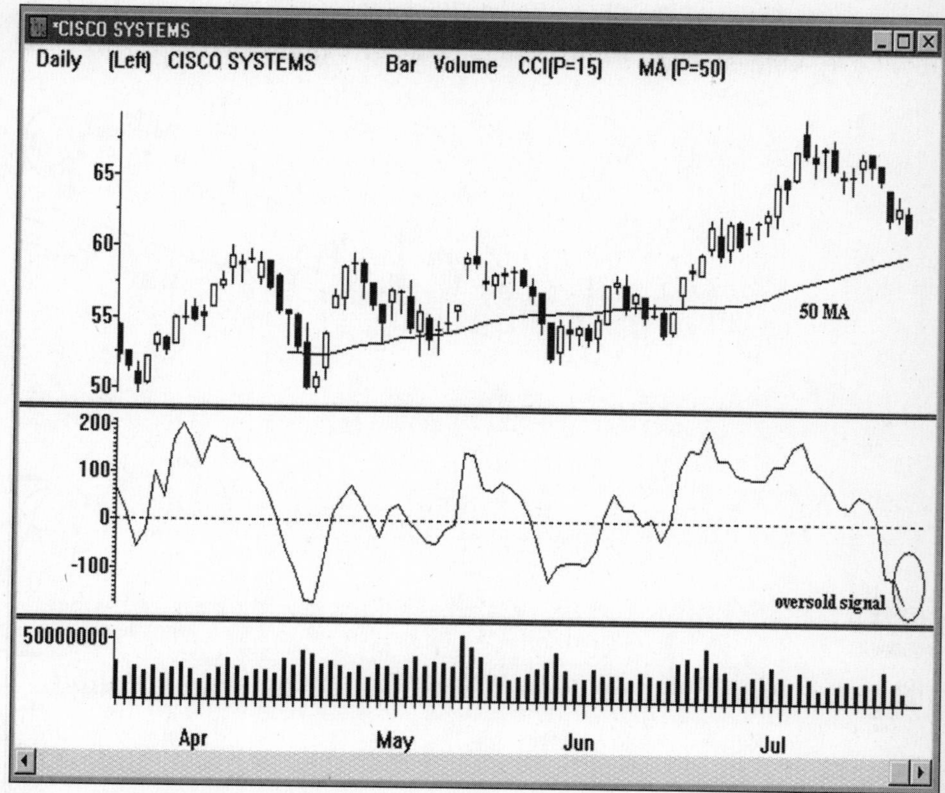

Figure 7-18

The Commodity Channel Index oscillator on this daily chart of Cisco Systems (CSCO) reads –150. an oversold reading. Couple this reading with the fact that CSCO is nearing its 50 MA. If it bounces off the MA, and the CCI hooks up, CSCO may become a buy candidate. If it falls through the 50 MA and the previous support area established in late June, CSCO could then become a short candidate.

Chart Courtesy of *The Executioner©*

stock's price is high, but the CCI reads –100, or –200), you can bet the stock will soon follow the direction of the CCI. Neat, huh? A crystal-ball effect!

As of this writing, the NYSE and Nasdaq alone list more than 8,000 stocks. If the one you're considering doesn't meet the best trading criteria, why play it? There are more than 7,999 others to choose from. Keep scanning. There's one out there with your name—and dollar signs—attached to it!

Now, please study Figures 7-20 through 7-22 and notice how the volume, moving averages, and CCI work together to tell you a story about a stock, and reveal its personality.

Figure 7-19

On this daily chart of Motorola (MOT), the CCI dipped below 100 to an oversold position, then bounced slightly. This is a bullish signal that you should look for when scanning CCIs. Although MOT broke its uptrend by making a lower low toward the end of July, it still hasn't broken its 50 MA and appears to be bouncing off of it. If it trades over its high of 94 made on July 22, and all other criteria is met, it should be a good intermediate-term buy.

Chart Courtesy of *The Executioner*©

QUIZ

1. True or false? A stock in a healthy uptrend displays higher volume on positive days, and lower volume on pullback, or consolidation days.
2. Is strong volume an important ingredient of a successful breakout? Why?
3. A stock breaks out on heavy volume, but the volume continues to increase on the pullback. What does this mean?
4. Is trading a stock with daily volume of fewer than 100,000 shares a good or bad idea? Why?
5. True or false? Moving averages form strong support and resistance areas.

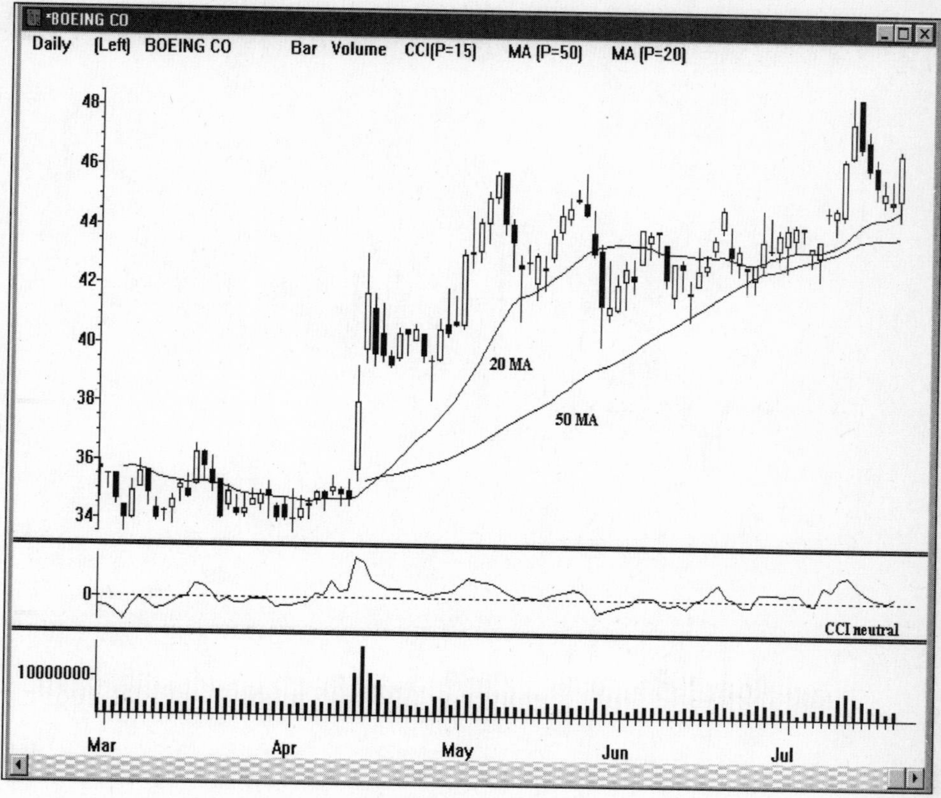

Figure 7-20

On this daily chart of the Boeing Co. (BA), the 20 and 50 MAs are properly positioned and rising—a positive signal. Also, BA is riding on top of the 20 MA, also very positive. The CCI reads neutral at zero. Volume broke out on the last breakout in mid-July and looks ready to increase again. This stock is ripe for a new breakout and is a possible buy candidate.

Chart Courtesy of *The Executioner©*

6. A stock you want to day trade is sitting on its 20 MA on a five-minute chart. Its 200 MA slopes overhead, just above the stock's price. Is this a good entry point for a long position? Why or why not?
7. A stock is moving sideways, trading in a range. Its 20 MA is also moving in a lateral direction. Is the MA currently a good storyteller?
8. The Commodity Channel Index is an effective ________________. It tells you whether a stock is __________ or ____________.

Figure 7-21

On this daily chart of Bristol-Myers Squibb (BMY), you can see that the stock just fell for a total of five days in a row. Now it's resting on its 50 MA in the form of a Dogi—a positive signal. The CCI has slid into oversold territory, also positive. BMY will be a buy candidate tomorrow if it trades over today's high of 70 3/8 on high volume.

Chart Courtesy of *The Executioner*©

ANSWERS

1. True. A stock in a robust uptrend invites more buyers than sellers. This accounts for high volume on positive days, and decreased volume on pullback, or consolidation days.
2. Yes, strong volume contributes in a big way to a breakout's success. The more buyers (demand + greed) a stock has pushing it up, the more the price will rise.
3. When volume increases on a pullback after a breakout, it means strong selling is taking place. This stock may fall as fast as it rose!

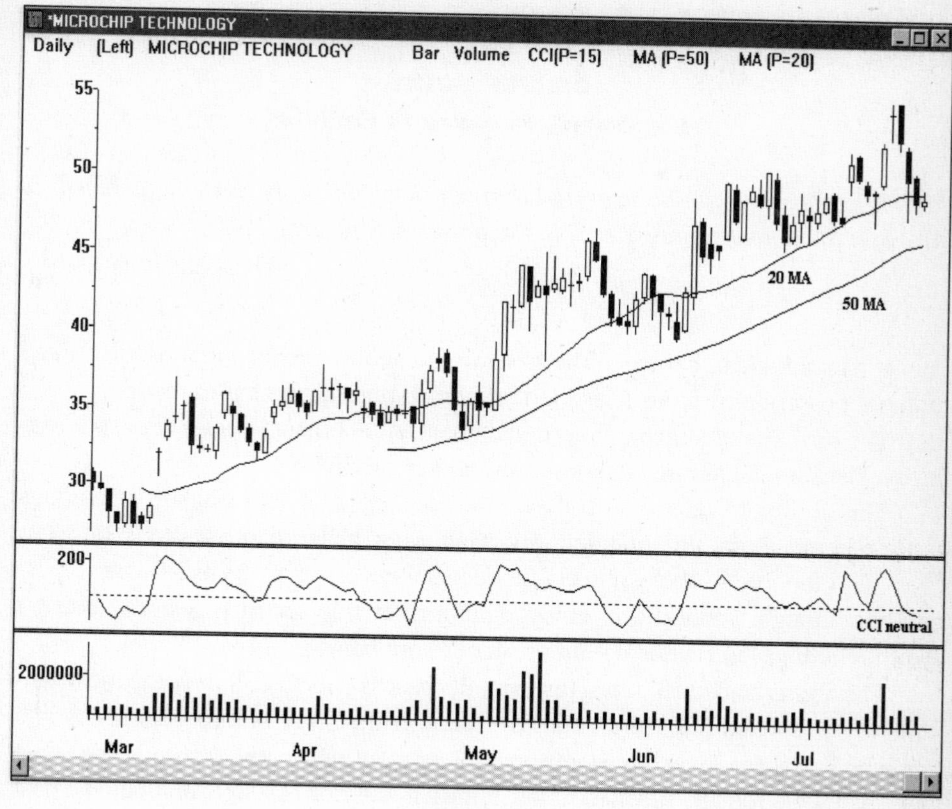

Figure 7-22

On this daily chart of Microchip Technology (MCHP), you can see the stock fell for three days, then had a narrow-range day barely under the 20 MA. The CCI reads slightly oversold. If it trades over the last day's high of 49 3/8 on high volume, the stock will be a buy.

Chart Courtesy of *The Executioner*©

4. Stocks with average daily volume under 100,000 shares make unsatisfactory trading stocks. Low volume means little movement, and high risk if you have to sell quickly.
5. True.
6. No, this is not an ideal entry point for entering long *or* short. Avoid buying stocks trading under their 200 MA, no matter what time frame you're trading in. As for selling this stock short, since it's riding on top of its 20 MA, that may provide support, at least temporarily. Wait for it to break *below* the 20 MA, then (if all other systems agree) short it.
7. No. Moving averages make effective indicators in stocks trending up or down. Moving averages become ineffectual when moving sideways.
8. oscillator, overbought, oversold.

✦ ✦ ✦

CENTER POINT

Detachment, Pathway to Freedom

Anything you want can be acquired through detachment, because detachment is based on the unquestioning belief in the power of your true Self.

—DEEPAK CHOPRA[1]

It's paradoxical, but true: The best way to acquire goals, circumstances, and material possessions in our lives is to relinquish our attachment to them.

The opposite of attachment is detachment. Attachment stresses fear and insecurity. Detachment assures freedom, joy, and creativity.

The ability to detach ourselves from the *need* of extravagant belongings assures peace, harmony, and security. Gathering material possessions into our lives, then looking to those objects for security never works. Why? Because possessions, though wonderful to enjoy, cannot offer true security. Security doesn't dwell in "things." It dwells within us, in our core being.

The ability to detach ourselves from the past sets us free. Surely the most limiting words spoken are, "We've always done it that way before." Mindsets and opinions like these leave no room for improvement or creativity. Along the same lines, when we remain attached to our family history or heritage, and believe past conditions define our future, that belief denies our self-enlightenment.

The ability to detach ourselves from our limiting opinions, and the way things "ought to be," is surely the most difficult detachment to attain! When we hold our ideas and beliefs in right and wrong in a viselike grip, when we refuse to consider alternative views, we erect walls around ourselves. We leave no room to grow. Loving relationships struggle to survive.

When we establish goals and desires, then attach rigid conditions to their outcomes, it leaves no room for serendipity. On the other hand, working on a goal with a nonjudgmental mindset opens us to new and higher possibilities.

As we free ourselves from the *need* of material possessions, the *need* to be right, and the *need* to control, the ultimate bliss of spontaneity and creativity draws exciting new circumstances our way that we never dreamed possible.

✦ ✦ ✦

1 Chopra, Deepak. *The Seven Spiritual Laws of Success.* (CA: Amber-Allen Publishing, 1994), p. 84.

CHAPTER 8

When the Tough Get Going: Beginning Trader's Boot Camp

If you've already been active in the stock market, perhaps as an investor, you've noticed that stocks, like people, have different personalities. Some you feel comfortable with, some you cross the street to avoid. Some are strong and calm; I always think of General Electric in that light (pun intended). Some are maniac depressives, rocketing up one day, crashing down the next, as the Internet stocks do right now. As I've mentioned before, securities on the NYSE are "kindlier and gentler" than those on the Nasdaq.

Most traders trade a group of favorite stocks. I know some, though, who make big bucks day trading the same one or two stocks—all day, every day—buying dips and selling rallies. As you learn your tolerance for risk and find your comfort levels, you will establish your own style.

Okay, now comes the fun. For the next two weeks, and the remainder of this chapter, you're going to attend boot camp. If you follow my directions, you'll build a step-by-step foundation constructed of the bricks and mortar of good trading—experience and knowledge.

Important note: From now on, unless otherwise indicated, I will be referring to *buying* stocks, not shorting stocks. Selling short requires a bit more finesse, and some different rules apply. Chapter 11 explains shorting techniques in detail.

BEGINNER'S BOOT CAMP: WEEK ONE

If you're a new trader, attending "Beginner's Boot Camp" introduces you to the trading environment gradually, without risking your capital. I wish *I'd* done this. I'd be richer for it, today!

Before we start, I have a request: During the following two weeks, *please don't place a trade*. The next ten trading days will acquaint you with the relationships between market and individual stock movements. This will be a special time for you. To learn effectively, it's best to observe without the emotion of having money involved.

Actually, this will be your first boot camp lesson. When you observe the market quietly, without trading, you learn the discipline of "sitting on your hands." Believe me, this *is* a skill! Most traders learn it *after* they lose money on impulsive trades. You, however, are going to experience it right away. Trust me, gaining the discipline to observe and listen without trading will represent one of the most valuable tools in your trading kit.

If possible, try to start boot camp on a Monday. Then only one weekend will break your momentum. Besides, Mondays usually set the market's tone for the week.

Monday: Welcome to your first day in Beginner's Boot Camp! Please settle into your home office, community trading center, or wherever you've chosen to trade.

Make sure CNBC is being televised. Though you don't have to see the television screen, it should be loud enough to hear, yet soft enough not to distract you from concentrating. Access to the news is a must. Trading without news is like fighting with one hand.

After a few days, you will learn to listen to CNBC with "one ear." Experience will teach you to automatically tune in to information that could affect your trades and filter out what doesn't.

Okay, let's get started. Choose an actively traded target stock from either the NYSE or Nasdaq. Try to chose an industry leader, for example, Pfizer (PFE) or Merck (MRK) in the pharmaceutical industry; Schlumberger (SLB) or Halliburton (HAL) in the oil industry; America Online (AOL) or Amazon (AMZN) in the Internet industry. Don't limit your observations to its opening and closing price. Display *all* the info you can obtain about it—real-time quotes, a five- or fifteen-minute intraday chart, a level II screen if it's available to you. Then watch this stock *all day*.

How does it act at the market's open? How does it react during the 9:50 reversal period, and the 10:25 reversal period?

Normally, you should leave your computer during lunchtime to refresh mind and body, and to avoid trading during most of this whippy time period.

But boot camp demands are rigorous! So eat a sandwich in front of your screen, and notice how your stock quiets down, or moves erratically, during the lunchtime "moody blues," from 11:30 a.m. to 2:30 p.m.

Bonds close their trading day at 3:00 p.m. EST. Since bonds and stocks are joined at the hip, that causes a market shift. How does your stock react? The 3:30 shift or reversal lasts until 4:00 p.m., when the market closes. During this final half-hour, institutions wind up their strategies for the day, which causes more volatility until the close.

If day traders play your target stock heavily—you can tell by extreme price movements and 100- to 1,000-share prints going off the majority of the time—look for it to sell off ten minutes or so before the close. Many day traders refuse to hold positions overnight. By the way, specialists and market makers know traders want to go home flat. So when you start trading, be careful. They may try to wash you out of the stock during this time by dropping the bid.

About five minutes before the close, the "shorts," or short-sellers, buy back their positions to close them, or "cover their shorts." *That* buying makes many stocks rise!

Tuesday: Today, pay attention to the way your stock acts in relation to the fluctuations of the Dow Jones Industrial Average and the Nasdaq Composite. Does it mimic them, or wander off on its own like a rebellious teenager? (Most NYSE stocks follow the Dow; Nasdaq stocks reflect the Nasdaq Composite. Naturally, this always happens, except when it doesn't.)

Find another active stock in your target stock's industry group or sector. Pair the two on your screen. Do they move in tandem, or separately?

Chapter 13 lists industry indices. If you can, bring up the sector index that applies and watch how your stocks move in relation to the index. Does the index move first, and the stocks follow?

By the way, boot camp is the time to paper trade, if you want to try it. Keep a record of your "trades," and relish every minute of it. It's fun making zillions of dollars on paper. Remember, though, paper trading is much different from the real thing. I've met many paper champions. Paper trading is a tool, not a barometer for success.

After the market closes, look at daily charts of your stocks. Are they in uptrends, downtrends, or trading in a range? Are they in congestion or consolidation patterns? Where are the next support and resistance areas? How did they move today in comparison to Monday's activity? Apply volume, and at least the 20, 50, and 200 MA. Bring in the CCI if you can. Do your stocks obediently ride their 20 MA, rising and falling in gentle curves, or do they hop up and down erratically between the 20 MA and 50 MA like a kangaroo on speed?

Wednesday: By now you may begin to sense, or internalize, the rhythms of the market. Fascinating, isn't it, how events that occur during the day weave the texture of the market? If you don't yet sense the ebb and flow of the market and individual stocks you're watching, worry not. It will come in time. When experience and knowledge sharpen that sense into a reliable "gut feeling," you'll know it! Spend today in the same manner you spent yesterday, watching the Dow, the Nasdaq Composite, and your target stocks.

Hot Tip

Most experienced traders wait until the market has been open for at least ten minutes before they place a trade. When the opening bell rings, specialists and market makers control the stocks and are in hot pursuit of leveling the field from the day before. So remember, when the opening bell rings, early birds don't get the worm—they get shot down!

Thursday: Today, add another stock to your target list. If your current stocks trade on the NYSE, add a Nasdaq stock, or vice-versa. Again, please choose a stock that trades actively to give you a feeling of how stocks move.

Also, before the market opens, examine daily charts of the Dow and the Nasdaq Composite. As usual, look for uptrends, downtrends, trading in a range, support, and resistance. Where are they in relation to their 20 and 50 MAs? This afternoon, after the market closes, revisit those charts. How did today's closing price affect the overall picture of the markets' direction?

Friday: By now, you should be watching three stocks and have developed the skill of watching them, related indices, the Dow Jones, and the Nasdaq Composite, all at one time. Check daily charts of your stocks, sector indices, and the Dow and Nasdaq before you start your weekend, so you have a feeling for what the next week might bring.

Congratulations on completing your first week of Beginner's Boot Camp! I promise your eyes will uncross before the weekend is over!

BEGINNER'S BOOT CAMP: WEEK TWO

Good morning, guys and girlfriends. It's **Monday** and I know you feel refreshed and ready to tackle a new week!

Did last week teach you how to watch a zillion numbers blink in front of you like hyperactive neon signs? Good. Now we're going to add three more indicators. Excuse me? Was that you moaning?

Don't worry, you're going to love these indicators. They're almost as good as finding three crystal balls sitting next to your computer.

Indicators come in two flavors: lagging and leading. Lagging indicators tell you what has already happened. For example, stock and industry cash indexes like the Dow, the Nasdaq 100, the Russell 2000 Small Cap Index, the OEX (S&P 100), and the Morgan Stanley High Tech Industry Index are lagging indicators. Volume and moving averages represent lagging indicators.

Leading indicators hint at what might happen next; the CCI is a leading indicator. So are the three indicators you're going to meet next: the TICK, the TRIN, and the S&P futures.

These numbers, along with other indicators like the advance/decline line, we label as "market internals." They divulge the true health of the market, a side of the market most people never see.

Just because the Dow and the Nasdaq 100 show positive numbers to the outside world doesn't mean all is actually rosy. Those two indices combined represent only 130 stocks out of more than 8,000. Market internals tell the real story. While the Dow smiles, internals can fluctuate wildly. We call their actions "whippy," and "choppy," and they lead traders on a merry chase.

On days like this, after the market closes, your friends inevitably stroll up to you and whomp you on the back. "Hey," they say, with a knowing cackle, "you must have made a fortune today. The Dow was up big-time."

You roll your eyes and bite your lip, recalling how you white-knuckled it through every trade you entered. You know only too well how the market can smile pretty as a beauty queen on the outside, but act witchy and fickle on the inside!

Nevertheless, internals such as the TICK, TRIN, and S&P futures give you the true, unvarnished facts. When they point in a certain direction—traders pay attention. Within seconds, the majority of stocks follow their lead.

Please access these today, and if possible, bring them up on your screen.

The first crystal ball is the TICK, and it is a short-term trading indicator. The number it shows represents the number of stocks ticking up minus the number of stocks ticking down on the NYSE. Even though the actual number measures listed stocks, it acts as an indicator for securities on all exchanges. You can see the TICK during market hours on the CNBC ticker at the bottom of the television screen. During market hours, it scrolls by as part of the "CNBC Market Summary." As of this writing, the TICK runs on CNBC fifteen minutes delayed.

I keep the TICK on a five-minute chart on my left-hand screen (I work on two monitors simultaneously). When the market acts squirrelly, I check the TICK's support and resistance areas. I also list the number, itself, in a market minder box right under the Dow and Nasdaq Composite.

If, for example, the TICK reads +332, that means 332 more stocks on the NYSE are ticking up, than ticking down. Any number over zero means the TICK is positive. If the TICK reads –587, it means 587 more stocks are ticking down than up, and that's a negative signal.

During a morning or afternoon trading session, when the TICK stays consistently in positive territory, stocks acting strong on the day generally keep their upward momentum. But if it screams skyward and soars over 1,000, don't get euphoric—get nervous. At this point, the market is trading in overbought territory and will likely reverse. It's like eating too much chocolate cake. It tastes so good while you're eating it, but afterward, you feel awful!

If you see the TICK climb over +1,000 and you have open day trades or scalps on the long side, lighten up. Chances are the TICK won't stay at such lofty levels for long.

Ditto to the downside. On really negative market days, when your entire screen flashes blood red (prices downticking on level II screens show in red), watch for the TICK to sink to –1,000, or lower. That's a signal things are as bad as they can get. The market's oversold and there's nowhere to go but up.

On a nasty day like this, when the bears rule, and the TICK plunges like a stone tied to a cement block, many traders lie in wait for the –1,000 and the subsequent reversal that may take place. (The operative word here is *may*.) When (if) the reversal takes place, they look for a pop up and buy stocks such as Cisco Systems (CSCO) and Applied Materials (AMAT), both which follow the TICK.

This tactic is fine for advanced traders, but if you're new at this game, please just observe. The TICK doesn't always behave as expected. If you so much as breathe funny, the TICK reverses to the downside. You can be dealt a burning loss before you know what happened!

I have a "TICK rule" I follow religiously. Other traders in the office where I trade have adopted it. It's simple: If the TICK falls below 0, I don't enter a scalp or day trade on the long side. My reasoning: When the TICK reads negative, breakouts to the upside tend to fail. They might poke over resistance, but many times they fall back—fast. Even getting out even means a loss because of commissions.

A trader I know who adopted my TICK rule, conducted an informal study. He told me that when the TICK stayed negative, eight out of ten breakouts failed.

My study, completed earlier in my trading career, resembled a whack to my head with a two-by-four! It took place one evening while I mulled over the day's losses in my journal. Each of my scalping plays began perfectly, but in the final outcome they all failed. A single common denominator stood out. In each case, the TICK was negative. Hmm. Lesson learned. Negative TICK, no trade!

As you can see, the TICK is a powerful indicator. Many stocks follow it like an obedient lamb, especially the listed large caps such as GE, AT&T, American Express, GM, Wal-Mart, and America Online.

Do any of your target stocks follow the TICK? To find out, run your stocks' charts and the TICK side by side.

The second crystal ball is the TRIN. Richard Arms developed in it 1967, and we owe him a debt of gratitude. An acronym for Trading Index, the TRIN is also called the Arms Index.

The TRIN measures volatility and has an inverse relationship to the TICK. A low TRIN means the bulls rule. A rising TRIN tells you the bears are fighting for supremacy.

You can access the TRIN on your level II system; most online brokers offer their clients access to it. On CNBC, it scrolls on the bottom ticker tape, following the TICK. As of this writing, the CNBC TRIN is fifteen minutes delayed.

Again, I keep a five-minute chart of the TRIN on my screen, along with the number on my market minder list, right under the TICK. It's advantageous to display the TICK and TRIN next to each other since their inverse relationship to one another is key.

If you calculated the TRIN, this is how you'd do it:

$$\frac{\text{Advancing Issues/Declining Issues}}{\text{Advancing Volume/Declining Volume}}$$

Like the TICK, the TRIN is a short-term trading tool. As you can see by the equation, it indicates whether volume is flowing into advancing, or declining, stocks. When advancing stocks dominate volume flow, the number reads under 1.0. When declining stocks command volume flow, the number exceeds 1.0.

Simply put, a falling TRIN signals a strong market. A rising TRIN foretells a weak market.

I find trading downright enjoyable when the TRIN stays below 0.9. If it moves into the 1.0 zone, my longs get jittery and start to slip. For good reason. When the TRIN hovers in the 1.0 area, it means the bears and bulls are fighting for control. Longs don't break out properly, and shorts don't fall down! At this point, you'll find me with a flat trading account, sitting on the sidelines. I don't take a picnic to the beach during a hurricane. And I don't jump between angry bulls and bears when they fight for supremacy.

In *Trading for a Living*, Dr. Elder agrees. He writes, "If bulls are much stronger, you should buy and hold. If bears are much stronger, you should sell and sell short. If both camps are about equal in strength, a wise trader stands aside. He lets bullies fight with each other and puts on a trade only when he is reasonably sure who is likely to win."[1]

For you ditty lovers out there, here's a new one—and a true one—for you: "The TRIN always wins!" Yup, it's true. Remember it.

Say the market feels depressed, with the TICK floundering in the –500 area, and the TRIN at 1.3, or so. Suddenly, the TICK makes a U-turn and leaps into positive territory. But the TRIN maintains its 1.3 to 1.4 level, refusing to sink. You're witnessing a sucker rally! Sucker rallies cajole newbies into jumping in headfirst and buying their favorite stocks. You—as a savvy trader—don't. You merely observe with short-lived rally with a smug smile.

---

1 Elder, Dr. Alexander. *Trading for a Living.* (NY: John Wiley & Sons, 1993), p. 47.

When you see an extreme, like the TRIN wallowing under 0.40, that's too good to be true. Watch for the market to sell off. The other extreme takes place when the TRIN climbs over 1.50, and you'd swear the end of the world draws near. Take heart. Buyers may start to nibble and a market rebound should appear.

Learn to watch the TICK and TRIN together, noting how they move in opposite directions. For the best day trading and scalping setups (on the long side), you want the TICK above zero and the TRIN below 1.0. Or the TICK up and the TRIN down. Simple, huh?

Days when the TICK is negative and the TRIN maintains a level over 1.0, you either sell short or practice sitting on your hands. If more traders had heeded these simple indicators, they'd still be around to talk about it.

At this point in your studies, you'll want to start formulating some of your own trading rules. My third rule, listed right under protect your principal and trade to trade well, is that I enter a scalp or day trade only when the TICK is over zero, and the TRIN is below 0.9. That rule has saved me a fortune. Try it!

The third crystal ball comes to you courtesy of the S&P futures.

In 1982, the Chicago exchanges introduced stock index futures to their growing number of financial futures contracts. Now the Standard & Poor's 500 Index Futures, or S&P futures, as it is known to traders, is a highly liquid commodity in its own right. More important to us, however, is that the S&P futures reflect public sentiment and the perceived state of the U.S. economy. That gives these futures incredible power in dictating market direction.

The futures usually correspond with the Standard & Poor's 500 stock index (except when they don't!). The S&P 500 stock index, also referred to as the S&P cash, is a benchmark index of 500 large stocks from the major exchanges. Standard & Poor's, a division of McGraw-Hill, maintains it.

I always have a three- or five-minute chart of the S&P futures, with 20- and 200-period MAs, smack in the middle of my screen. Scalpers may even use a one-minute chart. Because the futures are *the* primary indicator used by traders, to day trade or scalp without it would be like trying to breathe without a nose.

Put the futures up on your screen, in chart form, if you can. Now watch the TICK and the TRIN alongside. Interesting, isn't it? On an easygoing day, the TICK floats happily above zero, and the TRIN rests in the 0.50 to 0.90 area. The futures draw a nice uptrend, with a mild, but expected pullbacks. Mmm. Trader heaven. On those days, trading can be like printing money!

On a whippy, choppy day, though, the TICK flies into positive territory one minute, and dives into negative territory the next. The TRIN digs in and stays above 1.0. The S&P futures have no mercy either, drawing a jagged chart that resembles a kindergartner's first sketch.

After the opening bell rings, if you see the above pattern develop, get out of Dodge! Gather your profits, take small losses if you have to, and take your account flat. Stop trading. There's no way to outguess the market, and your chances of losing money are enormous.

Another warning: On any day, no matter the conditions, if you see the futures dive very hard and fast, make sure you know where your stops are. Watch any positions you have without blinking. When the futures talk, you listen!

Now, with the TICK, TRIN, and S&P futures on your screen, you may want to back off to one target stock, and its industry index. Watching more than one stock while acclimating yourself to these three indicators will drive you bonkers.

While you should still keep an eye on the Dow and Nasdaq Composite from time to time, from now on you'll depend much more heavily on your three "crystal balls" for market direction.

Tuesday: Continue to monitor the TICK, TRIN, and S&P futures, and your target stock's relationship to them. Is your stock in sync with the indicators? If not, why? One reason might be news, good or bad, that would propel the stock into its own trading pattern. Another reason might be that some stocks simply rebel against most indicators and do their own thing. When you trip over a stock like that, avoid day trading or scalping it until you internalize its behavior.

Wednesday: Let's add a level II screen. For those who whine that their vision is already blurred, that they can't add one more thing or their brains will short-circuit, chin up. This is the last item we'll add for a while.

Some traders, called momentum traders, use *only* level II screens to trade. They don't use charts, and they monitor few indicators. They use level II screens to trade volatile Nasdaq stocks as they rise and fall, and these traders execute hundreds, even thousands of trades per day. I *do not* advocate momentum trading for new traders.

Level II used in conjunction with charts, however, makes the ultimate trading weapon.

For our purposes, please choose an active NYSE stock as your target stock to watch. Now bring up your level II screen, making sure it includes "Time and Sales." Position the level II screen next to your target stock's intraday chart. Next to that, if you have it, add the index chart of the industry or sector your target stock represents. Don't forget your chart of the S&P futures, with a time frame that matches your stock's chart. (That is, make them both five-minute charts, or both fifteen-minute, or both sixty-minute charts—just so they match.) Nearby, keep the TICK and the TRIN.

Okay, I'm assuming the market's open. Let's get up close and personal with your level II screen.

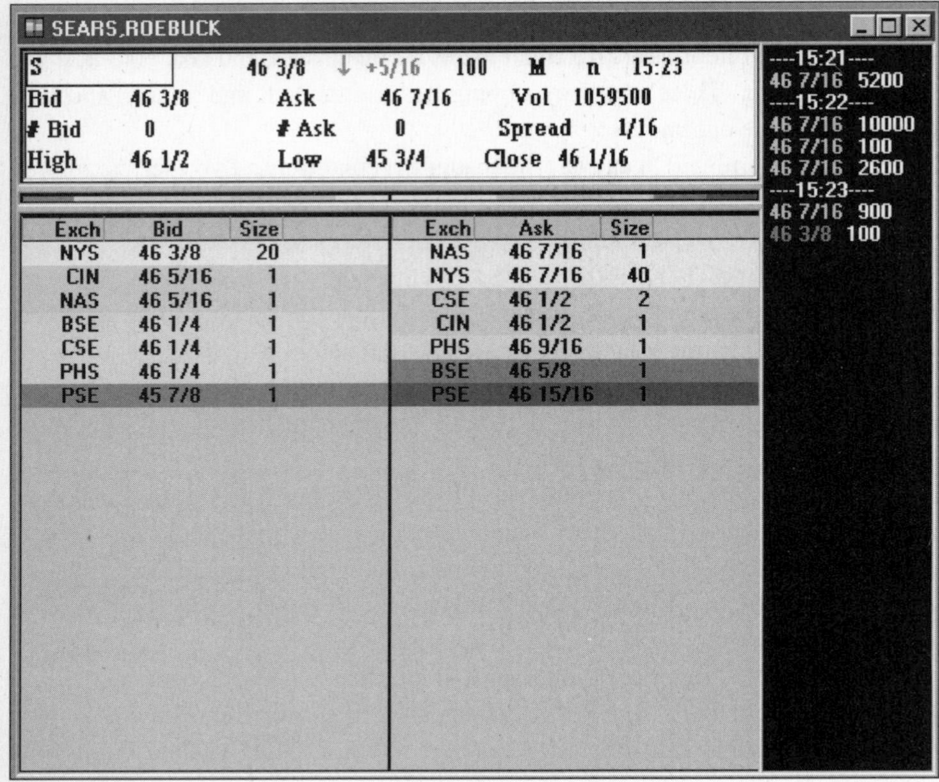

Figure 8-1

Level II Screen Courtesy of *The Executioner*©

A level II screen showing a listed stock is different from a level II screen displaying a Nasdaq stock. As mentioned before, NYSE stocks have only one specialist who orchestrates trading in that stock. Nasdaq stocks have many market makers orchestrating price movement.

On the inside bid/offer side of Sears (S) in Figure 8-1, you see the NYSE as well as the regional exchanges lined up, with lot sizes and price.

Let's evaluate what the level II screen shows us. First, Sears is trading at the high of the day. That's positive news.

Now notice the inside bid. The number of shares wanted to buy is 2,000 (at 46 3/8). On the inside ask, or offer, the number of shares offered out to sell is 4,100 shares (at 46 7/16). Since the number of shares on the bid side are less than the number of shares on the offer, that generally means there's greater demand to sell than to buy. You already know the equation: Selling = supply = price goes down.

But I qualified with "generally" because this falls under the "this is always true except when it isn't" syndrome.

Specialists to a certain degree, and market makers to a large degree, get their jollies by playing games with your head. No decent specialist or market maker will expose his entire hand (orders). They siphon your money away from you by masking their true intentions. The games are elaborate, and if I spell them out here, you'll end up confused, not educated.

Fortunately, the "Time and Sales" feature on your level II screen displays facts the way they are. Under the time of day, Time and Sales lists the "prints," or price and lot size for every trade. No amount of fancy maneuvering alters those facts.

Prints accompanied by "size" (size = large share lots) gives a reliable indication of current price direction. For example, look at all the green prints on time and sales trading on the offer of 46 7/16. They show size. You see buys going by at 5,200, 10,000, 100, 2,600, and 900 shares. Pay attention to size like 5,200, 10,000, and 2,600. Maybe an institution placed a buy order of a half-million shares, and the order is broken up piece by piece, then printing.

On the sell side, only one (red) print went by 46 3/8, and that for only 100 shares. Very little distribution (selling) is taking place.

Conclusion: Prints don't lie. Size is trading at the offer. More buyers than sellers = demand = stock should rise.

What if size is reversed? For example, imagine red prints going off at 2,000, 1,000, 5,000. Green prints show 100, 500, 300. Conclusion: More sellers than buyers = supply = stock should fall.

As you've surmised, when scalping or day trading NYSE stocks, it's wise to "trade toward size." After you've satisfied your other criteria for entering the trade, make darn sure you're headed in the same direction as the big prints. If size tells you you're swimming against the tide, wait on the beach until the tide turns.

Next, look at the inside bid and ask prices. When you sell a stock "at the market," you receive the price on the inside bid. Now, though, do the prints tell you traders are "splitting the bid and the ask"? If so, that indicates the specialist may let you sell the stock 1/16th or 1/8th of a point higher than the posted bid price. Or you may be able to buy a teeny (1/16) or an 1/8th lower than the current ask, or offer.

When you're buying, think of the inside bid and ask as retail prices, and the prices in between as "wholesale" prices. When you split the bid and ask, and buy a fraction lower than the "advertised" price at the offer, it's like buying the stock wholesale instead of retail (Figure 8-2).

Stocks are not always on sale, though. When the prints tell you the stock is being bought *at the offer price*, and not in-between, it's really a positive indicator.

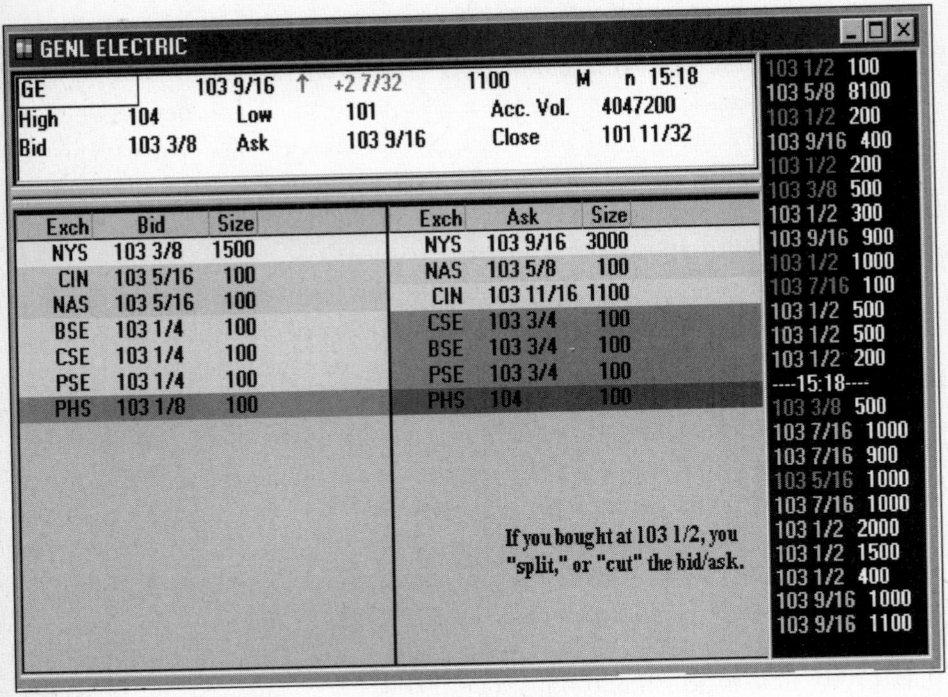

GENL ELECTRIC

GE	103 9/16 ↑	+2 7/32	1100	M	n 15:18
High 104	Low	101	Acc. Vol.	4047200	
Bid 103 3/8	Ask	103 9/16	Close	101 11/32	

Exch	Bid	Size
NYS	103 3/8	1500
CIN	103 5/16	100
NAS	103 5/16	100
BSE	103 1/4	100
CSE	103 1/4	100
PSE	103 1/4	100
PHS	103 1/8	100

Exch	Ask	Size
NYS	103 9/16	3000
NAS	103 5/8	100
CIN	103 11/16	1100
CSE	103 3/4	100
BSE	103 3/4	100
PSE	103 3/4	100
PHS	104	100

103 1/2 100
103 5/8 8100
103 1/2 200
103 9/16 400
103 1/2 200
103 3/8 500
103 1/2 300
103 9/16 900
103 1/2 1000
103 7/16 100
103 1/2 500
103 1/2 500
103 1/2 200
----15:18----
103 3/8 500
103 7/16 1000
103 7/16 900
103 5/16 1000
103 7/16 1000
103 1/2 2000
103 1/2 1500
103 1/2 400
103 9/16 1000
103 9/16 1100

If you bought at 103 1/2, you "split," or "cut" the bid/ask.

Figure 8-2

On this level II screen of GE, notice the unusually wide spread that GE has at this moment, between the inside bid of 103 3/8 and the inside ask of 103 9/16—or 3/16 of a point. If you want to buy the stock, this gives you a chance to split the bid and ask, by jumping in with a limit order placed at 103 1/2. Because the stock is rising, if you didn't get filled quickly, you would cancel your order and replace it at the inside offer, or 103 9/16.

If you owned GE and wanted to sell it here, you'd place a limit order for 103 7/16. If the stock starts to fall, you'd cancel your order and hit the inside bid.

Level II Screen Courtesy of *The Executioner*©

The specialist is demanding "retail" prices for his or her stock and is getting it. Demand = rising price.

When a NYSE stock I really want moves up fast, I'll pay retail rather than lose my chance to get in. If, however, the stock's moving slowly and I'm buying it as an intermediate-term trade, I'll try to buy wholesale by slipping a limit order into the middle of the bid and ask. (Limit orders are defined at the end of the chapter.) Sometimes it gets filled, sometimes it doesn't. If I really want the stock, and my order doesn't get filled quickly, I'll cancel it and buy at the offer price.

I do the same when I want to sell. If I want to get out fast, I'll accept the current bid price. If I have time and profits on my side, I'll enter a sell order that splits the bid and ask, and see if the specialist bites. If he or she doesn't, I'll cancel and reenter the order at the bid price.

LYCOS INC

LCOS		95	↑ +3 1/8	1000	Ot t
Bid ↑	94 15/16	Ask	95		
# Bid	1	# Ask	1	Spread	
High	96 11/16	Low	92 1/2	Close	91 7/8

Name	Bid	Size	#Best
ISLD	94 15/16	1	225
BRUT	94 7/8	1	1
HRZG	94 7/8	1	29
ARCA	94 7/8	2	21
MASH	94 13/16	10	11
SHWD	94 13/16	1	2
FBCO	94 3/4	1	9
INCA	94 3/4	3	77
STRK	94 11/16	34	1
PERT	94 1/4	1	6
REDI	94 1/16	5	18
MLCO	94	1	4
PRUS	93 11/16	3	5
SBSH	93 5/8	1	10
NITE	93 1/2	15	11
MONT	93 1/4	1	0
BTRD	93 3/16	1	56
SLKC	93 1/16	1	13

Name	Ask	Size	#Best
INCA	95	5	88
HMQT	95 1/8	1	1
USCT	95 1/8	1	0
MONT	95 1/4	1	0
ISLD	95 1/4	6	285
FBCO	95 1/2	1	9
GSCO	95 5/8	10	0
PRUS	95 3/4	1	2
BTRD	95 3/4	1	6
HRZG	95 3/4	1	39
SLKC	95 13/16	1	4
ARCA	95 7/8	5	15
CIBC	95 15/16	10	1
MHMY	96	2	0
NITE	96 3/16	10	5
BRUT	96 3/16	2	6
MASH	96 7/16	10	13
SELZ	96 1/2	1	0

94 13/16 900
94 13/16 900
94 7/8 100
94 7/8 100
----11:26----
94 7/8 500
94 7/8 100
94 7/8 800
94 15/16 500
94 15/16 200
94 7/8 100
94 15/16 300
94 15/16 600
94 15/16 1000
94 15/16 100
95 100
95 100
95 200
95 200
95 1000
95 100
95 900
95 200
95 200
94 7/8 100
95 600
95 900
95 1000

Figure 8-3

On this level II screen of Lycos Inc., notice that the "bid" side of the screen lists ISLD at the inside bid at 94 15/16 for 100 shares. BRUT, another ECN, is under ISLD, also bidding for 100 shares, but at 94 7/8. HRZG, a major market maker is next, also bidding 94 7/8 for 100 shares. Notice that HRZG has been to the bid 29 times so far today. The fact that he is highest #Best combined with the fact that he is has stayed at or near the inside bid for quite a while, continuing to refresh his bid, designates him as the "ax." ARCA, listed under HRZG, is an ECN. On the inside "ask" or "offer," you see INCA, another ECN, offering 500 shares for sale at 95.

Level II Screen Courtesy of *The Executioner©*

You can split the bid and offer with an online broker by issuing a limit order. The drawback: Without a level II system, you can't monitor your order on the screen; therefore, you cannot gauge the odds of it being filled.

For the remainder of the day, watch the prints, and keep close tabs on the other indicators on your screen as well. Notice how the stock price ebbs and flows with the TICK, TRIN, and S&P futures, as well as the industry index.

Thursday: Today, let's change the target stock to a medium volatile Nasdaq stock that moves at a reasonable pace.

For the level II screen shown in Figure 8-3, I've chosen an Internet stock, Lycos (LCOS). LCOS used to be a real party animal. It would scream straight up, quiver for one second, then crash so fast I referred to it as "a heart-attack on a screen." Lately, it's calmed a bit.

As you can see, level II screens displaying Nasdaq stocks have a slightly different content than listed stocks. The prices list in the same order on the bid and ask, but instead of the NYSE and regional exchanges, market makers wait in line. Just as on the NYSE stock, the inside bid and ask on this level II screen are colored yellow.

With New York securities, watching size is important. On the Nasdaq, size is important, but so are the actual players and their positions in the lineup.

Let's check out who's on the inside bid side. For future scalpers: *The inside bid/offer on the level II screen is the most important place to watch.*

The market makers (let's shorten market maker to MM) on the bid are buying the stock. They're the ones putting their money where their mouth is. When a lot of movers and shakers, like GSCO and MLCO, show up on the inside bid, that means they're buying (read: demand). The stock will probably shoot up.

When the same heavyweights show up on the ask, or offer, and the only MM on the bid is an ECN, that means the heavies are selling the stock (read: supply). It may dive, at least temporarily.

ECNs are proprietary, electronic communications networks that let customers display their orders to other customers. They also promote pairing of orders between customers. Think of an ECN as a trading cooperative, or "stock swap meet."

If you have a level II system, you'll receive access to one proprietary ECN dictated by your broker, and additional access to others like Island. ECN examples include ARCA (Archipelago), ISLD (Island), INCA (Instinet), BRTD (Bloomberg), ATTN (Attain), and REDI (Spear, Leeds & Kellogg). By the time you read this book, more ECNs will be in operation. Discover who they are and keep a current list.

If you're scalping, especially, you want to be buying when powerful MMs like GSCO are buying, and selling when they are selling. (You'll learn precise scalping tactics in Chapter 11.)

Next, let's find the "ax." The ax is the MM who has the most interest in your target stock. He's jumped to the inside bid/offer more than any other market maker. We want to identify the ax because he'll have more control over the moment-to-moment price than anyone else. Think of him as "the king of the mountain."

If your level II system has a "#Best" feature in the setup dialogue box, click on it. That displays the number of times each participating MM has come to the inside bid and ask.

ECNs don't count as the ax. Many times ISLD will appear to be the ax. Perhaps more than any other ECN, ISLD represents the public. On a popular stock, ISLD makes multiple trips to the inside bid and ask. Still, ISLD doesn't count as the ax.

Identify the ax by finding the highest #Best (disregard ECNs) that's a real-live MM such as GSCO (Goldman-Sachs), NITE (Knight), PRUS (Prudential), or MLCO (Merrill Lynch). The ax has a vested interest in how the price moves. Also, the ax has tremendous capital and order flow. Failure to pinpoint the ax compares to participating in a boxing match without knowing who your opponent is.

Now that you've found the ax, watch how he behaves. When the TICK is strong and the TRIN stays low, does the ax support the inside bid and even raise his price? If so, that's positive, and the stock should remain strong.

When the futures pull back, does the ax support the bid? Or does he back down a couple of levels? When the TICK tanks, does he flip to the offer and start selling? The last two moves are negative for the stock, at least in the short term.

Hot Tip

Identify the ax whenever possible when you scalp and day trade. Don't worry about the ax, though, if you're buying for a swing trade or intermediate-term trade.

Remember, you're not the only trader watching the ax. A zillion others are also watching and taking their cues from him.

For a quick refresher, let's confirm some points you've learned about the level II screen. The left side, or bid side, of the market maker screen is where MMs wait for you to sell your stock to them. (You sell, they buy.) The right, or offer side, is where MMs offer out stock for you to buy from them. (You buy, they sell.) Got it? Good. Now comes the fun.

When you're trading with a level II system, you get to play MM. You can buy on the bid and sell on the offer! The good news: This saves you the spread, and gives you an incredible advantage. The challenging news: It takes practice and market savvy to capitalize on it.

Say the stock you want to buy has broken over resistance. It's running up fast. Buy it on the offer (but no chasing) and be done with it. Trying to buy on the bid is a waste of time—the stock will run away from you. Why? If you're trying to buy on the bid, along with the other market makers (your order will be posted with the ECN of your choice), *somebody has to want to sell their stock to you*. When a stock looks as though it's heading for the moon, sellers are few and far between.

However, if your stock's just breaking out, the whole world hasn't noticed, *and* there's still a little selling pressure, post your buy order at the inside bid price, or a teeny or 1/8th higher (this is called "going high bid"). If it's filled, you're ahead of the game already. Assuming the stock rises when you take profits, you'll "make the spread" as well. If the stock reverses and heads down, you're in at a lower price than "retail," or the offer price and therefore, closer to your stop. That makes for a smaller loss.

Now it's time to sell the position. When your stock is still climbing like a jet bound for heaven, time and sales is full of green prints, and you have a tidy profit, *that's* when you post your sell order at the ask price. *Sell into buying pressure.* When everybody's still buying, your ask price should be filled in a heartbeat. Be assured the euphoria driving all the green prints skyward can reverse to fear, and falling red prints, in an ohnosecond. (An *ohnosecond* is that moment in time when you realize you've made a mistake, and it's going to cost you.) Whence comes the old trader saying: "Sell when you can, not when you have to."

If the trade sours, and the stock collapses like a punctured balloon, don't attempt to sell at the offer. You know the reason. To sell at the offer, someone's got to buy that ugly stock from you at a high price. Fat chance. You'd best "hit the bid," or if it's really falling fast, a level under the inside bid price.

Other factors come into these tactics, and you'll read about them later. For now, though, if your level II system offers a paper trading mode, during a calm moment, practice buying on the bid and selling on the ask.

Friday: Today, continue watching the interaction between the TICK, TRIN, and S&P futures, along with intraday chart of your target stock and its corresponding level II screen.

Pull up another chart for your target stock, if possible, and give it a different time frame. If your original intraday chart is a five-minute chart, pull up a chart of the same stock, and make it a fifteen-minute or sixty-minute chart. Add the same moving averages, say, the 20 MA and the 200 MA. Then, if you spot a breakout or breakdown take place on one chart, see if it comes out as a similar pattern on the other chart. Check the volume and moving averages.

The trick for making highly successful day trades and scalps is to have two different time frames correlate, like the 5 and 15-minute charts and both give you ideal setups simultaneously. In addition to the breakout pattern you've already learned, I'll give you more patterns to look at in the following chapters.

At the time you enter the trade, it's best when the stock sits *right on top of the moving average* on both time frames. If it's riding too far above the 20 MA, the stock is overextended, and may not rise too far. Today, watch stocks on intraday charts break out by bouncing off support. Support = areas formed by reversals, and support formed by moving averages.

Watch stocks break out by moving through key, or major, resistance. Observe how volume plays a part. Were the failed breakouts accompanied by weak volume? Or were they caused by deteriorating market conditions? Using what you've learned, try to analyze why stocks act as they do.

Okay, I know your eyes feel bleary and your brain fried, but stay with me. Learning these easy definitions completes boot camp.

You can buy or sell stocks using the following methods:

- Market orders. When you buy or sell a stock "at the market," you're giving the specialist or market maker *carte blanche*. That person chooses what price you pay or receive for your stock. Yes, you're supposed to receive the inside bid or offer when your order reaches them. But I've watched market makers, especially on a thinly traded stock, lower the bid when my market order reached them. If you *must* buy or sell in a panic, use a market order; otherwise, don't.
- Limit order: When you place a limit order, you give instructions with your order that you wish to buy or sell a specified number of shares of stock when it reaches a specified price. You place a limit order to buy at a price *lower* than the posted inside offer. Or you place a limit order to sell *above* the posted inside bid. *The specialist or market maker will fill your limit order only when the stock's price reaches your specified price, or better.*

You use a limit order to specify a price when you're buying and want to split the bid and ask, or when you're attempting to buy on the bid and sell on the offer. If a stock runs away from you, you can place a limit order to buy a certain number of shares at a certain price, *under* the current price. Of course, your order may get filled, or it may not. The same procedure takes place with a sell order. If you own a stock and want to sell it at a higher price than it's currently posted, you issue a limit order to sell your shares at a price *above* the posted price. Again, your order may be filled, but if the stock doesn't reach your specified price, you'll be left dangling. Limit orders can be either "day orders" or GTC, meaning "good till canceled." You may also have the choice designated AON. AON means "all or nothing." Translation: If the specialist or market maker cannot fill the total number of shares you request, you don't want the order filled at all. That is, if you put in a limit order for 500 shares at a certain price AON, and they can give you only 350 shares at that price, it tells them to ignore the order. I usually leave the AON box unchecked. Sometimes, on a moonshot stock, I get filled for funny, odd lots, like 26 shares out of my requested 1,000. If that happens to you, all you can do is laugh and "SOES it" or sell it on ISLD when you have a profit (more on SOES later). By the way, limit orders are the most frequent order you'll use as a trader.

- Buy stops. When you place a buy stop, it means you (again) specify a number of shares you want to buy at a certain price *above* the stock's posted price. Say Igloo Ice Cream is trading at $20, which is key resistance. If it breaks *above* $20, that's the perfect entry point. You're well aware, however, that when it moves over $20, everybody in the entire world will post a buy order for Igloo Ice Cream. How do you get an edge? You place a buy stop order for the number of shares you want, at $20 1/8. Then you sit back and wait. If Igloo doesn't trade over $20, your order will not be filled. Drawback: *Buy stops are filled when the stock trades at your specified price, or the next highest price.* If you place a buy stop with your online broker for 500 shares of Igloo Ice Cream at $20 1/8 *before* the market opens, then the bell rings and Igloo gaps open three points higher, *that's* where you get filled, at $23 1/8. *Gulp!* Stocks that gap open more than a 1/2 point higher than their closing price from the day before usually tank—fast. When the stock opens at $23 1/8, and your order gets filled, seconds later you could be staring at a posted price of $21. Lesson: Don't issue buy orders before the market opens. If you're going out for lunch, and there's a slow-moving stock you want to pick up if it breaks out while you're gone, that's good use of a buy stop order.

- Sell stops. Sell stops are often called stop loss orders. When you're holding a NYSE stock, you can place a sell stop, or stop loss, *under* the stock's current posted price. If the stock trades at that price, your stop loss reverts into a market order, and your position is liquidated. The Nasdaq doesn't grant stop losses. Some online brokers, however, provide stop losses on Nasdaq stocks as a customer service. You place a sell stop for the number of shares you own, at a specified price. When the stock trades at that price, the sell stop reverts to a market order, and your position is sold. Because your order reverts to a market order in both of these cases, your position may be liquidated an 1/8th or more away from your specified price.

Congratulations! You've completed Trader's Boot Camp! When you start trading you'll be glad you toughed-out the camp, and especially glad you finished it without placing orders. Without stress, you learn more.

In the following chapter, we'll discuss the exact criteria to place trades in each time frame. Then, with all systems "go," you'll execute a trade.

This chapter contains a lot of important material, and completing the quiz will crystallize it for you. To assure you've digested it, please answer the quiz questions by writing them down. Then refer to your answers during the next few weeks, until the terminology and concepts become second nature.

After that, you deserve a reward, so give yourself a treat over the weekend!

QUIZ

1. During what approximate time period in the morning does the market make its first reversal?
2. When does the next reversal, or shift, take place?
3. True or false? Experienced traders make most of their money on lunchtime trades.
4. What time of day do bonds close?
5. Stocks played heavily by day traders many times sell off ten to fifteen minutes before the close. Why?
6. True or false? Experienced traders wait at least ten minutes after the opening bell to place their first trade. What reason supports your answer?
7. Indicators generally fall under two headings: ____________ and __________.
8. Define the TICK.
9. True or false? When the TICK shoots over the 1,000 mark, that's a sure sign it's going to rise even higher from there. Smart traders add to their long positions.
10. What does the TRIN measure?
11. When the TRIN reads under 1.0, which stocks are the most heavily traded, advancing or declining?
12. When the TRIN hovers in the ________ area, the bears are fighting the bulls for control.
13. For the best day trading and scalping setups on the long side, you want the TICK _________ and the TRIN ___________.
14. True or false? The S&P futures are one of the most widely used leading indicators in the trading world.
15. On a level II screen of a NYSE stock, which specific factor in time and sales prints points to probable price direction?
16. If you want to sell a NYSE stock fast, do you try to sell by splitting the bid and ask? Why?
17. When you're considering a scalping breakout, is it best to have only ISLD or ARCA on the inside bid? Or is it better to see MMs such as GSCO, MLCO, and NITE?
18. Why is locating the ax, and then watching his actions, important?
19. How do traders "make the spread"?
20. When you're selling a stock position, is it safest to sell into buying pressure or selling pressure?
21. What is the "trick" for making the most successful scalps and day trades?

ANSWERS

1. Between 9:50 and 10:10 a.m.
2. The next reversal, or shift, takes place about 10:25 a.m.
3. Very, very false. Experienced traders rarely trade during the noonday hours.
4. Many day traders refuse to hold overnight positions, and so exit all of their trades before the market closes.
5. Heavily traded stocks may sell off before the close because most day traders do not take home overnight positions.
6. Experienced traders wait for ten minutes or so before placing their first trade. The reason: Specialists and market makers control the opening with prices they dictate.
7. lagging, leading.
8. The TICK is the number of stocks ticking up (trading at one tick higher than the last trade) versus the number of stocks ticking down (trading at one tick lower than the last trade) on the New York Stock Exchange.
9. False. When the TICK rises over the +1,000 mark, a reversal is in the wind. Smart traders take some profits off the table.
10. Market volatility.
11. Advancing.
12. 1.0.
13. up, down.
14. True.
15. Size.
16. If you want to sell a NYSE fast, you don't place your order between the bid and ask. You put it in at the bid and accept that price. Otherwise, you may have to chase the price down to sell your stock and, in the process, lose money.
17. When you're scalping or day trading a breakout, when you enter, you want heavy hitters like GSCO, MLCO, PRUS, and NITE on the bid.
18. Watching the ax is important because he has considerable interest (for whatever the reasons—maybe a large institutional order) in the price movement of this stock. If the ax keeps jumping to the inside bid, that's a positive sign. If he moves down a few levels on the bid side and stays there, or rotates to the offer side for a prolonged period, that's a negative sign.
19. By buying on the bid and selling at the offer.
20. To get the best and safest price when you're exiting a scalp or day trade, sell into buying pressure.
21. To execute the most successful scalps and day trades, find a stock that's breaking out on two time frames—for example, a five-minute and a fifteen-minute—with ideal setups on both charts.

✦ ✦ ✦

CENTER POINT
The Power of Intuition

It is only with the heart that one can see rightly; what is essential is invisible to the eye.

—SAINT-EXUPERY

How do we define intuition, our elusive "sixth sense"? Webster's says it's "the power or facility of attaining to direct knowledge or cognition without evident rational thought and inference. Quick and ready insight."

Western civilization teaches and even worships rational, logical thought processes. To depend on a "knowingness" that exists beyond what we can see, smell, touch, hear, and feel is pooh-poohed as quackery. What a shame! For in our strict adherence to judging all situations using only logic and reason, we've ignored a precious intelligent gift inherent in each one of us.

Science now admits that human minds operate on two levels: the conscious or rational mind, and the subconscious or intuitive mind. The conscious mind acts like a computer. It processes our experiential data, judges using previous input, and calculates conclusions.

Our intuitive mind, however, when respected and tapped into, accesses a vast storehouse of wisdom and insight beyond our own personal boundaries. It analyzes this information and presents it to us beyond our own personal boundaries. It analyzes this information and presents it to us as guidance exactly when we need it. We refer to this "quick and ready insight" as "woman's intuition" or a "gut-feeling."

Could it be that these seemingly random appearances of superhuman awareness are in fact our thread of communication with the universal mind?

When we honor and nourish our intuitive sense and allow it to become a guiding force in our lives, our sense of self-trust expands exponentially. Feelings of true security and empowerment strengthen all areas of our lives.

How do you go about accessing and following your intuition? By quietly going inside yourself and acknowledging its presence. By asking questions of this wisest part of you, such as, "What do I need to know now? What shall I do in this situation?"

A feeling may emerge immediately that you can identify and act upon. If not, trust that the answer to your questions will soon appear in an idea, conversation, book, movie, or event. The more you practice, the easier and clearer the communications become.

Our inner intuitive power is always available to us. It knows how to overcome challenges and achieve goals. We need only ask, then trust!

✦ ✦ ✦

CHAPTER 9

Plan Your Trade and Trade Your Plan

Say you're driving to Yuma, Arizona, from Boston, and you've never been to Yuma before. You wouldn't head up the highway without consulting a map, would you?

If your appendix needs to be removed, your surgeon wouldn't (we hope) take scalpel in hand unless he first studied an X-ray, would he?

The builder who constructed your home didn't throw pipes and bricks into a pile. He followed the blueprints, right?

Professional athletes don't run onto the ballfield without an established game plan. And, as a successful trader, you wouldn't *dream* of laying thousands of dollars on the line without an exact trading plan. Right? Right!

You plan your trade, and trade your plan. Once you've opened a position, the way you manage the trade determines whether it makes money or loses money.

First, we'll look at a basic spreadsheet you fill in the minute you buy (or short) the stock. Then, you'll learn final criteria for entering long trades in all time frames. More important, you'll learn where to get out!

HOW TO DESIGN YOUR TRADING LOGS

Buying a stock is a walk in the park. But consistently exiting trades with a profit involves planning, skill, and discipline. In Chapter 4, we talked about trading with confidence and self-trust. Nothing promotes that terrific feeling like a well-thought-out trading plan.

A simple written plan for each trade is one of the best things you can do for yourself and your account. They stop you from fudging on the stop losses and urge you to take profits realistically.

I keep an informal worksheet when the trade is in progress and complete a trading log when I exit the position. Both are very simple. If you like, combine the two. I just don't like too many numbers and columns staring me in the face when the market goes bonkers and I'm searching for stop loss points.

I trade with a yellow legal pad at my elbow as my worksheet. The trading log, or spreadsheet, lies next to it. (Did you know the color yellow promotes better thinking in us humans? Yup. That's why legal pads are yellow!)

When I'm eyeing a trade, waiting for the perfect entry point, I jot down the stock symbol on my worksheet. Then I calculate my sell stop and jot it down the stop column. Once I enter the trade, I circle the stop price.

The circle drawn around my sell stop means that stop is law! If the stock makes new highs, I might raise that stop, but I never, ever lower it.

Will I concede that the "circle is law" rule means I'm playing head games with myself? Certainly! Does it matter what kinds of crazy methods I use to keep my losses small, as long as it works? Heck, no. And it shouldn't matter to you, either.

Statistics show that people who store their goals mentally accomplish little. Those who write their goals down on paper accomplish a high percentage.

Guess what? The same result occurs when, instead of storing your sell stop mentally, you *write it down*. I found early on, that when my stock started to drop, I easily justified lowering my mental stop to the next support level. When I wrote that stop down, seeing that number on paper supports the discipline to execute it.

Conclusion: Written stops, obeyed automatically, equal smaller losses. Smaller losses equal higher profits. Good trading rule to add to your list, don't you agree?

When I enter the trade, I add the entry price and number of shares to my yellow worksheet. If the trade is an intermediate or swing trade, I'll check the daily chart to see where the next area of resistance lies and write that down.

When the stock nears the resistance area, I watch it closely. If it falters and it's an intermediate-term trade, I may take partial profits. If it's a swing trade, I may take all profits. If the market's strong, though, and my stock shoots through the resistance to a new high, I'll keep the position. Whatever the case, with the resistance number right in front of me, if I'm busy with another trade, I can glance at it and remain aware of the stock's activity (Figure 9-1).

With day trades and swing trades, I keep their intraday charts in front of me, so I don't write down resistance areas.

Date	Symbol	Buy/short	#shares	Price	Stop	Next Sup/Res Area
5/21	LCOS	B	800	120 ½	119 3/8	R123

Figure 9-1

Sample of yellow pad worksheet

When I close the trade, I mark a big X through the stock symbol. I start a fresh yellow page each day, transferring any open trade information from the day before.

My trading log, or spreadsheet, is shown in Figure 9-2.

I allow three spaces on my log to record multiple trade exits. Say you buy 1,500 shares of Igloo Ice Cream at 27. Then you offer it out in 500-share lots as it rises, taking profits at 27 1/2, 27 7/8, and 28 3/8. Great tactic, safe profits, and if you design your spreadsheet with multiple exit rows, you have enough room to record each sale separately and the net price, or proceeds. (The net cost and proceeds listed here are shown minus a $20 commission for each trade.) The last column shows your net profit or loss.

Please keep an accurate trading log and check your broker's numbers against your own. Brokers make mistakes, too.

VIEWPOINT: TOPS DOWN VS. BOTTOMS UP

Ask any trader if he or she is a "tops down" or a "bottoms up" trader, and that person will earnestly try to convince you why he or she is right in their premise.

Tops down traders assess the entire scene before they leap. They're like airline pilots who refuse to lift their plane off the ground unless all conditions, including weather and equipment, operate perfectly.

Before placing a trade, a tops down trader: (1) considers overall market trend; (2) checks internal market indicators; (3) inspects a chart of the target stock's industry group, if possible; and (4) studies the stock's weekly, daily, and intraday charts. If signals align, the trader waits for a perfect entry point and enters the trade. If the signals are out of sync or negative, the trader waits for a better time.

A bottoms up trader looks at the stock's chart and might glance at fundamental information, but rarely worries about industry or market conditions. These traders insist a chart tells them all they need to know.

Sometimes bottoms up traders are right. I've witnessed gut-wrenching days when the Dow tumbled 300 points, and the Nasdaq dove 70, drowning the most stalwart of stocks and making me wonder whether I should give up trading and sell lipstick at Macy's. Even so, when market conditions were at their goriest, a

Date	Symbol	Buy/ short	# shares	Price	Net Cost	Exit Date	# shares	Price	Net Proceeds	Profit/loss
5/21	LCOS	B	500	120 ½	96,420.	5/21	300	122 ¾	36,805	
							~~300~~	~~124~~	~~37,180~~	2,645
							200	125 ½	25,080	

Figure 9-2

Sample of trading log spreadsheet

few stocks marched by on the ticker tape, up two, three, or more points, blithely ignoring the snarling bears wielding bloody machetes.

Please start as a tops down trader. You want every possible odd in your favor before you risk your money. Bottoms up traders take extremely high risks.

Our goal in putting the Dow, Nasdaq, industry indices, and market internals like the TICK, TRIN, and S&P futures on your monitor was to show you how even during the rosiest moments, a strong indicator like the S&P futures can take a sudden tumble and drag a majority of stocks with it.

Lots of trading books show you a chart with a candlestick poking through resistance. They point an arrow to the breakout candlestick and say cheerfully, "Buy the breakout." This book may give a similar suggestion, but when I say, "buy the breakout," or "sell the breakdown," from now on, I'll assume you'll enter that trade *from a tops down perspective.*

Couple the tops down trading criteria with common sense. Why enter an intermediate or swing trade (or any trade) on a day when the "Mother Market" is in a rotten mood and odds are good you'll get stopped out? Everybody knows—when Mama ain't happy, ain't nobody happy!

On the other hand, when you're already in an intermediate or swing position, if the S&P futures undergo a few intraday hiccups, you can ignore them as long as your stock doesn't hit your stop.

Here is my tops down checklist. It applies to all trading time frames except scalping plays. (Scalps are so brief, they need not fill all the criteria, except the market uptrend or downtrend.)

- Is the market in an uptrend or downtrend? Remember ye olde trader saying, "the trend is your friend." Trading with the overall market trend increases your odds of success.
- Is the Fed (Federal Reserve Board) due to meet in the next day or two, with possible interest rate tightening? (The market *hates* interest rate tightening. Simply put, it means corporations pay more for their business loans, so their earnings aren't as high.) If so, wait until after the results of the meeting to place longer-term trades.
- Is your target company coming out with earnings in the next few days? Please don't risk holding a stock, especially overnight, when its earnings are due out. Most companies announce earnings right after the closing bell. Sure, if the earnings are good, the stock may shoot up, but if earnings are negative, it could gap down the next morning. Also, when giants like Dell, or Microsoft, announce negative earnings, they take at least their own industry and sometimes the entire Nasdaq down with

them—otherwise known as a "tech wreck." Stay on top of the dates when giants' earnings announcements are due out.

- Check your target stock's EPS ranking in *Investor's Business Daily.* (I equate buying stocks with an EPS ranking over 90 to dabbing number 15 sunscreen on my face before I go out in the sun. Sure, I can still get burned. But the lotion increases my odds of emerging burn-free.) EPS rankings over 90 add a comforting, if not foolproof, safety net to the trade.
- If your stock is on the NYSE, check the Dow's trend on the day; do the same with the Nasdaq Composite if your target stock resides there. Market averages may influence stock behavior and direction.
- You already know to check the TICK, TRIN, and S&P futures to make sure all systems are go (TICK positive, TRIN under 1.0, futures in an uptrend).

If this procedure sounds tedious, worry not. With practice, you will evaluate all this in a matter of seconds!

GET RICH SLOW

If you're a brand-new trader, you'll hone your skills best and lose far less money by executing successful intermediate-term and swing trades first, then tackling day trading and scalping second. It goes back to learning how to walk before you can run.

Those who succeed in this business take one step, and "get good at it." Then they take the next step, and "get good at that." Place one intermediate-term trade at the proper entry point, and follow your plan. With a cool head and the grace of the market, you will make money! Once you've mastered intermediate-term trades, tackle swing trades. Then move to day trades, and finally scalps, if you wish. Get rich slow. Beats the heck out of getting poor fast!

MONEY-MAKING CHART PATTERNS FOR INTERMEDIATE-TERM TRADES

Now let's look at chart patterns and then criteria for placing a trade. We'll start with intermediate-term trades, and in the next chapter look at swing trades and day trades plays.

Please note: Study the following patterns carefully. They apply to all time frames.

When you buy a stock as an intermediate-term trade or short-term investment, you plan to hold it for a week or more. These stocks represent your core holdings. As I mentioned before, they make a nice pillow when your day trades and scalps bounce you around on a hard floor.

On intermediate trades, expect multiple points. In fact, I make it a game to see how high I can ride the uptrend before I get stopped out. For these longer-term trades, the closer to the leading or initial breakout you enter, the more upside you have ahead of you. Some stocks double in value!

First, let's quickly review the basics: Stock prices move in three directions, up, down, and sideways. As they advance though time, these moves create patterns on charts. These patterns have predictive value to traders.

Patterns are divided into two basic groups: continuation patterns and reversal patterns. Sideways moves create continuation patterns. Up and down moves form reversal patterns.

Continuation patterns cast pauses, or consolidations, in the stock's prevailing trend. You could say the stock is resting, or taking a break, as runners do between laps. After the consolidation, the stock breaks out, and the prior trend resumes. I know we've already covered break out (and breakdown) patterns, but bear with me. We're going to move in for a closer look.

Remember to differentiate between sideways moves so you know you are looking at consolidation, and not a whippy, choppy, congestion pattern. Stocks in congestion patterns have no clue where they are going.

Also, I've talked about stocks moving sideways, "trading in a range," moving back and forth in two- to three-day or more increments, moving between a high and low price area. Trading in a range is *not* consolidation. (If none of this sounds familiar to you, please review Chapter 6.)

As you recall, consolidation means a stock is moving sideways in a tight, orderly fashion. The following interactive demonstration will explain.

Please get up now, and go sit on your bed. Yes, you read correctly. Please go into your bedroom and sit on your bed. Are you sitting? Good. Notice how your weight compresses the bedsprings?

When a stock consolidates, trading in a string of narrow-range days, it has pressure from buyers, or support, pushing it up from below, just as your box spring supports your mattress. The stock also has pressure from sellers, or resistance, who push the price down from above, as your fanny applies pressure to your mattress springs.

Now, stand up. Excellent! When you lifted your weight and released the tension by standing, your mattress springs sprang back up, right? Sproing!!!

The tension builds in a consolidating stock until the sheer volume of either bulls or bears overpowers the other. At that point, it releases, or even explodes to the upside. You could say it springs into a breakout (in a downtrend, the stock breaks down). As we stated, after a stock consolidates, it usually resumes it's prevailing trend.

Common and trader-friendly continuation patterns are called lines, triangles, flags, and pennants. A continuation pattern acts as the "pause that refreshes." It allows the trending stock to rest by moving sideways or pulling back; then the stock continues moving in its current trend. Figure 9-3 shows line consolidations in a breakout (uptrend) and breakdown (downtrend).

The next pattern (Figure 9-4) is a form of consolidation that coils even more springlike. Depending on the book you're reading, you'll hear it called a triangle or wedge. You can call it a turnip, if you want to, as long as you recognize it when you see it!

It consists of a wide range bar, followed by tighter and tighter days. Stay on the lookout for this pattern, and when you see it forming, monitor it for a breakout. It produces awesome trades.

A pennant is a small symmetrical triangle, a bit more horizontal in shape (Figure 9-5). At its conclusion, the prevailing trend usually resumes. This is a ter-

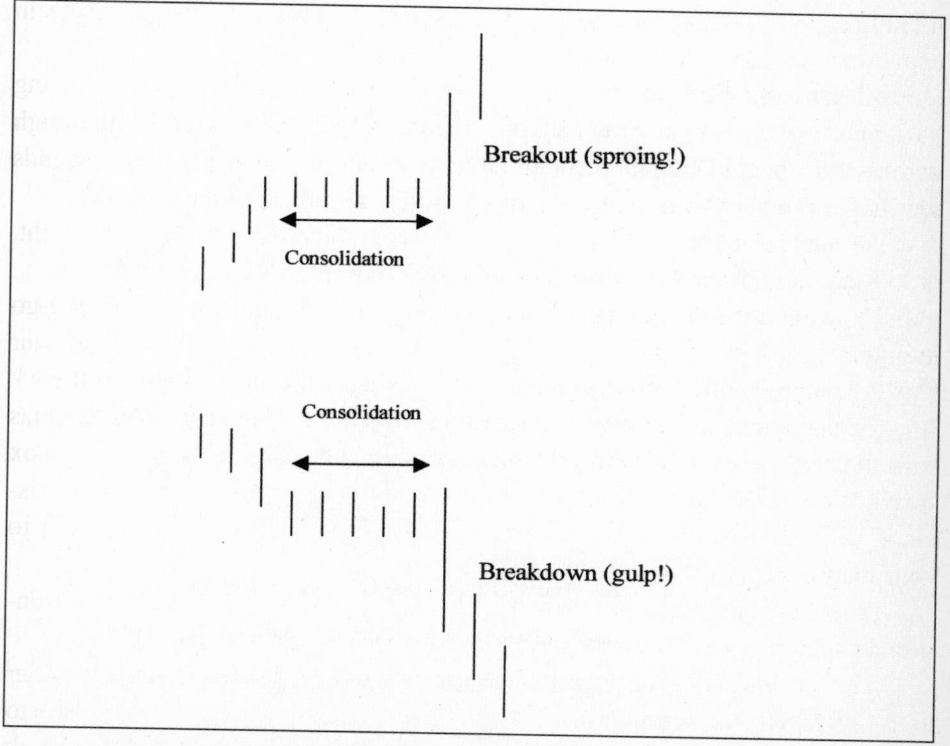

Figure 9-3
Line consolidation

rific long-term pattern, and it also forms nicely on intraday charts during the lunchtime moody blues. When it breaks out about 2:30 p.m., you buy the breakout.

A flag is when prices move sideways in a parallelogram, or rectangle shape, sloping against the strong, prevailing trend (Figure 9-6). Think: Pullback in uptrend, or rebound in downtrend.

As mentioned, patterns are either continuation or reversal. Reversal, as you know, means a trend changes direction. We'll talk about reversals as we progress. Please keep candlestick patterns in mind. Remember dogis? Evening star dogis and morning star dogis? How about hanging man and hammer? When you use these in combination with the preceding patterns, it increases your odds for success.

The following chart patterns, detailed in Figures 9-7 through 9-12, are reliable and easy to spot. Both the double-bottom and cup-with-a-handle are reversal patterns, with continuation patterns tacked on.

You can study additional books on charting and find many more to add to these. When you first start trading, though, you'd be smart to learn two or three patterns and learn them well. Keep it simple. You'll make more money and have more fun.

Double Bottom Pattern

This is one of my favorite patterns. It's one of the most powerful patterns for trading and works in various ways for all time frames. If you add two more legs in a V-shape, you get a triple bottom. Triple bottoms are rare, but even more powerful than the double-bottom.

A double-bottom formation looks like a W. For intermediate-term and swing trades, the pattern usually forms on daily charts when the stock is basing, or bottoming.

After the double-bottom completes its W shape, the stock should pull back slightly, then move in a sideways congestion pattern for a few days. The longer it consolidates, the more powerful the breakout should be (Figure 9-7).

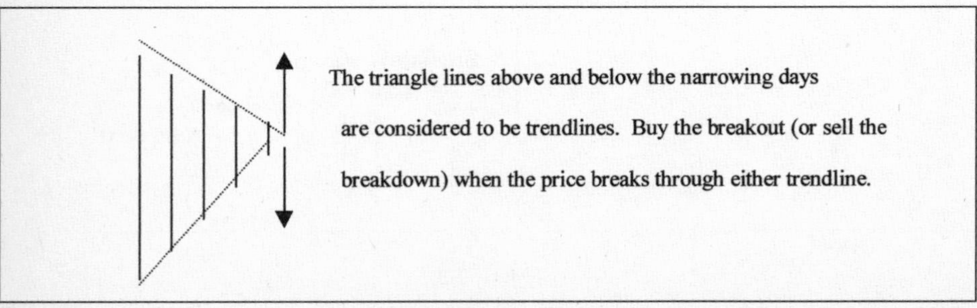

Figure 9-4

Symmetrical triangle. Bulls and bears are evenly balanced

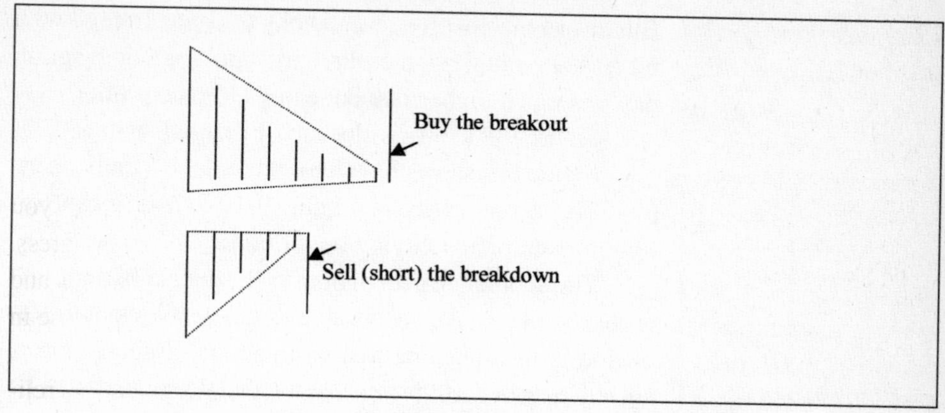

Figure 9-5
Pennant

When it breaks above the congestion, *on strong volume*, buy one-half your intended position when the stock trades 1/8 point over resistance.

During the initial pullback, monitor the volume. It should decrease.

On the *positive reversal* day that ends the pullback—on a daily chart, this would be a clear candlestick with a shaven head—check the stock a few minutes before the market closes. *Only if* the stock is trading near the high of the day, and the volume is strong, buy the second half of your position. If the stock doesn't close near its high on strong volume, don't buy.

For a safer entry point, wait until the following day, which I call a "nice spring day." When the stock trades 1/8 point over the reversal day's high, buy.

Very important: Pullbacks have to halt, reverse, then break out above their own resistance to be playable. Those breakout days I call "nice spring days" are the safe point to enter, once the stock trades 1/8 point over the reversal day.

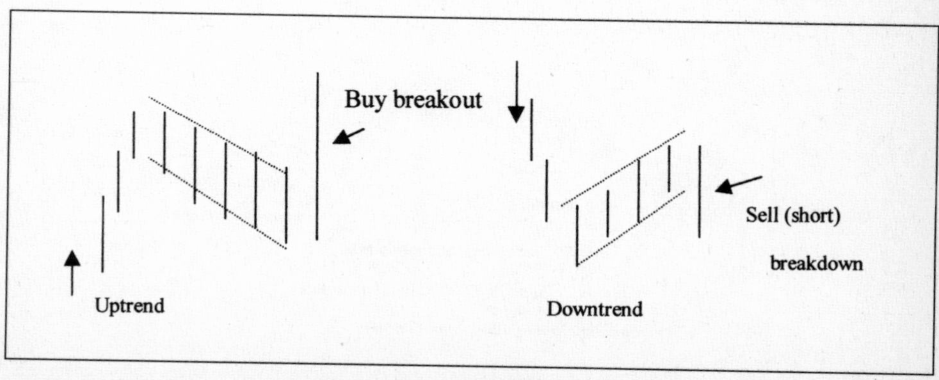

Figure 9-6
Flag

Hot Tip

If you're not sure which way a stock will head when it's finished consolidating, check where it closes at the end of each consolidation day. Closing near its high for the day is positive. Closing near its daily lows suggests it will break lower.

Buying on the positive reversal day (closing on high with increased volume)—the day prior to the nice spring day—is much higher risk but can yield nice profits.

Figure 9-8 shows a closeup of the pullback.

Figure 9-9 shows how it might look on a daily chart.

The actual chart in Figure 9-10 shows a double-bottom pattern and buying opportunities.

The double-top pattern mirrors the double-bottom, and is shaped like an M. As positive as the double-bottom formation is in foretelling a strong uptrend, a double-top is equally negative and warns that a lethal downtrend may be brewing. Short sellers can sell when a weak stock penetrates consolidation support. We'll talk about shorting techniques in Chapter 11 and show examples of double-top patterns.

Cup-with-a-Handle Pattern

William O'Neil, the founder of *Investor's Business Daily*, named this pattern. It crops up on all time frames and usually delivers wallet-fattening trades. For intermediate-term and swing trades, look for this pattern on daily charts when a stock is basing, or bottoming. It resembles a side view of a coffee cup with a rounded bottom and handle (Figure 9-11).

When the cup-with-a-handle is complete, a period of consolidation will assure the pending breakout rises on a full head of steam. Once the price breaks above resistance formed by the top of the cup, the handle, and consolidation, buy *on strong volume.* Buy one-half your position when the stock trades 1/8th point above resistance. Buy the second half when the pullback reverses into a nice spring day. For the safest entry, wait for the stock to trade 1/8th point above the high of the nice spring day.

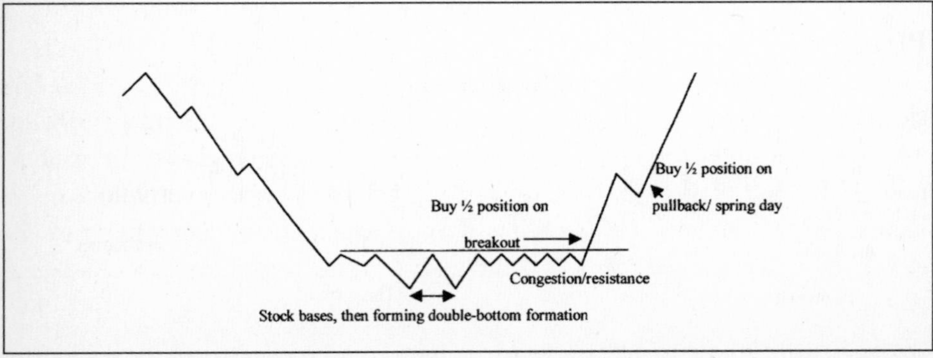

Figure 9-7
Double-bottom pattern

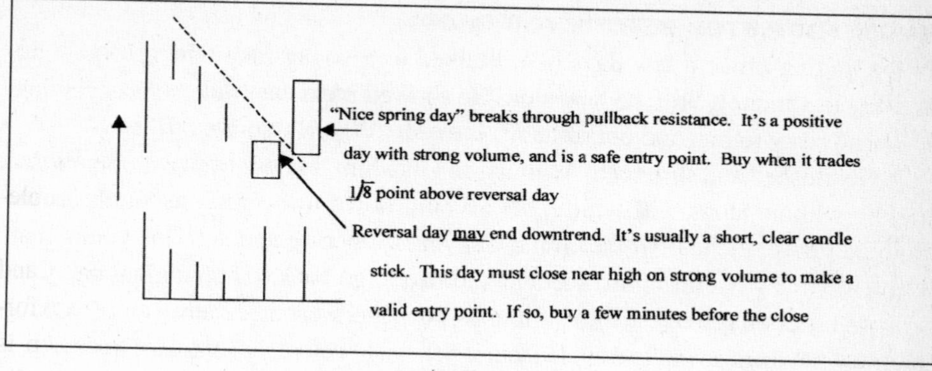

Figure 9-8

Closeup of pullback breakout with valid entry points

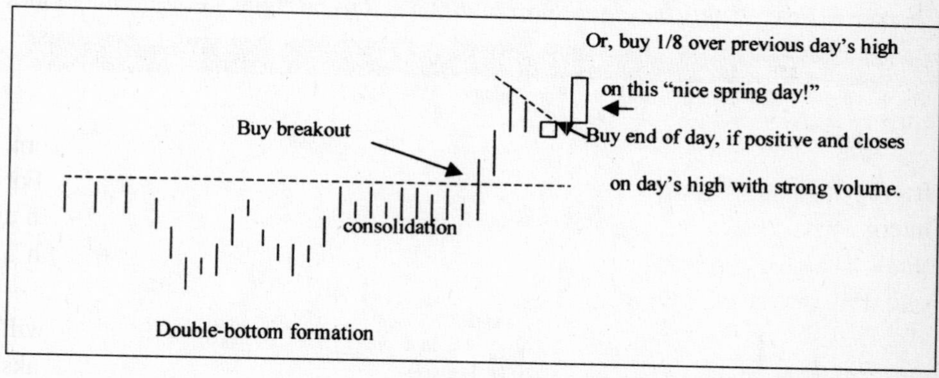

Figure 9-9

Double-bottom, breakout, and pullback/spring entry points

Figure 9-13 shows a sample chart showing a cup-with-a-handle, subsequent breakout and entry points.

Plain Vanilla Breakout

As you know, every stock has a different personality. When a stock wanders sideways in a basing formation, it may not cooperate by developing a cup-with-a-handle, or a double-bottom. It may just consolidate until good news or earnings propel it higher. It's still very playable. The tighter and more orderly the consolidation pattern, the lower risk play it will be. As long as it fits your tops down criteria and has strong volume, you can play it with the same criteria as discussed previously.

KNOW YOUR STOP BEFORE YOU SHOP!

In the trading office a few days ago, I talked to a young man whom I know has steadily lost money. Still, he hangs on. He showed me a day trade he was playing. It looked risky to me, and out of habit, I asked, "Where's your stop?"

He blushed and shrugged. As much as I like him, I know from experience that trading without stops will whittle his account down to bedrock as surely as the Colorado River etched out the Grand Canyon. (Sobering update: This young man eventually blew out his entire account and had to go back to his original day job.)

As I stressed before, the trick with stops, no matter what time frame you're working in, is to write them down (and circle them if you wish) before you enter the trade.

When the stock you're playing hits your stop—that's where the rubber meets the road! That's where you come face to face with the emotions we discussed in Chapter 4. Fear: *Is this the right thing to do?* Need to be right: *I don't have to sell*

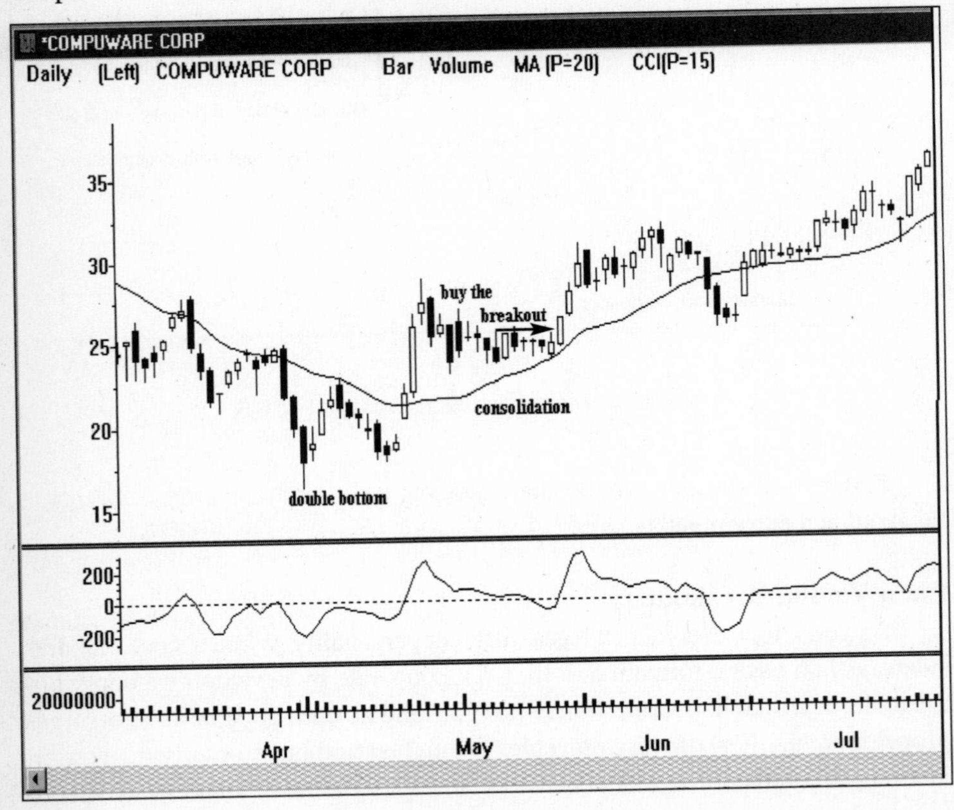

Figure 9-10

This daily chart of Compuware Corp. (CPWR) shows a classic double bottom pattern with subsequent consolidation. You would have bought the breakout over resistance on May 17, at about 24 7/8. Then CPWR rose to over 31 in the first week in June. At that point, CPWR broke support and gave a sell signal.

Chart Courtesy of *The Executioner*©

now. This is a good company. Greed: *If I sell now, I'll take a loss. I'll wait until it bounces.* Hope: *In just a minute, the futures will hit support. If I get lucky, they'll bounce, and this stock will recover with the futures.* Please shut your ears to these voices, no matter how insistent and tantalizing. When your stock hits its stop, execute your sell order swiftly, with no emotion. The old trader saying, "Your first loss is your smallest loss," speaks the truth.

Hot Tip

Many fund managers track stocks bouncing off their 50 MAs and their 200 MAs on daily charts. If you find a stock springing off its 50 MA at the same time it's breaking out, it should zoom to the moon!

For intermediate and swing trades, place your initial stop 1/4 point below the entry day's low. As the stock moves up, maintain a trailing stop by moving it up each day to 1/4 point under the day's low. If you're trading a NYSE stock, enter your sell stop order as soon as you place your trade. Adjust it each day. Then, if your stop is hit, you're automatically out of the trade.

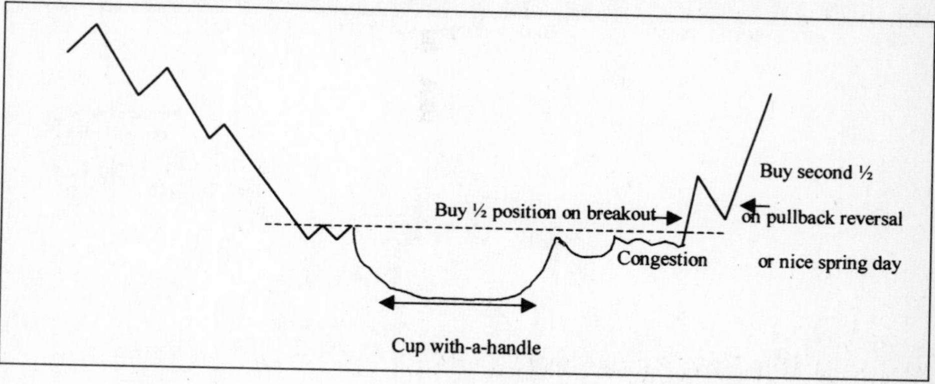

Figure 9-11

Cup-with-a-handle formation and subsequent breakout

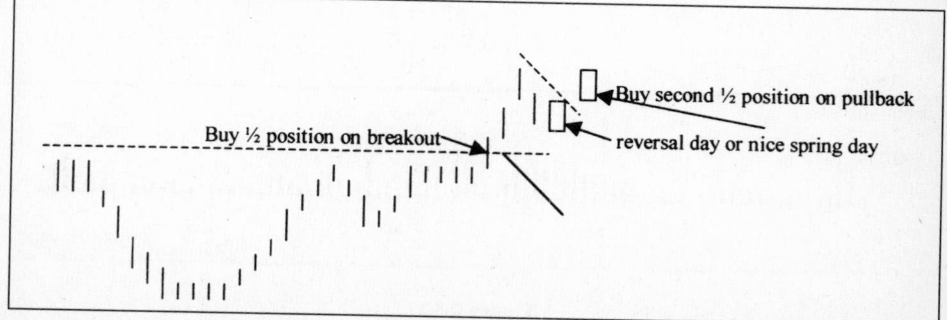

Figure 9-12

Cup-with-a-handle closeup

Here's an alternative stop method for intermediate-term trades: Adhere to the stop loss method just discussed until your stock's uptrend makes at least two pullbacks and two prominent highs. Then, connect the dots. Draw a trendline connecting the lows of the pullbacks, as you learned in Chapter 5. Next draw a line connecting the highs (Figure 9-15).

Place your stop loss 1/4 point below the bottom trendline channel. If and when your stock falls below the lower trendline channel, sell the position immediately. If it recovers, you can always buy it back. Otherwise, you've pocketed a tidy profit and can head for greener pastures.

Just as the bottom trendline acts as support, when you connect two or more highs with the top channel line, it defines the resistance area where the new highs of the uptrend will likely reverse. The next time your stock approaches this upper channel line, consider taking a portion of your profits. You can buy the shares back when it bounces off the lower trendline.

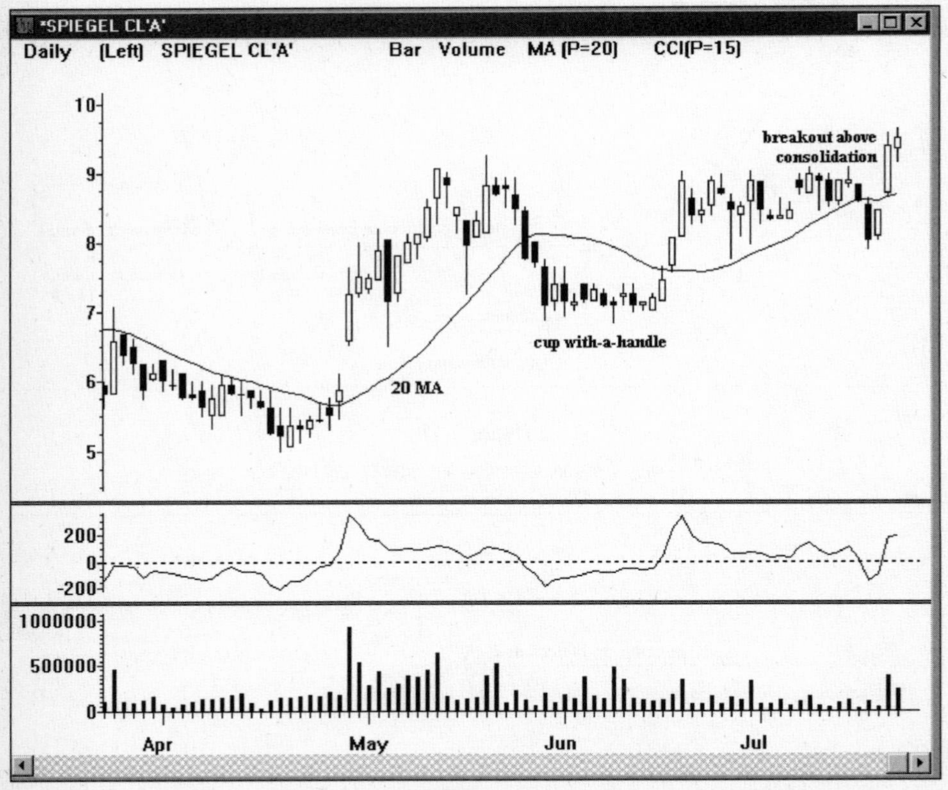

Figure 9-13

In this daily chart of Spiegel (SPGLA), you can see a cup-with-a-handle pattern, then consolidation. Since stocks don't always behave according to plan, on July 20, SPGLA dropped through resistance to 8. But on 7/22 it recovered nicely to break through resistance at 9, signaling a buy.

Chart Courtesy of *The Executioner*©

If you want to take profits early on—this is for intermediate *and* swing trades—wait until you have two points, then sell half or two-thirds of your position. If the stock continues to defy gravity, replace those shares at the pullback bounce.

Another profit point: If your stock gaps open to the upside two days in a row, grab your profits at the end of the second day. On the second gap open, shorts and sellers wait right around the corner, drooling and sharpening their claws. Few things are more irritating than riding a stock up to sky-high profits, then holding on while it drops back to your entry price, or worse, to your old stop.

Hot Tip

Ultra-strong stocks experiencing a breakout may rise three days in a row. At the end of the third day, the stock is considered overbought. By the fourth day, expect it to retrace, or pullback. Depending on market conditions and trading time frames, traders should consider taking half or all of their profits at the end of the third day.

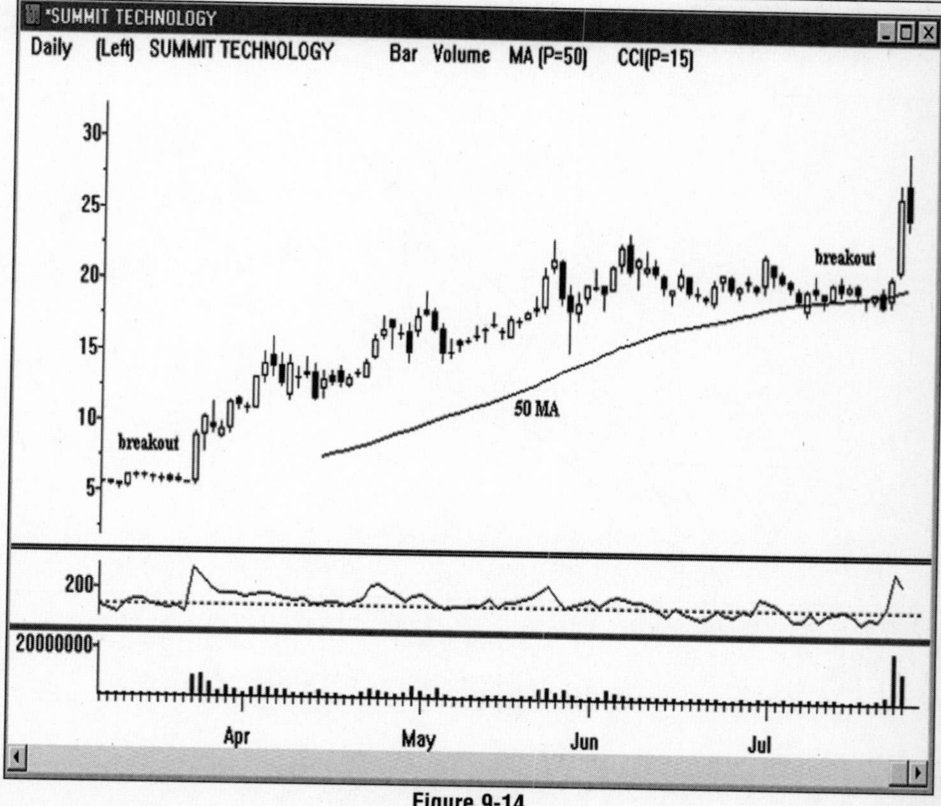

Figure 9-14

On this daily chart of Summit Technology (BEAM), the two "plain vanilla" breakouts are hard to miss. On both instances, high volume give BEAM a huge boost over consolidation areas for substantial breakouts. Can you see other pullbacks that were buyable?

Chart Courtesy of *The Executioner*©

Hot Tip

Now and then, when you jot down your stop *before* you enter, you realize the trade exceeds your risk–reward level. If it does—be thankful you looked before you leapt! Thousands of other stocks—with wiser risk levels—await your trading pleasure.

These stop loss points and exit strategies come with a caveat. If CNBC suddenly announces the world's coming to an end, or worse, the Fed chief appears on the screen and utters the words "inflation" or "tighten interest rates," forget your stops and exit plan. Don't wait for your stocks to crash and burn. Take profits fast. Then you can cluck sympathetically and hold the door open for the squealing slowpokes.

Okay, let's make a checklist to guide you through intermediate-term and swing trade entries. You may want to keep it next to your computer. Remember, before you run through the checklist and place your order, your tops down criteria should be satisfied. Be careful, and happy trading!

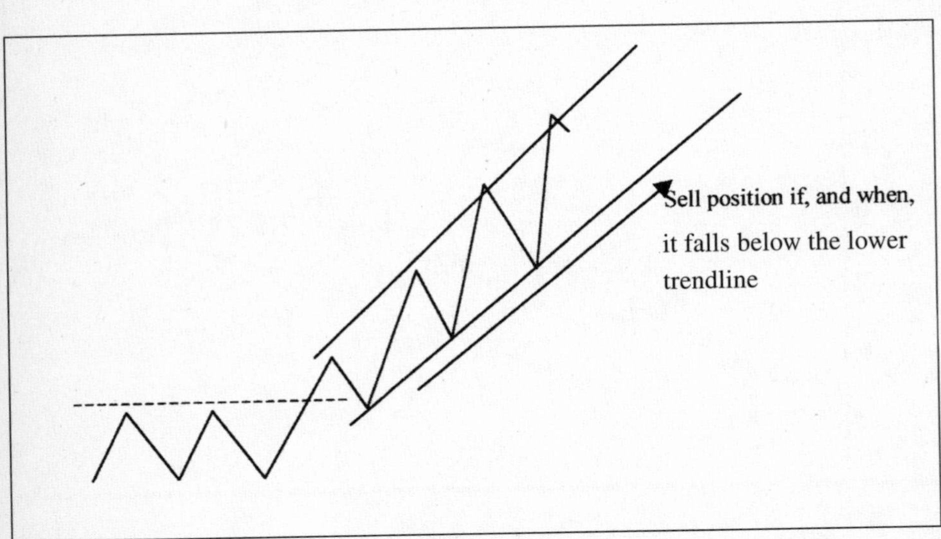

Figure 9-15
Channel lines

Buy Checklist: Intermediate-Term Trades

1. Either stock is in an uptrend (higher highs and higher lows) or it shows strong evidence of breaking out and initiating uptrend.
2. Stock is trading over its rising 50 and 200 MA (optimum: bouncing off of 20 MA).
3. MAs are layered in proper order (20 MA over 50 MA, and 50 MA 200 MA), not inverted.
4. High-volume day.
5. CCI is under zero median (optimum: CCI displays oversold reading).
6. Where's your stop loss? It should be 1/4 point below day's low. (If that's too far away, use the first thirty-minute high.) Jot down on worksheet.
7. Buy one-half position, 1/8 to 1/4 above initial breakout resistance.
8. Buy second half of position on pullback reversal day *only* if it's closing near day's high on strong volume.
9. Or buy second half of position when nice spring day trades 1/8 point above pullback reversal day's high.
10. Immediately write down entry point and circle stop loss on worksheet or trading log. If NYSE stock, enter a sell stop order.
11. After two days, raise stop to 1/4 point under each day's low. Or for intermediate-term trade, sell position if it falls more than 1/4 point below lower trendline.

In Chapter 10, we'll look at additional chart patterns and buy criteria that apply to both swing trades and day trades.

Does that make us swinging day traders? *Grin.*

QUIZ

1. Briefly describe the "tops down" criteria.
2. True or false? The best way to assure a successful trading career is to jump headfirst into scalping plays on your first trading day.
3. Price draws two types of patterns on a chart: ________ and ________.
4. A double-bottom formation on a stock chart looks like a big ____.
5. True or false? When the stock reaches the top of the last leg of the W, and breaks 1/8 point through resistance, it's a buy signal.
6. Every breakout, no matter the time frame, needs one common ingredient to assure its success. What is that ingredient?
7. How does a "trailing stop" work?
8. Describe an alternative stop loss plan for intermediate-term trades.
9. When you're ready to buy a stock, in which order, from the top down, should the moving averages line up? A: 200, 50, 20. B: 50, 20, 200. C: 20, 50, 200.
10. True or false? A wise trader buys 1/2 his or her position at the breakout and the other half at the pullback reversal or breakout.

ANSWERS

1. Before entering a trade, the "tops down" trader considers overall market trend; checks market internals; rates the stock's industry group; knows of no earnings or economic reports that would sour the trade; and studies the stock's weekly, daily, and intraday charts.
2. False, false, false, false, false, false.
3. continuation, reversal.
4. W.
5. False. Always wait until the stock finishes the W pattern, then pulls back and experiences multiday consolidation before buying the breakout.
6. Extremely strong volume.
7. After the stock is held two days, the trailing stop is adjusted each day to 1/4 point under day's low.
8. An alternative stop loss plan for intermediate-term trades is to exit the trade immediately if, and when, the stock breaks the trendline by a maximum of 1/4 point.
9. Always and forever, C: 20, 50, 200.
10. True.

✦ ✦ ✦

CENTER POINT

Practice Healthy Selfishness

Do you want to be a power in the world? Then be yourself. Be true to the highest within your soul and then allow yourself to be governed by no customs or conventionalities or arbitrary man-made rules that are not founded on principle.

—RALPH WALDO EMERSON

The quest for self-understanding takes time and effort. Those who believe time spent dwelling on inner growth is selfish, may want to reconsider.

Masters of the ages taught a dual path to self-enlightenment. To achieve balance and harmony in life, we must travel both the inner and outer path. Either one by itself will not take us where we need to go. The inner path is the most difficult—it's the path of self-knowledge, of consciousness development.

We've explored and transformed the frontiers of the outer world magnificently in the last two centuries. We've dissected the atom and delved into its secrets. We've invented wonderful gadgets, machines, and computer networks to modernize our lives. We've landed on the moon and sent cameras and telescopes to explore distant planets. Recently, the Hubbell telescope revealed that the universe is bigger and older than we thought it was. We humans find it quite acceptable to spend time investigating our outer world.

Yet, we've scarcely inquired into the other frontier—ourselves, our unique inner space.

Those who take time to reflect and study their emotions, beliefs, and potential, may appear selfish to those around them. Yet, is it truly selfish to spend time exploring your own inner self and communicate with that being? Is it selfish to learn your own power and discover your highest possibilities? Is it selfish to live fully, with a deep inner sense of meaning and satisfaction gained from self-knowledge? Is it virtuous to remain self-ignorant? To live in inner darkness, instead of inner light?

We cannot give to others what we, ourselves, don't have. We only forgive fully, once we've forgiven ourselves. We only love truly, when we love ourselves. We give authentic support, peace, and joy only when we bring them up from our own internal well of strength, serenity, and happiness.

We can share more good and enrich the lives of others if we spend time knowing, forgiving, and loving ourselves. Healthy selfishness not only improves our own experience, but it improves the world around us.

✦ ✦ ✦

CHAPTER 10

The Swinging Day Trader

Once upon a time, in the early 1100s, there lived an Italian man named Leonardo Fibonacci. Fibonacci, who was a mathematician, delighted in studying Egypt's Great Pyramid of Gizeh. In his studies, he discovered the unique relationship between a series of numbers. These numbers are now referred to as Fibonacci numbers.

The Fibonacci number sequence develops by starting at 1, and adding the previous number. The sum is the new number, for example: 0 + 1 = 1, 1 + 1 = 2, 2 + 1 = 3, 3 + 2 = 5, 5 + 3 = 8, 8 + 5 = 13. Therefore, Fibonacci numbers are 1, 2, 3, 5, 8, 13, 21, 34, 55, and so on.

For trivia buffs, a given Fibonacci number is about 1.62 times the preceding number. Also, any given number is nearly 0.62 times the following number.

Analysts anticipate changes in trends by using four popular Fibonacci studies: arcs, fans, retracements, and time zones. Those familiar with Elliott Wave Theory know wave counts adhere to the Fibonacci numbering sequence. Many level II systems offer Fibonacci studies as part of their charting features. Later, I will recommend you apply the retracements to your S&P futures chart.

"How fascinating," you mutter, scratching your head. "But what's that got to do with me making big bucks in the market?"

Plenty. Especially when it comes to the numbers 2, 3, and 5. From now on, we're going to keep the numbers 2, 3, and 5 uppermost in our minds. These numbers crop up repeatedly on charts, and we use them to help predict price movement.

Stocks in strong uptrends tend to move up three days, then down (pull back) for two. Or they move up for five days, then down three. In a downtrend, reverse those numbers. A probable pattern is three days down, two days up, or rebound. Or five days down, and three days up.

If a stock moves down for four days, you can bet it will continue into negative territory into the fifth day. (This always happens, except when it doesn't.)

In *Pit Bull*, renowned trader Martin Schwartz cites his Three Day Rule:

> Whenever a stock like a Microsoft or an Intel has had a large three-day move in one direction, you do not want to be buying on the third day, or selling [short] on the third day of a down move. That's a sucker play. Usually stocks will have big moves in three days. The first day the smart people are moving, the second day the semismart people are moving, and by the third day, the dunces have finally figured it out. This is an important rule. If the stock has bad news and it sells down, by the third day you may want to start looking to buy it because the bad news probably has been fully discounted.[1]

MONEY-MAKING SETUPS FOR SWING TRADES AND DAY TRADES

Picture a basketball, thrown with strong momentum, bouncing up a flight of stairs.

Some of the most successful swing and day trades you can enter entail catching stocks in powerful uptrends that are climbing their rising 20 MAs, or 50 MAs (the stairs) using the same motion as the basketball. They rise for two to five days (three is average), then pull back or consolidate for one to five days (two is common). As a savvy trader, you'll choose patterns that display orderly moves and that appear reasonably (!) predictable.

If tops down criteria is bullish, swing traders and day traders watch the pullback or consolidation for a nice spring day off the MA to enter. (Reverse this method to sell short.)

For swing trades, it's extremely profitable to discover the initial breakout and enter there, especially when it bounces off the 20 or 50 MA. If you miss the leading or initial breakout, don't worry. As long as the uptrend or downtrend stays intact, you can enter and exit at key points.

Once in the swing trade, if all goes well, you'll enjoy the ride for two to three days and should profit three points or more.

When you're day trading, you enter on the nice spring day that breaks above consolidation or pullback resistance as the stock bounces off the 20 or 50 MA. Plan to sell before the market closes and pocket one point or more.

When you're monitoring stocks with these criteria, especially keep the consolidation patterns and flag pattern in mind from Chapter 9. (All the patterns you learned are viable, however, in all time frames.) Then scan your daily charts for:

---

1 Schwartz, Martin. *Pit Bull.* (NY: Harper Business, 1998), p. 283.

- Strong stocks in an uptrend
- That are climbing up their 20 MA or 50 MA in an orderly fashion
- Have pulled back or consolidated for one or two days, and are nearing the supporting MA
- Have their CCI reads oversold, or at least under the zero median
- Have volume spiked on the last breakout, then decreased during pullback or consolidation

Don't forget to incorporate candlestick reversal patterns, such as dogis, morning star dogis, hammers, and bullish piercing patterns, shown in Chapter 5. They can either act as pullback reversal days at the conclusion of a consolidation or pullback, or predict that a nice spring day will soon appear.

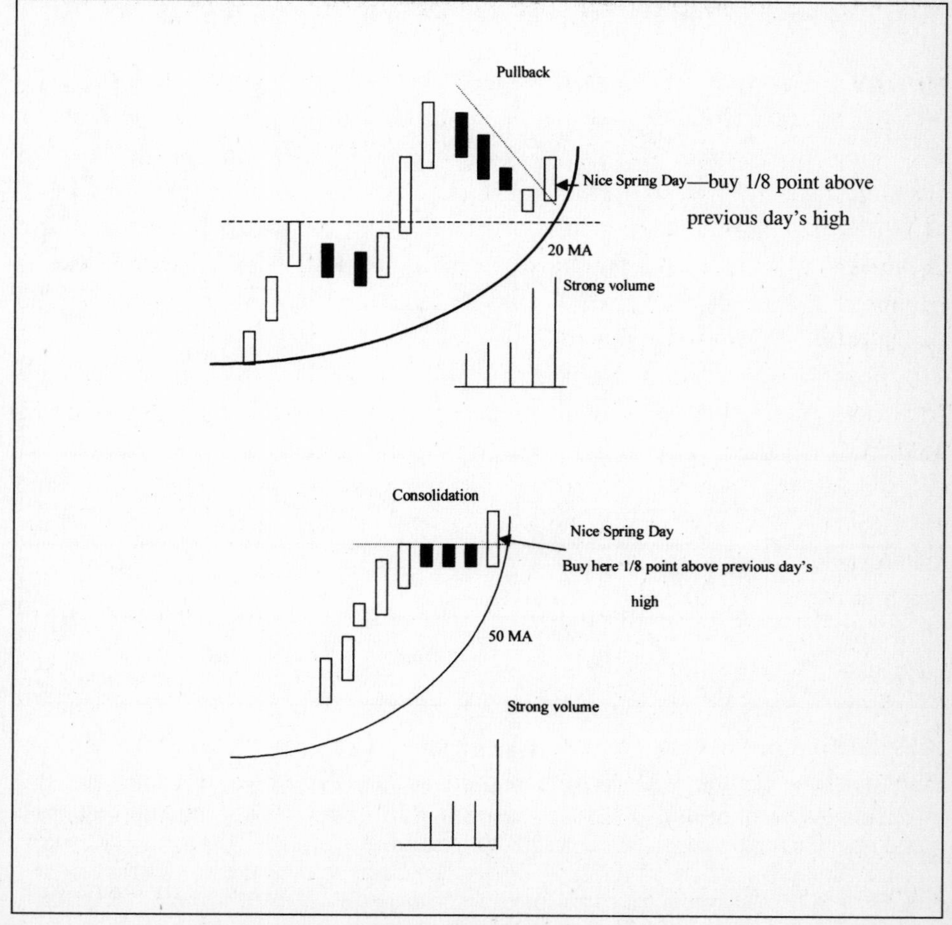

Figure 10-1
Pullback

For a quick review, these two "closeups" in Figure 10-1 show money-making setups you're looking for to enter a swing or day trade on the long side.

Learn to spot these two setups on daily charts. Then you can apply the tops down criteria to them, and enter at the proper points. Once in, adhere to your stops, and take safe profits. With these two setups alone, you can make a very nice living on swing trades and day trades.

Figures 10-2 through 10-4 show setups for swing trades and day trades using stocks in an uptrend, 20 and 50 MAs as support, and nice spring days on strong volume.

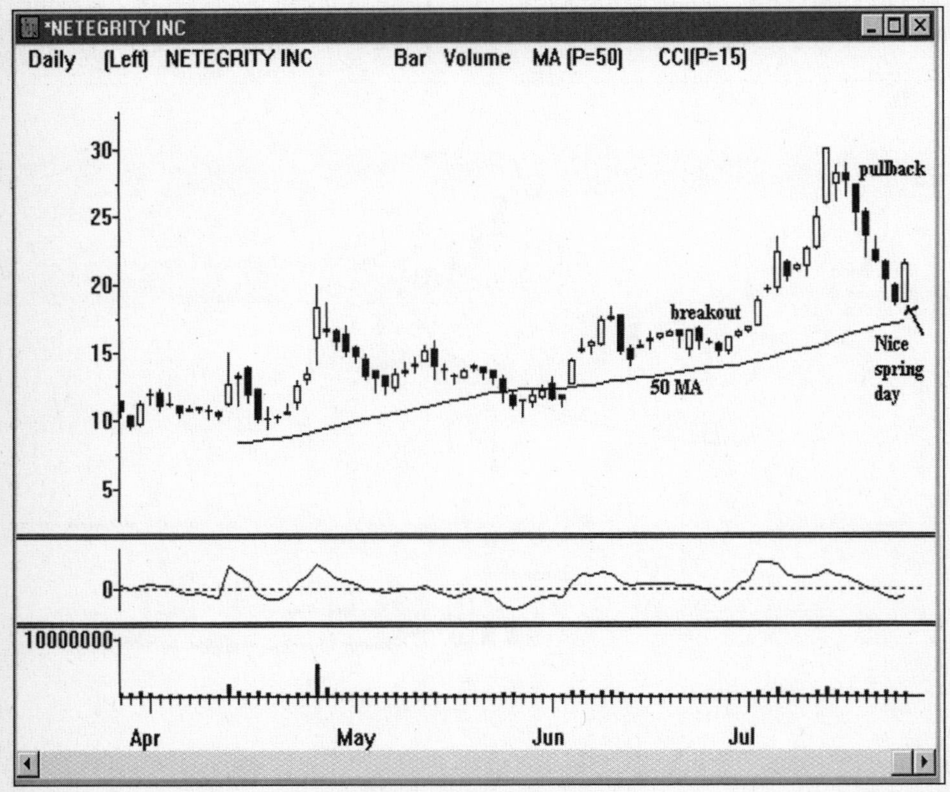

Figure 10-2

Opportunities for both swing trades and day trades exist on this daily chart of Netegrity Inc. (NETE). On July 2, NETE broke over consolidation of 16 7/8, signaling a buy at 18. Those who held on could have ridden the stock's perfect uptrend to a high of 30 on July 15. Notice that the stock rose smartly for the days of July 13–15, or three days up. Remember to exit a stock by the end of the third day up, since odds are it will pull back on the fourth. NETE pulled back to support and formed a bottoming bar on July 26, with a high of 20. On July 27, NETE rallied into a nice spring day. Swing traders and day traders would buy at 20 1/8.

Chart Courtesy of *The Executioner*©

GAP OPENINGS: HOW TO MANAGE THEM

Stocks gap open when they open higher or lower than the previous day's close. We say they "gap up," or "gap down."

Say Terrific Truck Lines closed Friday evening at 52 1/4. It opens Monday morning at 53. The 3/4 point difference in price might mean overnight traders or weekend traders (trading on Instinet) bid it up, or that the specialist opened it higher Monday morning because of order demand.

This gap up can be either a blessing or a curse. Those who owned Terrific Truck Lines at the close Friday evening woke up 3/4 point richer Monday morning. If you didn't own Terrific, but had been waiting for days for the perfect setup to enter long, the gap up negates your entry at the open Monday morning.

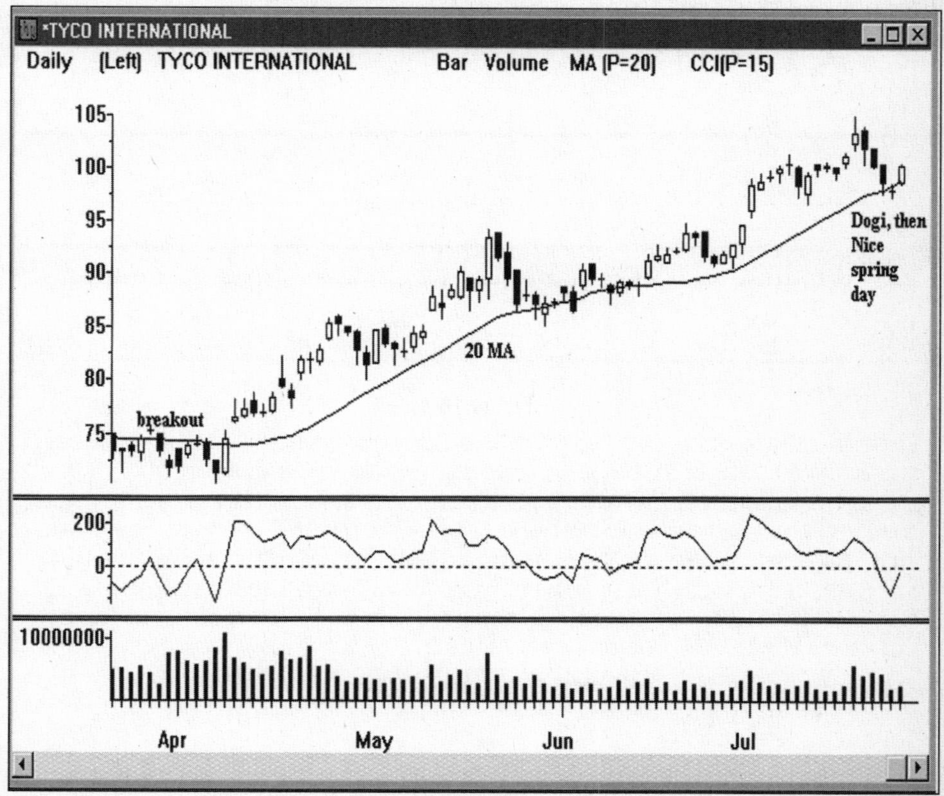

Figure 10-3

On this daily chart of Tyco International (TYC), note how the stock broke out after basing in March and April. On April 12, it broke out on high volume to rise over consolidation and the 20 MA, which also acts as resistance. TYC then rode its 20 MA from that breakout at 78 all the way to over 103. On July 26, the three-day pullback ended in a dogi, a good sign. Sure enough, July 27 produces a nice spring day. Day traders and swing traders would buy when the nice spring day trades 1/8 point over the high of the bottoming bar, or dogi, which was 98 1/2.

Chart Courtesy of *The Executioner*©

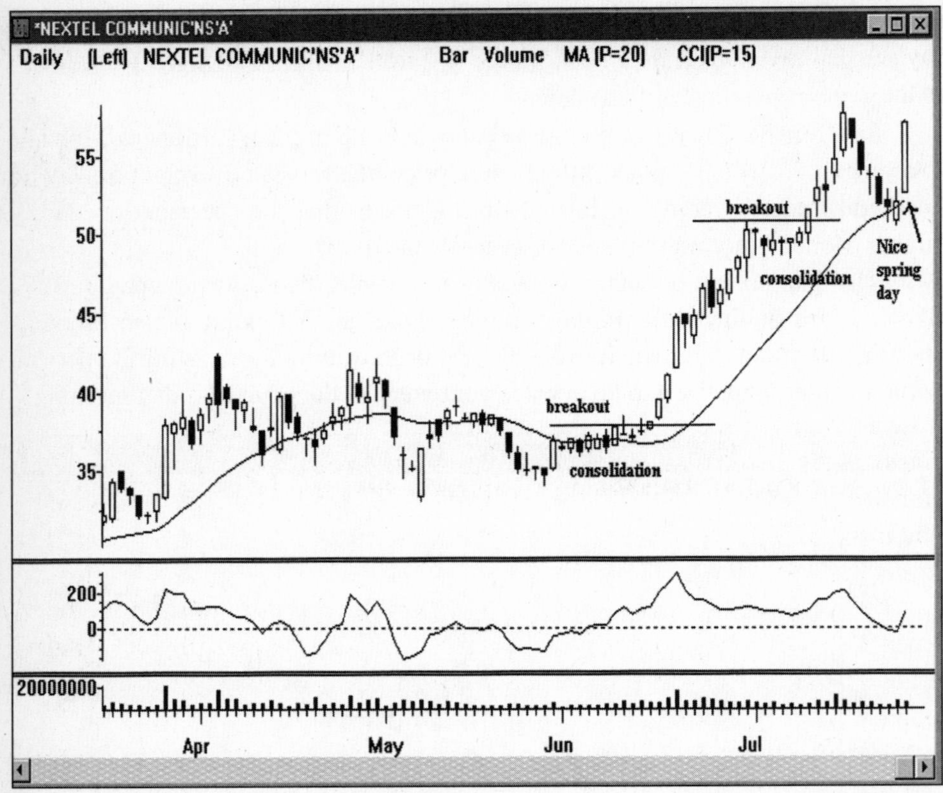

Figure 10-4

Consolidations and pullbacks on this uptrend in Nextel Communications (NXTL) make it a profitable play more than once. On June 16, NXTL broke over consolidation with high volume while sitting on its 20 MA, all good signs. It was a buy at 37 7/8. Intermediate-term traders could have held on easily until the stock topped at 58 in mid-July. Swing traders could have held for "3 days up" for a nice profit, and day traders would have made a point if the stock were bought in the morning and held until the end of the day. Finally, on July 19, NXTL started a pullback to the 20 MA in the form of five days down. On July 26, a positive bottoming bar right at the 20 MA halted the downtrend. The next day made a nice spring day by shooting past the previous day's high and was a buy at 52 7/8. It closed on the high of the day at 57, with all traders smiling!

Chart Courtesy of *The Executioner*©

When a stock gaps open more than 3/8 point from its prior close, it's best to wait for it to pull back, then enter when it trades over the first thirty-minute high. Pristine.com introduced me to the thirty-minute gap rule. It's a great technique to ensure that you avoid the initial risk of stocks that gap open, yet still gain the rewards.

Example: Terrific Truck Lines closed at 52 1/4 Friday evening. It opened at 53 on Monday morning. It might shoot up from there to 53 1/2, then—typical of most stocks that gap open—drop like a stone in the first ten minutes of trading to 52 3/8. It waffles around through the 9:50–10:10 reversal period. At 10:15, it starts showing life again. When it breaks above 53 1/2 (it formed resistance there, at the day's high), then buy it. The odds indicate it's strong, and will continue up as long as the market stays in positive territory.

Some stocks that gap open, however, use all of their energy during that first price spike, then tank and stay down for the day. That's why you avoid buying them at the open. Trader terminology for stocks that gap open, then fall—either for minutes or for a more extended period is "gap and crap."

Hot Tip

When a stock gaps up, trades above its opening price all day, then closes near the daily high, odds suggest that stock will move even higher. These odds improve if the stock closes over the previous day's high.

The reverse happens when stocks gap down at the open. This scene is one that causes sweaty palms for those holding long overnight positions. Terrific Truck Lines closes at 52 1/4 Friday evening, then opens Monday morning at 51 3/4. Typically, it will slide down a bit more, maybe to previous support at 51 1/2. Then the buyers come in. Maybe.

If they do, within minutes Terrific will recover. Just how much it recovers depends on market conditions, and the reason Terrific slid in the first place. Trader terminology for stocks that gap down, then recover at least some lost ground is "gap and snap."

If you're waiting to short a weak stock, and it gaps down, use the Pristine thirty-minute gap rule exactly as before—only upside down. Wait until the stock breaks below its thirty-minute low before shorting.

Since day traders look for faster profits than swing traders do, day traders who want to assume a higher risk can change the thirty-minute rule to a five-minute rule. That means, when a stock gaps open more than 3/8 point, wait until it passes its first five-minute high before buying.

TO HOLD OVERNIGHT, OR NOT TO HOLD OVERNIGHT

Swing trades necessitate holding positions overnight. The preceding explanation of gaps explains why holding stocks overnight make you yell with happiness, or pass out cold.

No clear-cut answer exists. Though one camp of day traders would sooner stop breathing than hold a position overnight, other traders make fine profits on overnight plays. I belong to the latter camp. I've made money buying a stock five minutes before the market closes, and selling it the next morning, just seconds after it opens.

Dissenters argue that holding a stock overnight exposes you to large risks. They're right. Occasionally, Mr. Big Shot Analyst from Mega-

Brokerage has to earn his pay by downgrading stocks. Of course, if Mr. Shot downgrades a stock you're holding after the market closes for the day, the stock will likely open much lower the following morning. It may, or may not, recover for a while. If you own a large position in that downgrade, the loss can dent your account, big time.

Hot Tip

These days, some moon-shot stocks gap open up five or more points on the day. To enter these high-risk stocks, please protect your principal and apply the thirty-minute rule without fail. It takes *lots* of buying energy for a stock to open halfway to the moon. Many times they gap open, fly even higher, then fall like bricks for half—or all—of their gains. Trading smart means you look, but don't touch, until the stock stabilizes. Remember an earlier lesson: Things that go straight up tend to come straight down!

One of my friends, bless him, has a flair for buying stocks that get downgraded overnight. I somehow escape with profits that far outweigh my occasional calamities.

Here's how I do it: I only take home stocks:

- In a sector engaged in a healthy uptrend.
- That represent the top pick of the industry.
- The overall market is powerful and making new highs.
- At the close, the TICK is high, and the TRIN is under zero.
- The stock, itself, is in a strong uptrend and *is closing at its high for the day.*
- It is the stock's first or second day up from a breakout, *definitely not the third day!*
- I take home small positions—300, 400 shares at the most. If any of these so much as breathes funny before the close, I either get out or reduce my size to 200 shares.
- When the stock gaps open the next morning, I sell *immediately*.

If you cultivate the knack of holding overnight and making money consistently, go for it. If you attract downgrades like ugly on an ape, leave overnights alone.

NITTY-GRITTY STUFF ABOUT DAY TRADING

Early on, I suggested opening two trading accounts, one for intermediate-term and swing trades, the other for day trades and scalping plays. I also stressed that if you did decide to manage dual accounts, it's very important to keep the two entirely separate.

Goals and risk–reward ratios differ between intermediate-term and swing trades, day trades and scalping plays. Time frames dictate those ratios. Intermediate-term and swing trades lean a teeny bit more toward investment objectives. With them, you focus on the individual stock's progress. If Mother Market slips into a rotten mood for a morning or afternoon, as long as your stop loss isn't violated, the trade remains in tact.

Day trades and scalps, however, use such abbreviated time frames that traders must factor in every nuance of market mood into open positions. When Mother Market frowns for even ten minutes, she causes many stocks to join her bad mood—whence came the saying, "When Mama ain't happy, ain't nobody happy."

In a swing trade, a 3/4 point drop may not cause concern. In a day trade, it could easily stop you out. In a swing or intermediate trade, your stop loss might be 1 to 1 1/4 points away from your entry point. In a day trade, your initial stop-loss perches a mere 1/4 point from your entry point.

Rewards match risks. In intermediate and swing trades, you look for multiple points. In day trades, you may offer out at a point, or even a half-point profit. Scalping plays grab 1/4 point, or even less.

Day trading demands keen concentration. You focus intensely on chart patterns while analyzing level II action. In your spare time you monitor market internals.

The heightened pace of day trading encourages many new traders to "over-trade." They jump at any stock with a decent setup and end up stockpiling five or more stocks into their account. Suddenly, they're in Panic City.

Hey, I've been there. When I started trading, I crammed eight or nine positions into my account at one time. Trouble was, I couldn't keep track of all of them. Instead of trading to trade well, I became a troubleshooter. And I shot holes in my principal at the same time!

Overtrading also leads novice traders to forget they should cherry pick the best trades. Instead, they jump in and out of positions far more than necessary, stockpiling losses, slippage, and commissions.

Experienced traders take their time. They pluck out the best trades and ignore the others. They also stop trading when odds go against them.

Hot Tip

Remember, when stocks gap open higher than they closed the prior evening, specialists and market makers have to take the other side of the trade. They must short those rocketing stocks. How do you think they cover those shorts at a profit? By waiting until the steam escapes from the initial run up, then bringing the stocks down—hard.

DOES YOUR STOCK WALTZ OR JITTERBUG?

When you start day trading, a good preventive against heart attacks is to learn your target stock's *modus operandi.* That way, when it pulls back two points, you won't faint at your desk.

Some traders call these intraday pullbacks "wiggles." Wiggles, shown in Figure 10-5, represent profit taking, just as they do on daily charts.

You recall that each stock has its own personality. Medium to mild-mannered stocks average 1/2 to 3/4 point intraday pullbacks on average. More volatile issues fall back a point, even more.

When you target a day trading stock, survey its intraday price action for the previous three days. Figure the average wiggle. Knowing what to expect helps you from exiting positions too soon. It also tells you how much room to give your trailing stop.

WHERE TO PLACE YOUR STOP LOSSES (SELL STOPS)

When you day trade, never take more than a 3/8 point loss.

After entering a trade, place your initial stop loss 1/4 point below your entry point (1/4 point above if you're shorting). Once the stock moves up the designated wiggle, or pullback amount, *plus* your 1/4 point stop loss, then you adjust your stop loss up to the current price on the day, minus the wiggle.

Example: Your entry point on Simple Software (SS) is 20 1/4. You place your initial stop loss—written down and circled—at 20. You've designated SS's wiggle to be 5/8 point. When (if) SS climbs to 20 7/8, you move your stop to 20 1/4 or 5/8 point below the current price on the day. Each time the stock makes a new high on the day, adjust your stop loss to 5/8 point under it. Now, if you see SS closing in on resistance, pay attention. Depending on the overall strength of the market,

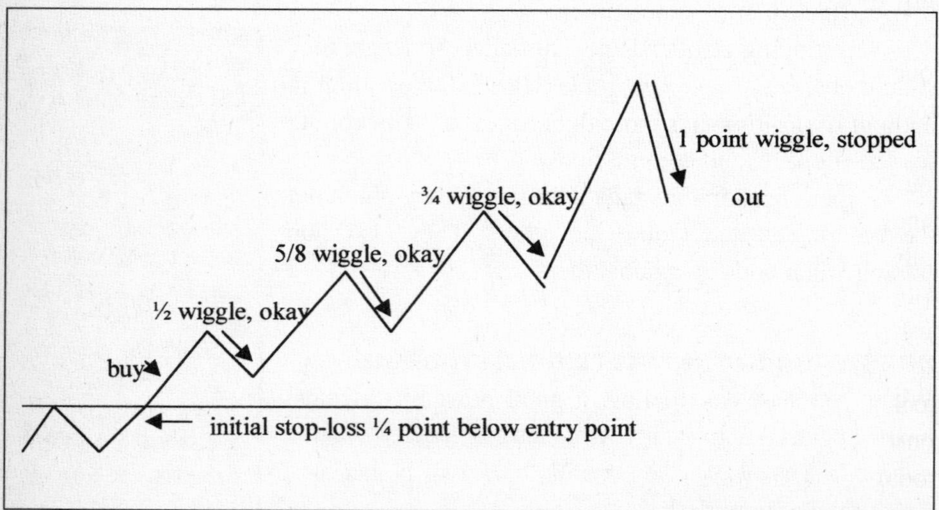

Figure 10-5

Do the wiggle

and whether or not your stock is losing steam, you may want to take some or all of your profits instead of waiting to be stopped, or "wiggled," out.

Reminder: Once you establish your stop loss, you may move it up, but never down!

DAY TRADING SETUPS: WHAT YOU'RE LOOKING FOR

Earlier in the chapter, you noted the illustrations and learned the two classic setups for entering swing trades and day trades: breakouts from consolidation and pullbacks. As I mentioned then, if you trade using only these two setups, complete with MA, volume, CCI, and tops down criteria, you can make a nice living.

For those who want more adventure, we'll look at additional setups and fine-tune the entries. You'll want to couple these setups with level II momentum, if possible.

Start by doing your homework. Analyze the previous day's (yesterday's) price movement; it tells you where and when you can or should not enter (in the case of a gap opening) today.

A given for the following plays: Moving averages play a role in day trading as well as longer-term plays. I use the 20 MA and 200 MA on all intraday charts because they're powerful support and resistance. (For scalping, I use one-minute charts and add the 10 MA.) As you develop your own trading style, you may add a 100 MA and/or 50 MA. Please remember to enter long plays only if the stock's current price rides above the 20 MA and 200 MA.

The 200 MA is particularly powerful on fifteen-minute charts. If it's above your stock's current price and ready to bop it on the head, it exerts pressure as the stock tries to rise.

Imagine you're in a swimming pool, treading water. A bully standing next to you keeps dunking you. Everytime you come up to gasp for air, he plunks his beefy hand on your head and pushes you back underwater. The 200 MA resembles the bully. Yes, of course, the stock can rise through the 200 MA and keep climbing. It's just that playing stocks with the 200 MA overhead (other MAs overhead can also push a stock under water) reduces your odds of winning.

Buy Setup 1 (Figure 10-6): Find a target stock in an uptrend (trading with a stock's long-term trend increases your odds of success) that has pulled back or consolidated for two to three days. Yesterday (assuming you'll enter the trade "today"), it shot up in a wide trading range, opening at or near its low, and closing at, or near, its high. Today, it opens slightly (within 3/8 of a point) above yesterday's high. Within the first few minutes of trading, it drops to quickly fill the gap. It reverses and moves back up, breaking the morning's high. Buy the breakout. Take profits in a reasonable period of time. This works best if captured in the first hour of trading.

Look for stocks that close at the high of the day. These make the strongest setups for the next day's buying strategy.

The five-minute charts shown in Figures 10-7 and 10-8 show Buy Setup 1 in action.

Buy Setup 2 (Figure 10-8): Once again, find a target stock in an uptrend. Yesterday was positive, and the stock closed near its high. A consolidation pattern into the close is preferable. Today, the stock opened at yesterday's close and broke out fast. During the 9:50 reversal period, the stock drops to a low on the day and holds on previously established support. A narrow-range bar, called a "bottoming bar," shows the mini-downtrend may reverse (at 10:00 a.m., or shortly after). Then, a nice spring candlestick confirms the reversal. Buy when the spring candlestick rises 1/8 point over bottoming bar. Place stop 1/4 point under entry point.

The charts shown in Figure 10-9 show Buy Setup 2 in action.

Buy Setup 3 (Figure 10-10): Again, target a stock in an uptrend. Yesterday was a sideways or positive day. Today, it gaps open much higher than yesterday's close—maybe a point or so (no more than two points). Wait until the stock trades for 30 minutes, then breaks above the high of the day. Buy the breakout and place your stop 1/4 point below entry. Consider taking profits by 11:00, or before the midday blues start around 11:20 a.m.

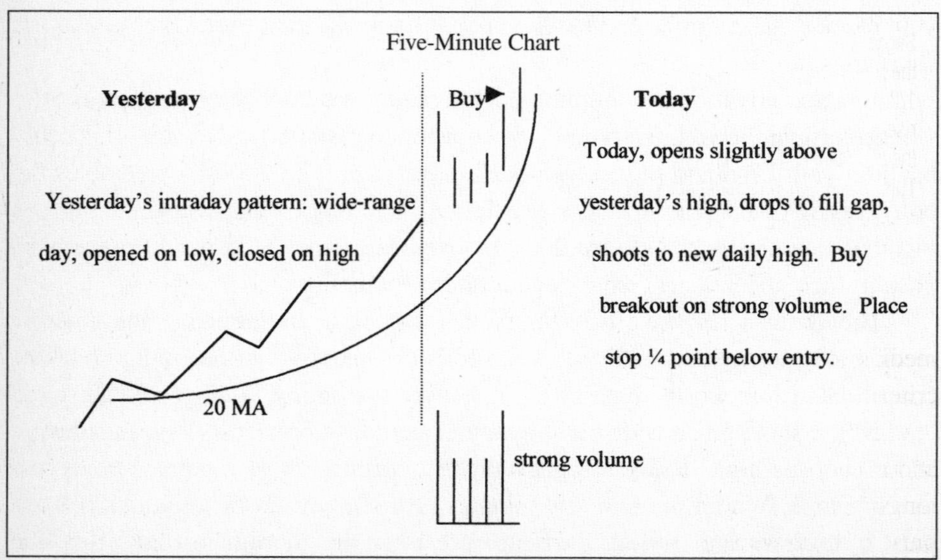

Figure 10-6

Buy Setup 1

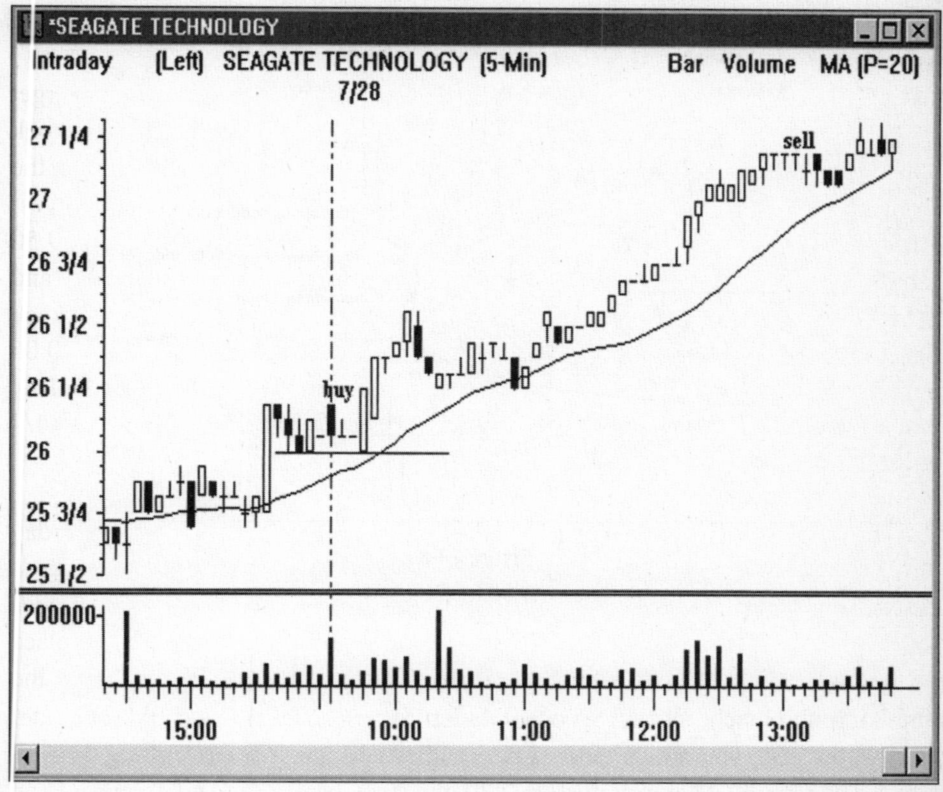

Figure 10-7

Segate Technology (SEG) follows Setup 1 perfectly. On July 27, it had a key reversal day (opening below the previous day's open and closing above the previous day's close). On July 28, it gapped open at 26 3/16, 1/8 point above the prior day's close. It quickly reversed to fill the gap, then bounced back up at 9:45 to rise over the day's high. Therefore, the stock was a buy at 26 1/4. Note how the stock rose right through the 9:50 reversal period. When stocks do that, they typically pull back around 10:25, just as SEG did here. This setup calls for quick profit-taking; SEG could have been sold before lunch at 27.

Chart Courtesy of *The Executioner*©

In all these plays, remember it's best if the CCI gives a reading of below the median zero, on the daily chart, yesterday and/or today. Of course, the tops down criteria is a given. Right? Right.

Buy Setup 4 (Figure 10-12): I love this one! It's easy to spot, trader-friendly, and reliable as long as Mother Market is in a cheerful mood. Target a stock in a long-range uptrend. Yesterday isn't that important, but today is. Today the stock must be positive and moving up into the midday blues. It reaches a high between 10:30 and noon, then pulls back, preferably to no more than 1/2 point or so from the high. (Use the stock's wiggle average to determine this.) The stock "straight

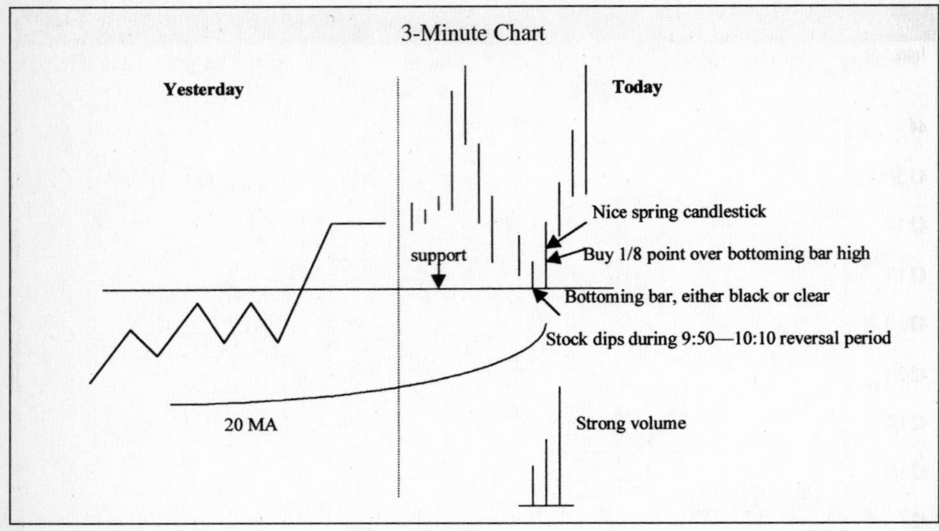

Figure 10-8
Buy Setup 2

lines" through lunch, forming a consolidation pattern so level you could set a ruler on it. After 1:30, you notice most of the candlesticks are positive, closing on their highs. Then, *voila!* At approximately 2:30, the stock breaks out and climbs into an afternoon rally. This one usually delivers nice take-home pay.

Figure 10-13 shows Buy Setup 4 in action.

DAY TRADING LISTED STOCKS WITH LEVEL II

You can make money on intermediate-term and swing trading using only an online broker. To profit safely and consistently on day trades and scalping plays, you're best using a level II system.

Since you've graduated from boot camp, you already have a good idea of how level II works. Let's brush up a bit.

On the NYSE, regional exchanges are listed under the bid and ask columns, with the lot sizes they're bidding for, and offering out for sale. The regional exchanges and their symbols are:

BSE—Boston Stock Exchange
NAS—Nasdaq Stock Exchange
CSE—Chicago Stock Exchange

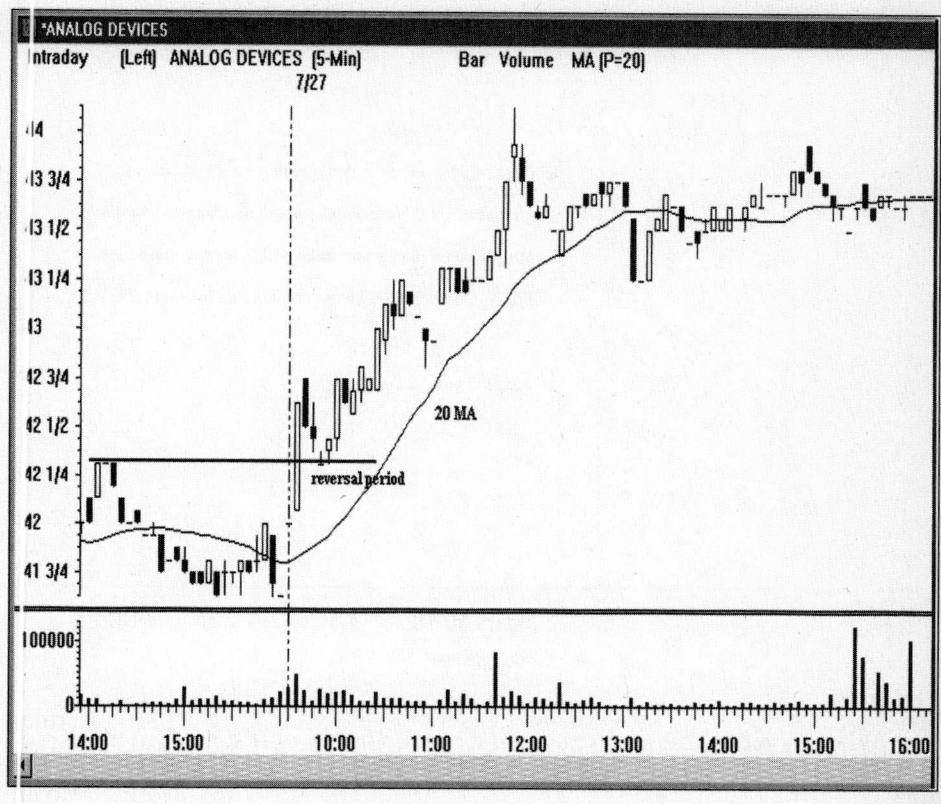

Figure 10-9

On this five-minute chart of Analog Devices (ADI), the stock opened very slightly higher than the previous day's close (3/8 point). As per Setup 2 critieria, it ran up fast, then dropped to previous day's support during the 9:50 reversal period. It shoots right back up to the day's high, consolidates for a few minutes, then breaks out at 10;25. It became a buy at 42 7/8. ADI topped out at 44 at 11:50, right before lunch. After such a good run, it's a good time to sell.

Chart Courtesy of *The Executioner*©

PHS—Philadelphia Stock Exchange
PSE—Pacific Stock Exchange
CIN—Cincinnati Stock Exchange
NYE—New York Stock Exchange

On the NYSE, it is the specialists' responsibility is to keep a fair and orderly market in their stock. Therefore, the spread on listed stocks usually stays narrower (less of a point spread) and more consistent than do the spreads of some wilder Nasdaq stocks. (The Nasdaq market makers have the same responsibility, but sometimes it slips their minds!)

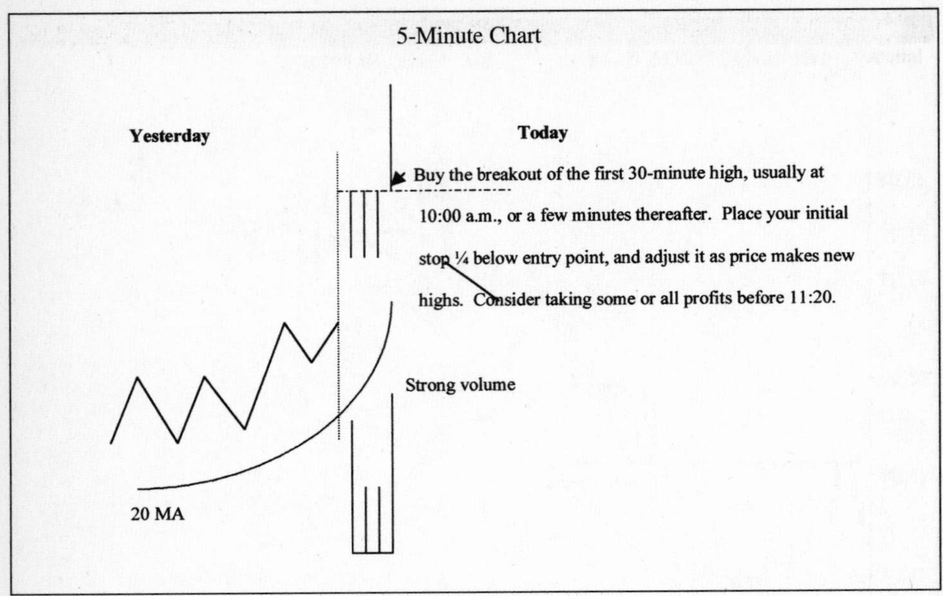

Figure 10-10

Buy Setup 3

When targeting a stock to trade, first check your level II screen for the spread between the inside bid and ask. *As a rule, trade stocks with a spread of 1/8 point, or less.*

Why do you only trade stocks with 1/8 point spread or less? To narrow your risk. Say the stock is trading at the offer, and not between the bid and offer. That means buyers will pay the inside offer, or market price for the stock. You'll see that on your time and sales screen.

Before you buy, you think: *Since I have to pay full price for the stock, if it turns against me the second I enter, where can I get out?* You look at the inside bid. The most desirable spread is 1/16 point, or a "teeny." Also acceptable is 1/8 point. But when the spread widens to 1/4 point or more, your risk increases. That means if the stock turns against you as soon as you buy the stock—and it happens—you'll have to sell at the market, or the bid (if you're lucky!). Your immediate loss, not including commissions, is 1/4 point. That's unacceptable.

Next, with listed stocks, always trade toward size. Watch your time and sales screen. Are the biggest lot sizes traded on upticks or downticks? Buys or sells? Please go with the trend here. If institutions or big investors are buying, that's what you do also. If they're shorting, and your setup agrees with that, go for it.

Figure 10-11

On this five-minute chart of PMC-Sierra Inc. (PMCS), at least two perfect day trading setups exist. PMCS gapped open 2 points. The trader waits until it trades over the thirty-minute high of 74 1/2 established at 9:35 a.m. At 10 a.m., right on time, PMCS shoots over the high and is a buy at 74 5/8. Depending on market conditions, many traders will sell before lunch in the 77 area. Notice how PMCS pulls back during the lunchtime moody blues. The trader will start monitoring volume about 1:30. When the stock shoots over consolidation at 2 p.m., it's a buy signal at 77 3/8. When it starts tiring around 3 p.m., the trader would sell at 79.

Chart Courtesy of *The Executioner*©

Once again, if the stock is trending up quietly, and the spread is 1/8 point, you can attempt to split the bid and ask by placing a limit order for the price between. Example: Igloo Ice Cream is trading 27 1/4 × 27 1/8. Issue your limit buy order at 27 3/16.

You can sell the same way as long as the stock is trading quietly, and you are not rushing to get out.

Use the time and sales screen as a storytelling device. Say you enter a stock on an early morning breakout. It consolidates into the 9:50 reversal, then at 10:25,

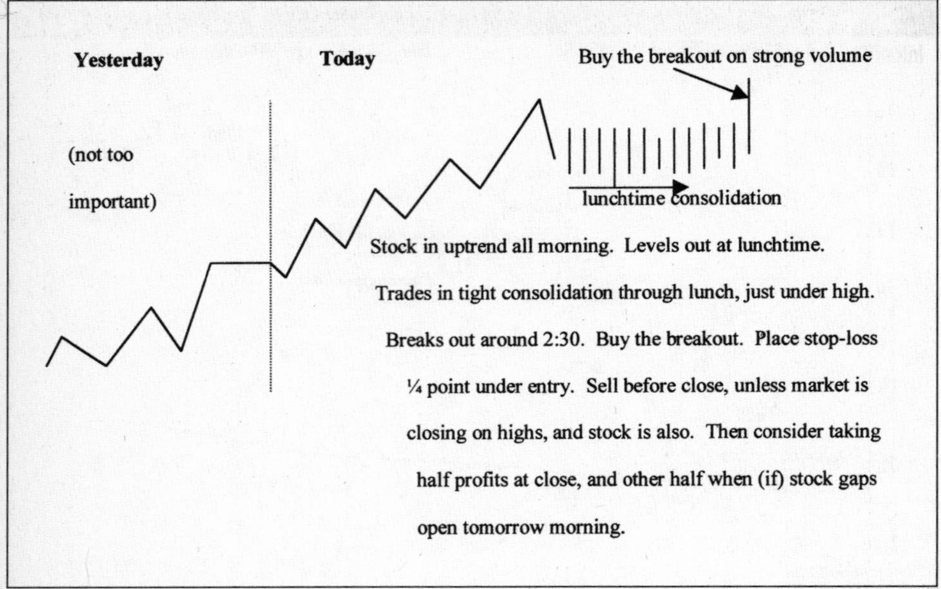

Figure 10-12
Buy Setup 4

it breaks through resistance again. If your time and sales shows you strong volume streaming into the buy side, you can add to your position.

Conversely, say you're in a profitable trade, and the price is nearing resistance. The market is overbought, and you see size being sold on the time and sales screen. Consider taking profits.

DAY TRADING NASDAQ STOCKS WITH LEVEL II

As you recall, Nasdaq level II screens display market makers at the bid and ask at each price level. Time and sales adjoins the market maker screen.

Once again, *before* you enter a day trade, check the spread between the inside bid and ask. One-eighth point or less is ideal.

A large percentage of Nasdaq stocks trade with a spread of 1/4 point or more. You must be extremely careful when you trade these stocks. What happens if the market turns against you before your stock has a chance to rise? Ouch!

Say you buy at the offer at 20 1/4, and the bid is 20. If the stock suddenly heads south, the market makers will drop the bid even lower. Prices get trampled as traders rush for the door, and you may suffer acute pain trying to get out of your position. As a wise novice trader, you may decide to avoid these stocks until you gain more experience.

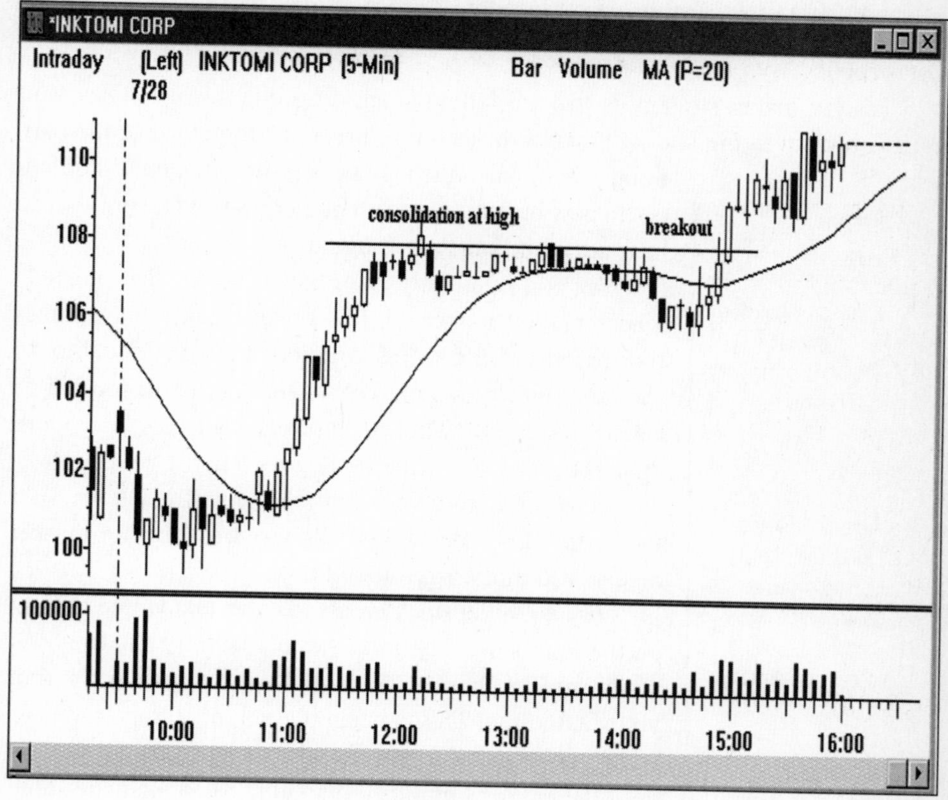

Figure 10-13

On this five-minute chart of Inktomi Corp. (INKT), the stock first breaks out about 11 a.m. and runs from 102 to almost 108. It then consolidates at its high all the way through lunch, then dips (with the S&P futures). At 2:50, INKT reverses and shoots through resistance, signaling a buy at 108. Day traders could sell before the close at 108.

Chart Courtesy of *The Executioner*©

After you note the spread, check your stock's level II screen for the depth of the market makers. Again, your foremost thought is to protect your principal. How many market makers line up at the inside bid to buy your stock if you want out fast? The longer the line of market makers at either the bid or the offer, the more "depth" it has.

When a breakout or breakdown occurs in an active stock, thousands of traders issue orders simultaneously. Market makers are swamped. And they play it for all it's worth!

When Igloo Ice Cream starts melting, and you and a zillion other traders issue sell orders at one time, those orders eat through one or two market makers on the bid in an ohnosecond. Market makers on the level below the inside bid will likely evaporate. That leaves the level below that—which will also disappear. Catastrophe City.

Market maker strategy is to let a falling stock drop like a stone. They wait until you're sweating and will take a rock-bottom price just to get rid of the darn thing. Then, when the selling pressure lifts, they'll dole it out to new buyers at a much higher price. (The noises you hear are market makers laughing.)

Hot Tip

With some hot-dog stocks, the spread between the bid and ask fluctuates wildly. One second it's 1/8 point, the next it widens to 5/8. It may even expand to a full point! Please don't jump into these stocks unless you're well aware of the acute risks involved. Getting in is always easier than getting out!

A good rule: Only enter day trades on the long side where market makers in line on the inside bid number four or more. Ditto with shorting on the offer side. Stocks showing one or two market makers on the inside bid or ask are too "thin." Thin price levels easily cost you more than 1/4 point loss if the trade goes against you.

In short, before you commit to entering a trade, first locate the door. If the spread's too wide, or the market makers too thin, forgettaboudit!

If your target stock is safe to enter, and you're trading on the long side, look to see who's buying. Are the 800-pound gorillas lined up on the bid side? 'Cause that's what you want to see! This concept plays a more important role when you're scalping, but it's wise to get a running start on *any* trade you enter. So check the bid for significant market makers. Here are some with their representative symbols.

Bear Stearns BEST
B.T. Alex Brown BTSC
Cantor Fitzgerald CANT
Donaldson, Lufkin & Jenrette DLJP
Gruntal & Co. GRUN
Goldman Sachs GSCO (lead gorilla)
Hembrecht & Quist HMQT
Herzog, Heine, Geduld HRZG
J.P. Morgan Securities JPMS
Knight/Trimark NITE
Lehman Brothers LEHM
Mayer & Schweitzer MASH
Merrill Lynch MLCO
Montgomery Securities MONT
Morgan Stanley MSCO
Paine Webber PWJC
Prudential Securities PRUS
Salomon Smith Barney SBSH
Spear, Leeds & Kellogg SLKC
Troster Singer Corp. TSCO

In Chapter 9, I mentioned the differences between market makers and ECNs. Obviously, the market makers in the list are big brokers or dealers who serve not only individual investors, but large institutional investors, including mutual funds and insurance companies.

Electronic communications networks (ECNs) display and handle orders from traders like you and me. They have no vested interest in the movement of the stock. They're electronic go-betweens. So unless an ECN waits at the bid with an oversize order of 3,000 shares or more, discount them as real buying or selling power.

Here is a list of some ECNs:

Bloomberg BTRD
Instinet Corp. INCA
Island Corp. ISLD
Spear, Leeds & Kellogg REDI
Terra Nova Trading LLC TNTO
Attain ATTN
Brass Utility LLC, BRUT

When you want to day trade on the long side, the ideal scenario is to find movers and shakers like GSCO, PRUS, MLCO, or MASH on the bid. Icing on the cake is to see big guys like these "lifting," or disappearing off of the ask, or offer. That means they're selling and leaving, not hanging around with big lots to get rid of.

If you *do* see a big guy hanging on the offer for a long time, and jillions of buys marching by on time of sales at his offer price, it means he's constantly "refreshing." He pretends as if he only has 1,000 or 2,000 shares to sell, but in fact he's got a large order to get rid of. Every time he fills an order from traders like us, he refreshes his position with more shares to sell. When you see this taking place, beware. If the inside offer stays at one price, and orders don't eat through the supply, the stock may stall. This is even more important when you're scalping since you intend to make profits in a matter of seconds or minutes.

Another dandy trick market makers play I call the MM fake-out. Instinet (INCA) services many institutional orders. Say you see GSCO, generally regarded as the lead gorilla, on the bid of your target stock. You naturally think: *Oh, boy, if GSCO's on the bid buying, this stock's gonna fly.* What you don't know is that INCA, who's sitting on the offer, may be selling a large order for GSCO. The stock could soon tank! How do you see through this ploy?

You don't. That's why you enter trades only where as many odds as possible are on your side. That's why you adhere to all stops. That's why you take profits sensibly.

The level II screens shown in Figures 10-14 through 10-19 will help you gain a better understanding of level II fundamentals.

SOES TRADING ON LEVEL II

Okay, we've scaled the mountain of criteria needed to enter a good trade. Now, if you're trading with a level II order entry system, you have to choose *how* you want to buy it.

One method of placing your order is with Nasdaq's proprietary system, called SOES. SOES is the acronym for Small Order Entry System. The Nasdaq implemented SOES after the October 1987 stock market crash. During the crash, many market makers avoided their phones. Brokers calling with customer orders (com-

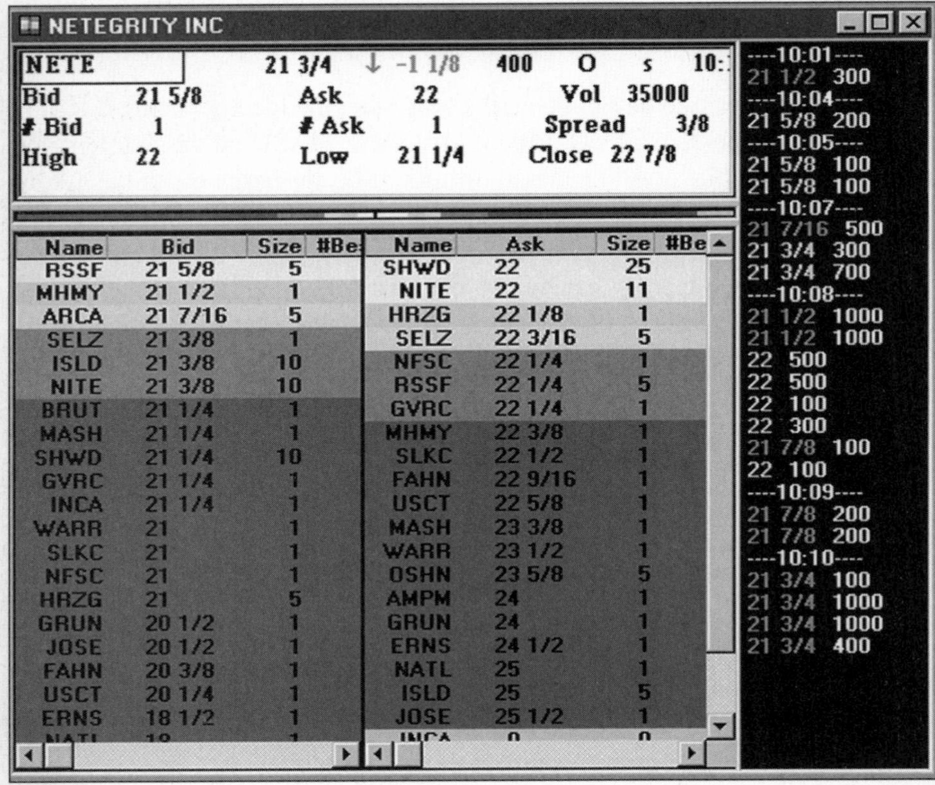

Figure 10-14

On this level II screen of Netegrity Inc. (NETE), note the wide spread, 3/8 point, between the inside bid and ask. A market maker, RSSF, wants to buy 500 shares on the bid at 21 5/8. On the offer, SHWD and NITE want to sell 3,600 shares at 22. If you buy on the offer, and the stock immediately turns against you, there are only 500 shares on the bid between you and the next bid down at 21 1/2. That's worse than it looks because MHMY wants to buy only 100 shares. The next level down in 21 7/16, at 500 shares. Then you go to the only level with depth, which is 21 3/8. Conclusion: If you buy on the offer at 22, and things get hairy, odds are you'll have to sell at 21 3/8 to get out. And 5/8 point is too much to lose on a day trade! This is called risk–reward ratio—and here the risk is too high for the reward!

Level II Screen Courtesy of *The Executioner*©

puterized trading wasn't as widespread then as it is now) couldn't get through, and the orders went unexecuted.

SOES is an execution vehicle developed for individual investors and traders. It provides liquidity by allowing the public direct access to the Nasdaq and its market makers who advertise to buy or sell Nasdaq issues at specified prices. After its inception, it mushroomed into a popular vehicle for day traders.

If a market maker places himself on the level II list (your market maker screen), he automatically becomes eligible for executions sent to him on Nasdaq's SOES system from traders like you and me. The automatic executions force him to accept orders at the price he advertises. He can refresh the bid or ask and restate

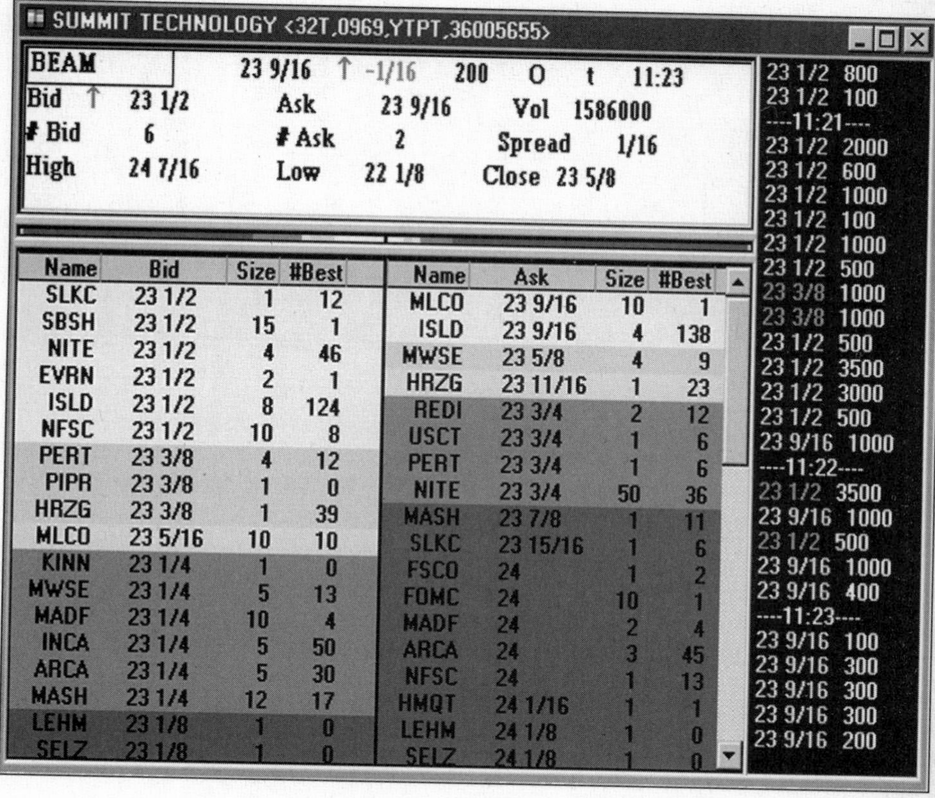

Figure 10-15

On this level II screen of Summit Technology (BEAM), you can see the spread between the bid and ask is 1/8 point. That is the maximum spread you want to play. If you buy on the offer, there is enough depth on the bid to beat a hasty exit with only 1/8 point loss. Since there are five market makers and an ECN (ISLD) on the bid, displaying decent size, you can assume for the moment that if market internals cooperate, BEAM will rise.

Level II Screen Courtesy of *The Executioner*©

APPLIED MATERIALS <32T,0969,YTPT,36005655>

AMAT	72 3/4	↑ -2 7/16	900	O	t	12:56
Bid ↑	72 11/16	Ask	72 13/16	Vol	4167900	
# Bid	4	# Ask	5	Spread	1/8	
High	75 1/8	Low	72 5/16	Close	75 3/16	

Name	Bid	Size	#Best	Name	Ask	Size	#Best
RSSF	72 11/16	1	13	FBCO	72 13/16	3	9
INCA	72 11/16	10	140	BRUT	72 13/16	2	13
ISLD	72 11/16	5	354	SLKC	72 13/16	1	51
MASH	72 11/16	10	23	INCA	72 13/16	14	152
SLKC	72 5/8	1	46	ISLD	72 13/16	10	421
HRZG	72 1/2	10	21	MLCO	72 7/8	10	3
NEED	72 1/2	1	28	MONT	72 7/8	10	4
JEFF	72 1/2	1	2	HMQT	72 7/8	1	5
GSCO	72 1/2	10	16	PRUS	72 7/8	1	3
LEHM	72 3/8	1	4	ADAM	72 7/8	1	0
MSCO	72 3/8	10	3	HRZG	72 7/8	10	29
PWJC	72 1/4	10	1	NEED	72 7/8	1	0
COWN	72 1/4	1	0	GSCO	72 7/8	10	14
CIBC	72 1/4	1	7	BTRD	72 7/8	5	28
AANA	72 1/4	1	0	DLJP	72 15/16	10	5
MLCO	72 1/4	10	2	LEHM	72 15/16	1	6
SBSH	72 1/4	10	9	JPMS	73	1	0

72 3/4 800
72 11/16 1000
72 11/16 500
72 3/4 500
72 11/16 300
----12:54----
72 11/16 300
72 3/4 300
72 11/16 100
72 11/16 500
72 11/16 100
72 11/16 100
72 11/16 4000
----12:55----
72 11/16 100
72 5/8 100
72 5/8 500
72 5/8 500
72 3/4 300
72 11/16 100
72 11/16 100
72 5/8 1300
72 5/8 100
72 3/4 200
72 3/4 100
----12:56----
72 3/4 200
72 3/4 900

Figure 10-16

On this level II screen of Applied Materials (AMAT), the spread between the bid and ask is 1/8 point, which is acceptable. The bid has good depth, with two market makers (RSSF and MASH) and two ECNs (INCA and ISLD) bidding. Four is the minimum number of market makers and ECNs you want to see on the inside bid when you enter a stock on the long side.

Level II Screen Courtesy of *The Executioner*©

his intentions to buy or sell the stock. He may also adjust his quote. At that point, he again becomes eligible for SOES orders.

SOES rules:

- You may execute a trade through SOES up to 1,000 shares, no more.
- You cannot split the bid and ask with SOES. You must buy on the inside offer and sell on the inside bid. You can issue them as limit orders, but to be filled, they must be posted at current prices.
- Market makers fill SOES orders. ECNs do not. Therefore, if you want to buy on the offer, and the only takers listed consist of ECNs such as INCA, ARCA, and ISLD, any SOES order you place will automatically cancel.

ORACLE CORP <32T,0969,YTPT,36005655>

ORCL 37 3/8 ↓ -5/16 100 O t 11:39
Bid ↑ 37 3/8 Ask 37 1/2 Vol 5147800
Bid 2 # Ask 1 Spread 1/8
High 38 1/8 Low 36 13/16 Close 37 11/16

Name	Bid	Size	#Best
INCA	37 3/8	15	77
ISLD	37 3/8	25	131
SBSH	37 5/16	5	22
BRUT	37 5/16	5	1
REDI	37 5/16	52	24
SLKC	37 5/16	1	12
MASH	37 5/16	1	14
MADF	37 5/16	4	11
PRUS	37 5/16	10	9
FBCO	37 1/4	10	11
MLCO	37 1/4	10	1
PIPR	37 1/4	10	3
CIBC	37 1/4	10	1
MSCO	37 1/4	10	4
FCAP	37 1/4	3	0
PWJC	37 1/4	2	4
BTRD	37 1/4	10	4
HRZG	37 1/4	3	15

Name	Ask	Size	#Best
WBLR	37 1/2	1	0
SHRP	37 1/2	1	15
MONT	37 1/2	10	0
DEAN	37 1/2	3	0
NFSC	37 1/2	1	4
WARR	37 1/2	10	4
EVRN	37 1/2	3	0
FCAP	37 1/2	2	1
SBSH	37 1/2	10	24
BRUT	37 1/2	1	4
NITE	37 1/2	10	19
SLKC	37 1/2	19	40
INCA	37 1/2	27	83
MADF	37 1/2	5	15
PRUS	37 1/2	1	11
ISLD	37 1/2	59	117
DLJP	37 9/16	10	1
NAIB	37 9/16	1	2

----11:39----
37 7/16 1000
37 7/16 1000
37 7/16 500
37 7/16 500
37 7/16 800
37 7/16 4400
37 7/16 200
37 7/16 1000
37 3/8 500
37 7/16 4800
37 7/16 100
37 7/16 1000
37 7/16 1000
37 7/16 800
37 7/16 1000
37 7/16 200
37 7/16 300
37 7/16 300
37 7/16 1000
37 7/16 500
37 7/16 200
37 3/8 100

Figure 10-17

On this level II screen of the Oracle Corp. (ORCL), the spread is 1/8 of a point, which is decent. Notice, though, that only two ECNs sit on the inside bid. If you jump in on the offer, chances are INCA and ISLD won't last long, and the next level down is 37 5/16. If the stock heads south the minute you jump in, you'll lose 3/16 for sure. To find the ax, look at the highest numbers on the bid under #Best. Market makers SBSH may well be the ax since he has come to the bid twenty-two times so far today, and is one level under high bid of 37 3/8. SBSM is also on the offer at 37 1/2 and has been "high offer" twenty-four times. If you're shorting ORCL, this is a great setup because there is huge depth on the ask, or offer. Keep in mind, however, that this stock moves extremely fast, and the level II screen changes many times a minute! New traders are better off trading slower-moving stocks.

Level II Screen Courtesy of *The Executioner*©

YOU AS THE MARKET MAKER

Another way to place orders on your level II system is through access with the ECN assigned to you by your level II broker. Some of those ECNs were listed earlier, and by the time you read this, additional ECNs will be operating. Using your designated ECN, you can "play" market maker.

INTEL CORP

INTC		70 1/16 ↓ -1/4		100	O	t	10:53
Bid ↓	70 1/16	Ask	70 1/8	Vol	16237700		
# Bid	5	# Ask	1	Spread	1/16		
High	71 1/32	Low	68	Close	70 5/16		

Name	Bid	Size	#Best	Name	Ask	Size	#Best
GSCO	70 1/16	10	16	SLKC	70 1/8	1	50
SBSH	70 1/16	3	8	PRUS	70 1/8	1	49
FBCO	70 1/16	1	19	REDI	70 1/8	8	100
INCA	70 1/16	23	127	MWSE	70 1/8	5	8
ISLD	70 1/16	29	231	INCA	70 1/8	25	141
CIBC	70	1	3	ISLD	70 1/8	16	186
DLJP	70	10	10	JOSE	70 3/16	10	3
PIPR	70	1	14	NITE	70 3/16	5	63
USCT	70	5	7	ARCA	70 3/16	2	76
HMQT	70	1	0	GKMC	70 1/4	1	0
MLCO	70	3	5	WARR	70 1/4	10	3
LEHM	70	1	20	DEAN	70 1/4	4	7
NITE	70	1	34	PWJC	70 1/4	1	15
ARCA	70	10	97	DLJP	70 1/4	10	9
PRUS	70	1	44	PIPR	70 1/4	1	29
REDI	70	5	91	USCT	70 1/4	5	10
MASH	70	30	24	NFSC	70 1/4	4	18
NFSC	69 15/16	1	5	HRZG	70 1/4	3	17
MONT	69 15/16	10	4	MLCO	70 1/4	24	3
HRZG	69 15/16	6	16	MADF	70 1/4	5	7
MADF	69 7/8	6	8	MASH	70 1/4	9	36
NTRD	69 7/8	50	4	MSCO	70 5/16	10	7

Time & Sales	
70 1/16	300
70 1/16	400
70 1/16	1000
70 1/16	1100
70 1/16	1300
70 1/16	100
70 1/8	500
70 1/16	100
70 1/16	300
70 3/32	500
70 1/16	500
70 1/16	500
70 1/16	800
70 1/16	200
70 1/16	1800
70 1/16	700
70 1/16	3000
70 1/16	1200
70 1/16	6400
70 3/32	200
70 1/16	100
70 3/32	300
70 1/16	700
70 1/16	2500
70 1/8	500
70 1/8	500
70 1/8	200
70 1/8	200
70 1/8	100
70 1/8	100
70 1/8	3800
70 1/16	100
70 1/16	100

Figure 10-18

On this level II screen of Intel Corp. (INTC), you have the perfect setup on the inside bid. GSCO (Goldman-Sachs, generally regarded as the lead gorilla of market makers) is on the bid, with SBSH and FBCO, also big guys, right under him. This means heavyweight market makers want tot buy INTC. That equals demand, so for the moment, anyway, the stock may rise. Another plus is that the spread is only 1/16th of a point, which is ideal. If you buy on the offer, you've got lots of depth on the bid side to escape with only 1/8 point loss or less if the market turns against you.

Level II Screen Courtesy of *The Executioner*©

Say the perfect setup for your target stock presents itself. If the stock moves slowly enough, you can *buy on the bid*: Post a limit buy order with your ECN for the inside bid price. I found ISLD orders work well for buying on the bid.

If your stock is climbing a little faster—but not too fast—and if there's enough room in the spread, you can "go high bid." That means you split the bid and the ask by entering a limit buy order a teeny higher than the current inside bid.

Now you're the high bidder. Your goal: to entice sellers. If nobody bites after a few seconds, believe it or not, that's good! It means that the stock is in such high demand, no one's selling. Do you want that stock in a big way? Cancel your order and buy on the posted offer.

MICROSOFT CORP <32T,0969,YTPT,36005655>

MSFT	86 31/32 ↑ -3 1/32	400	O	t	13:11
Bid ↑	86 15/16	Ask	87	Vol	16272200
# Bid	1	# Ask	2	Spread	1/16
High	88 13/16	Low	86 7/8	Close	90

Name	Bid	Size	#Best
MLCO	86 15/16	10	8
NFSC	86 15/16	10	9
SBSH	86 15/16	10	6
INCA	86 15/16	7	112
ISLD	86 15/16	7	122
FBCO	86 7/8	10	13
GSCO	86 7/8	10	9
DBKS	86 7/8	10	2
BRUT	86 7/8	2	9
SNDS	86 7/8	5	3
HRZG	86 7/8	3	30
NITE	86 7/8	5	29
MWSE	86 7/8	1	15
BEST	86 13/16	10	1
MASH	86 13/16	13	43
MSCO	86 13/16	10	2
PERT	86 13/16	1	16

Name	Ask	Size	#Best
PWJC	87	10	18
CWCO	87	1	0
GSCO	87	10	21
ARCA	87	3	89
DLJP	87	10	0
JPMS	87	1	3
MWSE	87	1	9
PERT	87	15	5
MHMY	87	10	1
ISLD	87	3	324
INCA	87 1/16	10	205
PRUS	87 1/8	10	10
SHWD	87 1/8	10	26
LEHM	87 1/8	1	3
SLKC	87 1/8	10	68
OLDE	87 1/8	1	6
REDI	87 5/16	3	91

87 1000
87 300
87 100
87 2200
87 200
87 100
86 15/16 1000
87 1000
86 15/16 1000
87 300
87 200
86 15/16 100
86 15/16 500
86 15/16 1000
86 15/16 1000
87 400
86 15/16 600
86 15/16 1000
86 15/16 500
87 200
87 100
----13:11----
87 2000
86 15/16 200
86 31/32 100
86 15/16 100
86 15/16 800
86 31/32 400

Figure 10-19

On this level II screen of the Microsoft Corp. (MSFT), the 800-pound gorilla, GSCO, and his buddies are offering quite a supply of MSFT for sale. This tells you that unless a lot of buyers suddenly show up, MSFT will likely stall here, or even slide a little.

Level II Screen Courtesy of *The Executioner*©

The times you do manage to get filled at high bid, the spread gained translates into more profit to you. Make an extra teeny four times a day, and it equals a quarter of a point. If you're trading 500-share lots, that equals $125 extra profit. Sweet, isn't it?

Before you place *any* order, though, please become proficient with your order entry system. When I started, systems sprang from their incubators directly into the hands of the guinea pigs who ordered them. We downloaded the software, and that was it. Limited training and support was available.

My total training (I swear!) on my level II system consisted of a man's voice on the other end of the telephone, who said, "Okay, honey. See that buy button? When you wanna buy something, click on it."

To this day, I can only whisper how much money I lost learning how to trade on my level II system by the trial-and-error method. Please learn from my mistakes. Study your system and make plenty of dry runs before you trade with real money. That's another excellent way to protect your principal!

THE ULTIMATE DAY TRADING SCENE

Okay, guys and girlfriends. If you've toughed out the journey thus far, you're on your way to reaping profits.

As a day trader, you're similar to the ringleader in a three-ring circus. You outthink tigers and lions (specialists and market makers), shoo the clowns from the tent when they act too rambunctious (exit stocks that act funny), hold the net for trapeze artists (adhering to stops under open positions), and at the same time, direct the remainder of the cast (monitor market internals and industry indices). This is a big role to fill. Are you up for it? I think you are!

One effective way to set up your screen—two monitors hooked to the same computer is better—is to position your market maker and time of sales screen, next to your five-minute, and fifteen-minute, thirty-minute, or hourly intraday charts. (Most traders rely on the five-minute chart as a staple, then add another intraday chart of their choice as they develop their own style.) Next to the charts, add your market maker and time of sales screen(s). Then add the TICK, TRIN, S&P futures, and the major market averages. Finish it off with industry indexes you're targeting, an interest list of stocks, and perhaps a ticker with those stocks on it.

Your goal is to find stocks where your tops down criteria, charts, market maker, and time and sales screen all agree.

Let's say that this is an awesome Monday morning, just after 10:00 a.m. Market internals glow with positive numbers. Yesterday, your target stock consolidated into the close near its high. It opened this morning 1/8 point higher, then consolidated nicely into the 9:50 reversal period. It's making a nice, tight edge across your five-minute chart. The 200 MA rides way below the current price, and the 20 MA sits just under it. The *same setup* is developing on the fifteen-minute chart.

Suddenly, you notice buy orders heating up on your time of sales. Three major market makers stalk the inside bid. Buy orders eat through the offer like a hot knife through butter. A quick check of your charts shows a volume spike forming. *The stock's going to break out any second*. You figure your stop and write it down on your worksheet.

You look for resistance on the fifteen-minute chart—none to worry about. (On the daily chart, you noted earlier that major resistance was more than four points away, and that was two months ago.) The stock noses over resistance. You pounce onto the offer. *Got it.* Buy recorded. Stop loss circled. Stock rising. See the trader smile!

Do you understand what I mean about everything coordinating? Now, that was the perfect scenario. Trader heaven. I've been there, and you will be, too. Only experience will teach you how to glance at each reading and weave them all together into a single decision—to enter or not to enter.

Please err on the side of caution and avoid trades you're not sure about. If you buy—and in the next ohnosecond wish you hadn't—sell immediately. Old trader saying: When in doubt, get out!

In the next chapter, we'll fine-tune day trading into scalping plays. Then we'll learn why your shorts fall down!

QUIZ

1. What are the first four Fibonacci numbers?
2. Give one reason why traders look to these numbers for guidance.
3. Strong stocks in an uptrend tend to bounce off their ____ or ___ moving averages.
4. Define a "gap opening."
5. When your target stock meets your entry criteria, but gaps open, how do you play it?
6. Describe an intraday "wiggle." Give an example.
7. When you day trade, what is the maximum loss you accept?
8. True or false? If your stock acts funny, you're justified in moving your stop loss down 1/4 point.
9. True or false? Odds of morning day trades increase (on the long side) when the target stock consolidates into the prior day's close and closes near the day's high.
10. When you enter a day trade, you automatically place your stop loss ___ point under (over, for shorts) your entry point.
11. Before you enter a trade, what do you check first on level II?
12. What is the ideal spread for safe trades? Why?
13. With listed stocks, always trade toward ___________.
14. The longer the line of market makers at the inside bid or ask on a Nasdaq stock, the more ________ it has.
15. Wise traders buy Nasdaq stocks when market makers on the inside bid number ____, or more.
16. When only ISLD is listed on the inside bid of your target stock, does that raise or lower the immediate odds of the stock rising?
17. True or false? With SOES orders, you can place a limit order and split the bid and ask.
18. At the end of this chapter, we pictured a Monday-morning scene. Please imagine the same scene again. This time, however, a total of three negative conditions suddenly crop up. Using everything you have learned so far, what might they be? Hint: Any one of the three causes you to reconsider the trade. All three together cause you to sit on your hands.

ANSWERS

1. 1, 2, 3, 5.
2. Because stocks tend to move in increments of these numbers. For instance, a stock may move up five days and down three, or up three days and down one or two.
3. 20, 50.
4. A gap opening occurs when a stock opens higher or lower than the previous day's closing price.
5. Play a gap opening by waiting until the stock trades over its thirty-minute high. (Short sellers reverse this. When the stock gaps down, wait until it trades below its thirty-minute low.)
6. A wiggle is the average pullback a stock makes during intraday profit taking. A stock moving in an intraday uptrend might wiggle, or pull back, 3/8 point on the first wiggle, 1/2 point on the next, 5/8 point on the next, then 1/2 point. We would assign a wiggle value of 9/16 to 5/8 of a point, and if the stock pulls back more than that after we enter, we exit!
7. The maximum acceptable loss for a day trade is 3/8 point.
8. Pul-lease don't tell me you dignified this question by reading it more than once! The answer is false, false, false.
9. True.
10. 1/4 point.
11. The width of the spread between the inside bid and ask.
12. The ideal spread between the bid and ask is 1/8 point or less. The narrower the spread, the quicker you can exit the trade if it goes against you the minute you enter.
13. size.
14. depth.
15. four.
16. When the only one at the inside bid is ISLD, an ECN, you know that at the moment, only traders are buying this stock. The big gorillas have no interest. Odds are, the stock will stall or fall.
17. False.
18. Any one of the following conditions should make you reconsider placing a (long) trade. More than one warns of low probability success. You'll be able to think of more, but these will get you started: (1) low volume on the breakout, (2) you just notice the 200 MA sloping above the stock's current price, (3) suddenly, the market makers lower the bid, (4) a truckload of heavyweight market makers appears on the offer—lots of supply, (5) the TICK takes a sudden dive, (6) the S&P futures drop like a rock.

✦ ✦ ✦

CENTER POINT
Release the Past

People are always blaming circumstances for what that are. I do not believe in circumstances. The people who get on in this world are the people who get up and look for the circumstances they want, and if they cannot find them, make them.

—GEORGE BERNARD SHAW

Do you know anyone who has fully left the past behind him or her? Few of us achieve that freedom. For all of us, at some level, the past is not really the past. Even when painful circumstances took place weeks, months, or years ago, at a deep emotional level we still hold onto them.

We try to bury them, but they still affect our lives. The energy we tie up in regret and resentments dwells at an unconscious level, so we don't realize why we are nagged by feelings of negativity or unhappiness. Yet, unless we somehow release that negative energy, the past lives in our present and shapes our future.

We cannot hold onto negative energy from the past in the form of grudges, resentments, and fears, and at the same time grasp our highest possibilities. Why? Because negative feelings block the flow of positive energy into our lives.

The best way to release the past is to forgive...forgive ourselves and those people and situations that hurt us. Just as our bodies heal physical bruises, our inner self wants to heal emotional injuries. We heal by releasing those injuries. We release by forgiving.

To forgive, we face the matter and own it. We acknowledge that the negative energy we've been carrying around no longer serves us. We choose to leave the situation behind and, in doing so, we forgive.

Forgiveness is a gift to ourselves. It releases us from the past, fills our lives with positive emotions, and frees us to shape abundant, successful tomorrows.

✦ ✦ ✦

CHAPTER 11

Scalps and Shorts, or the Quick and the Dead

"Level II trading is the closest you'll get to sitting in the cockpit of an F-14 Tomcat and flying into battle. Your rivals are professionals who capitalize on your errors if you interpret their actions incorrectly.

You must lock into your opponents' movement and accurately assess their intentions. Are they playing head games, or is what you see real? Once you decide, you take the appropriate measure to either engage or stand on the sidelines and live to fight another day.

The market is as unforgiving as any opponent you can encounter. If you choose erroneously, your best move is to retreat to safety and restrategize for the next 'battle'."

That's how Mike Campion, one of the finest traders I know, describes level II trading. I agree with every word.

Level II trading is an integral part of scalping. Our strategy is to use charts to find the scalping setups, then turn to our level II market maker screen as an additional guide to managing the trade.

NITTY-GRITTY SCALPING STUFF

When you're scalping, mental discipline dictates whether you make or lose money. Greed, fear, hope, or the need to be right play no role in a scalper's cool, calculating mindset.

Greed, especially, tempts traders to stay in scalping plays too long. Then it laughs and slaps them with a loss. How do I know?

When I first started trading, this was one of my biggest challenges. Once in a scalp, I stuck like ugly on an ape! Call it greed, or dignify it by calling it optimism. Whatever the name, I learned that clinging in hopes of an extra teeny nearly always boomerangs into a smaller profit, or a loss. If you're in the midst of a successful scalp and hear oinking noises emanate from your own mouth, cash in your profits.

When you scalp, time and risk–reward ratios compress into fractions. Since your reward is small, you keep your risk (losses) even smaller. Scalping plays usually last from seconds to minutes. Expected profit: 1/8 to 1/2 point.

To make money at scalping, you need a high percentage of winning trades. When you're swing trading or even day trading, one multipoint gain can erase two or three losing trades. Not so with scalping. You make 1/4. You lose a 1/8th. You lose another 1/8th. *Uh, oh.* You're not even, you're down on the day! Remember, commissions add up when you're only clearing 1/8th to 1/4 point.

Scalp stocks with a 1/8 point spread or less. This is an absolute! *When you scalp, you risk no more than 1/8 point loss.* Therefore, if you have to buy on the offer, you want no more than a 1/8 spread between you and a possible instant loss. The tighter the spread, the smaller the risk.

Enter only with good depth on the bid and ask, especially the bid. As with day trades, find the door *before* you enter the room. After is too late!

Certain numbers create natural support and resistance—such as whole and half numbers. Stocks moving up tend to stall at whole numbers, or they creep a teeny over, then pullback through them.

Example: Let's agree that Igloo Ice Cream represents typical intraday stock movement. It shoots from 25 5/8 to 25 7/8, then hesitates just below the whole number. If it's having an extremely strong day, it will rise through 26 to 26 1/16, then pull back, maybe to 25 3/4. That's why you consider taking profits—part or all—just below the whole number, or on it.

Be aware that whole numbers also act as support. When Igloo pulls back, it will slow or halt at 25. If it slips below 25 to 24 7/8, on a weak day it may slide lower—fast. Investors and traders know that stocks tend to bounce off whole numbers. Therefore, a truckload of stop loss orders generally sits just below a whole number. When a stock slips through a whole number and hits the 7/8 or 3/4 mark, the triggered stop losses increase supply. Supply = lower prices.

Half-points don't deliver quite as much support and resistance, but they definitely slow movement. If Simple Software rises to 25 3/8 or 7/16, watch for a stall and pull back at 25 1/2. When it rises to 25 7/8, or 25 15/16, then pulls back, it will probably stall at 25 5/8, just above the 1/2 mark.

As with longer time frames, scalpers use breakouts and breakdowns, capitalizing on the initial momentum. You grab a quick profit and leave.

Receivers on professional football teams must have "good hands." As a scalper, you need "fast hands." If you can (on the long side), you buy on the bid, then offer out on the ask, while the stock is still running.

In situations where the stock is trading on the offer—and running up too fast to buy on the bid—you take the offer. While momentum propels the stock higher, you offer out quickly (sell on the offer), grabbing as much of a point as you can before the sellers take over and the pullback begins.

Before you buy, check out your target stock's personality, just as you do for day trades. What is its average pullback or wiggle range? What is its average run-up range? That helps you anticipate how far it might run once you're in.

A note about lot size. After you become experienced, 500 to 1,000 shares are the minimum you'll want to scalp. You rarely make money scalping 200 to 300 shares at a time. Eventually the odds—commissions, slippage and losses—will swallow your profits.

When you're first learning, though, *do* practice with small lot sizes. Just don't overtrade. A novice pilot who's used to flying a Cessna asks for big trouble if he climbs into that F-14 Tomcat Mike Campion described at the beginning of the chapter. Similarly, a novice trader used to trading small lots in extended time frames may end up as the scalpee, instead of the scalper. Please go slowly and hone your skills carefully.

Successful scalpers use the S&P futures as a trigger. If Fibonnaci retracements come as an option on your level II system, apply them to your futures chart, especially when you're scalping. They give you high-probability support and resistance levels for the futures.

Keep in mind that industry giants, especially in tech stocks, are orchestrated by the shrewdest market makers in the business. The odds of either you, or I, outwitting them are Slim and None—and Slim's just leaving! Avoid entering scalps in giants such as Dell, Microsoft, Intel, or Cisco. Their respective market makers eat novice traders—and many experienced ones—for breakfast, lunch, and dinner.

From now on, as we talk about scalping techniques, please assume we're using Nasdaq stocks.

Most traders scalp NYSE stocks far less because of their decreased volatility. You can scalp listed stocks if you locate one breaking out or breaking down on big volume, but your strategies become limited. Watch your chart and your time and sales screen. Slip between the bid and ask if you can. If you can't, buy on the offer. Remember, always trade toward size. Before the run slows, grab your 1/4 or 3/8 point, and leave.

We'll also limit our discussion to plays on the long side. Shorting techniques are discussed later in the chapter.

SCALPING SETUPS

One excellent aspect of trading is that every reliable chart pattern you learn applies to every trading time frame. I've noted different patterns for intermediate-term to day trades and now scalping plays because certain setups and patterns appear with more regularity in different time frames. Still, a cup with-a-handle pattern, properly executed, works just as well on a daily chart for a longer-term play as it does on a one-minute chart for a scalp. So while you're perusing charts for scalping setups, know that you can use any breakout pattern you've learned thus far.

From my own experience, I find the best scalping plays set up by forming tight consolidation patterns. Those patterns move sideways in a range of 1/4 point or so, for at least twenty to thirty minutes. The longer the better! Optimum scalping setups:

- Consolidate at or near the day's high
- Move sideways in a tight, orderly fashion for twenty minutes or more
- As the steam builds, several candlesticks close on their own highs

Early morning plays don't always have the luxury to consolidate for a long period of time. As the day goes on, though, especially through the midday blues, those flatlines, shelves, or ledges they draw usually produce gratifying price spikes that deliver awesome scalping profits.

You can either enter at the usual breakout buy point, when the stock trades 1/8 point above resistance, or you can buy just before the breakout. When you buy just before the breakout, you need precise timing. That is, the majority of the candlesticks in the consolidation should start closing on their highs. Next, judge by activity on your level II market maker screen, time and sales, and the S&P futures that a breakout is imminent. Also, check the volume.

When you jump in early, you chance the stock reversing, falling through support, and diving fast. (When it breaks below supports, the short-sellers grab it and force it lower.) Please use extra caution and perfect your timing.

One strategy is to buy half your anticipated lot size before the breakout, and half at the usual 1/8 above resistance point. Then sell the first half when you make 3/16 point profit, and let the second half rise a level or two higher, depending on the play and the stock's strength.

The setups shown in Figures 11-1 through 11-4 apply to five-minute intraday charts. Depending on how fast the stock is moving, I use one-, three-, and five-minute charts.

The intraday charts shown in Figures 11-5 through 11-8 show actual scalping setups and how to play them. Study them carefully, then try to find duplicate patterns during market hours. Paper trade until you feel comfortable entering.

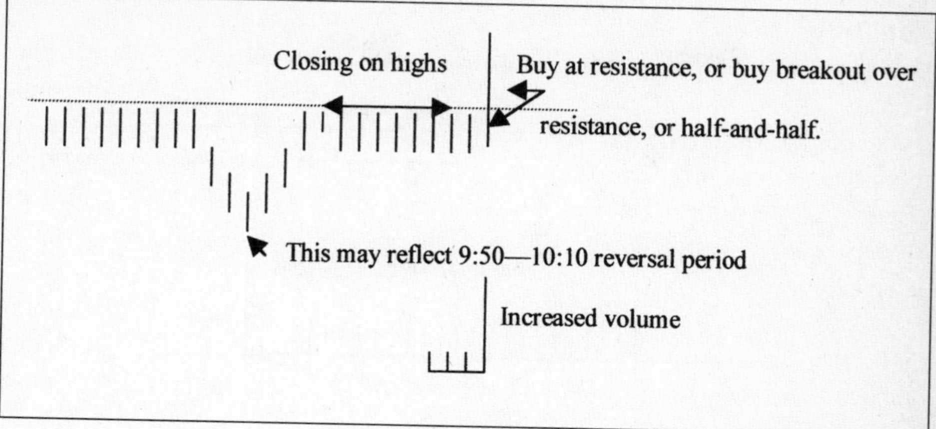

Figure 11-1
Scalping setup 1

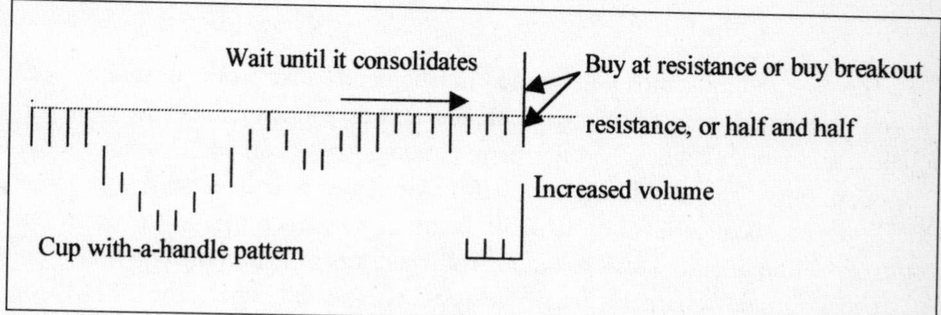

Figure 11-2
Scalping setup 2

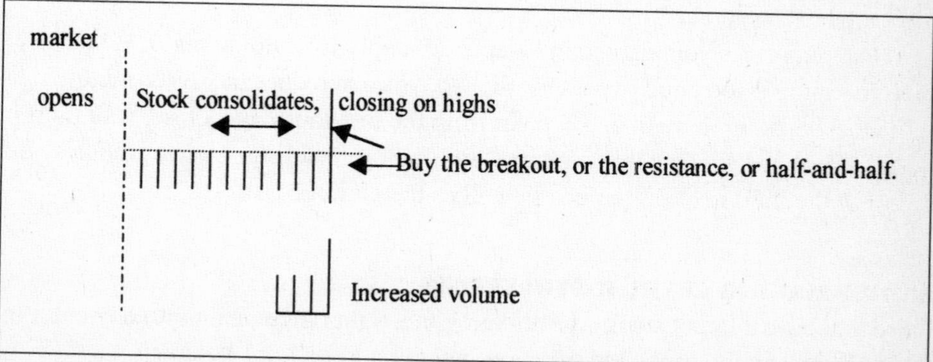

Figure 11-3
Scalping setup 3: Early morning setup, one-minute chart

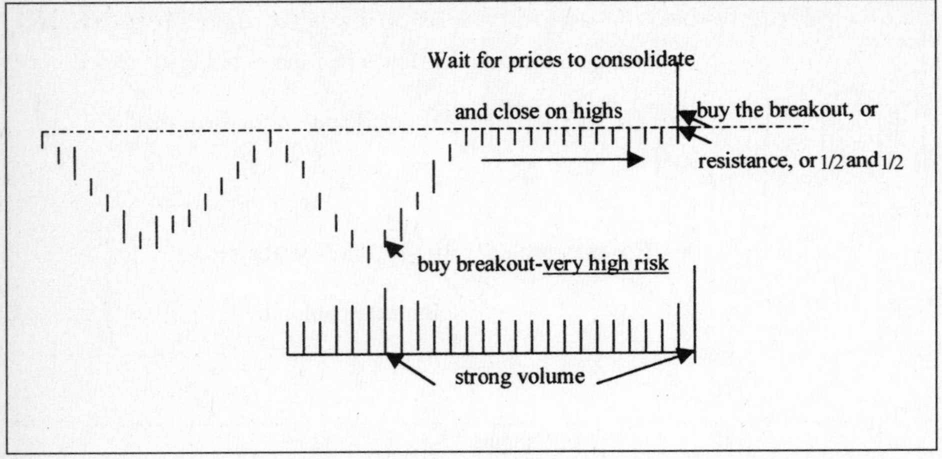

Figure 11-4
Scalping setup 4: Double bottom, high risk!

The day trading setups you learned in Chapter 10 also work for scalps. With all you've learned, zero in on two or three patterns and setups that fit your personality, and work exclusively with them. Gradually, you can add to your arsenal.

Also, please do your homework before you enter a scalp. Check your target stock's next resistance level on its daily chart. If resistance lies 1/4, or even one point away, find another stock to target. You want lots of headroom for your play! Also check intraday charts for nearby resistance; especially check the 200 MA on the five-minute and fifteen-minute charts. If it slopes down ready to dunk your target stock, look for another play. Remember, more that 8,000 stocks make up the major markets. Why choose a low-probability play when a really sweet one waits right around the corner?

Gapping rules you learned in Chapter 10 apply to scalping plays. If an early-morning setup is too good to pass by, though, you can reduce the thirty-minute rule (if a stock gaps up more than 3/8 point from the previous day's close, wait until it trades 1/8 above its first thirty-minute high before entering) to five minutes. Be aware of the 9:50 reversal period, as well as the elevated risk.

MONEY-MAKING LEVEL II STRATEGIES

Once you have a target stock consolidating in a tight range on an intraday chart in front of you, switch gears and turn your attention to its level II screen.

What you want to see on the ask, or offer:

The good news: A mixture of muscle market makers like GSCO, SBSH, and MLCO, along with some ECNs is fine, as long as aggressive buyers are eating

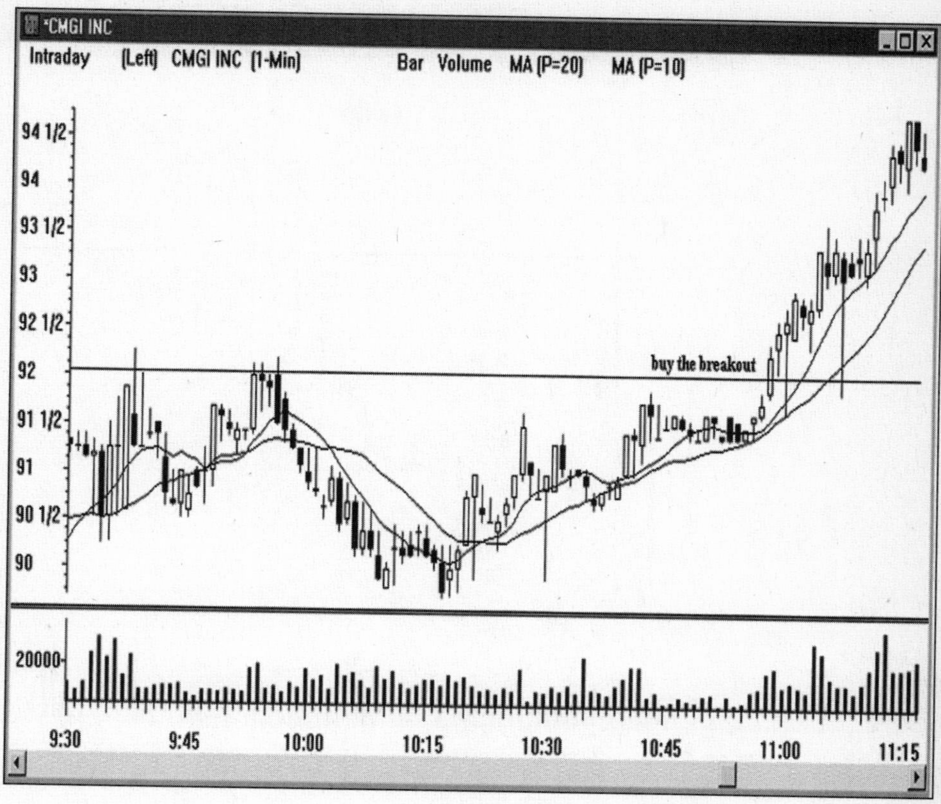

Figure 11-5

On this one-minute chart of CMGI Inc. (CMGI), you can see the dip-and-rally pattern that takes place mid-morning. It almost looks like a cup-with-a-handle. At 10:58, CMGI breaks over consolidation on strong volume at 92. It runs to 92 15/16 by 11:01, and most scalpers will be out by this small pullback. For those who hang on longer, the stock runs to 94 3/4 by 11:15.

Chart Courtesy of *The Executioner*©

through the offer, and the big guys are "lifting," or disappearing, quickly. The really good news: Time and sales shows trades firing *above* the market price. That means buyers are so anxious, they'll pay higher than retail to own this stock.

At the offer—bad news: Remember, what a market maker shows, sizewise, and the truth, are often two different numbers. If a gorilla like GSCO sits on the offer showing a paltry 100 shares to sell, yet thousands of shares at the offer march by on time and sales, GSCO's not showing his entire hand. He only *has* to show 100-share lots at a time, although he may have a big order to get rid of. Sooner or later, his selling pressure will push the stock south, especially if the S&P futures turn down. Lesson: Don't believe what market makers *say*. Believe only what they

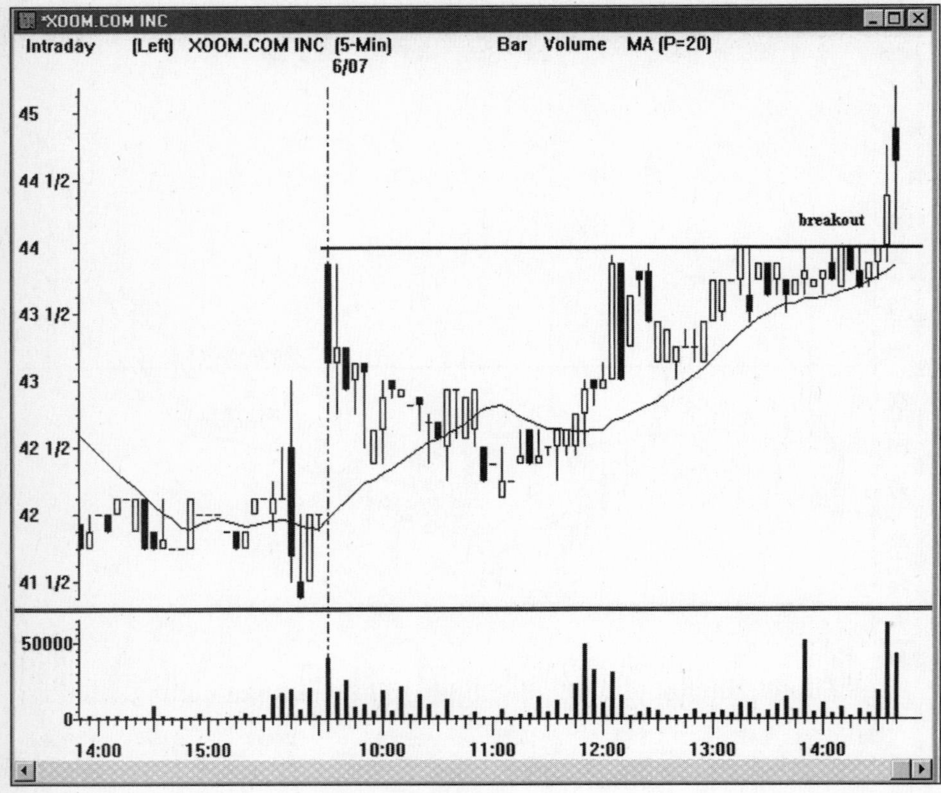

Figure 11-6

Although this is a five-minute chart of Xoom.com (XMCM), instead of a one-minute chart, it still could have been used for this scalping play. It is a perfect cup-with-a-handle pattern. As you can see, XMCM broke out just before 3 p.m. on high volume and was a buy at 44. It ran to over 45 fast, and a scalper could make out well—fast!

Chart Courtesy of *The Executioner*©

do. Time and sales will show you the facts. If you see a market maker sitting on the offer for minutes at a time, stay away from the scalp until the situation changes.

On the bid—good news: Big guys like GSCO and PRUS, SLKC on the bid, building plenty of depth. Who's the ax? Once you identify him (see Chapter 9), if he supports the stock by repeatedly appearing at the bid, and raising it to higher and higher prices, chances are the stock will rocket.

On the bid—bad news: Only ISLD and TNTO wait on the bid. *Uh, oh!* Not only is the depth too thin—ISLD and TNTO are ECNs. They represent the public. (INCA and BTRD are also ECNs, and represent institutions, as well as limited public orders.) If only ISLD and TNTO sit on the bid, it means gorillas like GSCO

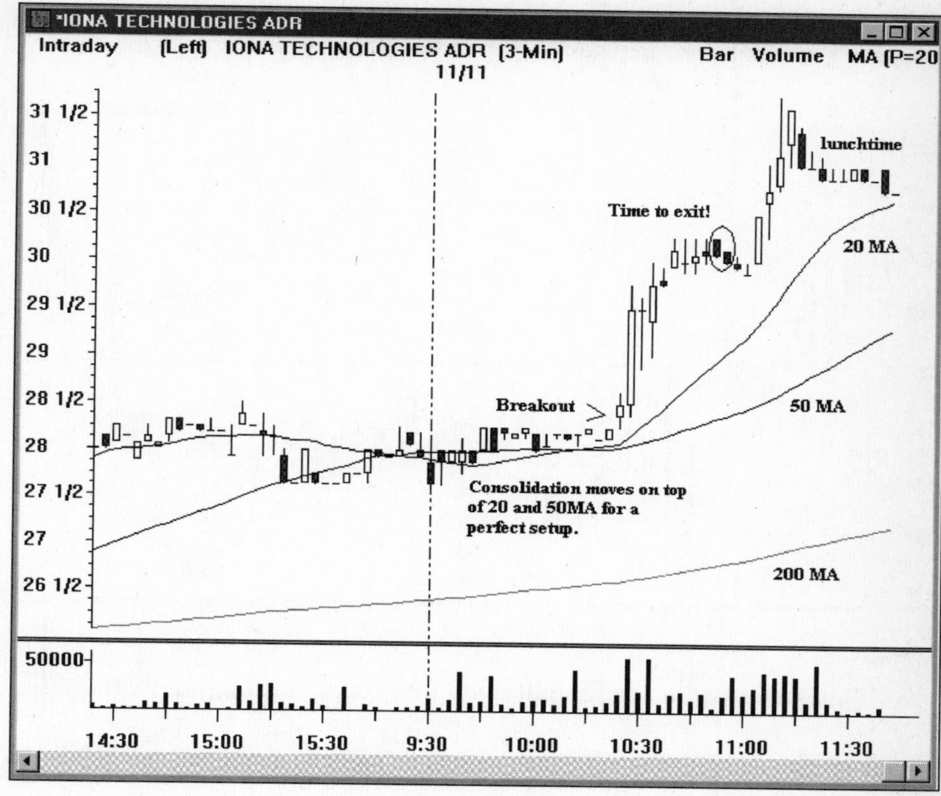

Figure 11-7

In this 3-minute chart of Iona Technologies (IONA), you can see it opened near the previous day's close. Then it moves sideways, building a shelf until the volume spiked and IONA broke above resistance of 28 1/4, at 10:27 a.m. This was the entry point. It rocketed to 29 3/4 on the next powerful bar, where most scalpers would have taken profits. Those who rode it to the top of the move at 30 1/4 got two warning black candlesticks at 10:51 and 10:54 to take gains and leave. Note how the stock pulls back and breaks out again at 11:03 for a 1 5/8 run, stopping at 31 5/8 at 11:12. The next black bar gives a stiff warning to all who haven't taken profits yet. The lunchtime moody blues start right on time.

Chart Courtesy of *The Executioner*©

aren't buying. The sellers on the offer may outweigh the lightweight traders on the bid. We know what more sellers than buyers do to the price of a stock. Next!

Again, if you can, play market maker. Buy on the bid by issuing a limit order for the inside bid price, using your assigned ECN. (Remember, you cannot cut the bid and ask using SOES.)

If the stock is running a little faster, you can attempt to go "high bid." Enter your limit order for 1/16 above the inside bid. *If you don't get hit in a few seconds, cancel your order.* Otherwise, other traders who already own the stock will notice

Figure 11-8

On this one-minute chart of Exodus Communications (EXDS), the stock makes a double bottom, then consolidates for a few minutes and breaks out at 1:10 p.m. at 131 1/2. A scalper would buy here, and could offer out all the way up to 133 13/16.

Chart Courtesy of *The Executioner*©

your bid just sitting there, and they won't sell to you. Instead, they'll assume selling momentum has stalled and will wait for a higher price.

When you buy on the bid, you may get filled a half-dozen times out of two dozen attempts. Don't let the odds disappoint you. Once in a while, the trading god will send a sleepy market maker or trader your way.

Every trader buys breakouts. As a result, when the ideal setup shows up you'll probably have to buy on the offer, or the stock will run away from you. When I want to buy a stock in a hurry, I use SOES or ISLD, if ISLD is on the offer.

ISLD matches orders when possible. If you see ISLD on the offer and catch it fast, the trade is instantaneous. If ISLD isn't on the offer, you can SOES your trade as long as any market maker *besides* an ECN is present. You can also issue a limit buy order, at the offer price, with your assigned ECN.

Please don't place a market order for a running stock. When the market maker sees your order coming his way, he'll collapse with laughter. After he struggles back to his feet, he'll fill your order at the highest possible price. Trust me. Been there, done that, got skewered!

NOW THAT YOU'VE GOT IT, WHAT DO YOU DO WITH IT?

Once in a scalp, some traders offer out immediately. That means they issue a limit order to sell their entire position at the ask price. They're content to make 1/8 point profit. Others offer out one-half their position at 3/16 point, and the other half a level or two higher. Still others, if momentum is hot enough, hold their entire position for two or three levels, grabbing 3/8 to 1/2 point. These moves boil down to personal preference, and what kind of metal your nerves are strung with.

When you first start scalping, I recommend you offer out at least half your position when you've made 1/8th point profit. That way, you've covered commissions and earned a little profit. Offer out the other half in another 1/8th of a point, or so, *before* momentum slows.

If no one takes your offer within a few seconds, cancel it. Then reissue a sell limit order for the bid price. Don't stay on the offer if you see momentum slowing. Cancel immediately and hit the bid.

Remember the old trader's saying: *Get out when you can, not when you're forced to.*

What if, midscalp, the S&P futures suddenly make a U-turn, and your stock follows? Get out fast. *Issue a limit order with your ECN for one or two levels under the inside bid.*

Translation: Say you're scalping 1,000 shares of Igloo Ice Cream. You're in at 26 1/4 . The stock is trading at 26 7/16 × 26 1/2. Suddenly, the futures drop like a stone. The TICK falls. The market makers on Igloo's 7/16 bid melt—fast.

What you do: Place a sell order with your ECN for 1,000 shares of Igloo at a limit of 26 1/8, or even 26. You want to be one or two levels *under* the inside bid. You may get hit at 1/4, 3/16, or 1/8. If things are really ugly, you may get hit at 26. In the ugliest of all scenarios, place a market order.

Why do you place your order under the current bid price? As I've mentioned before, it gets crowded when everyone's heading for the door at once. First come, first serve. Give yourself a price cushion. Otherwise, you'll find yourself in the gut-wrenching position of chasing the stock down. If no buyers want your stock, it could take one or two points, or more, before you finally sell. I've seen that happen a zillion times, and experienced it plenty when I was new. That's why you don't get greedy and wait for the extra teeny. That's why you get out while momentum is still positive. That's why you get out when you can, not when you're forced to. And finally, that's why you need fast hands and nerves of cast-iron to play this game!

Remember, on days market internals tell you a strong uptrend or downtrend rules, you can day trade and let your profits run. On choppy, whippy days, scalping—or better yet, washing your car—makes the wisest strategy. Only you can make that decision. Smart trader saying: When in doubt, stay out.

HANDY-DANDY SCALPING CHECKLIST

Here are some scalping guidelines. Consider making copies and keeping them handy until these steps become second nature to you.

When I was a novice trader, I'd forget one or two of these steps and pay the price. You don't have to! If more points to consider occur to you, by all means add them.

Handy-Dandy Scalping Checklist

1. Tops down criteria is in place. (Overall market, NYSE or Nasdaq, your stock's industry, TICK, TRIN, S&P futures, and so on in an uptrend.)
2. Resistance on daily chart and intraday chart (moving averages or overhead price congestion) will not hinder immediate price movement.
3. Intraday chart forms tight, orderly consolidation pattern, with majority of candlesticks closing on their highs.
4. Strong volume coming into stock; increased volume spike forming on breakout.
5. On level II screen: Spread between inside bid and offer is 1/8 point or narrower.
6. Good depth on inside bid—four or more market makers or more.
7. One or more market makers on bid are *not* ECNs.
8. Buy orders are eating through levels on the ask, or offer.
9. Double-check S&P futures—they are positive on the day and in an uptrend.

SELLING SHORT: DON'T SELL IT SHORT!

Rarely will you find a stockbroker or investor who likes to short stocks. Traders short more often, but even traders shun the technique. Why?

Number one excuse—The market has an upside bias.

Reply: Sure it does, but it's a long-term bias. Traders work short term. Plus, the market falls one-third of the time. Every stock moves through cycles; corrections and downtrends are inevitable. When they do fall, they fall faster than they rise because panic (the ultimate fear) drives stock prices down faster than euphoria raises them.

As I write, the Dow ended the week down 300 points. Many stocks are groveling near or under their 50 MAs. Savvy traders somewhere are much richer from shorting that drop.

Number two excuse: We Americans take pride in our optimism. We like our glasses half full and our endings happy.

Number three excuse: It's not nice to kick someone when he's down. We defend the underdog and shy away from capitalizing on another's downfall. And that's exactly what selling short boils down to—capitalizing on a beaten down underdog.

Snappy retort to the last two excuses: Short sellers eventually cover. That adds liquidity to the stock, and actually bolsters the price.

Number four excuse: There's an unlimited potential for loss. After all, if you buy a $20 stock, it can't fall below zero. What if you sell short a stock at $20, and the darn thing suddenly rockets to $100? When you cover, you lose a zillion dollars.

In practice, this is absolutely true. If you're silly enough to let *any* position go that far against you, all the rest of us can do is roll our eyes, cluck sympathetically, and pray you go back to your day job. (You won't have a choice!)

To limit your losses on shorts, place tight buy stops, (stop losses), just as you do with your long positions. Adhere to them. End of problem.

And, end of excuses. Let's learn how to make money shorting stocks.

THE SHORTING PROCESS: HOW IT WORKS

When you buy a stock, we say you're "long" that position, or you own it. You buy it with the intention of selling it later, at a higher price.

When you "short" a stock, you sell the stock with the intention of buying it back later, at a lower price.

Let's say Simple Software (SS) barks its way into an ugly downtrend. It's a real dog. You, as a wise trader, notice the breakdown, and feel sure SS will fall to its next support area at about $50.

So you sell short, or "short," as traders say, 100 shares of SS, valued at $60 per share. Total cost, $6,000, plus commission.

The brokerage house with whom you have an account removes $6,000+ from your account and tucks it away as a security deposit so you can return the stock if need be. Then he borrows that stock from another client's account. In its place, an IOU guarantees the stock returned on demand. Next, the broker sells the borrowed 100 shares of SS in the market for $60 per share. He puts the $6,000 away for safekeeping.

As you suspected, during the next week, SS falls to support at $50. Now, you issue an order to buy it back, known as "covering your short." Your broker takes $5,000 out of the safekeeping account, goes to the market, and buys 100 shares of SS at $50 per share, the current price. He returns those shares to the account of the other customer he originally borrowed it from and tears up your IOU.

Now your broker returns to you the $6,000 security deposit he took from your account, plus the $1,000 leftover when he bought the stock back, minus a commission. Your original $6,000 investment yields a $1,000 profit, minus commissions. Sweet, yes?

All stocks are not available for shorting at all times. The larger your brokerage firm, the larger the list of shorting candidates it has. If you trade with a level II system, your broker should furnish you with a list of stocks available for shorting.

The final quirky aspect of selling short: You cannot short a stock on a downtick. You can only short a stock on an uptick, or zero-plus tick. (A zero-plus tick means a stock trades on an uptick, then the following trade goes off at the same price level.)

The uptick rule, developed by the exchanges, is meant to prevent market sell-offs like the one in 1929. It also softens the blows to a tanking stock—a variation of "don't hit him while he's down." Specialists and market makers are exempt from the uptick rule.

CHART PATTERNS FOR SELLING SHORT: WHAT TO LOOK FOR

Before we go into shorting patterns, we'll discuss one of the best indicators you can use for this purpose, Bollinger bands. Created by John Bollinger, these bands duplicate moving average envelopes; they ride above *and* below the stock's price pattern on the chart, with the price moving between them.

Standard Bollinger bands are twenty-period exponential bands with two standard deviations. (Simply put, standard deviations measure volatility.) Most charting packages offer Bollinger bands as a basic feature (Figures 11-9 and 11-10).

One primary characteristic of Bollinger bands helps assure shorting success. That is, a price move that originates at one band is apt to move all the way to the opposite band. Read: A stock price that touches the top of its upper Bollinger band has a good likelihood of traveling down to its bottom band.

If possible, apply Bollinger bands to your target shorting stocks and monitor them. If your stock is at the top of its Bollinger band, chances are good it will fall.

My two favorite patterns for shorting in longer-term trades are the double top and the head and shoulders. Intermediate and swing traders will spot these two patterns on daily charts.

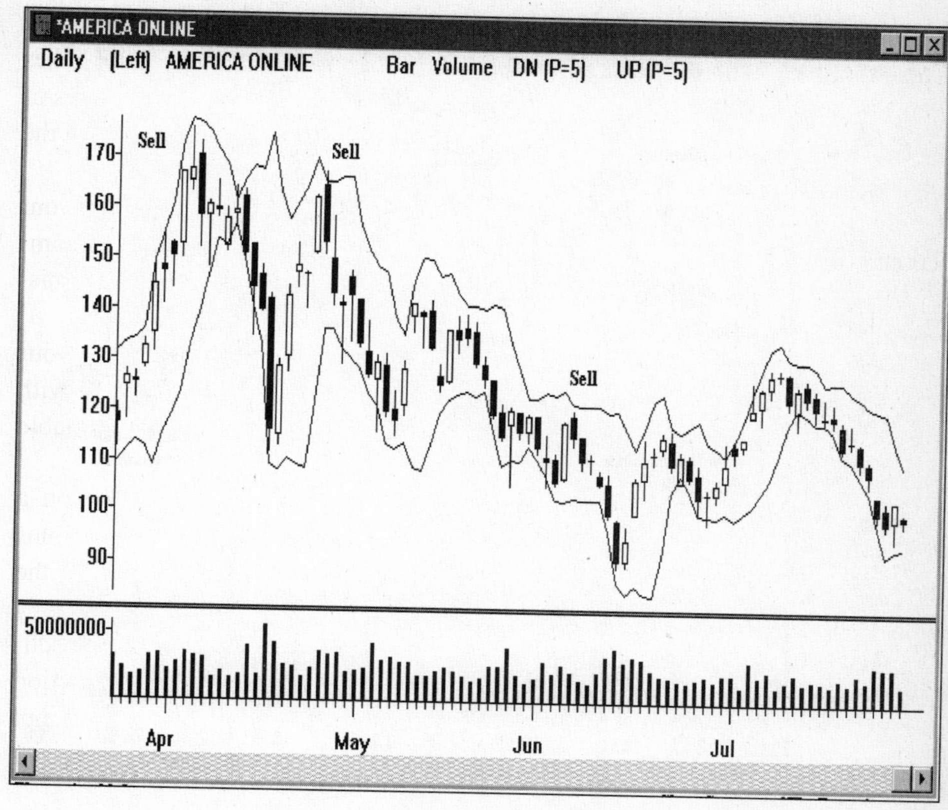

Figure 11-9

This daily chart of America Online (AOL) shows how Bollinger bands suggest good shorting opportunities. Notice that each time the stock soars to the upper band, it soon falls.

Chart Courtesy of *The Executioner*©

As you can guess, the double top, which, as you can see in Figure 11-11 resembles an M, forms a reverse image of the double bottom. Just as the double bottom can forecast a powerful uptrend, the double top presages a lethal downtrend.

The double top begins to form as a stock in an uptrend weakens. It makes a high, sells off, then makes another high. But the second high cannot break through resistance formed by the previous high. Buyers refuse to pay up, and those holding smell trouble and begin to sell.

Now the stock falls to prior support. It may rebound slightly, but weak volume can't propel it higher. The floundering stock tumbles into free-fall.

When you see a double top form on a daily chart, monitor it for a possible setup and entry to sell short. Remember to check moving averages. Make sure the stock has dropped *below* its 20 MA, and better yet, its 50 MA, on a daily chart. The entry point is the same as for going long—just reversed.

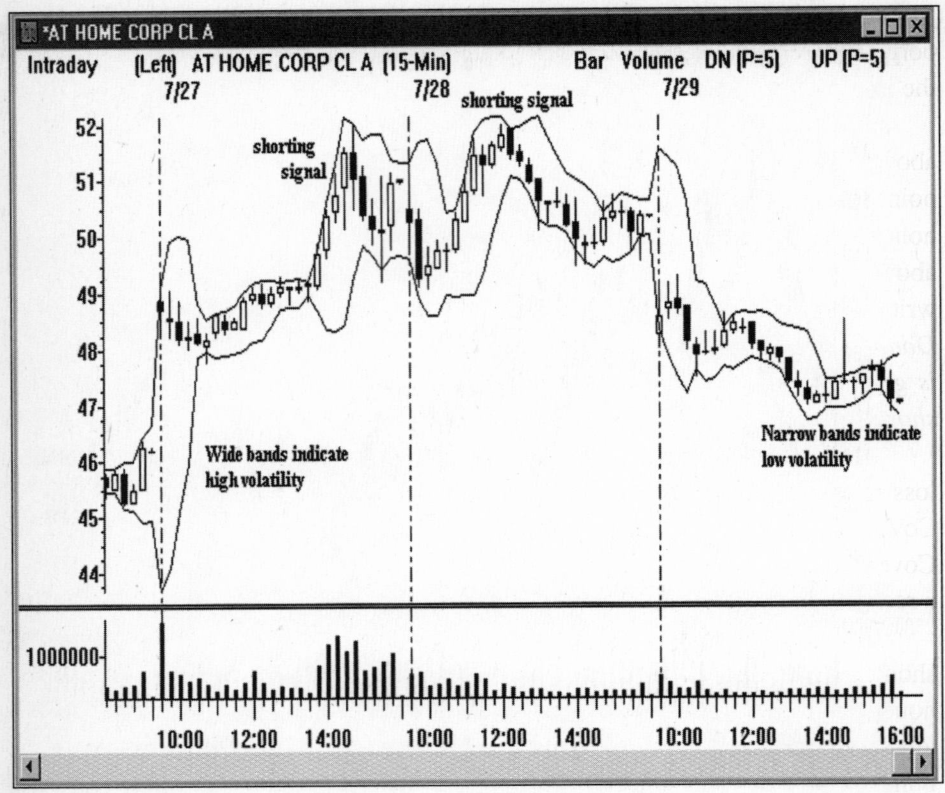

Figure 11-10

On this fifteen-minute chart of At Home Corp. (ATHM), you can see how both times the stock touched the upper band, it fell, at least short term. Bollinger bands should be used in conjunction with other indicators.

You may want to review the section on breakdowns in Chapter 6.

Figures 11-12 and 11-13 show a double top formation with Bollinger bands applied.

Now, Figure 11-4 shows two points to remember for big profits:

- Choose stocks with moonshot tops. The steeper the top, the steeper the drop!
- The less support available at the breakdown point, the more your shorts will fall down!

Just as you buy intermediate-term and swing trades when a stock pokes through resistance and trades 1/8 point above, you sell short when a stock penetrates support and trades 1/8 point below that support. Place a *limit* order to sell short the desired shares at the inside offer price.

> **Hot Tip**
>
> *What Makes Your Shorts Fall Down!* Increased volume fuels a downtrend just as it does an uptrend. Still, high volume is not necessary for a stock to break down violently. A stock can fall of its own weight through trader apathy, investor indifference, bad news or earnings, or negative market conditions.

If it's an NYSE stock, place a buy stop 1/4 point above the entry day's high as your stop loss. When that point is too far away, find a resistance area on the one-hour intraday chart, and place your buy stop 1/4 point above. Since you can't issue buy stops on Nasdaq issues, write down your exit point and circle it. Now it's law! *Don't even consider moving your stop higher. No reason is good enough. If the stock hits your stop, cover your short. No excuses.*

As the stock moves down, move your trailing stop loss 1/4 point above each new rebound on the daily chart. Cover 1/2 your position after you make a point or so. Cover the other 1/2 either when you get stopped out or at a reasonable profit. No oinking noises please.

The second pattern for intermediate-term and swing trades is the head-and-shoulders pattern illustrated in Figure 11-15. This pattern resembles a human silhouette. The stock rises in the conclusion of uptrend and pulls back, forming the left shoulder. It rises again, making a higher high, and forms the head. Again, it pulls back to previous support. This support line is called the "neckline." The last gasp is an upturn to form the right shoulder, then a retracement to the neckline

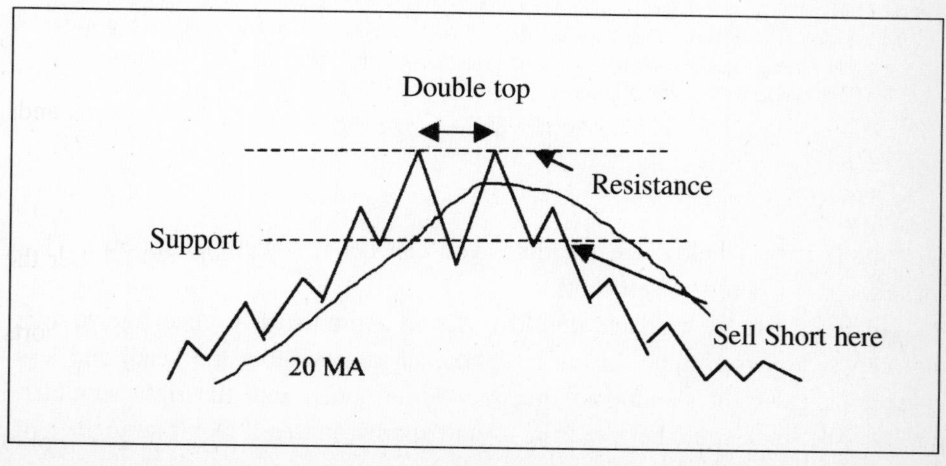

Figure 11-11

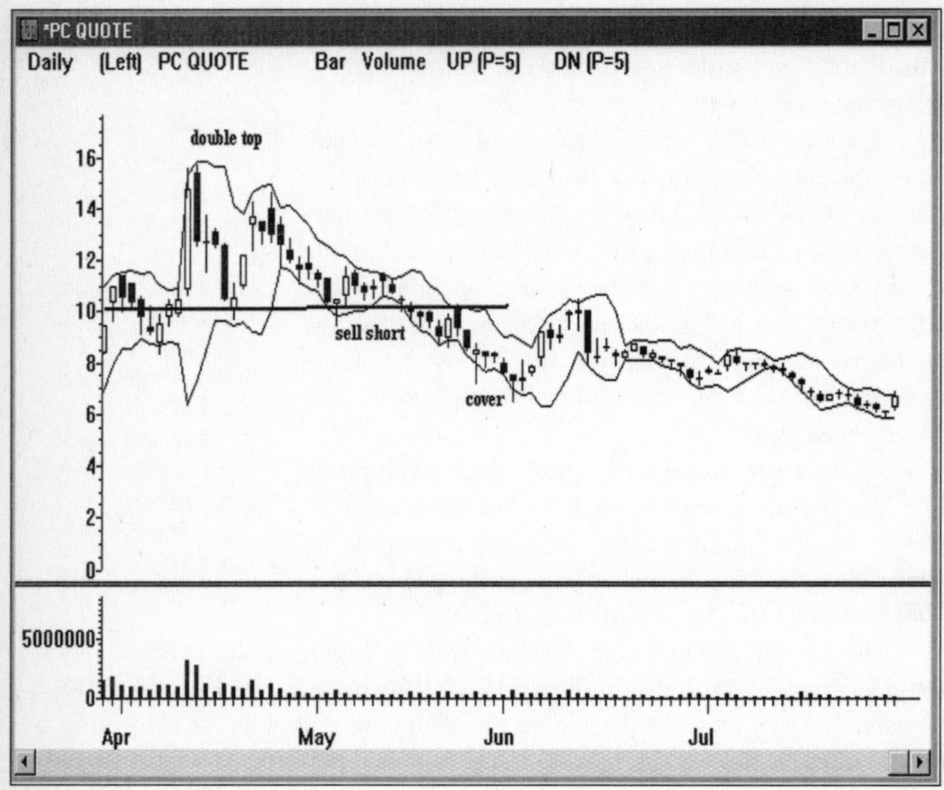

Figure 11-12

On this daily chart of PC Quote (PQT), you can see how the stock almost reaches 16 in mid-April, failed, then tried again and failed again. When you see a stock that fails to make a new high, it usually says that stock will fall soon. Here, PQT made a double top touching the upper Bollinger band each time. The first week in May it consolidated, then on May 14, it dropped below support and could be shorted at 10. By June 3, it fell to 6 7/8, where the dogi warned that PQT could reverse. (Remember, if you see a dogi after a protracted move up or down, watch for a change.) I deleted other indicators from this chart so you could see the Bollinger bands without confusion.

Chart Courtesy of *The Executioner*©

support. If it falls below the neckline, you can bet a downtrend follows. That breakdown is where you sell short.

In the case of the head and shoulders, for an optimum trade, check the volume as follows: higher volume on the left shoulder and possibly the head, and less volume on the right shoulder. If heavy volume comes into the right shoulder, beware. The stock could be preparing to start another uptrend! Don't jump the gun and sell short until the breakdown takes place.

Figures 11-16 and 11-17 show the head-and-shoulders formation.

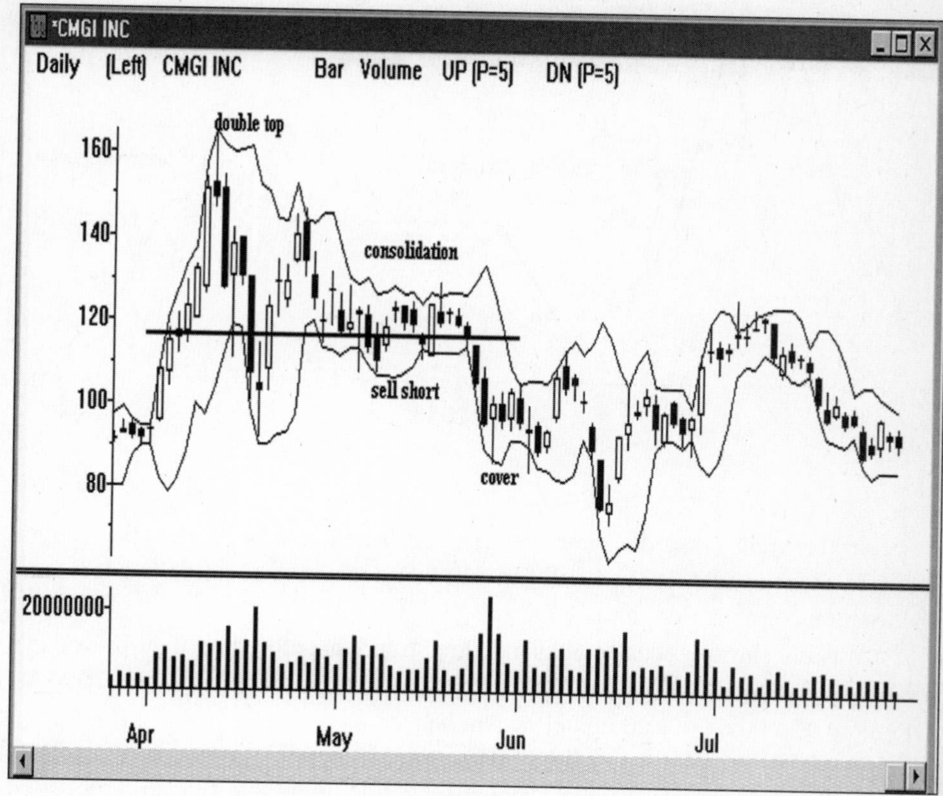

Figure 11-13

On this daily chart of CMGI Inc. (CMGI), notice how the stock rises rapidly in April from 90 to 160—in seven days! It dives back to resistance, then struggles up to 140—on less volume than the first peak, a dead giveaway that the stock's in trouble. On May 24, CMGI opened at 114 3/4 and closed at 105 1/2. Although the consolidation is disorganized, I set resistance at 111, and CMGI could have been sold short there. It fell, then consolidated for three days. On June 2, it opened and closed in the 95 area. Again, when you see a dogi form after a decent downtrend (or uptrend), beware of a reversal. Traders could have covered here with an eleven point gain. Do you see the next shorting opportunity in July? (Hint: CMGI clung to the upper Bollinger band on low volume.)

Chart Courtesy of *The Executioner*©

Besides the double top and head-and-shoulders pattern, when you want to short, look for a stock in a solid downtrend. You can short any valid breakdown as it stair-steps its way down through lower lows and lower highs. Just wait for the rebound and short when it weakens. Remember the nice spring day? Flip that pattern upside down and sell short on a "dark fall day."

This is an excellent time to brush up on candlestick patterns in Chapter 5, such as bearish engulfing patterns, hanging man, and evening stars. As you recall, these patterns warn of impending doom, which is good news for short sellers.

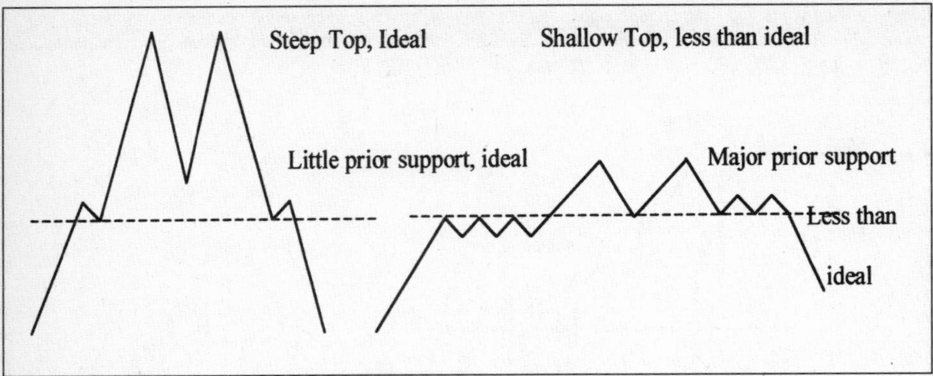

Figure 11-14

For day trades, use the same patterns you learned for buying stocks—again, just turn them upside down. Look for reversed cups-with-a-handle, wedges, and flag patterns on intraday charts.

Consider shorting weak stocks in a downtrend that closed on their prior day's low. Look for stocks on five and fifteen-minute charts trading under their 20 MAs. The more MAs they're trading below, the better.

Also, find intraday consolidations acting as support. Instead of consolidation candlesticks closing on their highs, look for vulnerable that may not hold stocks, with the consolidation candlesticks closing on their lows. This signals a possible breakdown.

Check out support levels on an intraday chart of the prior trading day, as well as the present. Where could a price reversal to the upside take place? It should be at least two points away. The closer it is, the higher the risk.

When all systems are go, and the stock penetrates the consolidation, then trades 1/8 point below, issue a sell short limit order at the inside offer price.

Figures 11-18 through 11-20 show shorting patterns and entry points for day trades.

When you're shorting, use the tops down criteria, only in reverse. Look for a weak overall market, or at least a weak NYSE or Nasdaq, depending on your stock's home. For good measure, the stock's sector should be downtrodden as well. The TICK should be negative, the TRIN positive (above 1.0, or higher.) Naturally, the S&P futures should be trading in negative territory. If you're using a CCI, look for an overbought reading, or at least a reading of *above* the median zero on the stock's daily chart.

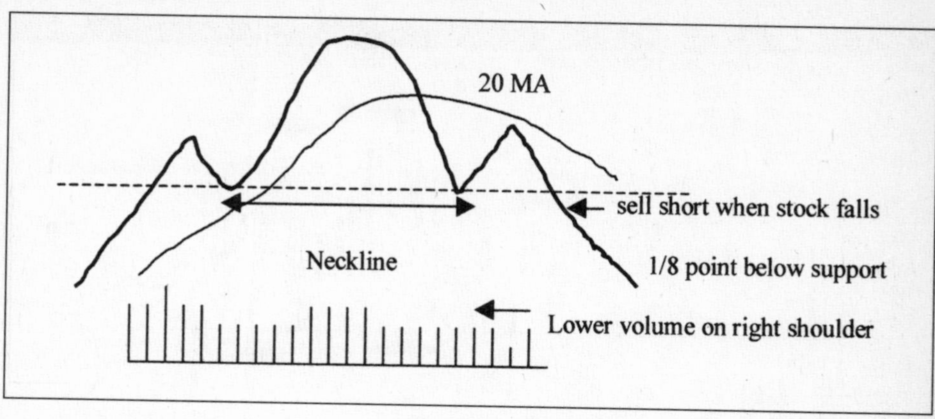

Figure 11-15
Head and shoulders shorting pattern

SHORTING DON'TS

- Don't sell a position short and then go to the beach for the day unless it's covered by a GTC buy stop. Besides, it's fun to watch your shorts fall down! Making money on a tanking stock is like watching the opposing team's quarterback get sacked. Maybe we feel as though we're getting revenge for all the times we entered long positions and got creamed. Now, we're the creamors!
- Don't short a strong stock in an uptrend. Also, when time permits, check your target stock's EPS rating in *Investors Business Daily.* Make sure the stock has a ranking of 60 or less.
- *Especially* don't short a stock because, in your opinion, it's flown way too high. Use indicators to tell you the facts. I remember when Yahoo (YHOO) was one of the first Internet stocks to soar into space. In March 1998, YHOO rocketed to the $100 mark, making multiple point leaps per day. Traders then weren't used to that kind of volatility. I remember a bunch of top traders who shorted the stock when it hit 99. They bet the ranch, shorting thousands upon thousands of shares. YHOO sped over the 100 mark. Still, disbelief that it could defy gravity much longer made short sellers hold. The stock didn't look back for a long time to come, and it wiped out many of those traders for good.

You would have known better. After studying this book, you would have looked at the strong volume on the continuing breakouts and surmised the stock might climb even higher. You would have been right.

Figure 11-16

On this daily chart of the Wisconsin Energy Corp. (WEC), I left the Bollinger bands off so you could clearly see the outline of the head and shoulders. Note that the volume is higher on the left shoulder than on the right—a good sign the stock will fall. It did just that, gapping down 3/4 point on June 28, to break the head-and-shoulders neckline. Traders could have sold short there at 27 and held two days until the wide range candlestick on July 30. The increased volume on that day signaled a possible trend reversal after a protracted move. Traders would cover at the day's end at 25.

Chart Courtesy of *The Executioner*©

- Don't short a stock just because it gaps down at the open. If it's a weak stock, and you believe it will head farther south, wait until it trades under its first thirty-minute low, then short it.
- If you're a new trader, please avoid scalping shorts. The uptick rule often makes entry difficult, time consuming, and imprecise. It's not worth it for a possible 1/4 to 1/2 point gain.
- Don't short a thinly traded stock, that is, a stock that trades fewer than 300,000 shares per day. That proposition is unwise on either the long or short side!

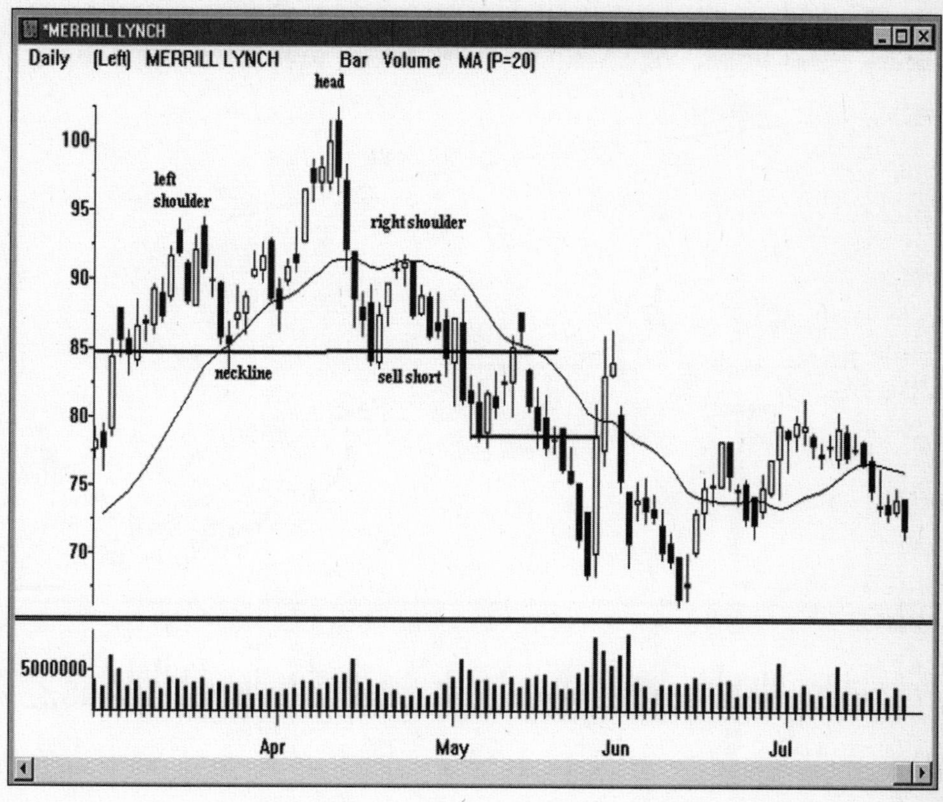

Figure 11-17

On this daily chart of Merrill Lynch (MER), note again how the volume is lower on the right shoulder than the left, a sign the stock may fall. On May 4, MER opened at 86 7/8 and closed at 81 1/4 on high volume. It broke the neckline and could be shorted just below support, at 84. The stock plunged for two more days to 78 5/8 and an oversold condition. (Again, I left some indicators and the CCI off the charts so you could clearly see the pattern.) Traders should cover on the third day down at 78 5/8 for a 6+ point profit. Notice the second support line I drew just below the neckline. If market internals agreed—and obviously they did since MER is considered a market bellwether—another shorting opportunity presented itself when the stock broke support.

Chart Courtesy of *The Executioner*©

QUIZ

1. When you're scalping, what fraction of a point spread do you look for?
2. Certain types of numbers play a role in support and resistance. What are they?
3. True or false? The safest scalping opportunities await in industry giants, such as Cisco, Intel, and Microsoft.
4. Name three ideal scalping setup components.

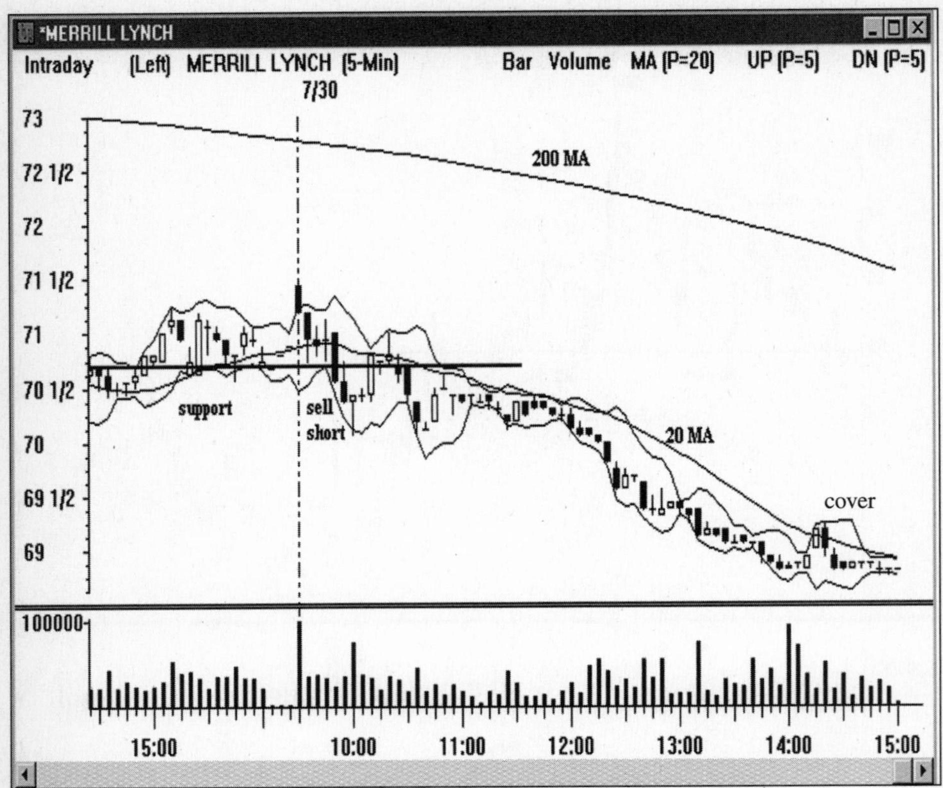

Figure 11-18

On this five-minute chart of Merrill Lynch (MER), the short seller has everything going his or her way. The stock is trading under its 20 MA when it opens, and has jutted through its upper Bollinger band. It quickly falls, hesitates at yesterday's closing consolidation, then falls through that support area and under its 20 MA as well. MER could have been sold short there at 70 3/4. It tried to rise, but alert traders would notice it did so on low volume, a signal the breakout would fail. It did, and by the end of the midday blues, the stock fell to 68 3/4. At the sudden rise in volume at 2 p.m., the stock should be covered for a two-point profit.

Chart Courtesy of *The Executioner*©

5. True or false? For an optimal scalping setup, you look for stocks on level II where only TNTO and INCA wait on the inside bid.
6. True or false? Never place a market order to catch a running stock.
7. Scene: You're in the midst of a successful scalp. Suddenly, the futures tank, the TICK drops, and the market makers evaporate from your stock's bid. How do you get out?
8. Define the shorting "uptick rule."
9. If you see a stock touching the top of its upper Bollinger band, where will it probably move next?

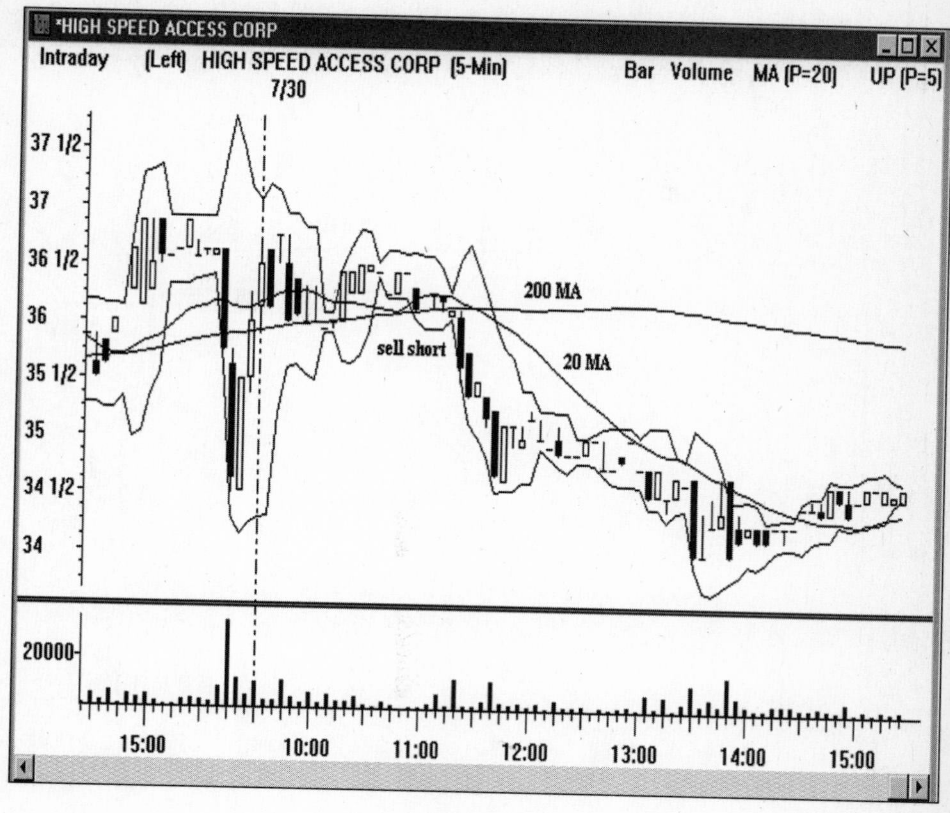

Figure 11-19

On this five-minute chart of High Speed Access Corp. (HSAC), you can see how the stock broke down on high volume the prior day, right before the close, then recovered (possible short covering). On this day, it wandered along its 200 MA until 11:15 a.m., when, with the help of failing S&P futures, HSAC dropped below its 200 MA and its 20 MA simultaneously. Traders could sell short here at 36, and ride along as the stock drifted to previous day's support at 34. HSAC could be covered here for a 1 1/4 point gain, or if market conditions remained negative enough, it could have been held through the midday blues until it bottomed at 34.

Chart Courtesy of *The Executioner©*

10. True or false? To find shorting candidates for intermediate-term trades, use daily charts and look for stocks in a downtrend, trading below their 20 MA, and better yet, below their 50 MA.
11. Is increased volume necessary for a stock to plunge into a downtrend?
12. When you're in a short and the darn stock starts rising, it's best to move your original buy stop, or stop loss, a resistance point or two higher. Right?
13. On the head-and-shoulders pattern for a good shorting opportunity, look for lower volume on the ____________ shoulder.
14. If a weak stock gaps down at the open, how do you handle it?

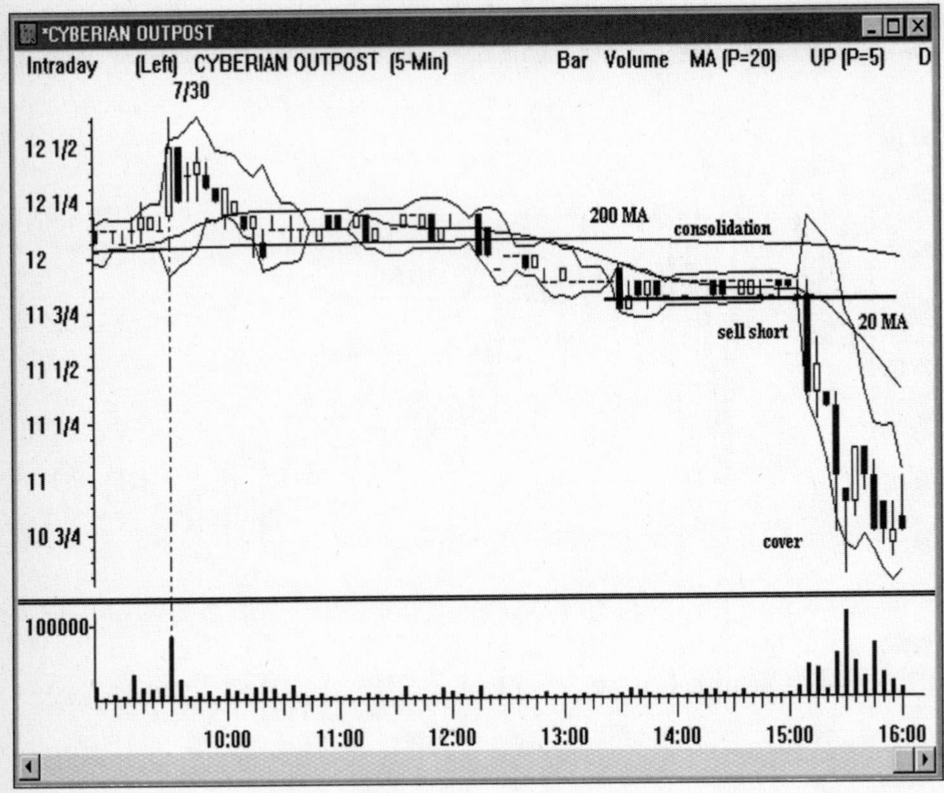

Figure 11-20

On this five-minute chart of Cyberian Outpost (COOL), the stock drifted sideways for most of the day, but as a short candidate, caught our attention watching when it dropped under its 200 MA and 20 MA during the midday blues. At 3:05, it fell through support on increased volume, a short signal. Traders who sold short here at 11 13/16 could have ridden it down to 10 3/4 at the close, a point profit in an hour. Please notice that short plays that drop through support from consolidation areas make great profit plays—fun and (relatively) easy!

Chart Courtesy of *The Executioner*©

ANSWERS

1. Look for a spread of 1/8 point or less.
2. Whole numbers, and to a lesser degree 1/2 numbers, play a role in support and resistance.
3. Very false.
4. (1) Stock is consolidating at or near the day's high. (2) It moves sideways in a tight, orderly fashion for twenty minutes, preferably longer. (3) Most of the candlesticks are closing on their highs.
5. False. INCA and TNTO are ECNs. They represent other traders, and as such, do not carry the institutional weight of muscle market makers like MLCO, GSCO, and SLKC. *These* are the guys you want to see on the bid!
6. As true as true can be!
7. When good scalps suddenly sour, issue a sell limit order one or two levels (1/8 to 1/4 point) under the inside bid.
8. The uptick rule: Stocks can be sold short only on an uptick. The trade can take place only if the stock trades above the last tick, or on a zero-plus tick, meaning the same price as the last uptick.
9. A stock touching the top of its upper Bollinger band will probably move down to its lower Bollinger band.
10. True.
11. No.
12. You're grinning, right? Answer: wrong, wrong, wrong.
13. Right.
14. When your target stock gaps down at the open, wait until it trades for thirty minutes. Enter after it falls 1/8 point under the thirty-minute low.

✦ ✦ ✦

CENTER POINT

Create a Prosperity Consciousness

You are an expression of the infinite creative flow, the infinite creative process. You have everything you need to achieve a life of abundance. You only need access it by claiming your entitlement from within. Know that you are a center within an affluent universe, and guidance, ingenuity, and opportunities await you."

—ERIC BUTTERWORTH

Each and every one of us is entitled to the boundless support of the universe. In order to claim this support in the form of abundance and prosperity, we must take charge of our beliefs and our thoughts. We must focus our consciousness not only on what we do, but how we think. How do we visualize our outer world?

Our prosperity, or lack of it, reflects the level of our thinking. As individuals, we may not have a direct impact on world economic conditions, but when we give them reality by focusing on negative thoughts or having conversations about them, we become synchronized with a negative energy flow that has a swift influence on our lives.

Do you hold onto the old belief that righteousness resides in poverty? Do you pepper your thoughts and conversations with phrases such as, "I can't," "I'm afraid, I don't know how," and "There's not enough"? Consider releasing those feelings of unworthiness. Instead, center your thoughts on concepts of abundance, sufficiency, and self-worth.

Know that you are a very special person. A unique consciousness dwells within you and flows through you. The universe is on your side. Life is biased on the side of healing, on the side of triumph, on the side of success.

Assume that inner and outer prosperity is your divine right. Center your thoughts on your blessings rather than on what you conceive as your lack and limitations. Lift your consciousness and stretch the boundaries of faith in yourself, and faith in life. Create conditions within your mind that make positive results inevitable.

Abundance and prosperity are ours for the taking! We need only claim them by taking responsibility for own thoughts, and in doing so, taking charge of our lives.

Each of us is entitled to the boundless support of the universe. When we hold this in our hearts, and minds, we act as magnets to attract prosperity and abundance as a natural function of life's process.

✦ ✦ ✦

CHAPTER 12

Love Your Losses: They're a Trader's Best Friend!

You probably read the title to this chapter and made immediate plans to have me carted off. But before you send me to the nut house, hear me out!

Losses represent one of the most important subjects of this book. That's why I'm taking an entire chapter to talk about them.

Here's a surprising, but absolute fact: The success or failure of your trading career does not depend on your gains. It depends on your losses.

Socrates wrote that an unexamined life wasn't worth living. Guess what? Unexamined trading losses will send you to the soup line! Trust me. I've approached the end of that line, spoon in hand, more than once.

The single most important thing you can do while you learn how to trade: Keep a journal of your losses. Please don't misunderstand. This is not a self-flagellation diary. In fact, call it your Success Journal—because if tended to properly, that's exactly where this exercise leads.

Buy a nice notebook with a cheerfully colored cover. (I like green, the color of money.) Put the day's date at the top of each page. When the market closes each day, record your entries. Write down the stock symbol, entry price, and exit price. Start the first sentence, "I entered this trade because…," then finish the sentence with your reason. Didn't have a good reason? Hmm. That's a point to ponder.

Maybe you entered for terrific reasons: perfect entry point, good tops down criteria, great chart pattern. Still, the trade turned sour. Begin this sentence with, "I lost money on this trade because…." Without criticizing yourself, list the reasons your trade went against you. No words like "stupid," or "dummy" allowed. Just the facts. Now study those facts and own the choices you made.

Once you understand what happened, think forward. Get on the other side of the loss.

Last, write, "The next time this situation arises, I will...." Finish this sentence with the steps you'll take the next time you encounter this circumstance. The next time, how can you better protect your principal? What would you do to make sure you're trading to trade well? When you execute a particularly awesome trade, include that in your journal also. Learn to repeat your successes.

The following trading morning, review your last Success Journal entries. If you have time, review others you have written.

As I've mentioned before, people who write down their goals prove to be far more successful than those who simply store them in memory. This premise holds for traders and their journals. The wealthiest traders I know completed this process early in their trading careers. It absolutely, positively, *always* delivers awesome results!

SEVEN "SUICIDE SCENES": HOW TO AVOID THEM, PROTECT YOUR PRINCIPAL, AND LIVE TO TRADE ANOTHER DAY

Let's haul some typical losses into the light of day, so we can inspect them. Since I've experienced every one of these losses, you don't have to.

Scene One: Stuff Happens

You buy a strong stock, in a strong market, at the right entry point. A few minutes later, though, negative economic news interrupts the routine commentary on CNBC. The market does a U-turn. Your stock joins the stampede to the south and hits your stop. You sell and are out with a small loss.

Loss avoidance tactic: There isn't one! You entered a strong stock, in a strong market, at the right time. Unexpected news happens. When you exited at the proper stop point, your loss represented a calculated risk of the business. Pat yourself on the back for a job well done.

This scene compressed into cold, hard reality boils down to: good trade, unexpected event, stock dives, proper exit action, small loss incurred. Study and reflect upon the sequence. Look simple to duplicate? It isn't. (You guessed it. The "proper exit action" usually gets in our way.)

This type of loss is the only justifiable loss you'll ever take. Losses like these are not the ones that hurt you. Those that follow are.

Scene Two: The Good News, Bad News Roller-Coaster Ride

Soon after the market opens up, you buy a strong stock at the right entry point. You've designated it a day trade. By 11:30, your stock rises to the next resistance area, two points away. Instead of exiting at this predetermined exit point with a $2 profit, you hold on. Surely after the market's midday blues, your stock will conquer the resistance area and make another point or two.

Fast-forward to 2:30 p.m., same day. Your stock and the market act listless and lifeless. Could it be the important economic news due out tomorrow? Your stock drifts down to your entry point, sinks beneath it, and hits your stop. You sigh and exit the trade.

I can't count the times I've ridden a good stock to fine profits, refused to sell, and ridden the darn thing all the way back down for a loss. Yes, it happens to everyone. No, that doesn't make it feel any better. Lethargy and optimism (greed?) are the operative words here. You get caught up in the euphoria of what may be, instead of looking at what is.

Loss avoidance tactic: Though this loss is acceptable because you sold your position at your established stop loss point, it was still avoidable. First, in a day trade, when a stock makes two points, then nears resistance, take your money and run! I don't care if the thing points to Mars. Do it anyway. Nine times out of ten, you'll congratulate yourself later.

Second, a stock that hits resistance at 11:30 a.m. will likely pull back. The midday blues will push it down, if nothing else.

Third, stay abreast of major economic reports, such as unemployment reports, the CPI (Consumer Price Index), GNP (Gross National Product), and PPI (Produce Price Index), usually announced at 8:30 a.m. EST. CNBC's S&P futures "bug" at the bottom right-hand corner of your television screen, and Squawk Box commentators discussing bond futures' reactions, will tell you whether or not the market liked the news.

The day *prio*r to the report, the market typically quiets in the afternoon. Many professional traders, including floor traders in the exchanges, go home for the remainder of the day. Pros refuse to commit to a position when economic news threatens to yank it from underneath. Join them. Exit some or all of your positions before lunch. If the market decides to rally, you can always jump back in.

Fourth, the market has become so volatile, you might consider the morning and afternoon as two different days. Many times, in the afternoon, the market reverses its morning action. So don't assume that because your stock is strong in the morning, it will continue its rise later in the day. Maybe, maybe not. Closing out winning trades before lunch promotes good digestion! Besides, hearken to the old trader saying: "You never go broke taking a profit."

Scene Three: Drop the Stop Game

You're scalping. After your target stock consolidated near its highs, it broke out and you jumped in at the proper entry point. Suddenly, the tide turns, really fast, and the stock drops like a bomb—right through your stop loss. You chase it down. Instead of issuing a sell order 1/4 point below the bid, you stubbornly shoot orders at the current bid. It gives way to the next level down. You cancel and shoot again. Oops. Bid gone. "Doesn't *anybody* want to buy this stock?" you wail. *No.*

When the stock grovels two points down from your original stop, a light bulb flashes in your head. *You'll switch this from a scalp to a day trade! No problem.* You check the day's low for a new stop loss point. *Uh, oh.* Stock's already crashed through that. What about yesterday's low? *Gulp.* That was 1/2 point ago. Worse, you're down almost three points. AAACK!

But, wait, your frantic mind flashes another light bulb. *This isn't a day trade. Doesn't have to be. As of right now, it's a swing trade.* Swing trades have much wider stop losses than day trades. *Sure. That'll work.*

With stomach churning and palms sweating, you pull up a daily chart and search for yet another reversal point, anywhere that the stock might find support. Glumly, you find it—four points below the current price.

Get the picture?

Loss avoidance tactic: When you enter a trade, designate the time frame, and stick to it no matter what obstacles jump into your path. All scalping entries do not a swing trade make! Or a day trade for that matter.

Okay, guys and girlfriends. Please raise your right hand and repeat after me: *"I swear on my mouse, I will never, ever, as long as I trade, lower my stop loss."*

Good. Got that done!

Scene Four: How to Catch a Falling Knife. Not.

It's a grim day at the ranch. Mother Market heard the word *inflation* muttered on CNBC by some Fed watcher, and she's fallen into a sullen mood. The TICK wallows in the –500 area, the TRIN is climbing over 1.2. Unhappiness prevails. You're flat, thank goodness, and you see nothing you want to sell short, but your trigger finger itches.

Hmm. There's a stock, a leader in the pharmaceutical industry that's plummeted for a week. It's got a bad case of the uglies. Makes sense because that industry is ailing as well. Betcha' that stock will reverse when it lands on its 50 MA on a daily chart. That should be today. You pull up the chart.

Oops. It just did! It just hit the 50 MA, and it popped 1/2 point. Yeah! *Just like the stockbrokers say, you'll buy low, sell high.* You buy.

After a brief rally, the market resumes its downward plunge. Your immediate profits wipe out, and the stock drops like a stone. It dives through your stop and plummets through its 50 MA on the daily chart. You stare at your screen, paralyzed. It slides another point, then another. You let it drop, unwilling to gag on such a large loss. By the end of the day, you are down four points. Numbly, still holding the position, you hear the closing bell.

Loss avoidance tactic: Another old trader saying goes, "Never try to catch a falling knife." Yet another states, "The trend is your friend."

First, if the market trends in a negative direction, and you feel signs of boredom—leave. Better you should take a walk, get a cup of coffee, or go shopping. If you're not in front of your computer, you can't commit one of the foremost new trader mistakes—overtrading, or trading for no reason.

What if the market reverses while you're gone and you miss a couple of opportunities? That's part of this game. Shrug it off.

Second, no matter which way the market trends, "the trend is your friend." Swim with the current.

Third, when stocks drop, they drop for a reason. More sellers than buyers. Nobody wants them! Traders call stocks like these "falling knives." Please don't try to catch one. The results can hurt.

"Buy low, sell high" works well in real estate. It rarely works as well in the stock market, especially in short-term trades. Remember, when you choose a stock to buy, it's like choosing players for your ball team. You don't choose the guy with a broken arm, or the girl who's clumsy. You choose the strongest people available to make a winning team. When you're trading, you choose the strongest stocks to make winning profits.

Scene Five: Hey, Wait for Me!

It's 8:30 a.m. on a weekday, and you're watching CNBC. The bug in the bottom right-hand corner of the screen says S&P futures are up nicely. The Dow flew into record territory yesterday, and things look rosy.

You're sipping your coffee, and smacking your lips at the money you'll make today. Your favorite brokerage stock on the NYSE reported earnings last night after the bell—and they were golden. Beat the Street by two cents. By 9:31, CNBC says the stock isn't open yet, but when it does, it will open higher. It dawns on you that you could get your order in ahead of the opening crowd.

You run to your computer. You've designated this a swing trade; you place a buy order for 500 shares, at the market.

When the stock finally opens, your stock opens up two points. You get filled a point higher. No problem. You know once it starts running it'll never look back.

Five minutes later—and you're right. It's up another point! Right on! Awesome trade!

You take a short break to call and invite some friends out for dinner—your treat—then return to your computer. Market's still going strong. Indexes, TICK, TRIN, futures, all fine. Your gaze moves to your stock. *Huh? Omigod.* It's fallen two points. Worse, it looks like it's in free-fall. The bid's dropping like a brick. When it tumbles through the day's low, you jump out with a loss. What happened?

Loss avoidance tactics: First, never place a market order to buy before a stock opens for the day. A market order placed before the opening bell, or before the stock opens, will get filled at the absolute top price possible. A subsequent gap-and-crap scenario can deliver an instant and devastating loss.

Second, monitor a stock with a good earnings announcement. Don't buy until you're sure of the direction it takes. Heard the old trader saying, "Buy the rumor, sell the news"? It's true. If the stock ran up bigtime *before* its earnings announcement on rumor of those good earnings, that run-up absorbed the pending news. What's going to happen when the news is announced? Profit-taking. Fast and furious.

"But," you reply, "the stock ran up when it opened. Somebody bought it. Who made it do that?"

You. You and Joe Public who acted on logic. You thought good earnings = rising stock price.

Sometimes. Not always.

Third, when the stock ran up in the days before the announcement, the specialists (in this case) had to sell their own shares. (Market makers are forced to take the same stance.) Remember, when buyers far outnumber sellers, specialists and market makers have to short the stock. Do you really think they'll let it run to infinity without slapping it back down again so they can cover their shorts? Nope. Specialists and market makers aren't known for their charity work.

They fill orders at the open, then drop the bid as soon as they can to make their own profits. After you panic and sell it to them at bargain-basement prices, they raise the bid—and sell it to someone else at higher prices.

Conclusion—don't jump into a good-earnings stock—until it calms down and you can lock into its genuine direction.

Scene Six: The Whipsaw Club

You're day trading. Strong market, strong stock. You buy at a good entry point. Stock moves up, then stalls. Uh, oh.

Market goes against you. The futures slip, and the TICK falls off, but the TRIN stays low. Good. You hold your position and start humming "The TRIN always wins."

Suddenly, the futures dive hard. The TICK follows. *Oh, no.* You're puzzled. Even though indexes and indicators edge down, the TRIN is holding relatively low, under 0.8.

Market makers vanish from the bid. Your stock slides through its immediate support area and through your stop. *Wince.* Support is an "area," isn't it? Lots of books say that. You'll give your stock another 1/8 point or two before you get out.

The 1/8 point leaves. Just when you're poised to click on your sell order, the stock rallies a 1/4. Whew. Close call!

Then, the downturn resumes. The TRIN climbs only slightly, while other indicators trickle through support areas. It's a slow decline, like Chinese water torture. This is a pullback, right? After all, nothing goes straight up. Retracements happen.

Your stock slides and you see high volume coming into each down candlestick. Enough already. Bite-the-bullet time. You sell and swallow your point loss. *Rats.*

Suddenly, you feel vengeful. If this stupid stock is going to fall, you might as well short it. You'll make money on the doggone thing one way or another. When it rallies (it's easiest to short on a rally where you have the upticks you need to enter the trade via the uptick rule), you short 500 shares and place your stop loss 1/8 point above the rebound price. There! *Take that, you stupid stock.*

The stock hesitates, falls 1/4 point, then stalls again. Suddenly the futures bounce, the TICK starts climbing. Your stock hits minor support. Muscle market makers appear at the bid. *Groan.* The stock shoots up two levels on your market maker screen. *Please stop.* Maybe…maybe this is just a rebound in the stock's downtrend. Do you get out now or wait?

The stock steps neatly over your stop loss and shoots even higher. You grit your teeth and cover your short. Another loss—one going each way. Now you're a card-carrying member of the Whipsaw Club.

Loss avoidance tactic: First, you let the stock slip through your initial stop loss without taking action. If you'd sold then, you would have shrugged off the loss as part of the business, and would have eliminated the need for revenge. "Don't get mad, get even" rarely works in the stock market!

Second, your anger caused you to short the stock just because it was going down. Anger = an emotion we can't afford when trading.

Third, the TRIN truly did tell a story, although prices are the bottom line. I've experienced a few days when the TICK dropped like a sack of moldy potatoes, and the TRIN remained under 0.8 for hours at a time. It's a strange divergence and certainly contradictory. The only way to read such diversion is "confusion." When events like this take place in the market, jump out and stand on the sidelines. We cannot outguess confusion, or a trendless market.

Scene Seven: Going Ballistic

You know the drill: strong market. You're scanning charts for a day trade on the long side. Suddenly an Internet mutual fund manager on CNBC mentions that Missile.com is the new darling of the "dot com" stocks. And, he likes it. He loves their new product, and their CEO is a wonder boy. Wow! That oughtta' do it! Internet stocks scream skyward whenever someone on CNBC sings their name.

You quickly bring up Missile.com's daily chart. Whoa! A week ago, it was 11. Today it's 44! It's trading miles over its 20 MA, and it's way overextended. Still, who can argue with success? A glance at its level II screen shows hungry piranhas eating through the offer like lightning. It's at 45, 45 1/2, 45 3/4, 46, 46 1/4. Awww. Just a 1/2 point. That's all you want. That's what level II is for, right? Ultimate speed. You throw in your offer 1/8 point over the current ask, and get hit in a nanosecond: 1,000 shares at 47. Sold to the highest bidder. You!

Missile.com quivers for a few seconds, then plunges. *No, wait. Hold it.* The time and sales screen turns blood red with downticks. The missile turns into a bomb. Your hand freezes on your mouse. It'll stop. *Please make it stop.*

Seconds later it screeches to a halt at 42. You're $5,000 in the hole. How do you climb out of it?

The fund manager on CNBC said Missile's a good stock, didn't he? Well…if you buy another 500 shares here, at 42, your net price per share would be 45 and change. Better than 47! So you buy 500 at 42 and dig in. Your scalp is now a swing trade.

The next day the market opens down, and the Internet sector sings the blues. When Missile hits 36, and holds through lunch, you take it as a sign from above. This is the bottom. Surely it'll breakout from its lunchtime congestion and turn north again. You buy another 500 at 36.

After lunch, though, the candlesticks in the congestion pattern start closing on their lows. *Gulp.* You know what that means. And it does. All fall down. Your stomach churns, your palms sweat. You're in so deep, how do you get out except with a horrendous loss?

You check Missile's daily chart again. You find support around 31. Surely it will bounce off that. By the end of the day, it slips to 31, and hovers there. Okay. Just one more time. Gritting your teeth, you buy an additional 500 shares, maxing out your margin.

During the next few days, the Internet sector, already overblown for weeks, gets punctured. You sell other stocks at a loss to avoid a margin call. Missile tanks again, through support at 31, and heads for parts unknown. Wearily, you check the daily chart. The next support is at 19. You can't take it anymore. You're out at 29.

Loss avoidance tactic: Before we start, if you think this can't happen—it can. This very situation happened…um…to a friend of mine.

First, it's easy to get caught up in the euphoria of a running stock. I swear, when the level II screen flashes a stream of green, we slip into a hypnotic state. In that trance, we click on the buy button. Next comes the *ohnosecond* when we realize what we've done. It's always followed by the standard prayer to the trading god: *Please, please get me out of this trade even. If you do, I promise I'll be good for the rest of my life.*

Setting sell stop for a wildly gyrating stock is a joke. It will probably hit it while your order to buy hangs in the ether. I've had my stop hit before my order was filled—but it was too late to cancel. It's obvious. If you get sucked into a screaming trade because of a momentary sanity lapse, get out as fast as you can. Old trader saying: "Your first loss is the smallest." Very accurate.

Second, when you see a stock trading way above its 20 MA on a daily chart, it's overextended. Like a rubber band stretched too far, it's likely to snap back soon. Leave it alone until it pulls back, at least to its 10 or 20 MA, which it will inevitably do.

Third, "averaging down" means you nibble on a stock in a downtrend at various points. You hope (uh, oh) when it rises, your average price will be low enough to reap nice gains, or at the worst, get out even.

When to average down: When a strong stock in a strong market pulls back to an expected reversal point, then breaks out, averaging down may reap gains.

When not to average down: When you're trading short term and your stock reverts from strong to weak, don't continue to buy more. Sell your position. If it sinks to a support area, holds, and breaks out on volume with a market reversal trending the same direction, that's when to consider reentering.

In conclusion, you see that scene one happens regularly as part of the business. Scenes two through six demonstrate how permitting a stock to initially penetrate its stop loss causes 99 percent of the subsequent agony.

The solution is so simple, and for some reason so hard to do. Please, as the saying goes, "just do it." Honor your stop loss points. Each time you make that choice, pat yourself on the back. The more pats you receive, the further along the road to success you've traveled!

QUIZ

1. What three questions will you answer in your Success Journal?
2. You're in a day trade. You have profits of $2 and your stock is nearing resistance. What should you do?
3. What usually happens to market mood on the afternoon prior to the announcement of an important economic report?
4. True or false? If you are in a trade and the situation gets ugly, simply change the time frame you've designated and lower your stop.
5. A market order placed before the opening bell will get filled at the open at the ______________ possible price.
6. Buy the ____________, sell the ___________.
7. When a stock comes out with a good earnings announcement, how should you treat it?
8. Some traders say, "If it's not a long, it's a short." Is that always true?
9. True or false? If a trade gone sour makes you angry, direct that energy to your next trade.
10. Define an "overextended" stock.
11. What's the least profitable situation in which to average down?

ANSWERS

1. Why you entered each trade. Reasons you closed it with a loss. Steps you can take in the future to avoid repeating those choices.
2. Take profits fast!
3. The afternoon before an important economic report, the market usually adopts a quiet, lethargic mood.
4. False, false, false.
5. highest.
6. rumor, news.
7. When a stock comes out with a good earnings announcement, wait until it trades for a while to see what trend it establishes.
8. No, it isn't true. Trendless stocks in a volatile market make neither successful long *nor* successful short candidates.
9. Don't you dare! You're not really angry at the stock. You're angry at yourself. Carried into your trading, that anger will cause huge losses. If you feel angry while you're trading, take your positions flat. Then go for a walk, or even take the rest of the day off. You'll feel better and so will your trading account.
10. We say a stock is overextended when it trades way above a major moving average. A good example is when a stock shoots way over its 20 MA on a daily chart.
11. The worst time to average down: You're trading short term (swing trades, day trades, and scalps) and your stock reverts from strong to weak.

✦ ✦ ✦

CENTER POINT

The Truth About Fear

Begin difficult things while they are easy, do great things when they are small. The difficult things of the world must once have been easy; the great things must once have been small...a thousand mile journey begins with one step.

—LAO-TSE

We are all acquainted with fear and the way it makes us feel. Regarded in the proper context, however, it's really a positive emotion. It warns us of impending danger so we can take steps to safety.

Unfortunately, we tend to hold onto fear after it's outlived its usefulness as a warning device. Then fear twists into all kinds of related detrimental emotions from low self-esteem, to stress, to panic. When fear digs its claws in deep enough, it takes a conscious effort to release it. Here are some thoughts that may help.

First, when you feel fear, acknowledge it. Notice how it feels and where it's located in your body. Many of us feel it in our solar plexus. Sit quietly; let yourself feel it in a nonjudgmental way. What thoughts come up around it? What message does it have for you?

Treat your fear as though it were a small child. If a four-year-old came up to you and cried she was afraid of the bogeyman, what would you do? You'd hug her and ask her to explain her fears. When she finished, you'd assure her that the bogeyman isn't real and soothe her with positive, affirmative thoughts. That's exactly how we need to treat that part of us that lives in fear, with love and positive emotions. After all, fear is not the truth. Fear is nothing, trying to be something. It has only the power we give to it.

Go back in your memories to a time when you felt supremely safe, secure, and loved. Draw upon the feeling that memory holds for you. Gently replace your negative feelings with the positive, loving feelings of those memories. Since love and fear are polar opposites, love drives away fear. Similarly, light is the reality, and darkness is the absence of that light. When you let light in, darkness disappears; it is not real.

Reality is this: Our lives unfold toward our best and highest good. We are guided and supported, and everything we need is available to us, right now, for the asking.

Knowing this, we recognize fear as the warning tool that it is. We acknowledge it, learn from it, and step another rung up the ladder to happiness and success.

✦ ✦ ✦

CHAPTER 13

Trading Survival Techniques

In this chapter, you'll find a "stew" of trading tips, techniques, and general knowledge I've gained through experience. They're the things I'd tell you if you called me on the phone, and we chatted as friends, and as traders.

THE "IF, THEN" MENTALITY: HOW IT BOOSTS YOU TO THE RANKS OF PROFESSIONALS

Remember a college math course called Logic? Logic used single sentences that we changed into a mathematical equation to gauge its validity. The first half of the sentence always began with "If"; the second half of the sentence started with "then." Briefly, if both phrases in the sentence were true, the sentence was true. If either phrase was false or uncertain, the entire sentence was false. Naturally, when both phrases were false, the entire sentence was invalid. Logic reveals the truth, and can be a terrific way to evaluate what a politician, for example, says in a speech.

I said all that to say this: The farther you travel in your trading career, the more you'll recognize correlations between diverse market occurrences. Every time you use those correlations to your advantage, you advance more quickly to the ranks of the victorious.

Therefore, learn to think in terms of "if, then." "If" might translate into a news event that causes the markets to react. Or it might state the positions of two indices used as indicators. "Then" represents probable reaction of the market to the "If" premise. Think: action = reaction. Or "When *this* happens, then *that* usually happens."

At different places in this chapter, I'll stress the "if, then" scenario so you'll understand why it's important to channel your thoughts along those lines.

STAY AWARE OF BIG PICTURE DYNAMICS

Even though you may be trading in short-term time frames, as a trader it's imperative you remain aware of major market trends. It is particularly significant when the market moves into the top of a cycle and reverts to a trendless interval. Cycle tops are always high-risk periods. Remember October 1987 when Black Monday wiped out many accounts within hours? (If you didn't experience it, you've surely heard of it.) Other high-risk periods were October 1997, when the Asian Contagion first infected our markets, and the disastrous summer and fall of 1998, ignited by a devalued Russian ruble, among other events.

High-risk zones, as illustrated in Figure 13-1, don't have to be accompanied by negative news, but often when the market balances precariously on the top of a cycle, bad news chooses that exact point in time to push the markets over the edge. High-risk zones *always* produce false signals and whipsaw conditions.

Interestingly enough, low-risk periods—when the market is bottoming, or basing—are not low risk at all on a short-term basis. They emit the same signals and conditions as toppy markets—false, whippy, and choppy. Why? Because they, too, occur when the market is searching for a new trend. During both periods, you'll hear announcers on CNBC quiz their guests with questions such as, "Is this the top?" "Can the market go higher from here?" Or "Is this the bottom?" Has enough panic-driven selling taken place that buyers will start nibbling here?"

Savvy investors and traders track market trends because it enables them to position themselves advantageously. At the culmination of a major uptrend, when the market rolls over into a high-risk zone, they build cash reserves and day trade, or scalp.

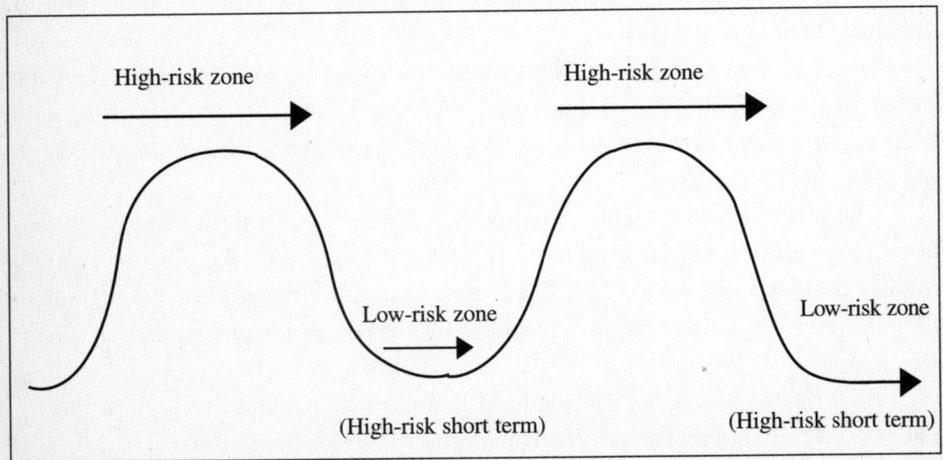

Figure 13-1

High-risk/low-risk periods in market cycles

When the market bottoms after a downtrend and begins to move sideways in a so-called low-risk area (remember, it's low-risk long term, *not* shortterm), it's time to cover shorts and again build cash supplies to prepare for selective buying.

See why traders say so often, "the trend is your friend"? During a definite uptrend or downtrend, we all agree on which road we're taking. When the camp divides after a protracted move, none of us agree on direction. We end up bumping into each other, and we both get hurt!

When the market turns into either one of these cycles, my advice is to observe without playing. A few scalps—maybe, occasional day trade—possibly, but more than that is gambling. I've traded through low-risk areas early in my trading career. Ouch, did I lose money. I couldn't get on the right side of anything. And I wasn't the only one. Disasters littered trading rooms everywhere!

So, how can you track big-picture dynamics? Simple. Periodically, pull up daily *and* weekly charts of the Dow, the NYSE, and the Nasdaq. Draw trendlines, and apply 20 and 50 MAs to them. Ask the same questions as usual: Are they trending or trading sideways? Where is support and resistance? Are they trading above or below their major moving averages? Which markets are overextended?

You don't buy a stock trading under the 20 MA, and especially the 50 MA. Smart traders tread carefully—or not at all—in markets exhibiting the same behavior.

If those who knew what to look for had checked a daily chart of the Dow in relation to its 20 MA the week before October 19, 1998, they would have exited positions the previous week and saved millions of dollars in profits. Now you're one of "those in the know." You needn't ride out such drastic moves ever again.

If, then: If *the market is in a high-risk/low-risk zone,* then *trading conditions will be whippy, choppy, and unpredictable. I will trade only short-term positions, if at all. I will save my cash for a stock-shopping spree when the market breaks out of this zone.*

THE ADVANCE–DECLINE LINE AS A SUPERB STORYTELLER

One of the most popular long-term indicators of market breadth—and thus overall market strength—is the NYSE Advance–Decline Line, or A/D line. A breadth indicator uses advancing and declining issues to measure participation in the movement of the market.

When we're in the midst of a strong bull market, a large number of stocks climb upward in a modest, orderly manner. If that market starts to deteriorate, only a *small* number of stocks make large advances in price. To the uninformed, it appears the bull still feels frisky because those stocks pull the averages up. The appearance is not the reality, though, and the A/D line tells it as it is.

Conversely, as a market bottoms after a downtrend, fewer and fewer stocks decline even though the market indices still slide.

The A/D line is calculated by subtracting the number of NYSE stocks that declined on the day from the number of issues that advanced. This is added to a cumulative total. Though the actual numbers that designate the line mean little, the pattern it draws tells us a vital story.

You'll find the A/D line published in *Investors Business Daily, The Wall Street Journal,* and other financial newspapers. Compare it to the Dow or the S&P 500. Now, look for divergences. Reassuring signs of a strong market combine a rising A/D line with new highs on the preceding indices. But when you see the Dow, for instance, making new highs in an uptrend, and the A/D line forming a negative divergence by rolling sideways and failing to make new highs, it's time to pull anchor on long and intermediate-term holds.

If, then: If *the Dow/S&P futures continue to make new highs and the A/D line doesn't,* then *this market may be headed for a spill.*

So go to cash, hop in and out nimbly with day trades and scalps, and get ready to hold the door open for those not as wise as you!

On a short-term, even intraday basis, keep an eye on NYSE advancing and declining issues.

If, then: If *declining issues outnumber advancing issues,* then *the markets are weak.* If *advancing issues outnumber declining issues,* then *the market is strong.*

MEET ANOTHER STORYTELLER: U.S. THIRTY-YEAR TREASURY BONDS

The thirty-year Treasury bond is the benchmark for all bond prices. Along with the S&P 500 futures, the T-bond futures indicate how the market will open. Since they trade twenty-four hours electronically, the bond futures react to international news, to foreign markets that trade while we sleep, and to U.S. issues active in those markets. Bond futures also watch and react to U.S. economic reports announced about 8:30 a.m. EST, along with company news of earnings.

Bond prices and bond yields, meaning their interest rates, move in opposite directions. As bond prices rise, their interest rates drop. When low interest rates generated by bonds make them less attractive to investors, those investors look to stocks for more attractive profits. Result? Stock prices rise. Finally, remember that interest rates equal the price of credit, which in turn reflects the growth rate of the economy.

When bond prices fall, their interest rates rise. Remember the late 1970s and early 1980s, when interest rates exceeded 20 percent? The stock market bottomed because investors had a safe place (bonds) to invest their money and earn 20 percent a year!

Check *Barron's* (published each Saturday) "Review & Preview" section for the following week's economic reports. As soon as CNBC announces those reports (usually 8:30 a.m. EST), the bond futures and S&P futures tell you how Wall Street interprets those numbers.

Say an economic report, like the GNP infers the economy is strengthening. Translate the report into an *if, then* equation, such as: *if* the economy strengthens, *then* higher interest rates follow, and bond prices fall. How will the market react?

In this case, the stock market may fall because a strong economy can goad the Fed into raising rates to curb inflation. Rising rates mean companies have to pay more to borrow money, which leads to lower earnings. Lower earnings = lower stock prices. Those reasons encourage investors to make "a flight to safety." They cash in their stocks and put their money in high-yielding bonds.

Or if the economy shows signs of mild strengthening, and general consensus holds that the Fed will not raise interest rates, the market rises because stockholders see higher earnings ahead. Again, the T-bond and S&P futures will tell you immediately which opinion prevails.

If, then scenarios—comparing thirty-year Treasury bond futures to S&P futures:

- *If* the price of bonds falls, and the S&P futures rise, *then* cyclical stocks (stocks that have cyclical earnings as opposed to stocks with earnings handcuffed to interest rates) show strength. Cyclical stocks include paper, aluminum, automobiles, technology, and retailers. Examples are International Paper (IP), Aluminum Company of America (AA), General Motors (GM), Motorola (MOT), and Outback Steak House (OSSI).
- *If* bonds weaken, *then* interest-sensitive stocks like banks (Citicorp-CCI), moneylenders (American Express-AXP), and homebuilders (Kaufman Broad-KBH) weaken with them. Higher interest rates mean banks have to pay more to borrow money and their spread between what they lend and what they borrow narrows. As interest rates rise, people stall on buying new homes.
- *If* bonds are strong and S&Ps are weak, *then* cyclicals usually recover strength first.
- *If* bonds are strong and S&P futures are strong, *then* look for banks, lenders, and homebuilders to climb.

OTHER "IF, THEN" SETTINGS

If oil prices rise, then airline stock prices fall, and vice-versa. When jet fuel prices rise, airlines' profits decrease.

If signs of inflation climb, then gold and silver stocks rise. Investors buy these instruments to hedge against inflation.

If the U.S. dollar strengthens, then imported goods become more attractive to Americans. So stocks like Nike and Toyota rise. Conversely, American products sold overseas cost more (Intel, Johnson & Johnson), so those stocks suffer.

If the CRB index (Knight-Ridder Commodity Research Bureau price index of seventeen commodities) falls, then inflation is not a worry. Bond and stock prices rise.

TOO MUCH CHOCOLATE?

The next two overall market indicators represent inverse sentiment. Translated, they suggest that too much of anything, whether good or bad, eventually causes the opposite reaction. Take chocolate, for instance. Chocolate (a good thing), when eaten in huge portions, causes a tummy ache (a bad thing).

- Bull/Bear Ratio:

  Investor's Intelligence in New Rochelle, New York, takes a weekly poll of investment advisors and publishes the Bull/Bear Ratio. CNBC routinely announces the Bull/Bear Ratio during market hours.

  The poll tallies how advisors feel about the stock market—bullish, bearish, or neutral. The ratio is calculated by dividing the number of bullish advisors by the number of bullish plus bearish advisors. (Neutral advisors don't count.)

  Since it's a contrary indicator, the more bullish the advisors feel, the more bearish the indication. For example, *if* 55–60 percent of the advisors polled are bullish, *then* that extreme optimism and euphoria usually signals the market is top heavy and ready to fall. *If* the reading dips to 40 percent, verifying extreme pessimism and bearishness, *then* the Bull/Bear Ratio implies a bullish reversal is in the wind.

- The CBOE (Chicago Board Options Exchange) Equity Put–Call Ratio:

  The CBOE Equity Put–Call Ratio tracks investors' trades in the options markets. (Puts and calls are options contracts that give participants the right to sell (put) or buy (call) the underlying security at a specified price, during a limited time period.) Most major newspapers list the weekly ratios for the CBOE Equity Put–Call Ratio.

  Since this is a contrary sentiment indicator, you interpret it like this: The higher the level of pessimism in the options players, the more optimistic the outlook for the market. The lower the level of pessimism, the more bearish the actual outlook.

  Or the higher the put (think, selling) trading, the more bullish the indication. The higher the calls (think, buying) trading, the more bearish the indication.

For example, a reading in the CBOE Equity Put–Call Ratio of 60:100 is considered bullish. Bearish signals flash when the ratio reaches 30:100.

WATCH OUT! IT'S OPTIONS EXPIRATION DAY

By the way, options, themselves, expire the third Friday of each month. These Fridays force options traders to close out their positions, so volatility and whippy conditions rule.

Quarterly or four times a year, options expiration is named "Triple Witching" because three types of options expire, instead of just two: stock options, stock index options, and futures options. (Added to that, it takes place on the third Friday of every third month.) Triple Witching Fridays cause extreme whipsaw and roller-coaster trading conditions. Please take the day off. I do.

PROGRAM TRADING: A JOLT OUT OF THE BLUE

If options expiration day feels like a roller-coaster ride, program trading resembles getting shocked by a hot lightning bolt. When a "sell program," especially, hits the market, the floor gets yanked from underneath most stocks in seconds. Your screen will turn blood red in a nanosecond with downticking stocks.

Program trading takes place when a divergence occurs between two closely related markets, like the S&P 500 cash (stocks) and the S&P 500 futures. Arbitrageurs buy one market, short the other, and profit from the difference.

Another definition of program trading is a computer-aided strategy generated as a hedge against falling stocks.

Either way, it's painful. Sell programs affect you by plunging many stocks straight down—so fast it takes your breath away. One defense tactic against program trading: Keep a ticker of the thirty Dow Industrials somewhere on your screen. If it suddenly turns blood red, a sell program probably went off.

Stay calm, while cutting your losses and taking profits as fast as you can.

LEARN HOW TO CHANGE GEARS—FAST!

The market never allows you to get comfortable. Just when you think you have it by the tail, everything changes.

When world or national events shape the market environment into a new paradigm, or pattern, you must keep an open mind so you can identify the changes. As soon as you spot them and analyze their effects, you can alter your trading techniques to fit the new paradigm.

For example, the Asian Contagion drastically altered U.S. stock market behavior. The Contagion started in October 1997, with the fall of Malaysia's market. It spread to Korea and Japan; much later, it contaminated Russia and Brazil.

Naturally, the U.S. market takes cues from the other markets as they open and close around the world. But the Asian Contagion, or "Asian Flu," as it was also called, severely tainted markets on a global basis.

Japan's stock market, the Nikkei, along with other Asian markets, assumed the role as a daily, leading indicator for the U.S. market. It was nerve wracking!

As I mentioned in an earlier chapter, I make money by holding stocks overnight. During the Asian Contagion, volatility in Asian markets brought that to an end. Just because the Dow or Nasdaq closed strong on the day, just because the TICK consolidated nicely near its high into the close, and the TRIN remained serene, didn't mean that it would carry through into the next day. (It doesn't mean it *for sure*, anytime, but in a sanguine market, the odds are in place.)

We traders began to watch CNBC much earlier in the morning than we used to. We kept a constant pulse on the Nikkei. Its close—weak or strong—pretty much dictated which way our market would open.

As you can imagine, holding stocks overnight became suicidal. Traders with any sense closed all positions, every night, no exceptions. We never had an inkling when the U.S. market closed whether the next morning would bring calm or catastrophe.

We also learned to shun stocks from companies with overseas exposure, particularly those who sold products to countries on the Pacific Rim. Technology companies, drug companies, and many others slid daily. Short sellers raked in profits.

Traders who refused to sell short spent their days hunting for stocks with no ties to Asian countries.

In other words, we had to change gears, and do it quickly, or get left by the side of the road.

When a major world or national event occurs, think: If *this event shapes our market into a different paradigm,* then *these industries and stocks (list) will benefit. These (list) should be avoided. In addition, I must alter my trading techniques to fit the changing market.*

TRADING DAY IN A CAPSULE

What does a typical trading day look like? Although it obviously changes from trader to trader, here's an encapsulated view of my day.

5:30 a.m. Rise and shine. While sipping coffee, read *Investor's Business Daily.* Focus on interesting stocks to pull up charts on later, along with news on currently held issues. Workout or run, shower, breakfast. While eating breakfast, scan *The Wall Street Journal* and/or *The NY Times* financial section.

8:00 a.m. Turn on CNBC. Check S&P futures "bug" in lower right-hand corner of screen. Are futures trading up or down? That, along with T-bond futures (announcers on squawk box talk about them) give a good indication of how the market will open. Start pulling up charts on stocks of interest, while listening to CNBC to get a feel for the upcoming mood of the market.

8:30 a.m. Check account balances for accuracy and cash available to trade.

9:30 a.m. Opening bell rings. Wait ten minutes before trading while ingesting futures movements on one-minute chart, along with TICK, TRIN, and other indicators. Only trades I make at the open: immediate sale (or short covering) of stocks gapping open from night before (just as I planned they would!), or emergency exits.

9:40 a.m. May or may not start testing the waters depending on conditions.

9:50 a.m. Change one-minute futures chart to three- or five-minute chart. Observe how open positions and possible new trades handle the 9:50 reversal period. Are they weak or strong? I find this to be a good weeding technique for discarding weak trades, and possibly beefing up strong ones.

10:10–11:20 a.m. Trade actively, moderately, or not at all, depending on opportunities and conditions.

11:20 a.m. Start taking profits on some day trades, depending again on strength of stocks and market conditions. I find lunch digests better with locked-in profits tucked safely under my belt. I especially take profits: (1) if economic reports are due out the following day that will cause this afternoon to slide into sluggishness, and (2) if a stock looks uncertain enough to capitulate during the lunchtime moody blues.

12:15 p.m.–1:30 p.m. Leave office for lunch.

1:30 p.m. Return from lunch and start scanning five-minute charts for strong stocks in an uptrend that have pulled back a fraction of a point from their daily high before lunch and are forming a tight shelf of consolidation. (You know the pattern. If not, review please!) Focus on the best candidates by zeroing in on those with consolidation candlesticks closing on their highs. (Reverse this scene for shorting.)

2:30 p.m. Watch for after-lunch volume to surge into breakout candidates. Begin to trade actively, moderately, or not at all depending on opportunities and market mood and manner. Check intermediate-term and swing trade holds for progress and possible profit-taking.

3:45 p.m. Begin taking profits before other traders exit and drive prices down. Consider potential swing trade entries and overnight holds if all systems agree.

4:00 p.m. Closing bell rings. Fall out of chair!

4:30–? Pull up charts and scan for tomorrow's opportunities.

WHERE TO FIND STOCKS TO TRADE

After you've been trading for a while, you'll have built a list of favorite, high-quality stocks that you know well, and profit from consistently. Where do you find those stocks?

Your starting point can be *Investor's Business Daily.* Although other newspapers like *The Wall Street Journal* and *Barron's* are invaluable and insightful, your subscription to *IBD* will pay for itself many times over.

In the Appendix of this book, I've listed the stocks in the S&P 100 Index and the Nasdaq 100. Other sources are The Dow Industrials, the S&P 500 (SPX).

The CBOE has its own indices you can pull from, including Automotive Index (AUX), S&P Banks Index (BIX), Biotech Index (BTK), S&P Chemicals Index (CEX), Software Index (CWX), Gaming Index (GAX), Gold Index (GOX), Health Care Index (HCX), Internet Index (INX), Oil Index (OIX), Telecommunication Index (TCX), and Technology Index (TXX). There's the Morgan Stanley Cyclical Index (CYC), the Morgan Stanley High-Tech Index (MSH), the Philadelphia Semiconductor Index (SOX), and The Street.com Internet Index (DOT.X).

When developing your list of trading stocks, you'll want to first make sure they have good daily volume (at least 100,000 shares, preferably 300,000+) for the reasons stated in Chapter 7.

Cross-check selections you make in the *Investor's Business Daily* stock tables. Make sure your selections are active stocks with high (over 90) EPS ratings, and have high relative price strength ranks (over 80). Also, stocks listed in these tables with high volume percent changes (+200 or higher) may offer good trading opportunities.

In the first paragraph of this section, you'll see the words *high-quality*. Please make sure *any stock* you trade represents a high-quality company.

Bulletin-board stocks and penny stocks are bad trading bets. So are relatively unknown stocks you find being hyped in some Internet chat rooms.

Unfortunately, greedy stock promoters, who have managed to dodge the SEC, run a few so-called investor chat rooms. These promoters goad naive traders and investors into buying small-cap and other "growth" stocks. The buyers run up the price of the stock. The promoters sell out for a profit, then disappear. The stock—which was worthless all along—crashes.

Please don't be a scam victim. *In every trading situation, think for yourself.* Remember your constant goals: Protect your principal, and trade to trade well.

YOUR BODY, YOUR MIND

Guess what? Bet you dollars to donuts that physically fit traders make more money than couch potatoes. Don't groan, please. Stay with me.

If you weren't aware of it already, the two weeks in Beginner's Boot Camp taught you that trading is stressful to the max. And it doesn't take a rocket scientist to figure out that sitting in a chair all day doesn't a healthy body make.

So do yourself a favor. If you're on an exercise regimen, stick to it, even if you have to get up a little earlier. If you're not—start. Drag yourself outside first thing in the morning and walk fast, ride your bike, run the dog, or swim for a half-hour. Exercise helps you think faster and produces wonderful feelings of well-being that combat stress. It will also ward off "the chubbies" from sitting all day.

An alternative is to use lunchtime as an exercise break. One guy in my trading office takes off at lunch and walks for an hour while pumping hand weights. Three other traders walk fast, from 12:30 to 1:30, then eat brown bag lunches when they return.

Some traders work out at the gym after the market closes. Some take long walks after dinner. Whatever it takes to keep your body "motating," just do it! You'll be a much happier camper.

Now, about your mind, and the attached emotions.... As you already know, trading demands every ounce of concentration you can muster. It also demands courage and self-confidence. When you walk in that trading room each morning, you better feel on top of the world! Not cocky, or self-important, but self-assured and in control.

Have you just broken up with your girlfriend/wife/boyfriend/husband, or had a fight with someone close to you? Is someone in your family critically ill? Are the kids home alone, and you're worried about them?

Did you by any chance party into the wee hours of the morning? Do you have the hangover-from-hell? Is your tongue wrapped in cotton and your head full of it?

Are you getting the flu? Or did you lose a bucketload of money trading yesterday, and you're extremely depressed?

Don't trade on the days you feel bad, whatever the reason! I mean it. *Please don't touch that mouse!*

The superraceway to losses originates in sad, worried, or even illness-fogged minds. I once traded the day right after a devastating romantic breakup. I imagined I could "trade through" my feelings, and that "working would be good for me." Wrong. By the time the closing bell rang, my trading account was squashed along with my heart. Oh, just great. Heart broken and broke, all in the same day.

Sadness, illness, nagging problems of any kind color your judgment and common sense. Count on it. I've watched good traders work with the flu. They *always* lose money. That's an *always* you can count on. So when you're not feeling up to snuff, don't brave it out. Stay away from your trading machine and live to trade another day.

And, by the way, if you're a brand-new trader, remember to breathe. Yup, I'm serious! High-stress and uncertainty causes some folks to stop breathing. Greg Capra at the Pristine.com Trading office regularly calls out to novice traders in the office, "Are you breathing?"

Most important, remember to laugh. Yes, indeedy, trading is a solemn matter (smirk). Why, we traders concentrate with herculean effort (snicker). Nothing's funny about trading, do you understand? (giggle). Doggone it, trading is war (chortle). We are the masters of the universe! (laugh out loud!)

Laughing is the best possible medicine. It lowers your blood pressure and raises your immune system. It brings oxygen into your system. It stops you from taking yourself too seriously, and it balances your outlook on life. Do it every chance you get.

One reminder about trading room manners. If you trade with other people nearby, and you close a killer trade netting you profits the size of Bill Gates's annual paycheck, please don't brag out loud. Nothing makes traders with dwindling trading accounts feel worse than someone who scores big and brags about it. When you do well, go outside, then holler for all you're worth. Whoop it up! Way to go—you deserve it!

TRADING RULES TO PROSPER BY

All successful traders I know post a list of trading rules near their computer. Please consider doing this, also. Written rules remind you of your goals and boundaries, and have the same effect on the psyche that written stops do: They make those points concrete, nonnegotiable. Think of them as your conscience. Written rules bring us back to "center" when the market hypnotizes us and we think we can fudge!

The following rules are my own. Use them, if you wish, as a base from which your own rules will evolve. Then keep your "Trading Rules to Prosper By" within full view at all times.

Naturally, the "I" in these rules refers to *you*.

Trading Rules to Prosper By

1. At all times, I protect my principal!
2. I trade to trade well, not to make money.
3. I trade only when tops down criteria are optimal.
4. I never chase a stock. Nor do I ever "bet the ranch" on a single trade.
5. I enter trades on the long side *only* when the TICK is above zero, and the TRIN is below 0.9.
6. I write down my stop loss for every trade. I adhere to that stop loss automatically.
7. If I have two open trades losing money, I stop trading and reassess what the market is telling me.
8. I never risk more than 1/4 point on day trades, and 1/8 point on scalps.
9. I never take home a losing trade.
10. When I have a reasonable profit, I take it.

QUIZ

1. True or false? A low-risk zone in a market cycle is the best time to initiate intermediate-term trades.
2. If the Dow is making higher lows and higher highs, but the A/D line rolls over from an uptrend to trade sideways, what does that indicate long term?
3. Bond prices and bond yields move in ____________ directions.
4. Interest rates equal ____ ________ __ __________.
5. If the Fed raises interest rates, why does that suggest stock prices will fall?
6. If bond prices are strong, and S&P futures are strong, what usually happens to bank stocks? Try to answer in an *if, then* format.
7. What do contrary or inverse sentiment indicators suggest?
8. True or false? Option's Expiration Days, and especially Triple Witching Days, make good days to go to the beach.
9. Name a good source from which to pull target stocks.
10. You have the hangover-from-hell. Your spouse is mad at you. You just got a margin call, and your car payment bounced. To top it off, you feel like you're catching the flu. This is the perfect day to trade hard because hard work is good for the soul. Right?

ANSWERS

1. False. A so-called low-risk area means the market is in a sideways, basing formation after a prolonged downtrend. The low-risk definition pertains to investors who buy long-term positions with reduced risk of the market going lower. For traders, a basing formation is trendless and produces whippy, choppy conditions. Placing intermediate-term trades before the market breaks out to the upside is chancy, at best.
2. If the Dow keeps making new highs, but the A/D line does not, long term the market may be ready for a major correction.
3. opposite.
4. the price of credit.
5. When the Fed raises interest rates, companies have to pay more to borrow money, which lowers their earnings. Lower earnings = lower stock prices.
6. *If* bonds and S&Ps are strong, *then* bank stocks usually rise.
7. Contrary or inverse sentiment indicators imply that too much optimism in the market leads to its downfall. Too much pessimism leads to an eventual uptrend.
8. True. Or go shopping. Or take your spouse/kids/dog on an unexpected outing. Just don't trade!
9. The S&P 500 Index is a good source to find target stocks. So is the Nasdaq 100. Another is industry indexes.
10. Poor baby. If you trade today, you'll end up even poorer. Take some aspirin, and some time-off to fix things. Tomorrow's a new day!

✦ ✦ ✦

CENTER POINT

Live Consciously, Succeed Miraculously!

Follow your heart, your dreams, your desires. Do what your soul calls you to do, whatever it is, and allow it to be finished; then you will go on to another adventure.

—RAMTHA

All of us have the choice to live our lives consciously, or unconsciously. When we live consciously, we come from a position of internal power. We tackle each day and the events it brings with proactive energy.

When we live unconsciously, life happens *to* us, and we react to it. Instead of learning from our problems, we shove them away and wonder why they keep reappearing in our lives.

The ultimate life process has a role for everything, everyone. One need only look at how perfectly nature orchestrates the forces on this planet to see the truth in this. Each of us has been given a unique talent, and a unique way of expressing it. We are meant to discover our potential, then express it. In doing so, we fulfill our own needs and help those around us.

When we look at life through the lens of our potentiality, we realize the urgency of purpose. Each day unfolds with new meaning. Instead of rushing through daily events in a helter-skelter, darned-if-I-do, darned-if-I-don't manner, we view each situation as a learning experience. Our decisions come from our core being, a peaceful, nonjudgmental, "knowing" that dwells deep inside. They are conscious, creative decisions based on our role in life's glorious plan.

When you choose to wake up and live thoughtfully and consciously, you totally transform your life. Suddenly, you realize you are far more than you thought you were—more than your background, more than your education, more than your "station" in life.

Let's carry out our everyday lives secure in the knowledge that we operate within the context of a greater plan. We are part of the ultimate life plan unfolding.

Every week, every day, every hour, we can choose how we will live in each moment. When we come from an inner place of peace, power, and consciousness, we bring a whole new intention to our lives. We transcend limitations and find our lives a miraculous expression of success.

✦ ✦ ✦

CHAPTER 14

The Future is Now!

Congratulations, guys and girlfriends, we're coming into the home stretch!

In this chapter, I'll give you a feast of Web sites filled with stock and trading information that you can download and devour.

Then we'll glance into the kaleidoscope of the future. How will the markets and trading change as we race into the new century?

MICROLIST OF HIGH-CALIBER FINANCIAL WEB SITES

Currently, the wealth of information on the Internet available to investors and traders boggles the mind. Type the word *stock* or *day trading*, into your search vehicle, and zap! a zillion sites nearly knock you down.

To get you started, the following Web destinations offer a cornucopia of stock news and information:

ABC News	www.abcnews.com/sections/
CNBC	www.cnbc.com
CBS Marketwatch	cbs.marketwatch.com
CNN Financial	www.cnnfn.com
New York Stock Exchange	www.nyse.com
MSN MoneyCentral	moneycentral.mas.com
Nasdaq–Amex Market Site	www.nasdaq.com
The New York Times on Web: Technology	www.nytimes.com/tech
News Alert	www.newsalert.com
Reuters MoneyNet	www.moneynet.com
TheStreet.com	www.thestreet.com
$Wall Street City	www.wallstreetcity.com

Wall Street Journal Interactive	www.interactive.wsj.com
Yahoo! Finance	quote.yahoo.com

These information sites are trader oriented:

AltaVista Finance	altavista.wallst.com
CyberInvest	www.cyberinvest.com
Financial Center	www.tfc.com
Interactive Investor	www.zdii.com
Invest-O-Rama	www.investorama.com
Investor Words (4,000 financial terms)	www.investorwords.com
The Motley Fool	www.fool.com
The Raging Bull	www.ragingbull.com
Silicon Investor (active bulletin boards)	www.techstocks.com
Stockpoint	www.stockpoint.com
Wall Street Research Net (links to 500,000 financial Web sites)	www.wrsn.com

TRADING WITH ONLINE TEACHERS AND FRIENDS

The following Web sites dedicate themselves exclusively to traders like you and me. Almost all give trial periods, from three days to two weeks. Most offer stock "picks" and recommendations that they e-mail to you, or that you retrieve each morning from their site.

Some offer active bulletin boards or chat rooms where you can hang out, and let us hope, learn something. (Whether you trade with an online broker or level II system, you can position your favorite trading site in a corner or to the side of your screen.)

Others offer "virtual trading rooms." During market hours, these rooms present intraday stock recommendations and information.

Investigate as many sites as you can before you designate one as your home base. Print out their educational materials and study like crazy. We—you and I—are traders-in-progress. We will never know everything there is to know about this business!

As far as stock recommendations go, even if they come from a reliable room, please compare the suggestions to your own criteria before you buy or sell.

At times you'll say, "I totally disagree with this recommendation. This stock is headed south, not north." (Good. You're thinking for yourself!) When that happens, follow your own reasoning. Then observe the stock to see how it plays out—and whether your assessment was on target. These situations make marvelous learning experiences.

Bear in mind that while you glean knowledge from trading rooms and sites, you're doing it with an eye to the future. Though you may enjoy subscribing to a service that gives stock suggestions, your goal is to trade from your *own* stock candidates, and make your *own* choices.

The descriptions of the following Web sites give you a small taste of their services. By the time you read this, their content may have changed. Also, new sites will have come online. (Investor or trader magazines are great sources for new online sites.)

The Daily Trader *www.dailytrader.com* daily recommendations from a computer-based system; previous and current market conditions.

Daytraders On-line *www.daytraders.com* daily recommendations, online stock info, intraday plays.

Elite Trader *www.elitetrader.com* day trading tutorials, news, bookstore, message board.

Mkt Traders *www.dtrades.com* daily picks, recommendations, virtual trading room.

Pristine Day Trader *www.pristine.com* daily picks, intraday trades telephone hotline, educational materials, virtual real-time trading room offering education and stock recommendations, nationwide training seminar schedule, level II software.

Tradehard.com *www.tradehard.com* trader's learning section with advanced trading techniques, updates, forums, online courses, level II software.

PUMP AND DUMP

As you try out different trading sites, please beware of one unfortunate situation that's cropped up. Although most online trading rooms are run by sincere, honest teachers, a few chat room and virtual trading room "gurus" employ a deceptive practice called "pump and dump."

Here's how it works: The guru puts a buy recommendation out on a certain stock; for example, he (or she) might say, "Buy AOL immediately—on the offer. It's going to fly." Fair enough. We'll assume that many subscribers on this Web site jump in and buy AOL. Result? The demand spikes AOL's price for seconds to minutes.

If the guru is a "pump and dumper," he quickly sells his personal AOL holding into the tremendous order flow generated by the recommendation. He may have bought the stock a few minutes ago, earlier in the day, or earlier in the week for that matter. His profit is assured—his subscribers buy and raise the price. Then he takes profits, in effect selling his shares to the people whom he urged to buy!

Now, maybe AOL really was poised to fly, and maybe it did. And maybe you made a profit. Fine and dandy.

But I've personally seen pump and dumpers make outrageous "it's gonna fly" comments about a stock that's tanking, in a market that's tanking, five minutes before the market close. New traders who didn't know any better jumped in and bought! Whose shares did they buy? They bought the guru's shares. He fled his position fast because the stock was crashing! If these gurus were registered stockbrokers, which they never are, they'd be behind bars.

Lesson: Never buy a stock just because someone tells you to. Always use your own measurements and criteria. And *always* think for yourself.

SHOULD YOU TAKE A TRADING COURSE? OF COURSE!

The more day trading explodes as a profession, the more courses and seminars crop up to fill traders' needs (or the needs of the seminar promoters).

Early in this book, I stated unequivocally that knowledge is the key to success in this field. It is. Period. When you're sitting in front of a computer screen with your finger on the trigger, about to make a split-second decision that involves thousands of dollars, it doesn't make a darn bit of difference how good-looking you are, what kind of car you drive, or who you know.

All that matters is what you know, and how you apply it.

That's why I recommend you research high-quality courses that teach day trading and technical analysis. Attend the one that most appeals to you, knowing it will be money well spent.

As day trading evolves, two kinds of seminars have emerged. The first is genuine trading courses, usually lasting one to five days. You'll find them listed in Web sites you know and trust.

The second type pretends to be a trading course. In reality, it trains you how to operate a trading company's level II system and requires you to open an account with them. If that's what you want to do, fine. Just be aware of the difference.

Some are pretenders, through and through. If they're not reputable, you'll end up learning a little and losing a lot. They'll get rich off the commissions. How will you know? Their reply to your questions will sound something like this: "Nah, you don't have to learn all that charting stuff to make money. Just open an account with us. In one evening flat, we'll show you how to make big bucks—guaranteed."

Baloney.

It's impossible to learn even basic trading techniques in one evening. Take time to learn traditional methodology and trading tactics, then continue to study while you trade. You'll end up as a prosperous, long-term trader, not a short-term loser.

QUANTUM LEAP INTO THE FUTURE

As I write, the financial markets are catapulting into the twenty-first century at mach two with their hair on fire! Nothing will stay the same. Venerable institutions like the NYSE, and its younger colleague, the Nasdaq, are being prodded by new technology and Wall Street's fickle nature to keep up, or pay the price.

New kids on the block in the form of ECNs have shown investors and traders that they don't have to pay retail for a stock. Broker-dealers recently clamored to the SEC (Securities and Exchange Commission) for permission to gain stature as stock exchanges in their own right. In April 1999, the SEC granted it. Island (ISLD) already has its exchange blueprints in the works.

FROM FRACTIONS TO DECIMALS

One of the first time-honored traditions to fall will be the U.S. financial markets' custom of pricing with fractions that represent part of a dollar, rather than pricing with cents.

On June 30, 2000, an industrywide conversion from fractional pricing to decimal pricing will take effect. Every system in every financial office that currently computes, compiles, stores, or displays fractional pricing will be converted to accommodate decimal pricing, the way all other U.S. products are priced. At the end of the book, you'll find a fractions-to-decimal table to place by your computer.

KEEP THE COFFEEPOT BREWING: HERE COMES TWENTY-FOUR-HOUR TRADING

No doubt goaded by the fact that more than 20 percent of the Nasdaq's orders from individual investors come after the traditional 4:00 p.m. close, the exchange plans to add a second trading session lasting into the evening.[1] By the time you read this, those plans will probably be in effect.

The NYSE also intends to expand its hours in June 2000. An early morning session beginning at 5 a.m. EST, will focus on trading European equities. The NYSE is also planning evening sessions that may last from 5:00 p.m. to as late as midnight.

ECNs like Reuter's Instinet (INCA) and Bloomberg's Tradebook (BTRD) already have extended hours, and other ECNs are jumping on the bandwagon.

---

1 Chernoff, Allan. "Nasdaq to add evening session." www.mscnbc.com/news/260718.asp, July 5, 1999.

Most market players believe that twenty-four-hour trading waits just around the corner.

MERGER MANIA INFILTRATES WALL STREET

The NYSE and the Nasdaq are starting to act more like corporate America than bastions of Wall Street. Merger mania infiltrates the two, and talk circles about combining their regulatory arms to enhance quality. The SEC is all for it.

Both exchanges are eyeing the huge impact ECNs are having on the marketplace. At the moment, ECNs execute one out of every five Nasdaq trades. Word's out that the NYSE may be planning a joint venture with an ECN, and may even purchase one.

In the meantime, the Nasdaq's parent, the National Association of Securities Dealers (NASD), took a cue from the Aussie's, who converted the Australian Stock Exchange from mutual ownership to a publicly traded company in October 1998. As of June 1999, those shares popped 135 percent.[2]

Now the NASD is mulling over a proposal to issue Nasdaq stock to the 5,000 + companies whose stocks trade under its umbrella. Eventually, a Nasdaq stock IPO (initial public offering) may come out. If the Nasdaq uses the funds it receives from such an offering to improve technology and oversight, the stock may prove a profitable investment for the public.

At the same time U.S. exchanges wade through the chaos of change, they're reaching out to global markets. A portion of the Nasdaq's eventual IPO money may support its foray into the overseas markets. The tech-heavy monolith recently set up a partnership with the Hong Kong Stock Exchange. The two will encourage stocks to trade in each other's markets.

Not to be outdone, the NYSE may turn to a for-profit operating basis and also issue an IPO. On the international scene, the home of the Big Board is communicating with the Paris Bourse about connecting the two exchanges. Later, Canadian and Latin American exchanges may join the party.

Globalization of the stock markets will open new opportunities to traders everywhere. Can't sleep? In the foreseeable future, you might crawl out of bed at 2 a.m., make yourself a snack, then pad over to your computer. You slip into an after-hours market and pick up a quarter-point on your favorite tech stock. Yawning, you wander back to bed. The fact that you bought the stock in a Hong Kong market, then sold it minutes later in an Australia exchange doesn't cause you to blink an eye. To you, future trader, trading globally will be commonplace.

---

2 Wyatt, Edward. "Want to Buy a Stock Market?" *New York Times*, July 5,1999.

NEW TRADING SYSTEMS AND YOU

Remember my high-risk warning in Chapter 9 about buying stocks with earnings pending? In the not-too-distant future, that risk may turn into reward.

Say America Online announces awesome earnings just after the market closes. You can use an after-hours system to pick up a position. Then, if the moon and stars stay in your favor, you'll sell it when AOL opens the following morning on the NYSE.

As new as after-hours trading is, already new spins are being added to it. The Digital Stock Market (DSM), based in New York, has traders haggling with traders. This after-hours, online trading platform allows traders to negotiate price and quantity between themselves; time limits on acceptance may be specified. When the traders meet on price, the system executes the transaction. DSM plans to focus on the relatively new and vast market segment of people who have to trade during evening hours.

The People's Stock Network already uses this format, with buyers and sellers trading a limited selection of stocks between them.

Optimark, based in Durango, Colorado, offers institutional and individual investors the opportunity to buy and sell large lots anonymously. Say you heard through the grapevine that thinly traded Teeny Weenie Small-Cap was a buyout candidate. So you bought 10,000 shares, thinking you'd make a killing. But the buyout fizzled. Now you want to dump your shares fast, without driving down the already faltering price. You go online with Optimark and sell off share lots at predetermined prices, similar to limit orders. Optimark's artificial intelligence software will attempt to match buyers with your order.[3]

In addition, the CBOE (Chicago Board Options Exchange), which executes nearly 70 percent of U.S. equity option trades, plans to offer online options trading via Optimark. Some heavy-hitters backing Optimark include Goldman Sachs and Dow Jones & Co.

ARTIFICIAL INTELLIGENCE SOFTWARE

Future traders may well incorporate artificial intelligence (AI) software into their strategies as a matter of course. Conceivably, you may someday send stock-trading search bots (a bot is an "intelligent" search engine) into cyberspace to comb global markets for competing prices on your target stock.

3 Ingebretsen, Mark. "Trading 2000." *Online Investor,* March/April, 1999, p. 24.

Of course, that opens a Pandora's box for all sorts of fraud. Stock promoters could flood the market with an army of bots inquiring about a stock. The appearance would be one of high demand. The reality would be deceiving to say the least.

As the world shrinks, and exchanges encourage traders to reach around the world to each other, it's not impossible to imagine playing head games with a Brazilian specialist, or a German, Dutch, or Japanese market maker! Funny? Maybe. Possible? Absolutely. Talk about learning new mindsets!

The last and perhaps most unnerving future scenario, especially to the old-timers, is the prospect that floor trading may fade into electronic execution systems. If it ever comes about, the games we play with specialists and market makers will become nostalgic memories. I, for one, will miss them.

Still, as traders, our future is bright. Every market, exchange, broker-dealer, and alternative trading system, on both national and global levels, is focusing on needs. Our sheer numbers give us strength, while we give the market liquidity.

It's a win–win situation that will fuel some exciting changes in the years to come.

IN CONCLUSION

Now, please let me congratulate you! You've made it all the way through a long discourse on a heavy subject. This shows courage and persistence, two qualities that mold fine traders. You are on your way to an exciting career in trading, and again, I commend you. You've got what it takes!

In composing this book, I have written each word from my heart. The techniques and tactics in these pages work for me. I hope they benefit you, help keep you safe, and assist in making your trading experience fulfilling and profitable.

May the trading god smile on you always!

✦ ✦ ✦

CENTER POINT
We Are All Connected

We have stopped for a moment to encounter each other, to meet, to love, to share. This is a precious moment, but it is transient. It is a little parenthesis in eternity. If we share with caring, lightheartedness, and love, we will create abundance and joy for each other. And then this moment will have been worthwhile.

—DEEPAK CHOPRA[4]

During interviews, astronauts who've orbited the Earth said that viewing our exquisite world from such a glorious vantage point has convinced them that a supreme, cosmic mind is at work.

Scientists tell us our planet formed billions of years ago from stellar debris. Out of that aggregation of cosmic dust, life evolved. The sun warmed the Earth, then one-celled plants and animals built the foundation for the chain of evolution that would unfold through time.

You and I represent an important part of that evolution. Our lives form a vital link in a much larger chain that stretches into the future.

When we celebrate our birthdays, we really are celebrating our participation on a planet that, since our last birthday, has orbited the sun one more time. We are part and parcel of the Earth's lifetime, just as the cells in our bodies are part of our lifetime.

When we stretch our minds to observe ourselves and our neighbors as life itself in the process of moving toward greater expression, we easily recognize that we're all connected. Though we have different beliefs, skin colors, and cultural boundaries, each of us is born of the ultimate intelligence and energy that begets all life. That common thread connects us as brothers and sisters in spirit.

As we go forth in our lives to meet new challenges and opportunities, consider if you will that we are each necessary to the evolution of life, the grand scheme of things. Further, that process of evolution connects you and me. We are separate parts of a perfect whole.

Let's honor one another and strive to make our world harmonious and peaceful. For together, we form links of a magnificent chain that reaches into infinity.

✦ ✦ ✦

---

4 Chopra, Deepak. *The Seven Spiritual Laws of Success* (CA: Amber-Allen Publishing, 1994), p.111

Appendix

RECOMMENDED READING LIST

How I Made $2,000,000 in the Stock Market, Nicolas Darvas

Japanese Candlestick Charting Techniques, Steve Nison

Market Wizards and *The New Market Wizards,* Jack D. Schwager

Reminiscences of a Stock Operator, Edwin Lefevre

Secrets for Profiting in Bull and Bear Markets, Stan Weinstein

Stock Patterns for Day Trading, Barry Rudd

Strategies for the Online Day Trader, Advanced Trading Techniques for Online Profits, by Fernando Gonzalez and William Rhee

The Disciplined Trader: Developing Winning Attitudes, Mark Douglas

The Electronic Day Trader, Marc Friedfertig and George West

Tools & Tactics for the Master Day Trader; Battle-Tested Techniques for Day, Swing, and Position Traders, Oliver Velez and Greg Capra

Trading for a Living, Dr. Alexander Elder

STANDARD & POOR'S 100

List of 100 Stocks in Standard & Poor's 100 Index (For the most recent listing, go to www.standardandpoors.com)

Company	Symbol
AT&T Corp.	T
Alcoa	AA
Allegheny Teledyne Inc.	ALT
American Electric Power	AEP
American Express	AXP
American General	AGC
American Int'l. Group	AIG
Ameritech	AIT
Atlantic Richfield	ARC
Avon Products	AVP
Baker Hughes	BHI
Bank One Corp.	ONE
BankAmerica Corp.	BAC
Baxter International Inc.	BAX
Bell Atlantic	BEL
Bethlehem Steel	BS
Black & Decker Corp.	BDK
Boeing Company	BA
Boise Cascade	BCC
Bristol-Myers Squibb	BMY
Brunswick Corp.	BC
Burlington Northern Santa Fe Corp.	BNI
CBS Corp.	CBS
CIGNA Corp.	CI
Campbell Soup	CPB
Ceridian Corp.	CEN
Champion International	CHA
Cisco Systems	CSCO
Citigroup Inc.	C
Coastal Corp.	CGP
Coca Cola Co.	KO
Colgate-Palmolive	CL
Columbia/HCA Healthcare Corp.	COL
Computer Sciences Corp.	CSC
Delta Air Lines	DAL
Dow Chemical	DOW
Du Pont (E.I.)	DD
Eastman Kodak	EK

Entergy Corp.	ETR
Exxon Corp.	XON
FDX Holding Corp.	FDX
Fluor Corp.	FLR
Ford Motor Co.	F
General Dynamics	GD
General Electric	GE
General Motors	GM
Halliburton Co.	HAL
Harrah's Entertainment	HET
Harris Corp.	HRS
Hartford Financial Svc. Gp.	HIG
H.J. Heinz	HNZ
Hewlett-Packard	HWP
Homestake Mining	HM
Honeywell	HON
Intel Corp.	INTC
International Business Machines	IBM
International Flavors and Fragrances	IFF
International Paper	IP
Johnson & Johnson	JNJ
K Mart	KM
Limited, The	LTD
Lucent Technologies	LU
Mallinckrodt Inc.	MKG
May Dept. Stores	MAY
McDonald's Corp.	MCD
Merck & Co.	MRK
Merrill Lynch	MER
Microsoft Corp.	MSFT
Minnesota Mining & Mfg.	MMM
Mobil Corp.	MOB
Monsanto Co.	MTC
National Semiconductor	NSM
Norfolk Southern Corp.	NSC
Northern Telecom	NT
Occidental Petroleum	OXY
Oracle Corp.	ORCL
PepsiCo. Inc.	PEP
Pharmacia & Upjohn, Inc.	PNU
Polaroid Corp.	PRD
Procter & Gamble	PG
Ralston Purina Group	RAL
Raytheon Co.	RTN.B
Rockwell International	ROK
Schlumberger Ltd.	SLB
Sears, Roebuck & Co.	S
Southern Co.	SO
Tandy Corp.	TAN
Tektronix Inc.	TEK
Texas Instruments	TXN
Toys R Us Holding Cos.	TOY
U.S. Bancorp.	USB
Unicom Corp.	UCM
Unisys Corp.	UIS
United Technologies	UTX
Wal-Mart Stores	WMT
Walt Disney Co.	DIS
Wells Fargo & Co.	WFC
Weyerhaeuser Corp.	WY
Williams Cos.	WMB
Xerox Corp.	XRX

NASDAQ

100 Stocks Listed in NASDAQ 100 (For the most recent listing, go to www.nasdaq100.com).

Company	Symbol
Bed Bath & Beyond	BBB
Biogen, Inc.	BGEN
Biomet, Inc.	BMET
BMC Software, Inc.	BMCS
Cambridge Technology Partners, Inc.	CATP
CBRL Group, Inc.	CBRL
Centocor, Inc.	CNTO
Chancellor Media Corp.	AMFM
Chiron Corp.	CHIR
Cintas Corp.	CTAS
Cisco Systems, Inc.	CSCO
Ctirix Systems, Inc.	CTXS
CMGI, Inc.	CMGI
CNET, Inc.	CNET
Comair Holdings, Inc.	COMR
Comcast Corp.	CMCSK
Compuware Corp.	CPWR
Comverse Technology	CMVT
Concord EFS, Inc.	CEFT
Corporate Express, Inc.	CEXP
Costco Companies, Inc.	COST
3Com Corp.	COMS
Dell Computer Corp.	DELL
Dollar Tree Stores, Inc.	DLTR
Electronic Arts Inc.	ERTS
Electronics for Imaging, Inc.	EFII
Fastenal Co.	FAST
First Health Group Corp.	FHCC
Fiserv, Inc.	FISV
Food Lion, Inc.	FDLNB
Genzyme General	GENZ
Herman Miller, Inc.	MLHR
Immunex Corp.	IMNX

Intel Corp.	INTC
Intuit Inc.	INTU
JDS Uniphase Corp.	JDSU
KLA-Tencor Corp.	KLAC
Level 3 Communications, Inc.	LVLT
Lincare Holdings, Inc.	LNCR
Linear Technology Corp.	LLTC
LM Ericsson Telephone Co.	ERICY
Lycos, Inc.	LCOS
Maxim Integrated Products, Inc.	MXIM
MCI WORLDCOM, Inc.	WCOM
McLeod USA Inc.	MCLD
Microchip Technology Inc.	MCHP
Micron Electronics, Inc.	MUEI
Microsoft Corp.	MSFT
Molex Inc.	MOLX
Network Assoc., Inc.	NETA
Nextel Communications, Inc.	NXTL
Northwest Airlines Corp.	NWAC
Novell, Inc.	NOVL
NTL Inc.	NTLI
Oracle Corp.	ORCL
PACCAR Inc.	PCAR
PacifiCare Health Systems, Inc.	PHSY
PanAmSat Corp.	SPOT
Parametric Technology Corp.	PMTC
Paychex, Inc.	PAYX
PeopleSoft, Inc.	PSFT
QUALCOMM Inc.	QCOM
Quantum Corp.	QNTM
Quintiles Transnational Corp.	QTRN
Qwest Communications International Inc.	QWST
Reuters Group PLC	RTRSY
Rexall Sundown, Inc.	RXSD
Ross Stores, Inc.	ROSS
Sanmina Corp.	SANM
Siebel Systems, Inc.	SEBL
Sigma-Aldrich Corp.	SIAL
Smurfit-Stone Container Corp.	SSCC
Staples, Inc.	SPLS
Starbucks Corp.	SBUX
Stewart Enterprises, Inc.	STEI
Sun Microsystems, Inc.	SUNW
Synopsys, Inc.	SNPS
Tech Data Corp.	TECD
Tellabs, Inc.	TLAB
USA Networks, Inc.	USAI
VERITAS Software Corp.	VRTS
VISX, Inc.	VISX
Vitesse Semiconductor Corp.	VTSS
Worthington Industries, Inc.	WTHG
Xilinx, Inc.	XLNX
Yahoo! Inc.	YHOO

FRACTIONS TO DECIMALS

Fraction (of a dollar)	Decimal (cents)
1/32	.03125
1/16	.06250
3/32	.09375
1/8	**.12500**
5/32	.15625
3/16	.18750
7/32	.21875
1/4	**.25000**
9/32	.28125
5/16	.31250
11/32	.34375
3/8	**.37500**
13/32	.40625
7/16	.43750
15/32	.46875
1/2	**.50000**
17/32	.53125
9/16	.56250
19/32	.59375
5/8	**.62500**
21/32	.65625
11/16	.68750
23/32	.71875
3/4	**.75000**
25/32	.78125
13/16	.81250
27/32	.84375
7/8	**.87500**
29/32	.90625
15/16	.93750
31/32	.96875

Index

H

I

J

K

L

M

N